YOURS
in
TRUTH

YOURS
in
TRUTH

A Personal Portrait of Ben Bradlee,
Legendary Editor of The Washington Post

JEFF HIMMELMAN

RANDOM HOUSE

NEW YORK

2017 Random House Trade Paperback Edition

Published in the United States by Random House, an imprint and division of
Penguin Random House LLC, New York.

RANDOM HOUSE and the HOUSE colophon are registered trademarks of
Penguin Random House LLC.

Originally published in hardcover in the United States by Random House,
an imprint and division of Penguin Random House LLC, in 2012.

GRATEFUL ACKNOWLEDGMENT IS MADE TO THE FOLLOWING FOR PERMISSION TO
REPRINT PREVIOUSLY PUBLISHED MATERIAL:

Alfred A. Knopf, a division of Random House, Inc.: Excerpts from *Personal History*
by Katharine Graham, copyright © 1997 by Katharine Graham. Used by permission
of Alfred A. Knopf, a division of Random House, Inc.

W.W. Norton & Company, Inc., and Benjamin C. Bradlee: Excerpts from *Conversations
with Kennedy* by Ben Bradlee, copyright © 1975 by Benjamin C. Bradlee. Electronic rights
throughout the world are controlled by the author. Used by permission of
W.W. Norton & Company, Inc. and Benjamin C. Bradlee.

Simon & Schuster, Inc., and Benjamin C. Bradlee: Excerpts from *A Good Life: Newspapering and
Other Adventures* by Ben Bradlee, copyright © 1995 by Benjamin C. Bradlee.
Rights throughout the world, excluding North America, are controlled by the author.
Used by permission of Simon & Schuster, Inc., and Benjamin C. Bradlee.

UCLICK Universal Uclick: DOONESBURY © 1974 G. B. Trudeau. All rights reserved.
Used by permission of UNIVERSAL.

Image credits can be found on p. 497

LIBRARY OF CONGRESS CATALOGING-IN-PUBLICATION DATA
Himmelman, Jeff.
Yours in truth: a personal portrait of Ben Bradlee, legendary editor of
The Washington Post / Jeff Himmelman.
p. cm.
ISBN 978-0-8129-8056-1
Ebook ISBN 978-0-679-60364-1
Bradlee, Benjamin C.   2. Journalists—United States—Biography.   I. Title.
PN4874.B6615H56 2012
070.92—dc23
[B]   2011044180

Printed in the United States of America on acid-free paper

randomhousebooks.com

2   4   6   8   9   7   5   3   1

Book design by Christopher M. Zucker

For my grandparents

To understand perfectly a new country, new situation, the new characters you confront on an assignment, is impossible. To understand more than half, so that your report will have significant correlation with what is happening, is hard. To transmit more than half of what you understand is a hard trick, too, far beyond the task of the so-called creative artist, who if he finds a character in his story awkward can simply change its characteristics. . . . It is possible, occasionally, to get something completely right—a scene, or a pattern of larceny, or a man's mind. These are the reporter's victories, as rare as pitcher's home runs.

—BCB memorandum to himself, for
"How to Read a Newspaper," a book he
imagined but never wrote, November 14, 1990
(quoting A. J. Liebling from *The Press*)

When Alan Pakula, who was the director for *All the President's Men*, was assembling the cast, he and the actors decided that they wanted Jason Robards to play Bradlee. He said they would pay him $50,000, a lot of money for Jason Robards at that time, and they gave him the script. And Robards was delighted. He went home and read it, and then he came back to meet with Pakula and the actors and said, "I can't play this part. Have you read the script?" And they said, "Yes, we have, what's wrong?" And he said, "Ben Bradlee, all he does in the script is run around and say 'Where's the fucking story?'" And they said to him, "What you're going to have to do is figure out fifteen ways to play that so it's different, so it's elegant," and that's actually what he did.

The genius of Bradlee will never be reduced to a sentence or a paragraph, but it is: he understood that that's what the executive editor does. He runs around and finds different and elegant ways to say, "Where's the fucking story?"

—Bob Woodward, at the awards ceremony for
the Illinois Prize for Lifetime Achievement
in Journalism, October 24, 2008

OPENING

I

I FIRST MET BEN ELEVEN years ago, when I was working as a research assistant for Bob Woodward. One spring night Bob and his wife, Elsa, threw a book party for a friend of theirs and invited me to join them when I knocked off work.

By the time I finished up, the party was in full swing. I walked out of my third-floor office, past the framed apology from Richard Nixon's press secretary, Ron Ziegler, that Bob keeps at the top of the circular staircase, and then down two swirling flights to the ground floor. The living room, study, and kitchen of the house were jammed with journalists of all stripes and sizes. I had grown up in Washington and should probably have known who everybody was, but I didn't. I was twenty-five years old and green in almost every way, a kid wandering through a grown-up dinner party.

I took some wine off a tray and looked for a familiar face. After a while I spied Bob standing next to the island in the middle of the kitchen. He was talking with a group of people, one of whom, an older guy, had his hand on Bob's shoulder. They were laughing.

When I got closer, I realized that the older guy was Ben Bradlee. I may not have known who anybody else at the party was, but I knew who *he* was. I'd seen *All the President's Men*, and, like most people who saw that movie, I came away with the impression that Ben was the living avatar of old-school journalistic integrity and rough-hewn charm. I'd also read his memoir during a slow day or two on the third floor, lingering over the pictures, marveling as much at the stories of women throwing themselves at him in the dimly lit arcades of Paris as at his descriptions of Watergate and the Pentagon Papers.

Bob always spoke of Ben reverently, respectfully. On rare occasions, which I always enjoyed, he would pause while talking about something we were working on to say what Bradlee might have done in a similar situation. We'd usually end up laughing, because a strategically placed "fuck" was involved most of the time. I was excited to meet him.

Bob turned, saw me lurking, and when the conversational waters parted he introduced me.

"Hiya!" Ben boomed. He was wearing a blazer and a shirt with an open collar, and he had a drink in his hand. As we shook hands, my mind raced back through his memoir, through everything Bob had told me, desperate for some nugget of casual conversational gold that would show him I was worth getting to know. The right phrase would identify me as a young writer of promise, and before long I'd be cozied up to the table at one of Ben's legendary dinner parties in Georgetown, sucking down cocktails and lapping my peers.

That particular bubble burst on contact. Before I could even get "It's a pleasure to meet you" out of my mouth, Ben had turned back to the conversation he'd been in before I pulled up. I stuck around for a few minutes, hoping that some fortuitous short circuit might route the conversation back to me, but it didn't. I finished my wine and went home.

It's odd to me now, how well I remember it: my excitement, the flash of his greeting, the dreamlike feeling that a door had opened and closed before I even knew it was there. I had no idea then that I would ever come to know Ben. But, looking back on it, that first meeting—all five seconds of it—contained most of the basics. You remember him. He's better-looking than you are. You want to please him. And if you hope to gain or keep his attention, you had better be quick on the draw. Otherwise, as he loves to say, the caravan moves on without you.

I didn't see Ben again until 2007, when Bob found himself short-handed for a couple of months and asked if I could help him out. One day he poked his head into my office and told me that he and Elsa had been out for dinner the night before with Ben and his wife, the journalist Sally Quinn, and the topic of Ben doing another book had come up.

"I told them they should hire you," Bob said. "You should do it."

Ten days later, I pulled up in front of Ben and Sally's exquisite home on N Street, in Georgetown, for an interview. The house and grounds take up almost an entire city block. As Evelyn, the maid, led me through the foyer and into the formal dining room, I tried to take in as much as I could without ogling. The phrase "Ben and Sally" has been synonymous with high Washington society and A-list parties for more than thirty years. The house, particularly the grand ground floor with its large foyer and cavernous living room, looked like a movie set.

Ben emerged from a door off the den with the remains of that morning's newspaper in his hand, and we all sat down at the table. Sally did most of the talking. Ben's memoir, published in the fall of 1995, had been called *A Good Life*. As Sally imagined it, this book would be "Lessons from a Good Life," filled with short and inspiring stories about Ben's time at *The Washington Post* interspersed with some words of wisdom from the man himself. She had the entire book mapped out already, down to the cover art.

"Ben's a writer, so of course he wants to write his own book," Sally said at one point, to be sure I knew what the rules were.* Ben rolled his eyes.

Two weeks later, I walked down to the *Post* building on 15th Street to meet with Ben at his office, on my own. On the phone, Sally had

*In ghostwriterland, that meant that only Ben's name would be on the spine, and I would be expected to be tactfully vague about my own contributions.

told me how thrilled Ben had been about our interview, how excited he was to get started, that he might huff and puff a little but that really he wanted everything exactly as she had described it to me. I didn't believe her, but I wanted to, so I went.

Ben's secretary, Carol, picked me up in the lobby and brought me up to Ben's office on the seventh floor. He was tilted back in his chair, reading a newspaper behind a great oval desk. A set of over-stuffed bookshelves lined the wall behind him. The far wall, looking out over 15th Street, was set with large windows that let in surprisingly little of the afternoon sun. Carol knocked gently on the open door, and when Ben looked up she led me in and introduced me.

To say that he had no idea who I was, or what I was doing there, isn't quite true. Carol and Sally had prepped him, so in the most minimal sense he knew. But, basically, he had no idea who I was or what I was doing there. I could tell by how he said hello to me. I took a seat, sweat cooling palpably in my armpits. Carol left the door open and went back out front.

"What can I do for you?" he asked.

I hadn't been nervous at their house, but now that I was alone with Ben in his element my mouth had somehow become untethered from my brain. I recited the things Sally had told me to say: We can take it slow, I can do some preliminary work and see if it turns into anything, if there's no book there then we won't force it. I have a vague, uncomfortable memory of saying something about what an honor it would be to work with him.

When I got done, he said simply, "I've already written one book. I'm not in any big rush to write another one."

I said I understood, which I did. I started to put my notebook away.

But he wasn't quite ready to kick me out yet. He asked me about my experience with Bob, and as I rattled on about it I hit on something funny and he laughed. The smile that the laugh brought with it completely transformed his face. It was like looking at a different person. His whole face sharpened, came alive. He leaned back in his chair.

I remember his being immaculately turned out that day: black sweater, gray slacks, shoes that revealed themselves to be leather ankle-zip boots when he put his feet up on the desk, glasses just so, hair swept back in a hard part. He was the most attractive eighty-five-year-old man I'd ever seen. Bob once described Ben as "Kirk Douglas as a submarine commander," and that's exactly it. His voice sounds like it comes from the bottom of Boston Harbor.

After a couple of minutes of back-and-forth, Ben mentioned that he had a bunch of boxes in storage someplace but had no idea what was in them.

"Would you like to look at those?" he asked.

It was an opening, a small one. Woodward had vouched for me, and now I had passed some sort of threshold. "I would love to look at those," I said.

"Carol knows where they are." He waved his hand, and that was it. He went back to his newspaper, and I saw myself out.

Ten days later, Carol called to tell me to come back down to the paper. The boxes were coming, and there were a lot of them.

II

THEY CAME IN TRANCHES OF four, seven, and nine—brown legal boxes, numbered sequentially and marked "Bradlee." Courteous custodial workers wheeled them out of the elevator and through the chiming glass doors that mark the entrance to the seventh-floor executive suite of the *Washington Post* building. I looked on with no small amount of apprehension as box after box dropped with a thunk, stuffed to the gills with the accreted professional life of one of the most famous newspaper editors in the world.

The first box I opened was so thoroughly filled with onionskin copies of Ben's correspondence that its sides were bowed. There were hundreds and hundreds of letters in this one box alone. I had to start somewhere, so I sat down at a desk in the temporary office the *Post* had given me and pulled one of the folders at random. The papers inside were so old and fine that I could see my fingers through them.

I didn't know what I was looking for, but after a few minutes I came across a letter to Kay Graham, then the *Post*'s owner and publisher, from a man named William H. Dodderidge:

October 17, 1977

Dear Mrs. Graham:

Messrs. Eugene Meyer and Philip L. Graham must be turning over in their graves because of the way you are dragging down what used to be a wonderful newspaper.

   In my humble opinion, I think the persons really responsible for The Washington Post's decline are Benjamin C. Bradlee and Philip L. Geyelin.* I hope the day is not far off when you fire those two peckerwoods . . .

Beneath it was Ben's response:

Dear Mr. Dodderidge:

Your letter to Mrs. Graham reminded me of the story about W. C. Fields sitting with a drink in his hand in his garden one afternoon.

   His secretary interrupted him repeatedly to tell him that a strange man wanted to see him and refused to say what he wanted to see him about. Finally Fields told his secretary to give the man "an equivocal answer—tell him to go fuck himself."

                                                          Sincerely,

This was going to be fun.

Many of the letters were to and from people with ordinary

---

*Geyelin was the longtime editor of the *Post*'s editorial page. Meyer was Kay Graham's dad, and Phil Graham was her husband; both men preceded her as publisher of the *Post*.

complaints—"You forgot the box scores," "I'm canceling my sub-
scription," "You're clearly a Communist." But some of them sang.
Ben, to an undergraduate who wanted to go into journalism but
wondered what to major in:

> I would major in something other than journalism. You could be taught
> how to structure a story pretty fast. You can't be taught the really
> valuable things like judgment and ethics and priorities and compassion
> and sensitivity. You've got to experience those or read about people
> who have experienced that. Journalism wants you when you're wise,
> not when you know how to structure a story.

And then there was this, also from 1977, which distills an entire (fool-
ish) debate into its essence:

> It is almost impossible to keep personal values out of a story. Don't
> think of objectivity; think of fairness. You can be fair while expressing
> values. A fire is big or it's small or it's tall or it's puny. You're still fair.

To one person who wrote in complaining about something he'd read
in another publication, Ben wrote simply, "I can only conclude that
you are an idiot." To another, who blamed Ben for everything that
was wrong with American journalism and threatened to spit in his
face if he ever "had the displeasure" of meeting him, Ben wrote
back, "The trouble with American journalism is readers like you. If
you spit in my face, you would regret it."

The publisher of *The Pueblo Chieftain*, in Pueblo, Colorado, wrote
to Ben in 1985, taking him to task for his recent appearance on a
panel at a publishers association meeting. "How ironic it was to watch
Ben Bradlee and Don Hewitt,*" the man wrote, ". . . display their
arrogance as they criticized a media credibility study which reveals
that the public views the press as being arrogant." After another paragraph of thinly veiled sanctimony, he signed the letter "Cordially and
sincerely."

---

*Hewitt was the creator and executive producer of *60 Minutes*.

This is Ben's response, in full:

To the Publisher:

Editors <u>do</u> run the risk of appearing arrogant if they choose to disagree with anybody who calls them arrogant.

You sound like one of those publishers who aims to please his pals in the community and give them what they want.

No one will call you arrogant that way. No one will call you newspaperman, either.

Cordially and sincerely,

Benjamin C. Bradlee

He was willing to stick it to pretty much everybody, from his friends and colleagues to larger public figures. He began one letter to Jesse Jackson, "You are one mean dude," and then proceeded to ream Jackson for his consistent attempts to influence the *Post*'s coverage of his agenda:

I'm telling you, as your buddy, that it really is getting counterproductive. And it's got nothing to do with race. . . .

If you are writing your letter of July 26 to me to show to some other people, well and good. So be it. But if you are writing that letter to help your cause, the cause of the good people in this world, you are close to being counterproductive. Next time you're in town, let's talk about that. Let's talk about what newspapers are for. One of the things they are not for is simply this: They are not to serve anyone's special interest. . . .

Your friend,

When Barry Goldwater, another friend of Ben's, took to the Senate floor to put up a stink about the *Post*'s publication of information about a signals intelligence satellite—information that was already in the public domain, it turned out—Ben wrote, "That's me you're recommending be tried for treason, friend, and I resent the hell out of it."

But there was humility, too. When he had to eat it, he ate it. In July of 1976, the *Post* ran a news story about Senator George McGovern's decision to rent his home in Washington to the Syrian ambassador. To any neutral eye the story was slanted, full of implication about McGovern's foreign policy views that had nothing to do with the rental arrangement. The *Post*'s editorial page disavowed the story, and so did Ben:

Dear George:

I think that our story about your house was bullshit, and I'm sorry it ever ran.

Sincerely,

Internally, he was as direct but more extreme. On a different story, during the eighties:

Dear Tom:

You fucked up big time.

I can't let yesterday's incident pass. You violated some basic rules, despite the fact that all the radars were on as a result of the Cooke case.

You took a quote out of context in a way that was guaranteed to get the quote denied by the FBI, and you were really daring me to cut it out.

I could easily have backed you. I wanted to because I trusted you and I believed you; and had I done so, I would have been in the same goddamn shit sandwich that I find myself in now.

You lost my trust, no matter how good that story was. And you lost the trust of some of your colleagues.

He seemed particularly irked by people—reporters, editorial colleagues, job applicants—who thought more highly of themselves than they should:

I have reviewed your clips, your letters, reports of your conversations, and I find you lacking. You lack courtesy, you lack flexibility, you lack any semblance of humility. You think you are better than you are, which is not sinful, but it is apparent . . .

I don't think you would be happy here, and I don't think we would be happy with you here.

But he didn't always bring out the rapier. Sometimes he could be much more gentle about the comedown, as with a young man who had written (as so many did) to "Ben Bradley" looking for advice:

Dear Mr. Patterson:

The first advice I would give anyone looking for a job in the newspaper business is that you spell the name of the editor correctly.

After you have learned that, I think I would advise you to decide what you want to do. You haven't convinced me you are interested in journalism yet, sounds more like you want me to choose something for you. I can't do that.

As a rule, he wasn't big on giving advice. People needed to figure things out for themselves. "Read a lot," he told one aspirant. "Work harder than anyone you know, and you will find it if it's there."

Sometimes there were tidbits you could use:

Dear Sandie:

I wish I had been told so many things when I was your age. But one special thing would have helped me enormously, and it is this: Any time spent convincing other people that you are or were important is wasted.

And in more than a few places there was a surprising tenderness, given Ben's reputation as a fire-breather:

Dear Susan:

That's quite the nicest letter I ever got.

I will miss you, no matter how unprofoundly we knew each other.

Your letter gives me credit for all sorts of virtues I don't have. You are an able and interesting person who seems to me at first glance to appreciate grace and lots of other things.

We will all miss you, but your reasoning sounds convincing. If the personal reasons why it is best for you not to be in Washington are what they sound like, he is wrong.*

Your friend,

He also rarely missed a chance to crack a joke. One reader sent in a crossword puzzle that he had completed backwards, and Ben wrote him a one-line response: "!SNOITALUTARGNOC." (Ben loves crosswords.) On a letter of complaint from George Allen, the reviled coach of the Washington Redskins, Ben simply wrote, "File under 'Assholes.'"

One of my earliest favorites was Ben's response to former president Ronald Reagan during the nineties, when Reagan invited Ben to California for a conference called "What's Wrong with American Politics?" Ben had written back, "Thank you so much for your invitation to attend your conference . . . I am really impressed that you think you can answer that question in two days."

---

*He was guessing—correctly, as it turned out—that she was leaving because of a breakup with an unnamed boyfriend.

III

Benjamin C. Bradlee
c/o Simon and Schuster, Publishers
Rockefeller Center
1230 Avenue of the Americas
New York, N. Y. 10020

Dear Mr. Bradlee,

Your new book, "A Good Life" is fascinating, informative and most interesting, with one important exception.

The crude, coarse, frequent degrading language - example: "shit sandwich, holy shit, shit hit the fan, fuck" used over and over to emphasize your opinion of a person, a situation - did <u>nothing</u> to enhance the expected maturity of a man of your age and experience.

I CAME IN EVERY AFTERNOON to read. I didn't spend much time with the real Ben at first. Half the time, I had no idea whether he knew who I was. One early "meeting" ended when I asked him how much thought he had put into some of his letters, and he said, "The number of letters I wrote twice you could put in your ear." Another ended when he started working on a crossword puzzle while I was in the middle of a sentence.

He didn't have much interest in the stuff I was digging up from the files, either. Whenever I found a letter that I thought was particularly incisive or relevant or funny I would bring it in to him in his office. He would hold it up, scan it for a couple of seconds, and then put it aside with the very clear intention of never looking at it again. I got used to it after a while.

One of the first things you notice about Ben, both the written and the in-person Ben, is his vocabulary, his vernacular, his penchant for one-liners and salty phrases. You don't have to hang around too long before you'll get a good, honest "fuck" out of him. It's a functional component of his charm. I could hear him cursing from the next office over, and so could the rest of the seventh floor. People would poke their heads out of their offices just to hear what he might say next.

Within days I found myself saying "fuck" or one of its equivalents in places where it didn't belong, under the misguided notion that it would give me street cred with him. I watched other people do it, too. Swearing with Ben makes you feel like you're part of his club, the club that doesn't take anything too seriously. Apparently even Kay Graham started doing it, after a fashion. But Ben's the master, and nobody will tell you differently. He can say the word "fuck" with Mandarin variation and tonal control.

The film version of *All the President's Men* is accurate in that regard. Jason Robards, who plays Ben, is constantly spewing curse words. "What kind of a crazy fucking story is this?" he says near the start. Then, later: "Fuck it! We're sticking with the boys." The movie had to be edited heavily in order to be shown on TV:*

---

*According to Gary Arnold, who reviewed the movie in the *Post* in April of 1976, Robards's performance single-handedly "liberalized the ratings system, making the most famous sexual four-letter word of them all acceptable for the PG classification as long as it isn't spoken in a sexual context."

THE WASHINGTON POST

From: BOB WOODWARD

ATPM / LANKINS

MEN

Bob –
This is obviously not
to be seen by too many
eyes.
Talk to you soon.
Best –
Robbi

To Bradlee —
This is why
ALL Pres. Men has to
be edited for TV.
Number of violations

Robards – 17
Hoffman – 17
Redford – 6

:o Redford about

their hearts and
Redford about Colson)

me to Redford)

is ass..." (Warden)
m)..."ass...bullshit"

ford and Hoffman

errace to Hoffman)

bout phone conversation)

Hoffman to Robards)

40' - "bullshit" (Redford talking to Holbrook)
40' - "goddamn" (Hoffman about New York Times story)
45' - "...why the hell...goddamn..." (Hoffman to Beatty)
53' - "Jesus" (Hoffman on phone to Redford)
54' - "Jesus" (Balsam to staff)
55' - "...their asses off..." (Paper staff meeting)
56' - "...frigging audit office" (Robards at staff meeting)
56' - "Goddamn...who the hell..." (Robards at staff meeting)
56' - "Then it's our ass..." (Robards)
58' - "Jesus" (Robards to man in office)

It's not just curse words, though. He uses all kinds of different colorful expressions when he wants to cut to the chase. In the middle of an interview with Woodward and Carl Bernstein in 1973, for the book version of *All the President's Men*, Ben's stepdaughter, Nancy Pittman, walked into the room:

BW: We're interviewing your father just for posterity.

B: They're writing a book and they're zeroing in on some of my mistakes.

BW: Do you get any feeling about what your reaction was when Nixon came out and said rather categorically in fact no one is involved—

B: The only one that tightened my sphincter—

BW: [To Nancy] Does he always talk like this around you?

The letters are also dotted with vintage phrases, the kind that only Ben can get away with:

Dear Frank:

I'm late in answering your letter. It isn't that I have all that goddamn much on my alleged mind, beyond imminent fatherhood, trying to thwart CBS's plans to steal Woodward for half a million bucks or thereabouts, worrying about some new raspberry plants I just put in, and generally feeling up to my ass in midgets.

A tough situation becomes, in Ben's mouth, "a basket of crabs"; an unaccomplished rich person a "busted flush"; somebody who disrespects a *Washington Post* reporter should expect to "hang by his thumbs for a month" before ever seeing his side of a story in print. On a transcribed phone call with a lawyer who had threatened to sue the *Post* preemptively about a story that hadn't yet run, Ben began by saying, "I've got to tell you that I think that letter has got more bullshit in it per square inch than any letter I've received in years. Honest to God."

Carol, Ben's secretary, likes to tell the story about the time her son met with Ben because he'd had a problem in college and wanted some advice. After the meeting was over and her son was walking out, Ben clapped him on the back and said, for all of the seventh floor to hear, "Keep your pecker up."

That's Ben.

The story that can't be topped is the one told at Ben's retirement roast in the newsroom, in 1991, by reporter Tom Lippman:

I had become a sort of freelance guru on style and grammar and usage for people around the newsroom. One day I had an almost hesitant, almost blushing visit from Debbie Regan, who many of you will remember . . . was Ben's secretary at the time. Ben had been dictating a letter on that little tape recorder, I guess, which Debbie had to transcribe, and she came over to my desk looking extremely uncomfortable.

She hemmed and hawed a little bit and she said, "Look, I have to ask you something."

I said, "Yeah, what is it, Debbie?"

She said, "Is dickhead one word or two?"

One night early on I rode out with him to the University of Maryland for a symposium in honor of Shirley Povich, the late and celebrated sportswriter for the *Post*. Ben loved Povich. He always says that when he first came to the *Post*, in 1948, Shirley Povich and the cartoonist Herblock were *The Washington Post*, the only true assets the paper had. Everybody on the panel was telling sports stories, and after a while Ben got bored. A couple of times he stuck both legs straight out in front of him and looked at his shoes, like a boy would. All the talk of blogs and the Internet wasn't doing much for him.

Then George Solomon, the former editor of the *Post*'s sports section, began to tell an anecdote about how Povich had helped integrate the press box at one sporting event or another. "Now *this* is a great story," Solomon said, launching into it with gusto.

He had barely gotten the words out of his mouth before Ben stirred on the other side of the stage. "*We'll* tell you if it's a great story, George," he said.

The crowd laughed, and so did the panelists. It did not require any great leap of the imagination to see a younger version of this man presiding as executive editor over a raucous story conference at the paper, cracking people up while also putting them in their place.

"It's good to know that at your age you still know how to take a cheap shot," Solomon said, blushing, amused, entirely unoffended.

At one point Michael Wilbon, the ESPN host who was then still a *Post* sports columnist, started talking about how much he had revered *The Washington Post* before he went to work there as an intern in 1979. He talked about how excited he had been to come to the paper that Ben Bradlee ran, how mythic Ben and the *Post* were in his own mind because of Watergate. He had watched *All the President's Men* the night before his first day on the job, he said. He was almost misting up about it.*

As Wilbon was wrapping up his spiel, the audience collectively caught sight of Ben in the next chair over. He was sawing on an improvised air violin and rolling his eyes for effect. The gesture was expertly timed and executed, playing to an audience Ben knew would be watching. He was poking fun at Wilbon for being sentimental but also showing that he didn't take his own mystique too seriously. The crowd roared, even Wilbon laughed. He'd been had by his old boss, and he loved it.

I've seen Ben whip that violin out on any number of people since then. He's pretty ruthless. When Sally got up at his eighty-eighth birthday party and started talking about how Ben was her hero, he didn't waste much time with it, either. When the spirit moves him, nobody is safe—not his wife or his friends, not other journalists or esteemed fellow panelists or anybody else. One step too far into sentimentality or self-importance and *blam*, there he is, taking the air out of the situation, showing you your pomposity (or preemptively leavening his own), demonstrating to everybody else that he's on to you. The mocking is almost always gentle; everybody laughs, because Ben is unfailingly charming and it's all in good fun. But the message is clear, consistent, unmistakably Ben down to its core: Cut the crap, keep it moving, save the self-serving details. Just get it out of your typewriter, kid.

---

*Wilbon retired from the *Post* in December of 2010, and in his final column he talked about "the complete awe, even 30 years later, I still feel whenever I'm in the company of Ben Bradlee, even if it's just seeing him in the elevator."

IV

Dear Ben:

On your 80th I want to say some of the things that seem never to get said. For reasons of maleness, and maybe time, I've rushed by too much that is important, the really, truly important. These things become too important to discuss. Let me try.

THE LETTER WAS DATED AUGUST 26, 2001, typewritten on Bob's personal stationery, with "AS SENT" jotted diagonally across the top left-hand corner in Bob's trademark scrawl. He pulled it out of an expandable manila folder marked "BRADLEE" and pushed it across the table toward me.

We were sitting at the back of Bob's living room on Q Street, at the same round table where hundreds of government officials have said things that they eventually regret saying into Bob's tape recorder. My own tape recorder was there now. It was still early on, before I knew Ben very well, and I had been making the rounds of the ten or fifteen people who knew him best in search of good stories. I had saved Bob for last.

We were talking about the first time he met Ben, and though he recited a version of it to me in person the letter catches it in a more complete way:

I'll begin with memory—my first of you. It was the first Friday in September 1971. I was waiting outside your office in the old Post. This was the last interview before being hired: Bradlee meets all the new hires; he almost never says no, but he might or he could. The rule was watch your ass, be careful and don't get into stray talk. Bradlee's got a short attention span. (At about this very same hour on this same day, unknown to both of us at the time, two guys named E. Howard Hunt and G. Gordon Liddy were boarding a plane at Dulles to Los Angeles so they could burglarize the office of the psychiatrist to Daniel Ellsberg.)

Could it be that you did not have a window in your old office? In any case that is what I remember. Maybe some renovations were underway? So the office seemed smaller than it should have been. You were already known as this energy force at the paper, and why should this force have such a small, cramped office, I wondered. For about two seconds. Then you turned on the lights—your face, eyes, the undivided focus—not exactly the short attention span of legend. The truth is that your strength is your attention span, when something is worth paying attention to. You were not particularly interested in what I had done at the Montgomery County whatever-it-was newspaper. You honed in on one thing. My time in the Navy, five years, not hard war years but a long time. You had been in the Navy, you said, as if it were the brotherhood. . . .

Everything after the Navy was easy, we agreed. After the Navy there could be running room. But somebody had to give you a job—a profession in which to run.

So that's what you gave me first—running room. It was a magnificent gift. I felt it every day, and it came directly from you. There was this huge sense that we were your boys, or girls or people—the entire newsroom—turned loose. Running room was a matter of pride and obligation. We didn't understand fully what it was, but we recognized daylight and went for it because that is where you were pointing. Daylight: news, the unexpected and surprising, and the daily folly and occasional generosity of mankind, that endless buffet.

Bob doesn't normally write like that. He tends toward the straightforward, the objective, the simple. When I worked for him, he would sometimes encourage me to "swing from the high vines," to take a chance, to go for it in terms of language or synoptic complexity, but he was always hesitant to do the same. It could be hard to tell how Bob really felt about anything, what it meant to him.

Evidently the occasion of Ben's eightieth had brought him out. The letter continued, going even deeper:

And when I screwed up in some well publicized and some less well publicized ways, what did you do? Never a harsh, judgmental word. Not one. Only human understanding and that wonderful motion with your arms in the air, shoulders in a shrug, and the tilted head and the momentary grimace that said, well, that's over, let's move on. No doubt there were times when you were angry or disappointed. Other than Elsa you are the only person who always stood by me in good or bad times.

Bob wondered what might have happened if Nixon had stayed in office, had the Watergate scandal never occurred. What would have come of the FBI, the CIA, "the habits and practices of concealment," the war in Vietnam? "Watergate upended a lot of things," Bob wrote. "You made it possible with goading and love and all of yourself, never a partial effort."

A few paragraphs later, the letter drew to a close. "The brotherhood lives," Bob wrote. "I feel connected to you like a son."

The way you and Sally have extended your family to ours in recent years is a cornerstone of our life. I'm feeling older. If the running room is a little less, and the rear end doesn't move as fast, the old fires of deep appreciation, deeper admiration and the deepest love still burn for you.

Sincerely,

[signed] BW

Later in our interview, he pulled another letter out of the file, this one from Ben to him. It was dated March 27, 1982, typewritten on Ben's office stationery, with "<u>CONFIDENTIAL</u>" written in Ben's blue pen at the top. That year, CBS had attempted to hire Bob away from the *Post*, and Ben made a memorable pitch for Bob to stay:

Dear Bob:

A light will go out in this place, if or when you leave. A light that never flickered, and generally burned strong and clean. That's for openers. You are quite simply the best investigative reporter I've ever met, or imagined. A team of investigative reporters [led] by you can reach levels of impact and importance that can hardly be conceived. (And without you, that team will probably disband.)

I'm not going to belittle television, or demean this latest offer now in front of you.

Instead, I'm going to outline what the POST will do for you now, and what the POST will do for you over the next 18 months . . . sure that you will do what's best in the long run.

Ben laid out a series of proposals—more money, more editorial responsibility (including weekend duty running the paper), management of Bob's own "SWAT" team of investigative reporters. I had never understood when I worked for Bob that he had once dreamed of replacing Ben as the executive editor of the *Post*. I knew Bob as somebody who reported and wrote and wanted only to do those two things. From the tone and substance of Ben's proposals in the letter, it's clear that in 1982 there was still a chance that Bob might succeed him, even though the Janet Cooke scandal had effectively put Bob out of the running.

The outlined proposal, Ben wrote, "should leave the POST in the best possible position to know you, and you in the best possible position to know us." That's the final sentence of the letter. Then, where

Ben would normally have written "Sincerely," he had written something different:

Yours in truth,

I had read hundreds of Ben's letters by then, but I had never seen that particular signoff before. It was a powerful way to close, so simple and pure and yet so loaded at the same time.

Bob showed me his response, composed four days later, on March 31, 1982, with "Personal" typed at the top of the printout. "Something will go out in me should I leave," he wrote, picking up on the opening metaphor of Ben's letter to him. "I don't want to." He would stay.

There were other letters, too, containing far more information than I was equipped at that point to understand. In the mid-eighties, when Bob was upset that some of his reporting on Libya and on Soviet secrets wasn't making it into the paper, he wrote to Ben that he was again thinking of leaving:

Dear Ben:

Something is dying at the Post, and I don't know what to do about it. Events, attitudes, decisions etc. have been nagging at me for months. You know that. I know that. And I know the displeasure you feel with my approach.

I say this with great sadness. Like you, I've been through two divorces. I know that what was once good and wonderful can turn very sour; the wise know when to depart. If that's what you want or what seems best, I'm gone. . . .

I wish there was not the evidence to support this. I hate to be a pain in the ass, your ass. I wish I did not have to say this to you, my friend and boss, a man I love. . . .

Four years ago almost to the day—it was March 27, 1982—you

wrote me a letter that began, "A light will go out in this place, if or
when you leave. . . ."

You tell me how to best handle this. I'd rather be part of the
ongoing solution to making a better paper, and not part of the problems
you have.

As you signed that 1982 letter—

Yours in truth,

There was no response from Ben to this one. When I asked Bob what
Ben had done about it, he said, "There was a story I was working on,
and it got in the paper the next day."

"Maybe that's one of the lessons," Bob said. "Simple solutions.
Somebody sends you a long, whiny, complaining letter, simple solutions. 'Okay. Give me a story I can publish.' And we did."

But wasn't there more to it than that? The language of these
letters—the references to divorce, to departure, to love and truth—
suggested currents that ran deeper than newspaper stories. Later I would
mention these exchanges to the reporter Pat Tyler, who for a time was
closer than most to Bob and to Ben. I said that I had been surprised to
see such an outpouring of emotion—almost like love letters—between
two guys who don't talk about their feelings all that much.

"They're both prisoners of very strong emotions," Tyler told me.
"But when they were still having their suits cut for dorsal fins, they
didn't show them. They suppressed them very strongly."

"At what point did you become friends?" I asked Bob as the interview was dying down. "When did you make that transition?"

"Well, you know," Bob started, "I think you've probably got other
people . . ." He trailed off, then tried again. "Ben and I are close and
we have this history," he said. "But he's not going to call me up and
say, 'Hey, come on down and have a beer.' I think he does that with
Lehrer and Wooten and Shelby some," he said, referring to three of
Ben's friends.* Then, a bit uncertainly, "Doesn't he?"

---

*Jim Lehrer, of PBS; Jim Wooten, of ABC News; and Shelby Coffey, a former *Post* editor.

"I don't really know," I said.

Bob paused, thought for a moment. "I mean, you know, it's ultimately like another father," he said. "Like with your father, you feel that you never close the deal."

Bob's father had recently passed away. I had never heard him talk much about him.

"In the sense of getting everything out on the table," Bob said.

"I'm not sure that anybody feels that they know him that well," I said.

It's true. I've never met anybody who claims to have closed the deal with Ben, except maybe for Sally. There is always a tinge of mystery and distance. As one former reporter and close friend told me, "Ben always kept some of Ben to himself." Earlier Bob had said that with Ben there was always "a sense that he's got a lot held in reserve." If these people hadn't closed the deal, I couldn't imagine that I ever would.

After we finished up, I went out in the garden at the back of the house to talk to Elsa. It was a sunny and slow Friday afternoon, with cicadas humming in the trees. Elsa agreed that it was hard to feel that you'd touched the bottom with Ben. "In a funny way, he's actually quite distant," she said, "for all of the bonhomie."

About an hour into our session, Bob brought out a bottle of white wine, and the three of us gossiped for a while. I mentioned that I'd uncovered some information in Ben's files that I didn't know quite how to handle, old letters that were torn up—saved, but clearly not sent and (perhaps) never meant to be seen.

Bob's ears perked up, as they always do when secrets get mentioned. He flashed a knowing smile and reached for the wine bottle.

"All biographers are concealers," he said.

At that point I was still writing a book with Ben, not about him, but maybe Bob already knew intuitively that that was going to change. I had the first flicker of the realization that writing about your mentor's mentor is a trickier proposition than it seems. The challenge hung in the air for a second or two, and then we clinked glasses and moved on to other things.

V

Porto Bello, 2008

"SO YOU WANT TO WRITE the book on me, huh?" Ben growled when he came onto the line. He was kidding around, but I almost never spoke to him on the telephone, so I wasn't quite sure how to handle it. I was a little scared.

It was now July of 2008, nearly eight months after Ben had decided that he didn't want to write another book. After some quick jujitsu from Sally, I had spent the intervening months helping their son, Quinn, with his memoir, but Ben's archives had never been far from my mind. Now I was making my big pitch.

"Not necessarily *the* book," I said nervously. "But *a* book." Too cutesy. I kicked myself for not just walking down to his office to talk to him in person.

He listened as I rambled on about how fascinating his archives were, and then he stopped me. He would be happy to cooperate, he said. Happy to. He just hoped it would be interesting. I told him that was the easy part, and we laughed. In exchange for his time and cooperation, he asked for nothing. As we were hanging up, he said simply, "It's your ass now, pal."

Over the course of the next three years, Ben opened his entire life to me, from his archives at *The Washington Post* to his friends, his colleagues, and his dinner table. We've shared birthdays and howled in pained unison at the television screen during Redskins games. We have conducted dozens of formal interviews in Ben's office and untold hundreds of casual ones over the dinner dishes, or in lounge chairs by the pool. My wife is in love with him. We're friends.

This is not to say that we bared our souls to each other. He didn't divulge all of his private thoughts about mortality and the meaning of human life, in part because I'm not sure that he has them. He just answered my questions. "I'm not hiding anything," he said to me one winter day in his living room. He sat back on the couch, and for a moment I thought he was going to tell me some big secret. Then he said, "I might have bopped a couple of dames that I shouldn't have, but I think I've been pretty honest about that."

What you see with Ben is what you get. The color is great but the substance is settled. Sometimes after an interview with him I would come away thinking I'd hit the jackpot and then find that he'd said the exact same thing, almost word for word, in his memoir or in a different interview. For a long time now, much longer than I've known him, he's had his story and he sticks to it.

But the files themselves were a different story, and in some instances a new one. In early 2009, a stroke of luck effectively doubled the amount of information that I had to draw from. Ev Small, Kay Graham's longtime researcher and friend, happened to be out at the *Post*'s storage facility to pull together some of Kay's old papers for the Library of Congress. While she was there, she noticed a bunch of boxes with "Bradlee" written on them. Carol had requisitioned everything for us a year before, but evidently these boxes had been missed in that first cull. Ev knew what I was doing and was kind enough to seek me out and tell me about them. Within a week or two, nearly twenty additional boxes had landed at my office door.

They were a gold mine: the Watergate files, a set of interviews that Ben did for his memoir in the early nineties, the complete files on Janet Cooke, verbatim transcripts of editorial meetings from the early seventies. There was new, never before published information about Deep Throat, about the Pentagon Papers, whole histories of events that never made the memoirs. One particularly happy day I came across three private interviews that Ben had done with Kay Graham for her Pulitzer-winning memoir, *Personal History*, each about fifty single-spaced pages in length. They traced Ben's entire career at the *Post*, and the back-and-forth between the two of them was priceless:

> K: Well, to ask Bradlee at that point what he wanted was very dangerous. And he said, famous quote, "Now that you ask I'd give my left one to be managing editor of The Post."
>
> B: If it became available.
>
> K: I don't think you said that, Ben.

People and relationships I'd read so much about came alive, and not just people from the *Post*. I knew, for example, that Ben and John Kennedy were friends; it's been written about ad nauseam by Ben and by everybody who writes about Ben. But one morning in January of 2009, at the back of Ben's Kennedy files, I found an invitation to a birthday party—a generic card, with furry animals aligned along the side and blanks for the handwritten time and place down the center. It looked modern, enough that at first I figured it had been filed in the wrong place. Then I looked more closely, and I noticed that the party was for John Kennedy, Jr., at the White House, to be held November 26, 1963. In a flash I realized that it was an invitation to a party that never happened, planned as it was for four days after Kennedy's death. I had to stop working and just sit with it for a while. Ben wrote a book about Kennedy, and has answered countless questions about him in countless interviews since 1963. Somehow the card did more to convey their closeness, and what was lost, than anything Ben has ever said or written.

One morning in the spring of 2010, we were making breakfast in the kitchen at Porto Bello, Ben and Sally's weekend place in southern Maryland.* Ben loves a country breakfast, fried eggs and bacon and sausage, the whole works. As he was firing up the skillet, he mentioned that *Post* columnist David Ignatius had spent the night there before I arrived. I asked him if he remembered an occasion, years before, when with Ignatius's encouragement he had ordered ever more expensive bottles of wine, ultimately nearly $1,000 worth, at a *Post* editors conference in Puerto Rico. Ben said that he did, and then chuckled.

"How do *you* know about that?" he asked.

"He told me about it," I said, "and I have the letter you wrote, telling the Post Company to charge the dinner to you, not to the company."

He turned around. "Jesus," he said. "You know all of my secrets."

That wasn't much of a secret, but sometimes I wondered whether he really understood how deeply I was digging around in his past. He

---

*By "weekend place," I mean magazine-quality restored historic manor house on a 200-acre former tobacco farm with several outbuildings and the requisite Bradlee-Quinn swimming pool and tennis court.

often seemed surprised by how much I knew. But other than that brief moment at the kitchen stove, he never expressed any concern when I quoted random documents in conversation or handed him inflammatory letters that he never sent. Once I showed him a tough unsent memo to his former number two, Howard Simons. Their relationship had started off well but deteriorated after Watergate, when Ben's star rose and Simons felt he never received the credit he deserved for his own contributions to the story. "There is a certain amount of shit that I am going to put up with," Ben had written, "and there is a definite amount of shit I am not going to put up with."

"It's interesting that you didn't send it," I said. I was fishing for some reaction from him, to see if he wanted to qualify it at all.

I should have known better. All he did was laugh as he looked the memo over and say, "Makes a pretty good case, though, doesn't it?" Then he pushed it back across the desk toward me.

There was only one time that he ever tried to steer me off something. I walked into his office with a faded copy of a play called "How, Please?" and plunked it down on his desk with a grin.

"Remember this?"

He looked at the title page and realized what it was: a play that he had written with a colleague at *Newsweek* during the late fifties, before his meteor ride with Kennedy began. He flipped through it, then looked back over at me.

"Don't kill me with this," he said, half imploring, half kidding. I promised him I wouldn't. That was the only time in three years that he ever, even jokingly, tried to stay my hand.

One of Ben's most basic traits as an editor was that, if he trusted you, he set you free and then backed you when it counted. At the *Post* he lived by that sword and nearly died by it, too. As much as I might have wished it, I never knew him at the peak of his powers, striding through the newsroom, dragging on a cigarette and scaring the shit out of the young reporters (and some of the old ones). That guy was gone by the time I showed up. The self-described "barracuda" for the news had been replaced by a kinder, gentler, more forgetful version. I could feel the old Ben, and see him in the eyes of the people who loved him, but outside of brief bursts I had to rely mostly on the archives to encounter him for myself.

As it happened, though, I did get to know the man who sets you free if he trusts you. At dinner with our families one night in March of 2010, he stopped in the middle of the conversation and raised his glass. "I hope we're as good friends when you finish your book as we are now," he said to me, across the table. "But I don't give a *fuck* what you write about me."

Access comes with pratfalls and trapdoors, but it also represents an uncommon opportunity, to look so closely at an uncommon life. I took it, because it was worth it. This is what I found.

IMPACT

ON APRIL 15, 1969, A man named George Vaillant met Ben at a coffee shop across from the *Post* building for breakfast. They had never met before. Vaillant was a young psychiatrist working for the Harvard Study of Adult Development, known colloquially as the Grant Study after one of its founding funders. He had come to interview Ben.

The Grant Study is still ongoing today, tracking the lives (and deaths) of 268 Harvard students from the classes of 1939 to 1944. Ben and the others in his cohort were selected because they looked like winners, no small feat in the narrow slice that was any Harvard class in those days. The founders of the study had set out to determine the factors that led to "intelligent living" and successful aging, and its researchers sought bright, well-adapted young men to track over the course of a lifetime. Ben was an obvious choice, from a good Brahmin family, the fifty-first Bradlee to go to Harvard, quick and good-looking and already, per a Grant Study intake form from his sophomore year, apparently quite self-assured:

HAS THE STUDENT:
ANY FEELING OF INFERIORITY ABOUT HIMSELF IN ANY
WAY? No.
ANY WORRIES ABOUT HIMSELF? No.
ANY WORRIES ABOUT HIS FAMILY? No.
ANY WORRIES ABOUT HIS WORK? No.

The subjects endured rigorous physical examinations and psychological evaluations while they were at Harvard. After college, they filled out questionnaires roughly every two years and sometimes met with researchers from the study for face-to-face interviews. Ben's 1969 interview with Vaillant, who would later become the director of the study, was his first such interview in twenty years.

Ben was forty-seven years old. He had been the executive editor of the *Post* for a little less than a year. The Pentagon Papers and Watergate lay just ahead, unseen over the horizon; Ben's friendship with Kennedy,* and the access and prestige that he had derived from that relationship, still largely defined his public reputation. He had been a naval officer on a destroyer during World War II, a reporter for multiple newspapers, a press attaché in the American embassy in Paris, and a foreign correspondent, Washington correspondent, and Washington bureau chief for *Newsweek* magazine. Now, in 1969, he had just started in on the job that would change his life forever, and he knew it:

> He said that the three years he had spent as managing editor were the hardest three years he had ever spent. He had not known anything about daily journalism and had showed up at the office at eight, worked until eight in the evening, and then often after supper came down to the office and worked until one in the morning. He continued doing this six days a week for two years. He said at <u>Newsweek</u>, where he'd been bureau chief, he'd been able to do it with "my left hand." Joining the <u>Post</u> was "a watershed" in his life.
> . . . [B]eing the editor of the <u>Post</u> interrupted his life but was the greatest job in the world—"there's nothing I'd rather do." He then said that he was an over-achiever, that he'd always operated at 100%, that he possessed no unused talent.

Vaillant took the interview along a pretty standard trajectory: work history, family history, medical status, psychological status. In addition to talking about how much he loved his job, Ben dug into some complicated feelings about his family—his love for his father despite his father's problems with drink, his conflicted relationship with his

---

*Not surprisingly, another Grant Study subject, three years ahead of Ben.

mother, his first and second wives. He spoke with such frankness that he seemed even to be surprising himself. "I'm letting it pour out," he remarked to Vaillant at one point, after stating that of the three Bradlee kids he had been the closest to his father. "That's what I'm supposed to do, isn't it?"

It was. But the most revealing part of Vaillant's report isn't his summary of what Ben told him. What's most revealing is the effect that spending time with Ben had on Vaillant himself.

At first, Vaillant records what Ben says without adding much commentary of his own. Gradually, though, as the report progresses, Vaillant begins to include some of his own observations. He notes parenthetically that Ben speaks in a "charming and urbane way," then later that Ben is "dressed in a dapper fashion." When the conversation veers into the relationship with Kennedy, Ben gives Vaillant a copy of "That Special Grace," the prose poem he filed for *Newsweek* the day after Kennedy was killed. "I had the feeling not of an artist pushing his wares," Vaillant writes, "but of someone giving me a profound gift."

In the final section of the report, entitled "Description of the Man," Vaillant tries to summon a more clinical assessment of how being around Ben has made him feel:

> [I]n walking over to the office there was a contagious quality about him that made me feel bigger than life just to be with him. It stemmed partly from his being completely generous with his own feelings, combined with a social gracefulness that must have been largely habit. . . .[H]is facial expression conveyed both tenderness and seriousness while making me laugh. He said many things that were funny, but never at his own expense and never to lead me off the track from something that was emotionally relevant to him. . . .
>
> He also possessed a contagious enthusiasm and constantly saw the positive aspects, not because he defended against them but because there were many things that he really enjoyed. I could easily understand why a President would have picked him as his closest companion during the Presidency.

The final paragraph takes it yet one step further:

> This was a man with a great capacity to focus his attention. He was a man who cared about things only as they related to people. Thus he gave up golf when he stopped playing it with Jack Kennedy. What he admired most about the latter was Kennedy's ability to love and his gracefulness. I left the interview feeling that I had greater capacity as a human being just from having known him.

That's the end of the eighteen-page typewritten report. Even Vaillant seems a bit stumped by the intensity of his own feelings; written in, by hand, is a concluding question, appended perhaps after he has read the report through and his inner clinician has had a chance to right himself. "An illusion, yes," he writes in a neat print, "but what in a personality creates that illusion in others?"

Reading through the final bewildered sentences of Vaillant's report is like watching a laboratory experiment in the real-time effects of charm and charisma, with a trained psychiatrist as the subject. It's hard to talk seriously about somebody being "bigger than life" without sounding like a fool, like a rube with stars in your eyes. In fairness to Vaillant, it's easy to imagine why he might want to pencil in a qualifying sentence about illusions before handing the typewritten report to his superiors.

But if I have learned anything about Ben over the time I've spent with him, it's that "illusion" is the wrong word. What happened to Vaillant was a real, observable phenomenon, part of Ben's primary functioning as a newspaper editor and as a person. Anybody who has spent much time with him will tell you that, even the people who don't particularly like him. This is not to say that he was perfect, or that he didn't hire the wrong people or have lapses in judgment or leave some emotional and professional carnage in his wake. He did all that, too.

But the truth at the heart of Ben's time at the *Post* is the infectious sense of possibility that he created for himself and for the reporters and the newspaper that he led. When you were around him, and when he focused on you, you were included in it, too. You can call that quality in Ben "larger than life," you can call it "charisma," you can call it "genius" or "instinct" or "focus" or "verve." Whatever it is, the most important thing to know about him is that he had it, and he knew it, and he used it.

NEWS

> People ask me when was the critical moment for this paper in its pursuit of Watergate. I tell them it came in my house in Georgetown when we decided to follow you with the Pentagon Papers, to chase you knowing we could never catch you. They don't understand, but you will.

—BCB to Abe Rosenthal, managing editor,
The New York Times, May 16, 1973

IN FEBRUARY OF 1968, MORE than a year before Ben would sit down with Vaillant for their interview, a *Post* reporter got his hands on a summary of an embargoed copy of the Kerner Commission's much anticipated report on race in America. ("Our nation is moving toward two societies, one black, one white—separate and unequal.") Joe Califano, the lawyer who would go on to represent the *Post* during Watergate, was serving as President Lyndon Johnson's top domestic aide at the time. When he found out the *Post* was planning to break the embargo, he was pissed.

"So I call Ben," Califano told me. "And Ben says, 'Well, we got a copy of the report with the embargo page torn off.'" He laughed. "You can imagine that conversation. We went at it. *Really* went at it."

Califano took the issue up with Kay Graham, who didn't think the *Post* should publish the summary, either. The government planned to release the report a couple of days later; what was the point? But Ben didn't bend, and he certainly wasn't going to be told what he could or couldn't publish by Joe Califano. On March 1, 1968, the *Post* ran the text of the summary in full, spread out over three inside pages in the front section.

That same day, Ben wrote a private memo to Kay to explain his decision:

Katharine:

You said yesterday that you didn't <u>really</u> understand why it was important to publish the summary we had in our possession.
. . . It is important to me that you understand my motives. . . .

My answer is simply that our duty is to publish news when it is news, and that means when we learn and when we have checked its bona fides and when we have secured the information legally and when we have checked it for libel and when we have assured ourselves that publishing is not against the national or public interest. . . .

A newspaper that yields to any one of these pressures takes a sure step—perceptible however small—out of the newspaper business. Of course no one of these steps would put us out of the business, but that is not the issue. Each such step yields the independence we all cherish to someone else. Often, in this town, to a President or his representatives, and that is unfortunate because the pressures are greater.

A newspaper that yields to any one of these pressures sacrifices one of [its] most precious assets—the vitality and commitment, and possibly the respect of its reporters. If only one man says "What's the use of getting the news first if we don't print it," we lose something vitally important unless our reasons are iron-clad.

Ben

Twenty-two years later, sitting with Ben for an interview, Kay Graham remembered the story, and the memo. "I still, as a matter of fact, if you . . ." She hesitated.

"Go ahead and say it, Katharine," Ben said.

"If you want to know, I'm still not thrilled with publishing an official report two days before they're going to issue it. I mean, it doesn't seem to me the end-of-the-world kind of wonderful journalism."

"But it didn't screw anything up," Ben said. "That's the other thing that it never does."

"I still think I'd call that one 50–50," she said, conceding that the memo was a "very good defense" of the rationale for publication but content for the moment to let the disagreement lie.

It was a small story, a twenty-four-hour victory, but that was Ben's whole point. They were in the business of twenty-four-hour victories, of pushing the limits, of getting it first and running it if you had it. That was the game, new every day. Ben was never a theoretician of the news. He was a practitioner, more interested in what happened than how or why, preferring his own instincts to abstract ideas. But if there is such a thing as a Bradlee philosophy of newspapering, that memo to Kay Graham comes pretty close. And there's no better example of how Ben and Kay practiced that philosophy together than the sunny day in June of 1971 when the Pentagon Papers arrived on Ben's doorstep in Georgetown.

Maybe it's a generational thing, but my eyes glaze over at the first sight of those words: Pentagon Papers. Before I knew Ben, whenever I saw a reference to them in a book I would reflexively start paging through to see how long it would be before the chapter ended. Whatever I learned about them never seemed to stick. Most people I know don't really have any sense of what they were, or why they mattered, beyond the facts that they were about Vietnam and that a man named Daniel Ellsberg leaked them.

The truth is that to understand why Ben cared about them, you don't need to know a whole lot more than that. But, for posterity, the Pentagon Papers were the forty-seven volumes of a top secret internal history of the Vietnam War, commissioned by Defense Secretary Robert McNamara in 1967. Ellsberg had been an analyst at the RAND Corporation who worked on the compilation of the papers but subsequently underwent a personal conversion about the merits of the war. He thought that if the American people really knew what was going on in Vietnam, they would rise up to put an end to it. He decided to leak the papers, first to Senator J. William Fulbright, the chairman of the Senate Foreign Relations Committee. When Fulbright didn't do much of anything with them, Ellsberg turned to *The New York Times*.

The most important revelation that the Papers contained seems now to be a kind of quaint confirmation of the obvious: the government, under both Democratic and Republican administrations, had routinely, and seemingly as a matter of policy, lied to the American public about the Vietnam War. Bombing missions that had been disavowed by presidential candidates were in fact being planned at the very moment of disavowal, by those very candidates. More Americans were dying than anybody knew. There were entire bombing campaigns, in Cambodia and Laos, that had never been reported. Though the media had harbored suspicions about all of these things, the Papers confirmed those suspicions on a scale that even cynical journalists hadn't quite imagined.

I had always assumed that President Nixon reacted so aggressively to the publication of the Pentagon Papers because they were made public in 1971, and therefore must have embarrassed his administration. It was actually quite the opposite: the Papers contained no information at all about the Nixon administration. They had been delivered to McNamara's successor as defense secretary, Clark Clifford, five days before Nixon's inauguration in 1969. Nixon was apparently quite pleased at first with how poorly the papers reflected on the Democrats, particularly his predecessor, Lyndon Johnson. It was only when he realized that he could find his own presidency damaged by similar leaks down the road that he decided to take action, thus setting in motion the Shakespearean mechanics of his own demise.

What mattered to Ben about all of this wasn't the substance of it. Ben cared only that Ellsberg had decided to leak the Papers to *The New York Times*. In the spring of 1971 everybody at the *Post* had been hearing for weeks that the *Times* was planning a major scoop, but nobody knew what it was. On Sunday, June 13, 1971, after months of top secret preparation—reporters working from an undisclosed hotel room, security guards at the door—the *Times* finally dropped the bomb.

This was the kind of thing that drove Ben wild. His mission, from the moment he walked into the *Post*'s newsroom as an editor in 1965, was "to get the world to refer to the *Post* and the *Times* in the same breath." That was his definition of excellence. Sometimes he would say publicly that his goal was to have "the best reporter on every beat," which was true. But the main reason he wanted the best reporter on every beat was so that he could stick it to the *Times*.

Now the *Times* had him licked. The only way for the *Post* to cover the story was to rewrite the *Times* on its own front page, the bitterest of pills. Ben has a flair for melodrama, and he always says that there was "blood on every word" of the story that ran in the *Post* that Monday. ("You know how grand he is," one *Post* reporter said when interviewed about it later. "I don't know what the hell he said. It was a professional kick in his face, and he didn't make any bones about it.")

After two more days of the same routine, big stories in the *Times* and baleful rewrites the next day in the *Post*, Ben finally caught a break. The Nixon administration, claiming national security privilege, had secured an injunction against the *Times*, restraining them from publishing any further classified material. This marked the first time in American history that the government had ever been able to enjoin, or prevent, a newspaper from publishing in advance. The granting of the injunction posed a series of First Amendment issues, and the *Times* immediately challenged it.

The break gave the *Post* an opportunity. Ben Bagdikian, the National editor, knew Ellsberg. On Wednesday of that week, he received a cryptic call instructing him to fly to Boston, where Ellsberg was waiting for him. Ellsberg was worried that the *Times* had been silenced, and he wanted the information out. He forced Bagdikian to extract a promise from Ben that the *Post* would run the Papers if they had them, and Ben relayed his assurance that they would. Bagdikian returned the next day with 4,400 sloppily copied and out-of-order pages, a subset of the original seven thousand that the *Times* had received. The large cardboard carton, full of small, disorganized bundles of paper tied together with string, sat in its own first-class seat on the flight down to Washington.

Fearing that the *Post* newsroom would be too public a place to review the documents—they didn't want to be enjoined before they'd even started—Ben summoned top editors and reporters to his house in Georgetown. The *Times* had taken nearly three months to comb through the papers and to determine how to present the material they contained. The *Post* didn't have that kind of time. To stay ahead of the government and the rest of the media, Ben and the other editors resolved to put out a story the very next day. Bagdikian arrived at Ben's house from National Airport at 10:30 on Thursday morning. They had roughly nine hours until the first edition deadline.

Ben calls it "bedlam." There were papers all over the place. The reporters were sequestered in Ben's library with their typewriters, trying to hammer out early drafts of stories based on whatever scraps of information they could process in so short a time. The lawyers and editors convened in the living room, to figure out exactly what they could and couldn't (or would and wouldn't) publish.

Chalmers Roberts, a veteran reporter and one of the fastest typists on the staff, had begun to put together a story about the Eisenhower administration's efforts to prevent elections in North and South Vietnam in 1954. As Roberts put it in a private interview some years later:

> I said, "It's not going to be sensational, but it will be different, it's something the Times hasn't printed." That's what Ben wanted, so I am printing something those bastards hadn't printed. Because Ben is a terribly competitive guy, as you know.
>
> Ben wasn't interested in the issue at all. He was interested in the journalism. He says he has no politics, he doesn't care whether the president is a Republican or Democrat. It's true. It's hard to believe about him, but it is true. . . .
>
> [H]e really is apolitical and he wanted good stories. He was still

trying to make it. He was not the Ben Bradlee of Watergate at this
point. We gotta think of him in a different context. He was a stoop
for the lemonade girl.*

"It was an almost personal thing," one editor said of Ben's approach
to the story. "It was almost manhood on the issue, it was macho."
Phil Geyelin, the editorial page editor, said that as Ben wandered
between the reporters and the businesspeople it was as if he were
back in the locker room at St. Mark's prep school. "Bradlee was go,"
Geyelin said. "That was his first instinct and I think it was his instinct
all along."

As the day wore on, Ben and the rest of the news side began to
realize that the decision to publish wasn't going to be automatic. For
starters, the *Post*'s lawyers didn't believe that the government would
make false claims about national security privilege just to cover its
own ass. The implicit assumption was that the government did what
was right, that the president was infallible, trustworthy, deserving of
the benefit of the doubt.† This is one of the hardest aspects of the
story to believe, forty years later.

One of the more convincing arguments that the lawyers offered
was that the *Times* had already been enjoined. The *Post* couldn't
claim that they didn't know what the stakes were. There was language in the statute about "willfully" publishing material that could
be "used to the injury of the United States," and that now meant
something different to the *Post* than it had to the *Times*.

And if that weren't enough, the Washington Post Company, which
in addition to the newspaper included *Newsweek,* three television stations, and three radio stations (among other holdings), had gone pub-

---

*Ben's ten-year-old daughter, Marina, had seen the comings and goings at the house and
had cannily hastened to set up a lemonade stand outside.

†The Nixon tapes reveal that the day after the first Pentagon Papers story ran in the *Times,*
Bob Haldeman said to the president: "But out of the gobbledygook, comes a very clear
thing . . . you can't trust the government; you can't believe what they say; and you can't rely
on their judgment; and the—the implicit infallibility of presidents, which has been an accepted thing in America, is badly hurt by this, because it shows that people do things the
President wants to do even though it's wrong, and the President can be wrong."

lic two days before, offering $33 million worth of Class B common stock. If the *Post* were to be charged with a crime for publishing sensitive information, the underwriters of the offering might back out of the contract. This would cost the company money in the short term, but more to the point it would put the entire strategy and public position of the corporation in jeopardy.

Over the course of the afternoon, positions sharpened. "We were not doing very well in the argument," Ben told me. Various compromise strategies floated around, including one in which the *Post* would notify the attorney general of what they intended to publish and then allow the Justice Department a day to respond. The reporters didn't like that strategy much. One piped in, constructively, "That's the shittiest idea I've ever heard." Chal Roberts threatened to resign.

Word that the *Post* had the Papers was already starting to travel. If they didn't print what they had, people would know—and the emerging reputation of the *Post* as a hard-charging, take-on-all-comers newspaper would suffer. "Here was this big new hotshot who was supposed to take the *Post* into the Promised Land," Ben would say later, imagining what the line on him would have been, "and yet the first time he had any kind of challenge he caved."

Late in the afternoon, somewhat desperate, Ben realized that the only person who could help him was his best friend, the famous trial lawyer Edward Bennett Williams. Williams was a grand Washington character, another larger-than-life guy, and one of a small number of people who could reasonably be called Ben's peers. They first met in the late forties, when Ben was a court reporter for the *Post* and Williams was an up-and-coming defense lawyer, and they had stayed friends ever since. Williams was working a case in Chicago at the time, but Ben eventually tracked him down by phone:

Edward Bennett Williams, private interview, late seventies, undated:

He outlined the case, and then I said, Bradlee, you and I have been friends a long time—and actually our friendship went back to 1949—and I said it's the first time I've seen you so far behind, it's

21–0, it's the fourth quarter, and there are eight minutes to go, and you better get going. . . .

I'd been watching [this] city for about 30 years, and I'd been watching responsible and respectable journalists tell the Congress to go to hell and to go fuck themselves, and every journalist, at a moment of crisis, if he was respectable and the Congress was pressing for information said, you know, go to hell. . . . Congress always [lost] its guts when it comes to taking on the press. [And] that's what I really was telling him. I guarantee that the Nixon people haven't got the balls to go after you, because Nixon doesn't have the balls to go for you. . . .

It was a political judgment and not a legal one, and I just knew that Nixon didn't have the guts to go after them, therefore in this town you went with it, you didn't sit there and be indecisive, you went to it, & you put the ball in their court.

Ben's summary of this conversation was that Williams had told him, "Fuck 'em, your job is to print it." The call bucked him up, right when he needed it. He also knew that Kay respected Williams, and that Williams's support for publishing would give him a card to play during what was rapidly shaping up to be the most important up-or-down phone call in the modern history of *The Washington Post*, placed later that evening from Ben's living room to the home of Kay Graham.

That evening, Kay was throwing a retirement party at her house for Harry Gladstein, the *Post*'s circulation manager. She had known since that morning that they had the Papers, and that various editors and reporters and business types had congregated at Ben's house to hash it out. But she hadn't realized how serious it was getting. It began to dawn on her only late in the day, when Eugene Patterson, the *Post*'s managing editor, arrived at the party and pulled her aside.

"This problem is going to come to *you*," Patterson told her. "You're going to have to make a decision. And when it comes to you, the *Post*'s immortal soul is going to depend on your decision to print."

"Oh God, no!" Kay said, somewhat stricken. She hadn't expected a decision of that gravity to fall to her alone.

She went on with the party as planned. Right in the middle of her toast to Gladstein, as she stood on her back porch addressing the assembled guests, the call came from Ben's house. This was it. Kay wanted to finish her speech but was told there wasn't time, they needed her right away. She wrapped it up and hurried in to the phone.

First on the line, by himself, was Fritz Beebe, the chairman of the Post Company, who had been at Ben's house for most of the day. He was an old family friend of Kay's, and he had been her father's estate lawyer. ("Old Man Meyer," as Ben always calls him, had bought the *Post* at auction in 1933.) After Phil Graham, Kay's husband, had died in 1963 and Katharine Meyer Graham had taken over the reins at the *Post*, Beebe's had been the one shoulder she could always lean on. His advice meant more to her than anybody else's.

"He crushed me," Kay later told Ben, of what happened with Beebe on the phone. She and Beebe had never been apart on anything before. She assumed he would say, "It's all right, go ahead and publish," but he didn't. What he said was, "I guess I wouldn't."

Ben, editorial page editor Phil Geyelin, and deputy managing editor Howard Simons came on the line. "I was ready to beg," Ben admits. "I would have done anything to get it published." He reported that Williams had told them to go with it, that they couldn't afford to wait. To fail to publish would indicate to the world that there were "considerations other than news that guided our decision-making," as Ben later put it.

Kay sensed that Ben was under enormous pressure, that the newsroom was going to go apeshit* if she said no. She asked Geyelin what he thought. He said that with everything hanging in the balance he knew it was a tough problem for her, but that he thought they should publish.

*Her word.

"Well, it could destroy the newspaper," she said bluntly.

"I've heard that in the argument," Geyelin told her, "and I can't easily dismiss it, but there is more than one way to destroy a newspaper."

The answer could come only from Kay. It was her family fortune, *her* newspaper. The fact that Beebe hadn't slammed the door as firmly as he might have had given Ben hope, but after he had made his case there wasn't much more he could do. She knew where he stood. The editors fell silent on their end, and so did Kay on hers. The sound of music from the party in Kay's garden drifted in and out over the open line.

"In a real sense," Ben would say in a speech a few years later, of the moment that followed, "it marked the beginning of the journey which placed the *Post* once and for all on the cutting edge of history and of journalism. Throughout 1973, I was asked to define the key moment in our coverage of the Watergate matters, the one moment when we took an irrevocable decision. The answer is plain to me: the moment when Kay Graham said, 'I say we print' the Pentagon Papers."

Kay agreed with that, particularly in hindsight, but later she needled Ben about that speech. That wasn't exactly what she had said, she finally told him, during one of the interviews for her memoir.

"What'd you say?" he asked.

"I just said, 'Oh, go ahead, go ahead.'"

"I couldn't say, 'She moaned, "Oh, go ahead, go ahead."'"

"I did, but I didn't *moan*," Kay protested. "I just said 'Go.' I mean, I was so tense that I would—the idea that I would say, 'I say we print . . .'"

"All I remember is hanging up the phone so fast," Ben said.

"Before she changed the wording?" an observer of the interview asked.

"Yes," Ben said.

"After you hung up the phone," the observer asked, turning to Kay, "did you have any regrets?"

"No," she said.

After two days of Pentagon Papers stories in the *Post*, the government attempted to enjoin them, too. Although the injunction wasn't granted at first, the appellate process tied the *Post*'s hands until the Supreme Court was willing to hear the case. For expediency's sake, the Court joined the *Post*'s case with the *Times*'s and heard them together, on June 26, 1971. There they were, the *Post* and the *Times* in the same breath on the national stage, fighting together for journalistic freedom. Ben's gamble had paid off.

On June 30, 1971, the Supreme Court ruled 6–3 in favor of the *Times* and the *Post*. Each justice had written his own opinion, and the verdict itself was something of a mixed bag. The upshot was that the Court had found that the government couldn't prevent publication of classified information in advance, but they could attempt to prosecute under criminal statutes after the fact if they chose. The case was seen as a narrow but important victory for newspapers and for the First Amendment, and in hindsight as a foreboding sign of the Nixon administration's willingness to abuse national security claims in order to obscure its own behavior.

At the *Post*, there was nothing narrow about the victory at all. When the word came in over the wire machines at the far end of the newsroom, Gene Patterson stood up on a desk to shout it out and the whole place erupted. It was a vindication of the burgeoning culture of the paper, of Kay Graham's ownership, of Ben's editorship, of everything that the *Post* as an institution believed about itself and wanted to stand for. Ben and the rest of the reporters and editors had asked Kay Graham to put her company on the line, and she had done it.

Ben always calls Kay a "gutsy dame" or some variation of that phrase, and he means it. Despite her many hesitations and uncertainties, that's what she was. A lot of people thought that Ben brought the bravery out in Kay, that he helped give her the confidence she needed when she couldn't supply it on her own, that she ran the Pentagon Papers stories because she wanted to be on Ben's team, to stand with him. I'm certain that's true. But it went both ways.

When I first started coming down to the *Post* in 2007, before new management installed a series of high-definition television screens, a set of large pictures of the paper's past faced the bank of elevators in the lobby. This was always my favorite of them:

Ben and Kay have just left the federal courthouse in D.C. during the early stages of the legal battle over the Papers. They seem so vital, so assured, like the real life you always thought you might lead if everything went right. This is what Ben stands for, and Kay, too: the golden era in newspapers that's gone and isn't coming back, as unrecoverable as the joke Ben cracked the instant before the picture was taken.

The Washington Post
1515 L STREET, N. W.   223-6000
WASHINGTON, D. C. 20005

BENJAMIN C. BRADLEE
EXECUTIVE EDITOR

June 30, 1971

TO THE STAFF

There is just no way of saying how
proud I am of this wonderful newspaper and everyone on it.

The guts and energy and responsibility
of everyone involved in this fight, and the sense
that you all were involved, has impressed me more
than anything in my life.

You are beautiful.

bcb

The Washington Post

Date 6/25/71

TO __Ben Bradlee__   FROM __Hal Willard__

RE:

I would like to say to you that I am proud
to be associated with a man who has guts.

Dear Mr. Bradlee,

Hooray!
The truth will keep us free.

FATE

"IF YOU WROTE THAT IN a novel, you wouldn't believe it," I said. We were sitting in Ben's office, talking about how he had first arrived at the *Post* in 1948.

He was twenty-seven at the time, three years back from the war and dead set on a career in journalism. He had spent two years working on a start-up weekly newspaper in New Hampshire, *The New Hampshire Sunday News*, but that paper had been sold and he was out beating the pavement. He had interviews, set up by high-placed family friends, at *The Baltimore Sun* and the *Post*.

As the overnight train from Boston approached the station in Baltimore on the morning of the interviews, Ben looked out the window and saw rain coming down in sheets. The *Sun* was the preeminent paper in Baltimore and a prestigious place for a young journalist to catch on, but it was raining so hard that Ben decided to stay on the train. He would take his chances at the *Post*.

When he arrived in D.C. later that day, he rented a room at the Willard Hotel (for $6) and then walked a block over to the *Post*'s old building on E Street for his interview. "It is hard to recreate the fear I felt," he would write later. "This was the city room of a newspaper where every reporter I admired would die to work." The *Post* didn't make much money, and the *Evening Star* was considered D.C.'s paper of record, but the *Post* was liberal in Ben's sense of the word—civil libertarian, anxious to tackle the tougher issues, unafraid to offend the big shots and the establishment.

As Ben made the rounds, one of the editors let slip that the *Post* just happened to have an unexpected vacancy; a reporter had quit the day before. Ben Gilbert, the city editor, and Russ Wiggins, the managing editor—two men who would get to know Ben and his ambitions quite well over the following decades—intimated later that afternoon that they wanted to hire him, pending the approval of publisher Phil Graham. The next day, the parsimonious Graham signed off on the hire, and after a whirlwind twenty-four hours Ben was the new low man on the city desk of *The Washington Post*.

"The continued intersection of your life with the *Post*," I said to Ben in his office, "through Phil Graham and then through *Newsweek*, I mean it really seems—"

"Fated," Ben said, interrupting me.

"Fated," I echoed, relieved that he had said it first. "It just seems like there was something pushing you . . ."

"Yeah."

". . . here. That this is where you were supposed to end up, and you got here."

"Yeah."

"But say that the wrong way and you look like a jerk."

"Yeah, well, say it the right way," he said.

The story of Ben's life has a lot of mythic elements to it—not apocryphal, but big, cosmic, blurring the lines between fate and luck and free will, like the story with the rain on his way down from Boston. He got his start in journalism, for instance, because his dad wanted him to have a job one summer and happened to know the owner of the *Beverly Evening Times*, a small paper near the Bradlee summer place. That was it. His dad picked up the phone and Ben's career in newspapers was born.

That's how things worked in Ben's life. When he got caught out where the waves broke, he was always able to ride them in. When he was fourteen, an epidemic of polio swept through his boarding school, killing one of his good friends, and he spent the summer laid up in bed as his body battled the disease. If you believe him, he never worried about whether he would walk again. Even the doctors at the Grant Study were mystified by his attitude, wondering openly about the relation between his confidence and his near-complete recovery:

> In spite of being unable to move his legs [for a couple of months] and in spite of one of his friends dying in the same epidemic . . . he never did consider that he would be paralyzed. This is a very interesting fact in illness. Do those people who develop a permanent paralysis have as much confidence while they are ill as this boy had?

Ben was just made that way. Even if you factor in the prerogatives of wealth and whiteness and WASPness and maleness and attractiveness and intelligence and charm and all of the other advantages that Ben was born with, you still can't quite reach his easy way with the world.

As David Remnick, a former *Post* reporter and now the editor of *The New Yorker*, put it to me, "He's not a Jew. You can quote me on that. 'Not a Jew.' " Richard Cohen, a longtime *Post* columnist and close friend of Ben's, once described the experience of staying at Ben's country place in West Virginia during the seventies:

> Actually, he always had two houses. One of them was a shack in West Virginia where Ben used to go on weekends to chop wood . . . and clip coupons. The place had no central heating. Just a pot-bellied stove. This was the WASP idea of Grossinger's.
>
> I went there once. Ben made your basic Protestant meal—hard boiled eggs, a pint of vanilla ice cream and a double scotch. Then

we all retired to our little Protestant bed rooms where the temperature was about 10 below zero.

I covered myself with 300-year-old quilts and stray pieces of export china. This was such a deeply Gentile experience that I awoke the next morning with a foreskin.

The point is less that he's a WASP than that people love to talk about what a WASP he is.* It's a crucial building block in the Bradlee myth, this tough-talking, profane guy whose dad was a member of the Somerset Club.

Ben's a Brahmin, even though he loves to play against type. Benjamin Crowninshield Bradlee, born in Boston in August of 1921 to two blue-blood parents who were both descended from the same Crowninshield line some generations before. His mom was Josephine deGersdorff, the daughter of a prominent and wealthy lawyer in New York.† If you ask Ben about her, one of the first things he will tell you is a simple but loaded detail: "Great teeth." That's a full sentence in his memoir. It took me a little while to realize that this wasn't a flattering comment:

> B: She was smashing-looking, spectacular, handsome, pretty lady. Very graceful, good figure, and pretty for a long time, I mean she was a pretty fifty-year-old. She smiled a great deal, laughed a lot, had no sense of humor, none. . . . She talked a lot, compared to my father. And she laughed easily. And some of us thought sort of thoughtlessly.

They clearly butted heads. "Bennie was the only one of my children who was spanked," his mother told the Grant Study interviewers in 1941, "and this was because he was a very obstinate child."

Ben's mother was the long arm of the law around the house. She was the one who made all of the children speak in French on Satur-

---

*More Cohen, to me: "I never met anybody like him in my life until I got to know him. I mean, I said to him, there wasn't anybody in my entire postal zone that had hair as straight as his."

†The law firm of Cravath, Swaine & Moore was, for a time, Cravath, deGersdorff, Swaine & Wood.

days, attend the symphony, and do all of the other things that the children of well-heeled WASPs did in those days. (Ben had an older brother, Freddy, whom he loved, and an older sister, Connie, of whom I have never once heard him speak.) Freddy was the oldest, but he was an outsider in the family—gay, destined for Broadway, bored by sports. He thought that Ben was powerfully influenced by their mother, even more so than by the father whom Ben adored. "Much of Ben's drive and competitiveness comes from her," Freddy told David Halberstam in the late 1970s. "She was a fiercely competitive, ambitious woman, ambitious for her children . . . that came from her."

His father, with whom he had a much stronger emotional connection, was Frederick "Beebo" Bradlee, a former all-American football player at Harvard. One of Ben's earliest and fondest memories of his house in Boston was the picture of his dad and the rest of the Harvard football team that hung in the waiting room at the top of the entry stairs. The coach was standing behind Ben's dad, with his hand directly on Beebo's shoulder. Father and son would go to the Harvard games on Saturdays, where Ben was always struck by his father's modesty. During one game a Harvard back broke off a long run for a touchdown, and somebody in the stands nearby yelled, "Shades of Be Bradlee!" Ben's dad had said quietly, "Yes, shades. Pull 'em down."

His dad had worked as a banker after leaving college, but he lost his job at the Blair Investment Company at the beginning of the Depression. Both Ben's mom and dad were set to inherit a fair amount of money, but Beebo's main trust didn't come due until after World War II. Ben's dad took on a series of odd jobs, keeping the books at country clubs and the like, sometimes doing things—like cleaning out a railroad car with a friend's commercial deodorant as a promotional gimmick—that embarrassed Ben and his siblings, even as they respected the industry. The Bradlees went from having a governess, a cook, and a maid to having nobody but themselves. (This is why Ben always notes that his family's house was on Beacon Street, but not on the "sunny side.") They were never going to be poor, by any stretch, but definitions like that are mostly relative when you're a kid. You

have no concept of worlds outside of your own. Ben and Freddy and
Connie were referred to as "scholarship" kids at school, because a
relative was paying their tuition. They felt it. Ben very clearly felt it.

And it also as clearly took a toll on Ben's dad. Asked in 1981 by the
Grant Study what blows in his life had hit him the hardest and upset
him the most for some time afterward, Ben responded, "Understanding that my old man drank too damn much, which I discovered
when I was about twelve and he drove me home drunk. But it curi-
ously brought me closer than ever to him. Off the pedestal into reality, etc." His dad had been driving him home from a dance at one of
the country clubs and was pretty bombed out—weaving back and
forth all over the road. Ben doesn't like to talk about it, but he was so
angry at the time that he actually tried to hit his dad, through his
tears. "Our real understanding dates from that," he told George Vaillant in 1969. Ten years later, he would tell a different interviewer that
"when you recognize frailty in your father it is a real milestone, and
it allows you in some way to love him as [you were] not able to before."

As an adult, Ben would look back on that time and say that the
Depression, on balance, was a good thing, because it forced the Bradlees to become a family for the first time. At the Bradlee country
place in Beverly, father and son worked out in the woods together,
often in silence. Ben noticed that whether they were chopping down
trees or clearing paths, his dad always did everything completely and
without complaint of difficulty. No task was too small to be done
well, and Ben admired that and took the lesson to heart. "He didn't
go disappear up his asshole," as Ben says, of the challenges his dad
faced during the Depression. "He went out and did things."

Though Ben remembers his upbringing fondly, the main reason
his WASPness is relevant is that he ultimately rejected it as a way of
viewing the world. That rejection was his first true step toward journalism as a calling. If you ask him why he became a journalist, he will
tell you "the war." And if you ask him to explain, he will say, "My
life had no purpose before the war," or "I gave a shit about nothing
before the war," and then he will look at you in a way that says, "I
hope you have another question."

You can't spend nearly four years on destroyers in the Pacific during a world war without undergoing some kind of transformation. "The war was the first marking experience as an adult for my generation," he says. "You were struggling for the first time with great issues. Most of all, what the hell were you doing here? Why were you fighting? Why was a nice little WASP from Boston suddenly in a goddamn destroyer off of New Guinea somewhere?" When Ben left for the Pacific, he was a relatively spoiled, insulated kid who had been on probation at Harvard twice and had decided to graduate early to fight in the war because "that was what you did before you thought anything through."

In November of 1946, the Grant Study questionnaire featured a special section titled "Armed Service War Record":

> Now that it is over, what effect has the war had upon you? Are you the same man who went into uniform or are you different, and if so, specifically in what way? What changes in your general outlook on life, especially in your religious beliefs, and ethical and moral standards have occurred? What is your present opinion as to what the world owes you and you it, and is this a change from views formerly held?

This is Ben's response, written in longhand, after he'd been home for a year:

> A better man, he cried, in that I know something at last of the human forces at work in America today.
>
> No changes—religiously. Today's #1 problem is how best to educate that great person & poor bastard, the average American. He gets us into troubles by an uninformed lethargy, but doesn't see how he did it.
>
> I value friends more & by friends I mean from Alpha to Omega. I defecate figuratively on the old school tie which I wore so proudly & misinformedly in youth—18.
>
> The world owes me nothing. I owe it everything. This is not maudlin & represents a complete metamorphosis.

The language is raw, more ardent than Ben would allow now, but it captures how he felt before he'd told the story a thousand times. The war opened Ben's eyes to people who lived outside the three-mile track between 267 Beacon Street and Harvard Yard, and also to the thrill of real responsibility in high-pressure situations. His job on the USS *Philip* had been to run the Combat Information Center, a position in which he had to cull information from various sources and tell the captain what he needed to know, when he needed to know it. (He proved to be so good at this, and pioneered such a successful methodology, that the Navy had him spend the second half of the war jumping from destroyer to destroyer, teaching other CIC crews what he had learned.) On the *Philip*, once he made officer of the deck, he ran the ship for four hours at a time—as a twenty-one-year-old kid.

In terms of his path to the *Post*, the most relevant part of Ben's war experience was the "complete metamorphosis" that it brought about within him, particularly with regard to the narrowness and privilege of his upbringing. There was no way he could return from the war to be a stockbroker with one of his dad's friends, which had been the informal plan before he left. When he lay in what he calls his "fart sack" at night, trying to sleep in the simmering heat of the ship, he wondered what he could really *do* when he got back to educate "that great person and poor bastard," to make some difference in the world.

"The only other thing I ever thought of," he once told me, "was teaching, and the more I thought of it the less it interested me." Floating somewhere out there in the ocean, Ben picked journalism, and when he got home he went straight for it.

Ben spent two and a half years as a city reporter at the *Post* during his first go-round, from 1948 to 1951. These were the days of newsboys yelling "EXTRA!" in the streets, when the small, scrappy *Post* ran third in a four-newspaper town. He covered the courts, the gamblers and the vice squads and the part of the city that people love to call the underbelly. He climbed out on a ledge next to a suicide jumper that he'd spotted on the ninth floor of the Willard as he walked out of lunch one day, taking notes for a front page story while the cops talked the guy down. Once he heard shots while he was on his way to work on the trolley car and saw bodies in the street. He stepped off the trolley and walked into the middle of the assassination attempt on President Harry Truman, who was staying at Blair House, the presidential guesthouse, while the White House was undergoing some remodeling.

The most historically important moment of Ben's first stint at the *Post* occurred in June of 1949, when he and another reporter covered the attempted integration of one of the city's public swimming pools in Anacostia. There had been a near race riot, with whites attacking blacks and vice versa, which Ben and his colleague had witnessed and then filed by phone with the rewrite desk. (In those days, many of the stories in newspapers and magazines weren't written by the reporters themselves, but by "rewrite men" who stayed in the office and converted the raw files, dispatches, and telephone reports into a finished product.) The riots were a front page story, without question.

Later that night, when the bulldog edition* of the paper came up from the press room, Ben saw that the story had been buried inside the local section of the paper, with the "race riot" element severely downplayed as an "incident." He was pissed. "The great liberal *Washington Post* was scared to tell the truth," as he put it. He was sitting in the city room of the paper, making his displeasure known, when all of a sudden he felt a tap on his shoulder. Behind him was Phil Graham, the *Post*'s publisher, wearing a tuxedo.

"All right, Buster," Graham said. "Come on up with me."

Without Phil Graham there is no "Ben Bradlee," and there isn't

---

*The "bulldog" is the first edition of the next morning's newspaper, often produced at about 11:00 the night before and distributed in those days to movie houses and newsstands for the late night crowd looking for a jump on tomorrow's news. When *New York Times* copyboys began swiping copies of the *Post*'s bulldog out of the alley behind the building in the late sixties, Ben viewed it as a sign of great progress at the paper. When Robert Kennedy was killed in 1968 the bulldog had already come out and Ben actually yelled, for the one time in his career as an editor, "Stop the presses!" so they could remake an entirely new front page.

really a "Kay Graham" either—not as the historical figures they became. Kay's father had bought the paper, but in 1946 he had made his
son-in-law the publisher and part owner. From then until his death
in 1963, Phil shaped the *Post*, more so than any of its editors or reporters. And he wasn't just the boss in name; out of the five thousand
Class A shares that Old Man Meyer made available to Phil and to Kay
to purchase as a couple, he allotted 3,500 to Phil and only 1,500 to
Kay. "As Dad explained to me," Kay wrote in her memoir, "no man
should be in the position of working for his wife."

David Halberstam memorably introduced him in *The Powers That
Be* as "the incandescent man," and Ben always says that Phil Graham
was the most interesting person in the room, no matter what the
room was or who else was in it. He crackles in the pages of books.
Everybody who encountered him remembers him as brilliant in
every sense of the word, irreverent, obstreperous, unstoppable. As a
young man he had been president of the *Harvard Law Review* and
clerked for two Supreme Court justices, and as the publisher of the
Post he had become one of the most influential operators in town.
John F. Kennedy and Lyndon Baines Johnson took his phone calls
and relied on him for advice. "You could give him the most complex
problem and he'd solve it in three sentences," Arnaud de Borchgrave, an old colleague of Ben's and Phil's, told me. "And so we all
followed him. He and Ben had a lot in common."

Phil was six years older than Ben, and they moved in some of the
same social circles, but in June of 1949 Ben was a cub reporter and
Phil Graham was the boss. Up in Graham's office, Ben discovered
that the secretary of the interior (Julius "Cap" Krug) was already
there, along with famed counselor-to-presidents Clark Clifford,
who represented President Truman. Heavyweights. The secretary of
the interior had jurisdiction over D.C. pools at that time, because
D.C. was still run completely by the federal government. (There was
no elected mayor of D.C. until 1975.) As Clifford and Krug looked
on, Graham asked Ben to recite the story of what he'd seen at the
pool and then dismissed him. Ben didn't know it at the time, but
later he discovered that his version of events became a bargaining

chip in a deal that Graham struck with the government that night: close the pool in Anacostia at once and then reopen all of the city's pools on an integrated basis the next year, "or Bradlee's story runs on page one tomorrow." The government took the deal, and that was that.

"Probably pretty wise," Ben said of it later. "Probably a good deal. But unthinkable to me. I don't think you can pay too great a price for telling the truth." D.C. would be ravaged by race riots in 1968, in the wake of Martin Luther King, Jr.'s assassination. If Phil Graham had run the pools story on page one in 1949, those later and larger riots could well have happened much sooner. "It might have been better if we had," Ben said. "I can't make the judgment and I'm sure no one else can either."

After a couple of years on the city desk, Ben realized that his options for immediate advancement at the *Post* were limited. He wanted to work on the National desk, but the paper was so small and so broke at the time that in order to get a new slot, he says, "you had to wait for some poor bastard to die." Ben asked Phil Graham if he would support his application to the Nieman Fellowship program at Harvard, which would give Ben a chance to change his surroundings and maybe result in some kind of promotion when he got back.

"Fuck you," Graham said. "You've already been to Harvard."

So much for that. But in Ben's life there's always a door that opens, and in this instance it was opened by a letter from a friend at *The New Hampshire Sunday News* who had become the press attaché in the American embassy in Paris. He was being transferred out soon, and he knew that Ben spoke French and had always wanted to live in Europe. Would Ben have any interest in being his successor? Phil Graham wasn't overly pleased with it, but he granted Ben a leave of absence to go.

Ten days after he started the job at the embassy, Ben knew that he was going to end up hating it—"cookie pushing," he called it. You always had to cover your ass, and you could never say what you really thought. He had to tell a white lie here or there to make sure the stories came out right. It was an important job, but even after six months you can tell that he missed the *Post*:

> I wanted to change because I wanted to get foreign experience: it was as simple as that. I hope to return to the POST either as a foreign correspondent, or as a reporter. . . .
>
> My work is very much the same, except for its geography. I suppose I am now more sedentary, since I no longer chase fires, rapists, gamblers or disasters. I suppose I feel more satisfaction, because the experience is new, and I feel necessary in the making of a successful journalistic career. But I did not change jobs because I was disinterested in the one I left.

That's Ben's Grant Study questionnaire from January of 1952. By July of that year, he was already openly campaigning for a return to the *Post*. He wrote to the higher-ups at the paper from the French countryside, where he and his first wife and some friends had rented a château,* living "as high on the hog as we will ever be":

> Re return to Washington. I have entered negotiations with M'sieu Wiggins, but situation is complicated. Believe it or not, I am a fair-sized cheese (not too big, mind you, but ripe, solid) in this job, and I fought like hell to get it. I have just been upped a class. I am making $10,000 a year, living in a beautiful city, seeing parts of life and the world that I will never have the chance to see again. If I leave before June, I have to pay my way back—call it an even grand. There is something in me that says I would be crazy to leave this for anything. We want to come back, don't get me wrong, but not to Municipal Court. I bet when I took this that I could go faster from here, than from there. And I don't want to lose, without an effort.

---

*At dinner one night, when my wife discovered that Ben had rented a weekend place outside Paris for a couple of summers, she asked him, "Was it some kind of timeshare?" Ben turned to her, incredulous, and bellowed, "*Timeshare?* It was a fucking *château!*"

Phil Graham read this letter and then composed a response to Russ Wiggins, the managing editor of the *Post*, on July 31, 1952:

> Here are my views on Ben Bradlee's letter, and you can send the attached copy along to him if you like:
>
> (1) Ben is an exceptionally able person—the kind of person we would like to have on the Post.
>
> (2) His experience—in terms of value to the Washington Post—is still a little short of that of Folliard, Albright, Friendly, et al.
>
> (3) From our point of view, Ben's return amounts to the same thing as though he had stayed here—i.e., he'll have to come back without benefiting over other people who have not been away. That means, as I figure it, $98.25 per week salary.
>
> (4) Much as I wish we could, we cannot compete for Ben with public relations jobs at $10,000. My own feeling is that ten years from now he'll prefer newspapering to public relations—but that is conjecture. This personal choice obviously must be his.
>
> (5) If I were Ben I would come back to the Post, because: (a) it's the brightest, best paper in the U.S.; and (b) it's young and growing. But, again, that is to some extent conjecture and cannot, of course, be considered as safe a prediction as one about the stability of, say, Metropolitan Life.
>
> P. L. GRAHAM

It's a rare chance to see Ben as his old boss saw him. Phil would never know just how right he had been.

But the loop didn't close quite yet. Having made it to Europe, Ben wasn't going to rush back to D.C. to take a job that offered no advancement from the one he'd left behind. This was his only shot abroad and he wanted to make the most of it, so he cast around for other opportunities. The Hotel Crillon was across the street from the American embassy, and in those days a number of foreign correspondents used to go there for a drink after work—Art Buchwald, who became one of Ben's great friends, and Arnaud de Borchgrave, who was the European correspondent for *Newsweek,* among many others.

"Today, nobody even knows who the press attaché is *anywhere,* but in those days it was a major media presence," de Borchgrave told me. "Everybody knew Ben. In those days, if you were writing a serious piece about the United States, for a French newspaper, you would go and see Ben. That was how powerful the position was."

One night they had a drink after work and de Borchgrave told Ben that he was thinking of leaving his post as European correspondent at *Newsweek,* to move up to become a foreign editor. He needed to find somebody to succeed him who could speak French and was well connected. Instead of offering advice, Ben leapt at the opportunity for himself.

"It hadn't occurred to you before?" I asked de Borchgrave.

"No," he said. "Because in those days press attaché was more important than *Newsweek* bureau chief." But Ben was bored at the embassy, and he knew an opportunity when he saw one. After some back-and-forths with the editors at *Newsweek,* Ben was hired.

"You couldn't help but like the guy," de Borchgrave told me. "I never saw a side of Ben that I didn't like. You were happy to be in his company, and you looked forward to having that drink at the Crillon bar."

I made a joke about how Ben refers to his days in Paris, after the dissolution of his first marriage and before the beginning of his second, as his "brief swashbuckling phase."

"We used to kid him," de Borchgrave said with a chuckle, "that there were women queuing up in front of his apartment for fifteen minutes of his time."

The arrival of Antoinette (Tony) Pinchot Pittman in Paris in the summer of 1954 would bring an eventual end to Ben's swashbuckling days and ultimately set in motion his return to the States. Tony was blithe, blonde, and descended from the landed gentry—daughter of Amos Pinchot, a wealthy lawyer, and niece of Gifford Pinchot, who was twice the governor of Pennsylvania and a conservationist who served as the first chief of the U.S. Forest Service. Tony and Ben had moved in some of the same WASPy circles in D.C. in the late forties, and he had always noticed what he would later describe as her "inner light," but they didn't fall in love until she arrived in Paris. That summer Tony and her equally alluring sister, Mary, were traveling through Europe without their children—on a "toot with the diaphragms," as they called it:

B: That summer we had rented a chateau just west of Paris, southwest of Paris, in a little village called Boissy St. Leger and it was, god, it was the most beautiful place. It was not an old, old castle, it was a sort of post-Napoleonic castle, 1829, 1830. Four hundred hectares, walled-in acres, owned by a man called Rodolphe Hottinguer, who was a baron. . . . They rented this place to us for a hundred thousand francs a month, that's three hundred bucks a month. It had sixty-five rooms in it, it had two ballrooms. . . .

There were a lot of children, we had a swimming pool, we had a pond. It was just a gorgeous place, and it was probably thirty-five, forty minutes from Paris. And we used to give these big parties every weekend which Tish Noyes would cook up a lot of chili or spaghetti or something like that, because none of us had any dough, we really didn't. . . . We had a lot of people from the embassy, we had a lot of French types, we had a lot of—I mean there was a party going from Saturday through Sunday night and Tony and Mary came to one of those and Tony and I fell in love.

Q: That day?

B: That day. It was very complicated, very difficult, very—I probably am not terribly proud of that in the sense of although Jean and I were not a viable family we were a family. But nothing really happened for years. That was 1954 and Tony and I got married two years later. She had a family, she had four kids, she went into analysis, I did and—

Q: Jean knew?

B: Jean knew.

Q: Right from the start?

B: Yeah. And we separated. And there was no deception, no dissimulation.

Tony was married with four kids, and Ben and his first wife, Jean
Saltonstall—a Boston Brahmin whom Ben had hurriedly married
just before the war—were still officially together, though their marriage had been dying on the vine for a while. Over the course of the
next two years, both Tony and Ben would break up their marriages
and uproot their lives in order to be together. Eventually they struck
a deal: they would get married, Tony would come to Paris for one
year with all four of her kids, and then the following year Ben would
return to the U.S. with his new family.

This meant Ben was going to have to find a new job in Washington. As the *Newsweek* correspondent in Europe, he had been his own
boss, leaving to cover a war in Egypt on a whim, traveling between
Algeria, Morocco, and Tunisia with luxurious weekend respites at
the home of Marion and Irwin Shaw near Biarritz. That was hard to
give up, but Ben worked it out so that he could return as a correspondent in the Washington bureau of the magazine. He hadn't
wanted to make a lateral move when he was in France with Jean, but
he was willing to make one in order to be with Tony. In 1957, the
newly combined Bradlee family moved into a house on N Street in
Georgetown, and Ben set about working his way up the ladder at
Newsweek.

Two important things happened next. The first was that, shortly
after Ben and Tony moved to 3321 N Street, Senator John F. Kennedy
and his young wife, Jackie, would buy the house at 3307. The second
was that a couple of years after Ben returned to D.C., *Newsweek*'s
owners decided to sell the magazine.

Ben often says that you really only make a couple of major decisions
in life, that everything else is window dressing and logistics. He would
later write, of Watergate, that "a chance like this comes only once in
a lifetime, and I suspect our contribution was simply to recognize it
when it came." He recognized another of those opportunities—
outside of Watergate, perhaps the most important opportunity of his
life—in February of 1961, when he picked up the telephone and
called his old boss, Phil Graham, to pitch him on buying *Newsweek*.

Ben and Oz Elliott, the managing editor of *Newsweek* in New York, had been wondering for months who was going to buy the magazine and what that would mean for them. Eventually, Ben decided he was going to try to find a buyer himself. He knew people with money, and Phil Graham was at the top of his list. "In my circle, when you said publisher, that's what you meant," he once said, referring to Graham. "If you were going to buy *Newsweek*, you weren't going to see some buddy of yours who was also making nine grand a year."

It was late when Ben decided to call, somewhere around eleven o'clock. (Over the course of that evening he had downed "a couple of pops," as he likes to say, and the liquid courage helped.) To Ben's surprise, Graham answered the phone himself and told Ben to come over right away. Ben hurried over to Phil and Kay's house on R Street, where he and Phil spent most of the night in conversation. "I didn't have a goddamn clue as to whether I was getting anywhere," Ben says, but as dawn neared Graham asked him to put together a memo about who he thought were the best people, who should play an important role at the magazine if the Post Company were really to take a serious interest. Graham was using words like "we."

Ben didn't know it—nobody knew it yet, really, except for Kay—but Phil Graham was a manic-depressive, and he was in one of his up phases. Had Ben caught Graham at a lower moment, the outcome would surely have been different.* As it was, Ben went home and hammered out a long handwritten memo, "stream of consciousness stuff," all about who was good and who wasn't, making the hard sell

---

*K: Well, now, Ben, after Phil bought Newsweek he was pretty involved, very involved with it until that summer.

B: He was and then . . .

K: . . . and then he got depressed.

B: And then he got depressed.

K: But you all didn't know it.

B: We didn't really know that.

K: No . . . Well, you know, he was, when he bought Newsweek it has to be said, he was manic.

for the *Post* to take the chance. (Sadly, this memo is lost to history, one of the few things that nobody can find.)

Graham bit, and so did Fritz Beebe and the rest of the Post Company. A couple of weeks later, after a fair amount of secrecy and intrigue—code names on the telephone, the invention of a fictional "Uncle Harvey"—the sale was final. Fifteen million dollars, but very little of it in cash, one of the best deals in the history of the Post Company.

However good a deal it might have been for the company, it was a far, far better deal for Benjamin C. Bradlee. In the first instance, Graham offered him the role of Washington bureau chief at *Newsweek*, and Ben took it. His days as a lowly correspondent were over. Now he would be the boss, managing the bureau, directing coverage, assigning reporters, answering only to Oz Elliott. He had officially become a fair-sized cheese.

But that was only the start of it. Because Ben had brought the deal to Phil Graham and the Post Company, the company awarded him a finder's fee of Washington Post Company stock in the form of options. In the years to come, Post stock would skyrocket and Ben's allotment would yield millions of dollars. Ben had some family money, and he was always paid pretty well, but nothing like this. "Without putting too much arithmetic on it," he once said, "it made me many times the millionaire, it bought me houses, it allowed me to do things I never could have done otherwise. With the most innocent, naïve of motives." He had been far more motivated by the prospect of professional advancement than by any grand dreams of a finder's fee. The payout was a wonderful surprise, a bonus in the true sense of the word.[*]

The purchase of *Newsweek* brought Ben back into Phil Graham's orbit, and into the *Post*'s, for good. He would never work for any-

---

[*]B: Just for one good idea.

  Q: It was a pretty good idea, though.

  B: Yeah, it was a pretty good idea, but was it a multi-million dollar idea? I don't know. "Hey, let's call up Phil Graham." Doesn't seem in retrospect.

body other than a member of the Graham family again. But there was also a deeper symbolic meaning:

> B: [I]t occurred to me that we, me, should try to influence who bought us. Therefore influence our own future. That if we could persuade somebody to buy it who shared our goals in journalism that it would be a wonderfully worthwhile thing to do.
>
> Q: Did you have an epiphany?
>
> B: No. I just—no—I just said that—perhaps even a moment of introspection whether man did have control of his fate, in any way. Whether you could influence your own future. Whether you could do something that would decide history, that would make your history. I don't want to leave the impression that this was an epiphany of any kind. . . . Suddenly I was determined to try, that's all.

You can wait a long time and never hear Ben admit to "a moment of introspection," so you know it meant something to him. He was never a shrinking violet; when de Borchgrave said he was looking for a replacement, Ben hadn't hesitated to recommend himself for the job.

This was different, though, more broadly gauged and fundamental. You had to raise your hand. You could shape history, and certainly your own history, but you had to be willing to put yourself in the hunt. Throughout the rest of his career, Ben would always cotton most to the people who were willing to go for it, to take a chance, to run with something. The people who wanted instruction or guidance from him never fared all that well. After the sale of *Newsweek*, with his star on the rise and his good friend newly installed in the Oval Office, Ben was in the hunt in a way that he never had been before.

Ben's story from there is such a happy one that it's hard to stomach what would happen over the course of the next two years to the man who had made so much of it possible. Phil Graham played a pivotal role in Ben's life, and they were roughly the same age, yet in a basic way Ben never felt that he knew him. He wasn't alone. "His wit was a way of keeping people away from intimacy," Kay once said privately of Phil, who could keep dinner parties going for hours with his command of fact and humor. "He had no intimates. He had a lot of people who were friends of his, but he had no real intimates." Phil was so supercharged that nobody could ever get a handle on him, and he struggled to get a handle on himself.

In August of 1963, on leave from a psychiatric institution and stuck in the grip of a deepening disease, Phil took his own life with a shotgun at Glen Welby, the Graham farm in Marshall, Virginia. He had been acting out, carrying on an open affair and even threatening to divorce Kay and take the paper away from her. There's no way around those uncomfortable facts, and it's all a part of the path that Kay Graham would have to walk toward her own unexpected future.

There's also no way around the fact that Ben and Kay would stand on Phil Graham's shoulders. He left them a newspaper and a media company on the rise, financially secure and growing after long years of scraping by. His decision to buy the *Washington Times-Herald* in 1954 (and to continue to print the two pages of exclusive comics that came along with the deal) had established the *Post*'s morning monopoly and made the modern *Post* possible.

When he was starting to lose it toward the end, Phil had called President Kennedy and berated him, shouting into the phone, delusional, "Do you know who you're talking to?" And JFK had answered, "I know I'm not talking to the Phil Graham I have so much admiration for." As crazy as things got, people loved him. When Ben came back over to the *Post* as an editor in 1965, he had his old boss's distinctive oval desk brought down to use as his own. All of the big decisions that have come to Ben's desk since then have come to Phil Graham's desk, too.

PREZ

Mrs. John F. Kennedy (right) listens intently as her husband announces his candidacy

By Bob Burchette, Staff Photographer

Ben and Tony with Jackie Kennedy, *The Washington Post,* January 4, 1960.

Ben and Antoinette Bradlee, interview with Arthur Schlesinger, Jr., March 26, 1964:

Q: Were you and Tony with him [JFK] the night of the West Virginia primary?

AB: Yes.

Q: Do you remember anything about that evening?

AB: I do. We had dinner with them, at their house, and then Jack was so restless after dinner that we all decided that we'd better go to the movies . . .

B: . . . and they wouldn't let us in because it was a horror movie—one of those things that "We won't open the doors after the show started." And we said, "This is Senator Kennedy. He's running for President." And there was a big yawn from the guy.

[They ended up across the street at a movie called *Private Property*, which was on the list of banned films for Catholics, "a nasty little thing . . . starring one Katie Manx as a horny housewife who kept getting raped and seduced by hoodlums," as Ben once put it.]

AB: . . . But he spent most of the time there leaving and going next door to a drugstore and telephoning to see how things were going.

B: Two or three times.

AB: And then we sort of finished the movie out and we went back to their house, and he put in a phone call to—I guess Larry O'Brien.

B: Bobby.

AB: Was it Bobby?

B: Yeah.

AB: In West Virginia. And I remember seeing his face as he got the news. He was absolutely stunned. . . . This seemed to be the first realization he had that he really might make it. It was that night. And it came upon him that he might be the next President of the United States. . . . Jackie rushed out into the kitchen and got a bottle of champagne.

B: Our champagne.

AB: Was it our champagne?

B: Yeah, we brought it.

SO MUCH BAGGAGE HAS BEEN LOADED onto Ben's relationship with John F. Kennedy over the years. All anybody ever wants to ask Ben is whether he knew how much Jack was screwing around, and when Ben gives his standard answer nobody believes him anyway. And if it isn't the philandering, it's the relationship itself. Journalists love to take shots at Ben for having been too close to Kennedy while he was covering him for *Newsweek*. The Nixon people had a field day with it, for obvious reasons, but they're not alone. The uniform perception is that most editors today would never allow a friend to cover a friend the way Ben covered Kennedy.

There are some uncomfortable moments, to be sure, places where Ben and Kennedy each crossed a line that Ben would never have crossed later in life. In a few key spots the relationship would veer more toward transaction than friendship. "Did he use me? Of course he used me," Ben said in an interview in 1975. "Did I use him? Of course I used him. Are those the ground rules down here in Washington? Hell, yes." They both knew that ambition had been baked into the cake from the start.

But most of those complexities wouldn't emerge until later. There is something simple and satisfying about Ben tucking that bottle under his arm and walking with Tony over to the Kennedys' for dinner on the night in the spring of 1960 that JFK realized that he might be president. Just the four of them, having dinner, taking in a movie, sharing a celebratory bottle of champagne. What a moment in life, in anyone's life, to watch the key turn in the lock and the door swing open, to see history in such personal terms. Within a couple of hours, Ben and Tony would be on the *Caroline,* the Kennedy campaign plane, for an impromptu victory trip to West Virginia. Ben was still just a correspondent at *Newsweek,* and *Newsweek* ran a distant second to *Time,* but when he walked off Kennedy's plane in Charleston behind the now likely Democratic nominee Ben saw a welcome flicker of fear in the eyes of *Time*'s White House correspondent.

One of Ben's favorite expressions is to say that something put somebody "on the map." When I came across a copy of an expulsion order from the French government in March of 1956, kicking Ben out of France for having made illicit contact with French double agents posing as Algerian rebels, I noticed that he had put a yellow Post-it on it: "This incident put me on the map as a foreign correspondent."* Later, at the *Post,* hiring David Broder away from *The New York Times* "put me on the map as a personnel person." Woodward and Bernstein "put me on the map in ways that no one could have predicted." And, of course, "Nixon put me on the map."

In 1957, newly returned from Paris and low correspondent in the Washington bureau of *Newsweek,* Ben was starting over. Instead of

---

*The order, for Ben to depart Paris within twenty-four hours, had been rescinded shortly after it had been issued when some of Ben's Parisian friends intervened on his behalf. For a few weeks, Ben had been the talk of expatriate Paris—without filing a word of copy on the story.

choosing his own assignments in exotic locations, he now had to make do with other reporters' crumbs. He could report the hell out of the annual conference of the Organization of the American States, but he didn't care and neither did anybody else. That was never going to get him where he wanted to go.

He needed to get back on the map, and in 1958 he found his chance when he and Tony ran into the young Senator Kennedy and his wife, Jackie, near their house on N Street.* Ben and Kennedy had met before, but now they were neighbors, and so they spent much of the afternoon in the back garden of the Kennedy house at 3307, making small talk with the wives. That night, in the luck-meets-fate way of Ben's life, the two couples found themselves not only at the same formal dinner but assigned to seats at the same table, with Jack next to Tony and Ben next to Jackie. Tony—beautiful, inquisitive, charmed, unafraid—asked Kennedy whether he thought it strange that he should all of a sudden decide to be a presidential candidate. "Yes," he told her, "until I stop and look around at the other people that are running for the candidacy. I think I'm just as qualified as they are." The couples rode home together from dinner, a new friendship under way.

That Ben and Kennedy would and should get along seems a foregone conclusion. They had both been born to privilege in Boston and gone to Harvard; each had had what men of that generation euphemistically call "a good war" in the Pacific with the Navy. They were both cool—handsome, charming, ambitious, ironic, self-deprecating in the slightly underhanded way that the people with the best cards can afford to be. They both loved gossip, and not surprisingly they both loved the news business. As Ben says, Kennedy was "one of the great news junkies that ever lived." And though they apparently never discussed it with each other, each had been through severe trials with his own health, Ben with polio and Kennedy with his back, colitis, jaundice, Addison's disease, you name it.

Much has been made of Ben's verve, his appetite for life, and of

---

*The official date of this meeting isn't fixed. In his book *Conversations with Kennedy,* Ben says first that it happened in January of 1959, then that it was "a sparkling late summer day in 1958." In *A Good Life* he goes with "a warm Sunday in early 1959," a kind of compromise.

Jack's similar spirit. At one point the two men were riding alone in a car together, with Ben's son Dino jumping around in the backseat. Kennedy watched Dino admiringly and then turned to Ben and said, "Really, if you could only have one thing it would be energy, wouldn't it?" Each man had been given what amounted to a second chance in life, a third if you counted surviving the war. "The war was such an unusual experience and dislocation," Kennedy once told Ben privately. "Everybody turns suddenly in a different direction." Each intended to make the most of what he had and was comfortable with that kind of intensity and desire in other people.

All that said, the two men built a lasting personal relationship largely because their wives liked each other. Ben himself told an interviewer in the late seventies that "a lot of the friendship was forged by the wives getting on very well. Jackie was very lonely in those days, I mean she did not like most Washington women, and she said to Tony at one point, 'Will you be my best friend?' And that's what did a lot of the connection." They spent most of their time together as a foursome.

Ben admits that he had heard rumors about Kennedy being a "fearful girler," but he insists that he and Kennedy never talked about it and that he never had any understanding of the extent. As Ben always puts it, imagine that you're at a table having dinner with Jackie and Tony and the president. "You're not going to talk about screwing other women," he says.

> B: . . . The times I was alone with him, a couple of times when we went sailing together, couple of times we played golf together, couple of times we went riding together. It's not a situation that breeds the kind of intimacy that must exist before that subject is going to be brought up. . . .
>
> I'm trying to think if I ever had a conversation with any man about a conquest of his. They just don't do it. Anyway, that's the way it was. Whether people believe it or not, I don't give a shit now.

He does acknowledge, in *Conversations with Kennedy*, that at one White House party stocked with particularly attractive females, Kennedy had turned to him and said, "If you and I could only run wild, Benjy." He also describes being invited by Kennedy to a party in a hotel room in Jackson Hole, Wyoming, while accompanying the president on a trip out west, and then being hastily uninvited by one of the president's aides.

"That second call has interested me more than the first one did," Ben would write later. "I wondered why, but without the obvious thought that occurs to me now. I didn't think of investigating to see who might have been a special guest of the president. I figured someone had pointed out to him that he might risk alienating some reporter, if only one reporter was present. Is that so naïve?"

Ben's deepening association with the candidate Kennedy was a boon to his status in the *Newsweek* bureau. As Kennedy's star rose and his decision to run for president appeared more certain, Ben became the go-to guy for quotes from the candidate. He also spent a good deal of time out on the campaign trail.

"The Wisconsin weather was the worst of the season," Ben opened one dispatch for *Newsweek* in November of 1959. "Blowing snow, glare ice, and ear-tingling cold . . . But Jack Kennedy, at a springy 42, was equal to the elements." This is typical of Ben's prose style at the time, and of the style of newsmagazine writing in general. Jauntiness was clearly a goal. Ben's coverage of Kennedy in *Newsweek* was favorable, but that was somewhat unavoidable; Kennedy did win, after all. To note that crowds enjoyed Kennedy's youthfulness, humor, and vigor is likely an honest accounting of what most people would have seen had they been there.

Behind the scenes, things were a little less clear-cut. In May of 1959, before Kennedy had officially announced his candidacy, Ben covered a speech of Lyndon Johnson's in Harrisburg, Pennsylvania, for *Newsweek*. At the time, Johnson was widely perceived to be one of Kennedy's potential rivals for the Democratic nomination. Ben filed for *Newsweek*, but he also wrote a private, critical assessment of the speech in a "Memorandum for Sen. John F. Kennedy" that definitely crosses the line between what a reporter should and shouldn't do for a friend. (He never mentions having written this memo in any of his books or interviews; I found it at the Kennedy Library.) After calling the speech "a masterpiece of corn," Ben deconstructs Johnson's entire presentation:

> My own response to Johnson is that, almost all other considerations aside, he could never make it. The image is poor. The accent hurts. . . . [He] really does not have the requisite dignity. I watched closely. His personal mannerisms are destructive of the dignified image. He's somebody's gabby Texas cousin from Fort Worth.

LBJ never trusted Ben. He always thought that Ben was a Northeast elitist Kennedy partisan who couldn't accept somebody like him as president. To a certain extent, LBJ was right.

Playing to his audience, Ben proceeds with more strategic advice:

> For safety's sake, I think your present assumption, that he is a candidate, has to be the one. . . .
> The danger is, of course, not that he makes it or that he can hand his strength intact to anybody else. What is to be feared is that he will come to Los Angeles with a block of 300 or more delegates and hold them off the market for three or four ballots. . . . Not only do you have to advance steadily, but you have to do it in pretty big leaps. . . .
> This is the peril of Johnson. Every piece written that touts him as a candidate should, it seems to me, be read in this light rather than on its apparent face value. . . . He's to be feared not as a potential winner but as a game-player who might try to maneuver you right out of the contest in Los Angeles.

Somebody in Kennedy's office, perhaps Kennedy himself, underlined that last sentence.

For the most part, Ben stuck to being a reporter.* Kennedy never

*Before the election in 1960 rumors swirled that Kennedy might tap Ben as press secretary. Ben told me flatly that he never wanted that job, but in his Grant Study form from October

gave Ben big scoops, particularly during the campaign, but he handed out tidbits. Ben flew out early to the Democratic convention in Los Angeles in July of 1960 to prepare for *Newsweek*'s cover story on Lyndon Johnson. Tony followed a few days later, in a seat on a commercial jet next to the presumptive nominee himself. She was carrying a page of questions spelled out by Ben for her to ask, playing reporter as she had the first night she and Jack met. "Will you pick LBJ?" she asked. JFK, battling a sore throat and wanting to save his voice, had taken to writing out his responses. "He won't take it," Kennedy wrote. (In Los Angeles, Phil Graham, in one of his episodes of manic brilliance, would help engineer the deal that put Johnson on the ticket.)

Ben was in the room for nearly every important moment, from the night of the West Virginia primary to the famous televised debate between Nixon and Kennedy in September of 1960, where he was in the studio for the taping as one of the pool reporters. (According to Ben, Nixon looked like a "cadaver.") He and Tony also flew up to Hyannis on the night of the presidential election. The election was so tight that it wasn't clear Kennedy had won until the next morning, Wednesday, November 9. That evening, the Kennedys invited Ben and Tony and Bill Walton, Kennedy's advisor and confidant, for a private dinner in their home on the compound.

The famous line to emerge from that dinner, which at the time was officially off the record, was Kennedy's quotation of his telephone conversation with Chicago mayor Richard Daley the night before. "Mr. President," Daley had said, "with a little bit of luck and the help of a few close friends, you're going to carry Illinois." When Ben published Daley's prediction in *Conversations with Kennedy* in 1975, people went crazy. Since then it has become part of the lore of that election and fodder for the notion that Daley had "stolen" it for Kennedy.

But more simply, Kennedy's invitation to Ben and Tony that night says a good deal about their friendship. On the day that he found out

---

of 1960 he was significantly more open to the idea. He was happy at *Newsweek,* he wrote, "but this might change if some job in a Kennedy administration were offered."

that he had been elected president, Kennedy wanted to have dinner with *them*. From the interview with Schlesinger:

> B: When he came down the stairs we were there. It was very emotional. The terrible problem was what do you call him? You know, whereas Tony could just say "Oh Jack, how wonderful!" and kiss him, I couldn't do that. And then was when he said, "You can call me Prez." That's what Bobby and Teddy had decided on that afternoon. And then we went to the movies, didn't we, again? In the early moments of John Kennedy's great historical life, he went to the movies. When in doubt go to the movies.

Edward Bennett Williams used to joke that the way to get something in the newspaper was to tell Ben, "Don't say anything." "He's pretty ruthless, even with me," Kay Graham once told an interviewer. "I'd tell him something and ask him not to say anything and he'd use it." "I asked him what people criticized him for," Vaillant observed in his Grant Study report in 1969, "and he said, 'being a barracuda with regard to the news,' that people said of him that they should say nothing to him or he'd put it in the paper." Asked once when this ruthlessness began, Ben said, "I learned that covering Kennedy. I was a newspaper person first and foremost because if I'd been less of a newspaperman, I would have been more of a friend."

That statement is hard to evaluate and may not be true—not only because Ben wasn't technically a newspaperman when he was covering Kennedy. After Kennedy reached the White House, Ben realized that he had rare access to a president and resolved to make the most out of it. A couple of months into JFK's presidency, Ben started writing up detailed summaries of their social visits—dinner, which he and Tony had with the Kennedys at the White House every week or two, or the occasional weekend trip to Hyannis or Newport or Camp David. He didn't tell Kennedy he was doing it, and Tony didn't like that. "I felt one shouldn't have dinner with one's friends and then write about it," she told *Vanity Fair* in a rare public comment in 1991. She and Ben argued about it. Ben eventually came clean with Kennedy, but not until March of 1963, nearly two years after he had started.

Kennedy might not have known that Ben was taking notes on their interactions, but he did know that Ben would push it if given the chance. The most romantic passage in Ben's memoir describes an evening in February of 1962 when Kennedy gave him a scoop at one of the big dances that the Kennedys held at the White House, back when presidents did that kind of thing. At 12:30 in the morning, as Ben was standing and chatting with Kay Graham in the Green Room, Kennedy pulled him aside and gave him an exclusive: the U.S. was going to trade a high-ranking Soviet spy, Rudolf Abel, for Francis Gary Powers, the CIA U-2 pilot who had been shot down near Sverdlovsk. The trade was set to be announced in a few hours, and Kennedy wanted to know if it was too late for *Newsweek* to change its cover.

It was, but Ben wasn't about to let the opportunity pass him by. Without asking Kennedy's permission, he found Phil Graham and told him what was going on. Within a few minutes, Ben was on a White House telephone line, dictating a story to the night managing editor at the *Post*. When the paper led with the story the next morning, Kennedy was so unsuspecting of Ben that he considered starting a leak investigation.

By the time Ben and Tony arrived at the White House for dinner the following week, Kennedy had figured it out. "By the way," he said to Ben during cocktails, "who do you work for, anyway?"

"Are you making any charges?" Ben asked, playing it cool.

"No," the president said. "Do you have any statement you want to make?"

"Not at this time," Ben said.

Ben also got burned sometimes. Kennedy tolerated the Powers scoop in the *Post*, but he didn't take it very well when Ben spoke to a reporter for *Look* magazine a couple of months later and complained about how tough Kennedy and Bobby were to please. "It's almost impossible to write a story they like," Ben had told the *Look* reporter (believing, he claims, that it was off the record). "Even if a story is quite favorable to their side, they'll find one paragraph to quibble with." Seems minor, but it set Kennedy off and he put Ben in the freezer for three months. No dinners, no phone calls, nothing.

The only contact Ben had with Kennedy during the freeze was one of the sketchier episodes in their relationship. Rumors had been circulating for a while that Kennedy had been married once, before Jackie, and that he had gotten a quickie divorce. Untrue, evidently, but lingering—probably because of some of the widespread extracurricular skinny-dipping that Kennedy was engaged in. Pierre Salinger, Kennedy's press secretary, negotiated to have Ben come up to Newport, Rhode Island (where Jackie's family had an enormous waterfront estate, Hammersmith Farm), to review FBI files that would prove that the organizations spreading the rumors about Kennedy were shady themselves. This would discredit the opposition and advance a story line that the administration wanted to advance. On top of that, the president demanded approval over anything that ran in *Newsweek*.

"This is a right all presidents covet," Ben wrote later, "but which they should normally not be given. This one time, the book seemed worth the candle, however, and we decided to strike the deal." The phrase "this one time" does not normally qualify acts of which one approves, either in prospect or in retrospect. Ben and *Newsweek* were being used, in an explicit way. The next morning, Kennedy signed off on the story and then almost immediately made sure that Ben knew he was still in the doghouse. The British ambassador entered Kennedy's office as Ben was on his way out and asked if Ben would be joining them for the America's Cup races that afternoon. Kennedy pointedly said no. Shortly thereafter, Ben was out the door and on his way back to Washington.

Ben would remain in the doghouse until November, when he and Tony were invited to a White House dance.* Tony, always the grease for the wheel, sealed the Bradlees' return to Kennedy's good graces.

---

*The dance had originally been scheduled for June; otherwise, they might not have been invited.

"The president and Tony had a long session about the difficulties of being friends with someone who is always putting everything he knows into a magazine," Ben wrote later. "Everybody loves everybody again."

In a review of *Conversations with Kennedy* in *Harper's* magazine in 1975, the historian Taylor Branch likened Ben on the trip to Newport as "more jilted lover than journalist" and ridiculed him for accepting the terms that Kennedy demanded. Twenty years later, Michael Lewis would beat Ben with the same stick in a tough review of *A Good Life*: "The access journalist is forever deciding whether to protest when, during the waltz, the hand lands on his bottom." Journalistic standards and expectations were different in 1975 or 1995 than they had been in 1962, and *Newsweek*'s editors had signed off on the deal, too. They always delighted in Ben's friendship with Kennedy, pushing him ever closer and then dining out on the details that didn't make the magazine. But the core truth remains: at that moment, stuck out in the cold, Ben needed Kennedy more than Kennedy needed him, and so he kept on dancing.

Once Ben was back in, he was back in. Kennedy was like Ben that way. He couldn't remember why he was mad after a while. They dropped back into their routine of dinners at the White House and gossipy phone calls often only tangentially related to work. Kennedy didn't feel any pressing need to distinguish between the working Ben and the nonworking Ben, usually assuming now that he was seeing the working Ben but that they could be friends at the same time.

Jackie was different. She felt threatened by the lurking presence of the barracuda. When the president let revealing details slip at dinner, Jackie would look over at Ben as if to say, "This is not to be repeated." Every so often she would actually say it out loud, that some part of a conversation was private and never to be printed in *Newsweek*. (Ben always says that after Kennedy found out that he was writing up their interactions, he was usually more interested in telling Ben what to put *in* his notes than what to take out.)

The sudden blow of Kennedy's assassination would point up all of these dynamics at once. Ben was in Brentano's bookstore in downtown D.C. on his lunch break when the news came in, and he raced back to the office. It was a Friday, and *Newsweek* closed (was readied for the press) over the weekend. In addition to dealing with his own personal grief, he had a bureau to run and a magazine that had to be almost completely rewritten, all in roughly two days.

That afternoon Oz Elliott added to Ben's burdens by asking him to write a tribute to Kennedy, and Ben said that he would try. As soon as he sat down at his typewriter, he started to cry and couldn't stop. Late in the afternoon the call came in:

> B: Jackie's secretary called up and said, will you please go up to Bethesda Hospital where Jackie was coming in that night with the President's body. And so we said yes and met at the White House and I was trying to write what turned out to be That Special Grace. . . .
>
> We went up to the umpteenth floor and there came a time with Jackie in a pink suit covered with blood walked into the room and she made a beeline for me. So I put my arms around her and hugged her for a minute. She said do you want to hear about it. I said of course. And then she said, but you're not working, okay? That was always between us that she had to worry about that, would I be taking notes. Sort of made me sad.
>
> Q: That she said that at that particular time?
>
> B: Yeah, right at that time, which must have been one of the worst moments of her life and there she is having to remember that.

The next morning Ben went into the office and finished his piece, "That Special Grace," which ran in that week's edition of *Newsweek* and later was published as a small book by Lippincott. The Grant Study researchers were fascinated that he was able to function so well in the midst of so much grief, referring to his reaction as "sublimation." As Vaillant described it to Ben many years later, "It's taking enormous pain and being able to keep good enough hold of it so you can make it publicly acceptable. You can do this with affairs, you can

do it with anger, you did it with grief. It's anything that usually im-
mobilizes people." Ben's method for overcoming rough spots has
always been hard work.

"History will best judge John F. Kennedy in calmer days," "That
Special Grace" began, "when time has made the tragic and the gro-
tesque at least bearable." It was a short, plain, sentimental piece, "half
elegy, half eulogy" as Ben describes it. He wrote about Kennedy's
physical gracefulness, his taste, his humor on the golf course, his love
for politics, for his kids, and finally for Jackie. Many of the images in
the piece were drawn from private memos that Ben had written previously for the editors at Newsweek, detailing his own impressions for
the kinds of "what he ate for breakfast" stories that newsmagazines
used to distinguish themselves from newspapers in those days. He
hadn't ever imagined stringing those observations together for this
kind of purpose.

A few days later, he wrote another private memo for the Newsweek
editors, this time about Jackie at the funeral, at which he had been an
usher. The lede: "Jacqueline Kennedy added majesty to the American dimension last week." He talked about how she had refused for
a time to take off her pink suit spattered in blood, and about how
angry she had been. "After her anger, drama came to Jacqueline
Kennedy; she always had a sense and an understanding of the
dramatic—visual, historic, and compelling." The memo ends:

> It was Bobby—perhaps alone among the mafia whose devotion and
> involvement with John Kennedy was so total—who was completely
> unsurprised at the great quality that emerged in Jacqueline. The
> others were amazed at how great she was. Not Bobby, and not the
> friends that she and Jack shared.

After the funeral, Ben and Tony spent a couple of weekends alone
with Jackie out at the Kennedy retreat in horse country near Middle-
burg, Virginia. These were difficult weekends, full of tears and tor-
ment and not a whole lot to talk about. "We proved only that the
three of us had very little in common without the essential fourth,"
Ben would write in his memoir.

During one of these visits, Ben and Tony encouraged Jackie to marry again someday. Shortly afterward, Jackie sent them a hand-written note on a small mourning card with black trim, explaining that she couldn't even consider the idea. Her husband was dead, and in every important way so was she.

It's a sorrowful note, and it also holds the seeds of a rift between Ben and Jackie that would intensify in later years and last for the rest of Jackie's life. Ben always moves on, but Jackie couldn't, at least not yet.

MUMS

K: And so then time passes and . . .

B: Well, time passes and the telephone rings and it's you. That's the next event in my life.

K: And I say, "Would you like to have lunch?"

B: Yes.

—BCB interview with Kay Graham, October 9, 1989

ONE DAY, AT THE BACK OF one of Ben's boxes, I encountered an undated document titled "A case-study in prestige institution building." There was no author listed on the cover page, only the designation "rough draft" and a handwritten note from Ben's old secretary referring to the author as a "French b-school professor."

I eventually figured out who wrote the report, and why, but for two years I knew him only as "The Frenchman." It really is as if de Tocqueville had materialized in the *Washington Post* newsroom. The Frenchman was an outsider, observing the operation and culture of the *Post* clinically but with a distinctly French sense of whimsy. "With an elusive smile," he writes of Ben at one point, "I would say that the Executive Editor is a fundamentalist." You can almost smell the cigarette smoke.

He fully grasps Ben's vision for the *Post*:

In our case, as the French would say, Mr. Bradlee's <u>coup de genie</u> has been first to visualize the intuitive relevance of a new image for the <u>Post</u> and then to give it an appropriate formulation. . . . The mid-sixties conceptual breakthrough was (to use an old fashioned military catch-word) to provide <u>The Washington Post</u>

with a <u>mission</u>. In brief, it was to move <u>The Washington Post</u>
from a parochial and liberal newspaper to a prestigious national
one.

He saves some of his most incisive analysis for the relationship between Ben and Kay:

> In what respect can the [goal] formulation and the concomitant
> vision of <u>The Washington Post</u> have been the seeds and means of a
> committed working <u>psychological contract</u> between Mrs. Graham
> and Mr. Bradlee? Serious professors would label this operation the
> formation of a "dominant coalition" between Mrs. K. Graham and
> Mr. B. Bradlee, I will rather use the more musical French term
> "duo." Cheap talks of pop-psychoanalysis speculate a lot about the
> "duo." In fact, social scientists are better off—and better
> novelists—if they stay with the plain facts of human action. . . .
>
> Pundits are delighted to guess who is in charge at the <u>Post</u>? It's
> like making waves in a glass of water. Both can attempt to carry the
> mission and try to become "number 1" in their respective domains.
> Mr. Bradlee's line of conduct was restricted to gaining the support
> necessary to lead an autonomous news room dedicated to making a
> prestige institution. Mrs. Graham's opportunity [lay] in directing the
> paper as an organization, to control its editorial component and, of
> course, in the area of "critical decisions" to have the last word. The
> rationale of the "duo" is that of a positive sum-game: both actors are
> dependent upon each other, the two of them have stakes but the
> more they cooperate the greater the chances to win together—and
> in that case, to win big.

There is a lot of truth packed into those two grafs. The Frenchman
couldn't have known how right he was, even in terms of how Ben
and Kay saw themselves. This is an exchange the two of them had in
January 1974, during Watergate, when a media report named Kay
"Outstanding Newspaper Executive" and Ben runner-up:

Dear Katharine:

When I was at boarding school too long ago, I chased one classmate for
five goddam years in the scholarship department. In forty months of
grades, he finished first, and I finished second . . . except for one month
when he was recuperating from undulant fever or something.

So I was accustomed early to being runner-up. But it pissed me off!

It is one of the pleasures of working for you to tell you that I don't
mind being runner-up to you one damned bit. In fact, I'm all-out
flattered.

Love

Kay wrote back to Ben the next day:

Dear Ben:

That note was a Bradlee gem. It was full of charm; I loved it. . . .

The reason you and I get along so well, notwithstanding the fact
that we are both innately endowed with a primordial urge—not at all
competitive, mind you—to be No. 1, is because of this—our routes run
parallel and synchronize.

I know I'm No. 1 because you are No. 1. You know that I know
that I am No. 1 because you are No. 1 . . . I don't mind it and even
quite like it. That's why it doesn't piss you off and you don't wish for
me undulant fever.

It's a privilege to work with you, in the words of a great man.

Love

"If you go over the whole of Kay Graham's life," Don Graham, Kay's
son, told me one afternoon in his office, "Ben was the biggest right
decision she ever made."

Graham succeeded his mother as publisher of the *Post* in 1979 and
as chairman of the Post Company when she retired in 1991. When I
asked him what had stuck with him about Ben over time, he said,
"Obviously his relationship with Kay was something you had to see
to believe. I don't know if you've read her book . . ."

"I have. I loved it."

"She is not overstating how self-doubting she was."

"And Ben's the opposite."

"He was the best thing she had going," Don Graham said.

They didn't know each other very well when they got together for their fateful lunch, at the private F Street Club in downtown Washington, in December of 1964.* If anything, they had actually gotten off on the wrong foot. The main obstacle between them had also been their main point of contact: Phil.

In the last year or so of his life, as his bipolarity worsened, Phil had taken up with a young woman named Robin Webb, a stringer who worked in *Newsweek*'s bureau in Paris. In addition to all of the marital hurts inherent in such a betrayal—Kay found out by mistakenly picking up a second telephone in their home on Christmas Eve of 1962—it turned out that Phil had retained Ben's friend Edward Bennett Williams to draw up a new will excluding Kay and leaving his controlling interest in the paper and in the Post Company with Robin.

It's hard to convey what an affront this was to Kay, and to her family. Her father, Eugene Meyer, had bought the paper in 1933, right before Kay turned sixteen, and the *Post* had been central to her life since then. Meyer was a successful financier who had mapped out and then executed his life in thirds: the first for education, the second for asset accumulation, and the third for public service. He viewed the ownership of a respectable newspaper as a kind of public trust, and the *Post* was his baby. He had nurtured it back to life from near-financial ruin with sound management and adherence (generally speaking) to the seven principles of running an effective newspaper

---

*As with the date of Ben's first meeting with Kennedy, this lunch date is a little uncertain, too. Ben wrote in his memoir that it happened in March of 1965, but Kay wrote in her memoir (published two years after Ben's) that it had occurred in December of 1964. She knew what Ben had written and clearly chose the different date for a reason, in the manner of setting the record straight. Having seen a few of her archival files and all of Ben's, I feel pretty good about sticking with hers.

that he set out when he bought the *Post*, principles that even in this digital age still sit in hard copy in the *Post*'s lobby.*

"He is a Jew, a Republican, and rich as hell," Phil Graham wrote of Eugene Meyer, with typical directness, to his own father after deciding to marry Kay in 1940. According to Kay's memoir, Meyer was worth somewhere between forty and sixty million—in actual dollars at that time, not adjusted for inflation—when he left Wall Street shortly before the First World War to begin the public service portion of his life in Washington. In accordance with principle number six, he would pump more than $20 million of his own funds into the struggling *Post* before it became consistently profitable.

Kay and Ben shared an elite pedigree, which was one of the reasons Kay felt so comfortable around Ben, but her upbringing was much posher than his. There was an apartment on Fifth Avenue, a vacation home on seven hundred acres in Mount Kisco, New York—indoor swimming pool, bowling alley, tennis court—and a large mansion on Crescent Place, off 16th Street, in downtown Washington. Kay attended private schools, took French lessons, made her debut, and generally lived the life of one of the richest young women in Washington.

For all of the privilege, there was also a heavy dose of loneliness and distance. Kay's mother, Agnes Ernst Meyer, was an intelligent, imperious woman who cultivated intense friendships with writers like Thomas Mann and didn't have a great deal of interest in mothering her children. Shortly after Kay was born, in New York, Agnes

---

*1. The first mission of a newspaper is to tell the truth as nearly as the truth can be ascertained.

  2. The newspaper shall tell ALL the truth so far as it can learn it, concerning the important affairs of America and the world.

  3. As a disseminator of news, the paper shall observe the decencies that are obligatory upon a private gentleman.

  4. What it prints shall be fit reading for the young as well as the old.

  5. The newspaper's duty is to its readers and to the public at large, and not to the private interests of its owners.

  6. In the pursuit of truth, the newspaper shall be prepared to make sacrifices of its material fortunes, if such a course be necessary for the public good.

  7. The newspaper shall not be the ally of any special interest, but shall be fair and free and wholesome in its outlook on public affairs and public men.

departed for Washington to be with Eugene, leaving her children in the care of paid staff in the Fifth Avenue apartment for more than *three years.* "I can't say I think Mother genuinely loved us," Kay would later write in her memoir, one of that book's sadder sentences.

Kay worked as a copygirl at the *Post* between high school and college (two years at Vassar, two years at the University of Chicago). She claimed to have read the paper every day while she was away at school, sometimes offering her father welcome suggestions about how to improve it. He added a famous, prophetic postscript to one of his letters to her while she was at the University of Chicago:

> P.S. If you don't soon get down here on the Post there won't be anything left to do but the routine jobs of trying to hold our position. You ought to be in on the job of putting it to the top. It is much better sport fighting to get there than trying to stay there after you have gotten there. When we get there I will go out looking for some trouble somewhere, and let you, Mother, [and two editors] keep the machine running.

After graduation, she spent a year working as a reporter for the *San Francisco News*, but she knew that she was only postponing the inevitable. In early 1939, she came home to work for her father as an editorial writer at the *Post*, and later that year she met Phil.

The Meyers embraced Phil Graham, and he them. He and Kay started a family (the only time that Kay stopped working for the *Post*), and when Phil got back from service in the Army during World War II Eugene Meyer brought him in as an associate publisher. From then on, but officially beginning in 1948, Phil ran the paper with Eugene Meyer's blessing, and Kay generally supported Phil. He was voluble and hated to be alone. When he took a bath, he wanted her to sit in the bathroom with him. When he worked late down at the paper she would often join him and hang out on the couch in his office.

Eventually, supporting Phil became harder and harder, publicly and privately. His drinking accelerated, and his unpredictability wreaked havoc on their lives. She knew he was on a manic upsurge when he decided to buy *Newsweek* in 1961, and she was so worried about his health (and the success of the deal) that she didn't even tell him, when she arrived in New York, that she had been preliminarily diagnosed with tuberculosis. She began to understand that the gutting depressions that followed the up phases were symptomatic of a true sickness.

And then came Robin Webb.

In those days Washington "society" still existed, and the Phil-Kay-Robin situation caused a stir. The idea that Phil would both leave Kay and then take the paper away from her and the Meyer family didn't sit well with the prim matrons who called the social shots. Much of high Washington society rejected Phil and wouldn't allow him to come to dinner without Kay. People took sides.

This is where Ben comes back in. As he says, "I worked for Phil Graham." He didn't know Kay all that well and felt no particular allegiance to her. It was Phil who had bought *Newsweek* and promoted him. And so when Phil called once from New York and asked if he and Robin could come to dinner that night at Ben and Tony's house, Ben checked with Tony and then said okay. News of that kind of thing got around. Worse, Kay had heard rumors that Ben had been making jokes about the situation in public, saying that the only thing Phil Graham needed was a divorce.

Kay never confronted Ben directly about any of this until decades later. During their interviews for her memoir, she remembered an interaction they'd had sometime just before Phil's death. "I said something about Phil being sick," Kay told Ben. "You said that there was nothing wrong with him except that he needed a divorce and that I should give it to him."

"I said that to you?" Ben said. "Absolutely made up. I would never do that, Katharine."

"I don't know," she said. "I think you did, Ben."

Whether Ben said it or not matters less than that Kay *thought* he did. "She says, 'There are only two people I thought I would never forgive, and one was Ben Bradlee,'" David Halberstam noted after one of his interviews with Kay in the late seventies. "Ben going around saying that [Phil's] unhappy and all he needs is a divorce."

When Phil died, the tension between Ben and Kay deepened when Ben didn't attend a small gathering that Kay held at her house, on R Street, after the funeral. Ben had flown home for the service on an emergency basis, interrupting a vacation in France with Tony, and he wanted to get back to Europe as quickly as he could. He also felt Kay hadn't explicitly invited him to her home. Word eventually trickled down to him that she resented him for not showing up.

"[Fritz] Beebe said that you were furious at me because I hadn't gone to [your] home," Ben said to Kay when they finally talked about it all for the record, years later.

"See, I don't remember that," Kay said. "I wouldn't know that."

"I said I didn't go because I wasn't invited," Ben said.

"I wouldn't have thought I would have noticed," Kay said.

It seems likely that she *had* noticed, and that in the interview she was playing it cool for posterity. Either way, it's striking that there were still such uncertainties and unresolved feelings on both sides regarding a funeral that had happened more than twenty-five years before. If it was that way in 1989, after all that they'd been through together, it's hard to imagine what simmered between them in 1963.

Kay had been ready to fight Phil for the *Post*, but his effort to take the paper away from her died when he did. When he drew up Phil's revised will, Edward Bennett Williams had also written a memorandum saying that he didn't think Phil was in his right mind when he made the changes that left the company to Robin. After some minor hiccups, the paper was Kay's. Largely because she was a woman, people expected her to sell it, and the vultures circled. "Sometimes you don't really decide, you just move forward," she once wrote of this time in her life—sounding, incidentally, a lot like Ben. "And that is what I did—moved forward blindly and mindlessly into a new and unknown life."

On September 20, 1963, Kay assumed the presidency of the Post Company and set about conquering her own fears about being a female boss and running a newspaper. There were a number of sideways steps at the start. ("She spits out executives like tobacco juice," Edward Bennett Williams once said, of Kay's capriciousness as an early manager.) As she got deeper into the job, she began to hear from her friends around town that the paper had been coasting for a while, that it had been losing steam even while Phil was still alive. Scotty

Reston, the famed *New York Times* D.C. bureau chief, once asked her, "Don't you want to leave a better paper for the next generation than the one you inherited?" She had been so busy getting her legs under her that she hadn't had time yet to think about it that way.

By December of 1964, she had started actively to think about what she might do to put some spark back into the *Post*. Even though she didn't particularly like Ben, she was curious about him. She knew he ran a good bureau, that the people who worked under him were happy. *Newsweek* had twice tried to promote him to positions of higher editorial authority in New York, and he had refused each time. She worried that he would leave the Post Company, maybe for a job in television, and she felt that she should try to keep him. "In some ways it still rankled her years later," a close associate of Ben and Kay's would say privately, "the idea that that son of a bitch was dining out all over town, going the wrong way on her and making fun of her. And yet she's very tough and she knew she needed him. A lesser person might have held it against him."

October 9, 1989

K: I just wanted to have lunch with you and talk to you. And it was such an awkward thing for me to ask someone to lunch that I took you to the F Street Club because there would be no bill.

B: There would be no bill? . . . Oh, because you could charge it.

K: Yes, that's why we went to the F Street Club.

B: Oh, no. Really?

K: Yes.

B: Isn't that wonderful? I'd have paid, Katharine.

K: And I asked you the question. I mean we chatted and then I said I've just noticed that you have twice turned down New York. And what is it that you kind of want to do?

B: When you grow up, yeah.

K: Yes, and you instantly said, well, now that you ask me . . .

B: No, no, no. That's not true. I'll tell you exactly what I said. I said that Phil had always said that there should be continuity in the bureaus, that changing the bureau chiefs of these weeklies every [two] minutes prevented . . . giving the person who had the job enough time in the job to assume a leadership position of some kind. . . . I was really quite happy where I was. And thought it was honorable work. But then you, then something happened in which I bit.

K: Well I must have said what do you want to do in the long run? Next question. And that's when you said, "Well, now that you've asked me, I'd give my left one to be managing editor of the *Post*."

B: "If it ever came open," I must have said that.

K: Yes.

B: That's a little rough even for me.

K: I'm not sure what you said, Ben, but we'll amend that for history.

B: Whatever you say I said, I said. I'll have my innings later.

Kay's openness to the possibility of a return to the *Post* lit a fire under Ben. Whatever lessons he had learned from the sale of *Newsweek*— about seizing your own destiny and making your own history—he had clearly made part of his permanent practice. And whatever reservations Kay harbored about him at the start, she admired how ferociously he pursued her for the job. This is from a private interview that Kay did in the seventies:

[Ben was] pushing like hell. And it made me like him. From then on every time I saw him—when are we going to do this? . . . And he was pushing in a very decent way. I mean, Ben's pushing is somehow attractive. . . . It was almost sort of like you know the old Perils of Pauline, and Pearl White, and the villain you know has the woman strapped in bed, and you're about to do some awful thing and then it's continued for the next week . . . and he's always pushing, and he was relentless. . . .

I sensed that he was right, that there was a drive and ruthlessness about him and I felt I needed someone to push.

In November of 2010, stuck after two days of trying and failing to write about the beginning of Ben's real working relationship with Kay, I decided to go down to the paper and talk to Ben about it. The last few times I'd been in to see him he had seemed tired and a little uninterested in my questions, so I wasn't sure how much more I was going to get.

"Hey there, young man!" he said when I walked into his office.

"Got a sec?" I said. We chatted for a few minutes and then I made my usual segue. "If I can scratch your historical memory again a little bit . . ."

"Of course."

I had caught him at a good moment. We started with how little he had known about Kay before he went to work for her, and then we moved on to the famous lunch, a story that's been told so many times it was hard for Ben to recall anything new.

"Do you remember when it started to become a relationship that you enjoyed, and felt connected to her?" I asked.

"She originally, as I remember it—and even this maybe is a little cloudy—but it was in terms of a year," Ben said. "Would I come over for a year, just to see whether there was a fit. I was on the ladder to go up to New York"—to move up in the chain of command at *Newsweek*—"and she knew that. So I think that made her wonder whether there was something for me at the *Post* here. And what that might be. And could that be explored by my going over there for a year and just nosing around. I think she admired what she called my 'energy.' She thought the *Post* was kind of sleepy."

"When you would have come over, were you already thinking, 'I want to run this place'?"

He hemmed a little bit, not wanting to seem immodest. "As I was there and got involved, I got more and more interested in the fact that I had skills that fit. I saw the *Post* needed an injection of—it was a *sleepy* paper. There was no energy kicking around the place." He thought about it a little more, and then said, "Energy is the word. There was just none of it."

We circled back to Kay. "I guess what I'm interested in is that you really don't know her and then you get to know her," I said. "And how important that is for the newspaper. The relationship between the two of you—her knowing she could trust you and you knowing you could trust her, that that's what made all of this stuff possible."

"If you really want what . . ." he said, and then he trailed off. He seemed to sense what I was driving at. "I mean, the mystery is how . . ." Again, a pause. I waited.

"We had to decide to become close," he finally said.

"Right."

"And to keep that out of the physical is amazing."

It was the question I had wanted to ask but hadn't quite known how to ask directly.

"Because it's unlike me," he continued, and we laughed. "I don't know whether it was unlike her or not, but it never—there was never a question, you know. I mean, I would tell you if there was a glance or something."

"Of course."

"Nothing," he said. "And that's hard. And I bet it was hard for her."

The "Perils of Pauline" image that Kay used to describe how she felt when Ben was pursuing her for the job had always stuck in my mind, along with the act of ravishment it implied. You don't have to dig very far to find people close to Ben and Kay who will tell you that she was always in love with him.

I brought up another of their better-known exchanges on the subject. When Ben retired in 1991, *Vanity Fair* ran an extended profile of him in which a former city editor at the paper claimed that he watched Ben roll up his sleeves right before a meeting with Kay, just so she could see his muscular forearms. "He came into the room and the sexual energy of him and her titillation was about as obvious as my stomach," the editor claimed. "She was very much, and I don't mean this in a carnal way, she was very much in love with Ben. But then again, so was I."

At Ben's seventieth birthday party, a month or so after the *Vanity Fair* piece ran, Kay gave a toast. "I'd like to use this opportunity to knock down many of the rumors about Ben and me. One is that I was in love with Ben. This is nonsense," she said. "Another bummer was that I was impressed with Bradlee's muscles and when he rolled up his sleeves, I keeled over. What I really did is say to myself, 'This man wears cheap shirts.'"

She got off another good line toward the end. "Someday when I reach my seventieth"—she was four years older than Ben—"I hope I'll be as sexy as you are. It's difficult when you're seventy years old to be described in the press as a sex symbol. It's even harder to prove it."

"It was clear that you guys felt comfortable joking around about it," I said to Ben.

"Very comfortable. But that was the magic of the relationship, is that it was comfortable. I hadn't had all that many bosses. And certainly none of the opposite sex. But it was she who made it comfortable. And she didn't make it comfortable by flirting with me. There was none of that."

A little later I asked him if he had ever thought consciously about trying to preserve some boundaries as they began to get closer to each other.

"Oh, I was worried about it," he said. "I was scared of it. You know, because I could see that we were getting to be friends. And I think I worried . . ." He paused. "I never *thought* of fucking her."

He looked right at me as he said it, as if to say, "There's the answer to your real question," and I laughed, hard.

"Put it that way," he said. "And I didn't get any sense that she thought of fucking me. I thought that she wanted to be friends. And I started to call her Mums. And that, you know, that describes the relationship. You wouldn't call a girlfriend 'Mums.' And yet, I didn't feel maternal—I mean, you know."

I could easily envision how much charm Ben had poured on, first to convince Kay Graham to hire him despite her initial skepticism, and then later to keep her happy when they hit rocky spots at the *Post*. He gave her a lot of his energy, and a lot of Ben's energy is a very seductive thing. He would have needed to preserve the space between them somehow.

As we continued to talk about Kay, I made reference to having been surprised by the almost comical stiffness of her upper lip in an interview with Mike Wallace on *60 Minutes*, right before Nixon resigned.

"Can you say to me truthfully, Mrs. Graham, that you never said to Ben Bradlee, 'Ben, come on, we're having—it's beginning to cost us'?" Wallace asks.

"*Heavens* no," Kay replies, in the most aristocratic way you can possibly imagine. "I wouldn't *say* that, and I *don't* think it would move him a *bit* if I *did*." Total lockjaw. It's like a parody of somebody trying to sound like a rich person, and yet she's saying exactly the right thing. The paradox of Kay Graham.

"She's got this upper lip that just—it doesn't move," I said to Ben, trying to convey this point as our interview drew to a close. I wasn't criticizing her, but I realized that he thought I was. He pointed toward a framed picture hanging on his office wall, of him and Kay laughing together in a *Post* meeting room someplace. He's grinning widely and her head is thrown back in a full gleaming belly laugh, as it is in so many of the pictures of the two of them together.

"It moves in *that* picture," he said.

IMPACT

He was determined to make the paper into what it could be: A great paper. Exciting. You had to read it. It was just, impact. He wanted impact. You ought to have impact, goddamnit. Instead of this namby-pamby stuff. And impact isn't cheap. It ought to have power, authority, and be well written; it ought to say something, and tell you about something you wanted to know; and it ought to be displayed so you don't miss it. That's what it's all about.

—Haynes Johnson, Puliter Prize–winning journalist and one of
Ben's early hires at the *Post*, October 11, 2007

ON SATURDAY, JUNE 3, 1965, at 4:30 P.M., McGeorge Bundy, LBJ's national security advisor, sat down to write a "Memorandum for the President" describing a dinner he had attended the night before at Kay Graham's house. Bundy was a friend of Ben's family's. His father, Harvey, had been a trustee of the estate from which Ben's parents had bought the country place in Beverly, Massachusetts, where Ben spent much of his childhood.

> The most important piece of conversation was one which Kay asked me to pass on privately to you. She has decided to move Ben Bradlee from NEWSWEEK to the POST. He is to be Al Friendly's deputy on the news side, and is to move into Friendly's place in a couple of years if all goes well. Kay knows you have reservations about Bradlee, but she also knows that he has the respect of the professional press and she has had to go on her own best judgment. She wants you to know this decision from her.
>
> This may be as good a time as any for me to repeat my own

judgment that while Ben Bradlee is a very determined and inquisitive reporter, he is not hostile to us or in anyone else's pocket. It is certainly true that he was a great personal friend of President Kennedy. But he has never been close to Bobby—they are temperamentally opposites. What made Bradlee and President Kennedy friends was a shared coolness and irony and detachment, which was the side of JFK that does not appear in his brother.*

Bill Moyers, LBJ's close advisor, once said that Johnson viewed Ben as "a metaphor for a kind of journalism and culture that he did not like, and he personalized it very much. I mean, Bradlee, he particularly disliked him . . . it was almost emotional." Johnson apparently referred to Ben, disdainfully, as "the one with the Stacomb hair."

At the end of 1964, Ben had written a piece in *Newsweek* stating with authority that the search for J. Edgar Hoover's replacement as the head of the FBI had begun. Shortly thereafter, Johnson held a press conference at which he reappointed Hoover essentially in perpetuity. On his way out to deliver the statement, Johnson turned to Bill Moyers (who was the source for Ben's story), and said, "You tell your friend Ben Bradlee, 'Fuck you.'"

On Monday, August 2, 1965, Moyers's friend Ben Bradlee officially returned to the *Post* for good, as the deputy managing editor for national and international affairs. As he tells it, he never considered the fact that his career as a reporter was over. He was too busy throwing himself into the job. He worked the longest hours of his life, going home for dinner and then coming back at night to learn the mechanics of production, the editing processes, the people— everything. He often stayed until one or two in the morning, watching as the paper got put to bed, as it's called, each night.

"There was really no holding Ben down after he came back," Russ Wiggins once said in an interview for Ben's memoir. Wiggins had

---

*Ben didn't see Bundy's memo to Johnson until 1991, shortly before he retired from the *Post*. "Get a load of this!" he wrote on a covering note as he passed a copy of the memo along to Kay. "Our dear, independent friend McGeorge Bundy reporting slavishly to Lyndon Johnson about dinner with you. . . . This gives me the willies." He signed it by hand, and then, underneath his name, wrote in, "For the memoirs!"

been the managing editor of the *Post* during Ben's first stint at the paper in the late forties, an erudite and well-read man of the old school. In the first months after Ben's return to the *Post*, Wiggins— now the head editor—watched as his former Municipal Court reporter ate up the ground between them. "He had cranked himself up to where he was really ready to take over responsibility," Wiggins said. "There was no doubt about it."

A young Don Graham talked to his mom during the first week Ben spent on the job. "What she talked about was his energy," Graham said years later. "That he was working nights, he was trying to figure out how the paper worked and what everybody did, and his ambition. He walked in the first day wanting to make it much, much better. And that feeling only got stronger."

Al Friendly thought he had at least a year left in the managing editor's chair while Ben learned the ropes. This was a delusion that few others shared. "There were no Friendly-Bradlee run-ins," *Post* reporter and historian Chalmers Roberts wrote later. "It simply became a question of when Bradlee would take over." In October of 1965, less than three months after Ben had started back at the *Post*, Friendly was sent packing, first as an "associate editor" on the "new ideas" beat—whatever that meant—and then, after a couple of months, off to London. This was all labeled as a promotion, but everybody in the newsroom knew what it meant. Ben was the new managing editor of the *Post*, and he had Kay Graham standing right behind him.

"I think back on those months as some of the greatest ever," Ben says, of his days gathering steam. "I had the best goddamn time. It was so exciting. I mean, you felt that you were doing what the hell you were put on the world, on the earth's surface, to do."

"When Ben became managing editor of the *Post*, what he did was go hire people," Don Graham told me. He went so far as to say that Ben did his job by hiring, and that the utility of hiring as a management technique was "Bradlee's first lesson." As Ben puts it, he didn't yet know everything about newspapers but he did know what a good

reporter was, so he started there. One of the key points he'd negotiated with Kay before he came over was that she would hold all vacan-
cies for him, and she held five—no small number, given the size of
the paper at the time.

One of the first, and most important, of Ben's hires was David
Broder. At the time, Broder was a well-respected but somewhat disgruntled political reporter at *The New York Times,* unhappy with that
paper's stodgy bureaucracy and its stifling effects on his reporting. He
had just written a long internal memo about exactly what he thought
was wrong with the *Times,* and somehow Ben had gotten wind of it
and decided to pounce.

"I romanced him like he's never been romanced," Ben wrote later,
"in coffee-shops, not fancy French restaurants, because Broder was a
coffee-shop kind of man." He sold Broder on the idea that the *Post*
would give him a better platform to do the kind of political reporting
that he had sought and failed to do at the *Times.* When Broder finally
agreed to come over to the *Post,* the victory was twofold: Ben had
just landed a young talent who would become one of the finest political commentators in the history of the modern newspaper, and on
top of that he had managed to lure him away from the enemy.

This was a pattern that would repeat. Jim Hoagland was another
early hire, also lured away from the *Times* by the promise of what Ben
was building. As Hoagland told me, a friend of his had urged him to
meet Ben and he had taken him up on the offer, without any intention of making a career change:

> "You ought to go talk to this guy named Bradlee, who's just taken
> over at the *Post.* They say he's gonna do great things" . . . and I say,
> "No, I'm happy at the *Times,* I've got my career path set there."
> "Just go talk to him." Ben and I talk for ten minutes, he offers me a
> job, and I take it. Because in that ten minutes I figured out
> something I'd never seen before. This is a guy I want to work
> *for.* . . .
>
> Before that conversation with Ben, the idea of coming to the *Post*
> had never entered my mind.

As Haynes Johnson, whom Ben hired away from *The Washington Star*, told me, "There wasn't any doubt, after I had met him and we talked. He reached out, held out his hand, and I grabbed it, and that was it. There was no contract, nothing. It was just, 'Come, we want you,' and I've never forgotten that."

Others in the business took notice of the *Post*'s hiring spree. In August of 1966, almost a year after Ben arrived, his old friend Tom Winship—who had worked as a reporter with Ben at the *Post* but had since moved on to *The Boston Globe*—wrote a note to Kay praising her for her "conquests."

"Don't you and Ben feel a little bit greedy," he wrote, "grabbing up . . . three or four of the best young reporters in the country, the hottest columnist property, and stealing the second best political writer in the country from the *Times*? You have the *Star* eating tacks with frustration."

Kay forwarded Winship's letter to Ben with her own handwritten notes in the margin. Underneath his list of their acquisitions, Kay wrote simply, "It does sound great."

"The other thing you have to remember," Carl Bernstein told me of Ben's early days, "is that *The Washington Star* was a great newspaper. When I went to work there in 1960, it was still a better paper than the *Post*." From the start Ben wanted to compete with *The New York Times*, but in a very real way he had to outdo the *Star* first. With the purchase of the *Times-Herald* in 1954, the *Post* had become the only daily morning newspaper in town. But the *Star*, an afternoon paper, was still preferred to the *Post* as the paper of record in D.C.* "Not only did we beat the *Post* regularly," Carl says, "but the *Post* was not an honest newspaper in its coverage. It had agendas."

If Ben had a single journalistic goal in his effort to revamp the *Post*,

---

*Even in later years, when the *Post* was passing the *Star* in circulation and importance and profit, Ben would say that "people lived in the *Post* but they died in the *Star*," meaning that the *Post* was a livelier and better paper but that the death notice in the *Star* would be more official, and mean more.

it was to remove the agendas from the *Post*'s news reporting and from the paper's general posture in the community. He wanted what he called "a harder news edge," in addition to vitality and flair. In an early memo to a correspondent who complained that the editors in Washington had mutilated one of his stories, Ben laid it out as clearly as he could:

> We are not trying to make this paper flatter. We are trying to make it fairer. What you interpret as an effort to remove flavor, individuality and allusion is in fact an effort to remove the tipped hand, the veiled stand, the editorial phrases that make your position clear while they cloud the news. . . . If we flattened [your] vivid writing to colorless mush, the *Washington Post* would be a loser. We want flair, audacity and a flashing quality to wax in this paper. You've got those qualities. They're valued. But we're talking here about something entirely different: tilt. Tilt flaws the effort we're making to become a newspaper distinguished by flavor, individuality and allusion—while being, above all, fair.

Toward the end of 1965, Ben had a chance to send his first hand-picked correspondent to cover the war in Vietnam. Ward Just had been a young reporter at *Newsweek* whom Ben had taken a liking to, and when Ben came over to the *Post* he brought Just with him as one of his first hires. Just was a strong, subtle writer—Ben called him "Ernie" as a joke, in reference to Hemingway—who would eventually leave the newspaper business to write a series of successful novels. He brought that sensibility to his reporting. "I think he saw my highest and best use as probably not a beat reporter," Just told me. "He had very, very good instincts about what to do with the people he had, where to place them."

As the story goes, at a meeting in Ben's office before Just left for Vietnam, he asked Ben, "Well, what do you want me to do over there?"

"What do you mean, what do I want you to *do* over there?" Ben barked. "I want you to be a goddamn reporter, that's what I want you to do!"

I say "as the story goes" because I didn't hear it from Just himself, but rather from somebody else who cited it as a typical Bradlee story, the kind that was always floating around the newsroom in one exaggerated form or another. When I called Just to confirm it, he said the story was "too charming to deny."

"I have to tell you," he said, "it sounds like him. I was certainly not given any instructions." He referred to his stint in Vietnam, where he was given free rein to report on anything that he wanted, as the greatest time he ever spent in journalism. "I never got a call or a cable from the office telling me to do something, never," he said. "Not once in a year and a half did that happen. They absolutely allowed me to write it, to define whatever it was I found and then write it up."

Just also contributed a series of increasingly dark analysis pieces about the war, including one concluding with the pithy assessment that "we are here defending freedom as we understand it for people who don't." When he was seriously wounded by shrapnel from a grenade in the course of reporting a story, he insisted on going back after a short period of recuperation at home.* This was exactly the kind of person Ben wanted covering a war. Kay paid Just the highest compliment that she could, and summarized exactly why Ben had sent him in the first place, when she said of Just that "not a single person on the *Post* could tell where he stood from his news stories."

Peter Osnos, another of the young highfliers at the paper in the late sixties, remembers that Ben called him into his office one day and said, without small talk or fanfare, "Do you want to go to Vietnam?"

"Just like that?" I asked.

"Mmm-hmm," Osnos said. "That's the way it worked. If Ben

---

*Just's firsthand account of his own wounding ran on July 17, 1966, under the headline "Ain't Nobody Been Walking This Trail but Charlie Cong." The writing is superb, and Hemingwayesque: "Verlumis walked up and offered me his .45 pistol. I refused it, arguing that it was bad luck for a non-combatant to be armed. Verlumis persisted. He said anyone who wandered around Kontum province unarmed ought to have his head examined, and besides, it was a fair trade for the drink of whisky the night before. So I took the .45 and Verlumis shouldered his M-16 and we moved out. I never fired the .45 and Verlumis was dead before dusk."

Bradlee calls you in and says, 'Do you want to go to Vietnam?' you don't say, 'Listen, I've got to talk to my broker.' You say, 'When can I leave?'"

This kind of management strategy didn't apply only to Vietnam. Across the board, Ben did his job by picking people he trusted, firing them up, and then setting them loose. (The flip side of this was that he wouldn't give you the work if he didn't trust you. One of Bernstein's beefs with Ben, prior to Watergate, was that Ben refused to send him to Vietnam.)

The main knock on how Ben did things flowed directly from the best aspects of how he did things: critics, even within the paper, thought he was too agnostic and dispassionate about the war, too unwilling to push toward conclusions and judgments about Vietnam. Ben is the first to admit that this is true, that he was hesitant to take sides. He never wanted anybody to accuse him of "whatever the fucking editorial policy was," as he once put it. "It wasn't in me to preach. I can say somebody's a horse's ass, but I can't tell people what to do."

During Ben's years as managing editor, editorial policy was set by Russ Wiggins, and it was openly, disproportionately supportive of Lyndon Johnson and his administration's war effort in Vietnam. Wiggins played by a different and older set of rules. He had come up during the Phil Graham days, when the *Post* meddled in policy debates and tried to steer the political process toward the "right" outcomes. Ben could do whatever he wanted to make the news coverage fairer and flatter, but for his three years as managing editor he didn't have much say (by choice, but also by design) in the editorial page's posture on the war. Even as Ben ran Ward Just's reports of the carnage in Vietnam, the editorial page walked in lockstep with the sanitized version of the war that Johnson was trying, with increasing lack of success, to peddle to the American people.

When Ben replaced Wiggins in 1968, one of his first orders of business was to split the editorial page off from the news operation. Wiggins had been "Editor," in charge of news and editorial. Ben created the title of "Executive Editor" for himself, with a responsibility solely for the news, and appointed Phil Geyelin (a deputy to Wiggins) to run the editorial and opinion pages. This division between the news and opinions about the news was one that Ben had always maintained within himself, but now it was an institutionalized value. As Ben once put it, when Jim Lehrer asked him why he didn't care about editorials: "I think that what I think is not important."

Though Ben's philosophy differed from Wiggins's, the two men liked each other and worked together well. Wiggins had gotten an awful lot right during his days in charge at the *Post*, from removing most racial signifiers from news coverage (saying simply that a man had been shot, for example, instead of a "Negro" man) to building a newspaper that was willing to call Joe McCarthy what he was. In March of 1950, Herblock, the *Post*'s famous cartoonist, had deployed and coined the phrase "McCarthyism" in a cartoon, emblazoned atop a stack of buckets of tar. Ben maintains that Wiggins charted a positive course for the *Post* that "ten Bradlees couldn't change."

During his three years as managing editor, Ben also created a small sideline in collecting some of Wiggins's oddball remarks. He called them "Thoughts of Chairman Wiggins," a play on the *Quotations of Chairman Mao* that had come out in 1964. A sample, typed out by Ben: "We're never going to get anywhere in this business until we abolish people. What we need are good looking girl computers."

In preparation for a speech after his career as an editor was over, Ben wrote down twelve "Editor's Lessons." They're pretty simple, particularly the first five:

1. <u>Owners</u> are everything
2. <u>Energy</u> is vital; yours & staff's
3. A vacancy is a beautiful thing
4. Hire people brighter than you are, & listen to them
5. Don't micro-manage (over-edit)

The sixth lesson is different, and subtler: "Pick your fights. Don't duck 'em, but don't fight 2nd rate opponents." Underneath this rule, Ben wrote in "Libel—Gilbert."

The most fundamental confrontation about news independence and the direction of the *Post* wasn't about Vietnam, and it didn't unfold between Ben and Wiggins. The real battle was fought in the city room, between Ben and a man named Ben Gilbert, the deputy managing editor for local news and Ben's chief rival from the minute Kay brought him back to the paper.

Gilbert had been the city editor during Ben's first run at the *Post* in the late forties, and Ben had learned from him but never much liked him. When Ben came back in 1965, a rumor circulated among some of the reporters that he had punched Gilbert in the face in the old days, a rumor that Ben didn't hasten to dispel. Various old-timers at the *Post* described Gilbert to me as "a terrible person," "a sad creature," "abrasive," etc. "Many people detested him," former *Post* editor Robert Kaiser told me, adding that Gilbert was "really deeply manipulative and profoundly insecure personally." Ben says simply that Gilbert had "the people's touch of a Gorgon."

Ben never cops to much in the way of bureaucratic maneuvering, but he does acknowledge that he knew right away that he would have to find a way to "get on top of Gilbert," as he put it. Though Ben outranked him after succeeding Al Friendly, Gilbert controlled the structure of the paper, from how many pencils went to each desk to how the *Post* played stories. He also enjoyed his status as a kind of unofficial mayor of Washington. He was well wired in with the black establishment in the city at the time, and he was particularly close to Walter Washington, a black politician who ran the housing authority in D.C. during the early sixties and was one of the city's prime movers. Washington and his wife, Bennetta, stopped by Gilbert's house most nights for a social call, a drink or a cup of coffee. The fruits of this relationship were blatantly apparent in the paper. "Walter Washington was a good public servant," Ben told me. "But the worship of him by Gilbert and the *Post* was embarrassing."

In 1967, LBJ decided to appoint Washington as the first mayor-commissioner of the District of Columbia. Washington naturally tipped Gilbert, and Gilbert in turn told Kay and Ben, but it was explicitly off the record and not for publication. Gilbert also arranged for Washington to be invited to an informal lunch at the *Post* during which the *Post* higher-ups would mingle with him and, implicitly, approve of him.

Ben didn't like that idea. In accordance with his sixth rule, he decided to pick a fight. Behind Gilbert's back—there is no other way to put it—Ben assigned a female reporter named Elsie Carper to the story, without telling her what Gilbert had told him. If Washington were really about to be appointed mayor, the FBI would be running background checks and there would be a paper trail somewhere. Carper nosed around and confirmed, on the record and on her own, that Washington was indeed going to be the appointee.

At the White House, when top domestic aide Joe Califano got wind that the *Post* had the story, he called Kay to complain. If they ran it, Johnson would hold up the appointment, Califano said. Kay stood with Ben. "We just had to think about what our job was," she said later, "and our job wasn't to make Walter Washington mayor."

Somehow, with all the back-and-forth between Ben and Califano and Kay, Gilbert still hadn't heard that a *Post* reporter had confirmed the story independently. Every day at a newspaper, the production department creates what's called a "dummy" of the front page, so editors can get a sense of what the morning's paper is going to look like. The day before the Washington story ran, Ben and the rest of the editors who were in cahoots with him dummied a phony story in place of the Washington story so Gilbert wouldn't know what was happening.

Later that evening, Ben realized that the secret still wasn't safe. Like most people in positions of authority at the *Post*, Gilbert had the bulldog edition of the paper delivered to his house as soon as it came off the presses. The bulldog would have the real story, and when Gilbert saw it he would go ballistic—and possibly try to pull the plug for later editions of the paper. And so, in one last twist, Ben sent an editor to swipe the bulldog from Gilbert's front stoop. Gilbert didn't figure out what had happened until the final edition of the paper hit his doorstep the next morning, August 24, 1967. The headline that led the paper read, "Walter Washington Seen as Top Choice for D.C. 'Mayor.'"

The entire escapade is somewhat surprising, given Ben's image as a brash and fearless commander. "I can tell you authoritatively," Len Downie, Ben's successor as executive editor, told me, "Ben does not like confrontation. He does not like having arguments. He's this bigger-than-life character so everybody assumes that he's a bruiser, but he's not. He retreats from that." Of the Walter Washington story and the confrontation with Gilbert in particular, Downie said, "Ben just wanted him out of there. He didn't want to have to argue with him."

There would, eventually, be real blowups between Ben and Gilbert, including shouting matches over two different stories that were also related to the black community. But the Walter Washington story was a major marker, and after that episode Gilbert knew that his days were numbered. "The whole city room was watching the struggle between us," Ben told me, and in that theater he had bested Gilbert and staked a claim about what the *Post* would and wouldn't do.

"It was a very nice announcement that something new had begun," Robert Kaiser would say later of what had unfolded between Ben and Gilbert, "and we called that the Bradlee era."

SUBSTANCE

The whole country has their eye on your bold new venture. I like it.

—Tom Winship to Jim Truitt, the first editor of the Style section,
February 4, 1969

IN 1991, WHEN BEN WAS thinking of writing a book called "How to Read a Newspaper," he and a colleague, Tom Wilkinson, commandeered a microfilm machine and went back through every issue of the *Post* printed after Ben's arrival in 1965, searching for signs of his influence. They ran a tape recorder, and it makes for pretty good listening.

"I'll tell you what strikes me about this," Ben said, looking at one early front page. "How unimportant it all is." Asked what he took from another, he replied, "That the papers are boring and not reader friendly is what I take from it."

As the papers scrolled by, Ben grew dispirited. "Boy, I'll tell you, the change is really gradual, isn't it," he said, clearly hoping for more visible proof of his hand at the wheel. "All this talk about what a killer I was and what a shark I was, and I don't see any blood on the floor at all."

A little later in that same session, you can hear the microfilm machine whirring and then a finger suddenly tapping on its glass screen. Ben had been talking distractedly, but at the moment that he tapped on the screen he stopped mid-sentence.

"Now there!" he said.

This was the front page that he was tapping:

"Now *that's* a Bradlee . . ." he said, trailing off.

"What's the guy's name?" Wilkinson asked, referring to the person who drew the caricature of Senator Everett Dirksen.

"David Levine," Ben said. "That's a gorgeous picture. I mean, you never saw that in a newspaper in your *life*."

"It's a Bradlee *what?*" an observer asked.

"To order the caricature and to put a profile on page one, we started doing that."

"Was there resistance to that?"

"Sure."

"Do you remember from whom?"

"Gilbert?" Wilkinson asked.

"Yeah, the traditionalists," Ben said.

"Did you just go ahead and do it, or did you argue with them?"

"Yeah, I mean, I've got the A-bomb by now," Ben said, meaning that by January of 1966 it was clear that he was running the show. "That's the story, right there!" he said. "No jump, no nothing. You're really leading with that picture. *That's* the story." There is real excitement in his voice. "For a newspaper you have no idea how shocking that was at the time."

Three years later, nearly to the day, the first edition of the Style section would appear in the pages of *The Washington Post*. The same spirit that inspired the Dirksen caricature would inspire Style, on a much grander scale; from the minute he came over from *Newsweek*, Ben had wanted to give the *Post* a sense of vitality, of soul. He also wanted to shock people, to get them talking about more than just the news. Though he began to make incremental progress toward those goals shortly after his arrival at the paper, with the creation of Style in January of 1969 Ben made a huge leap forward.

"When my life is written as a journalist," he once told me, "the Style section is going to be the most important thing."

"*Really?*" I said. "I think a lot of people would be surprised by that."

"That's the most significant," he said.

In pure newspaper terms, he might be right. In a profile of Ben in

Esquire in 1976, James Fallows referred to Style as Ben's "clearest personal monument," even after Watergate. "Bright people were set free to write about the soul of the town," Fallows wrote, and that's the essence of what Style became.

"The Style section was Ben's great invention and a huge contribution to the modern newspaper," Carl Bernstein told me.

"Within ten years every newspaper in America had a lifestyle section just like it," Don Graham said in 2008, when Ben won the Illinois Prize for Lifetime Achievement in Journalism. "But Ben was the first, and Style was the first."

The precedent for Style in Ben's life dates back to before he was born. His great-uncle on his mother's side, Frank Crowninshield, was the first editor of *Vanity Fair*, a post he held for twenty-one years. Crowninshield was a fixture on the Manhattan social scene, natty and elegant (and "gay as a goose," as Ben says), but more important he took a frivolous fashion magazine and turned it into one of the better literary journals of its era. Like his great-nephew, Crowninshield excelled at identifying and attracting talent, though the talent in Crowninshield's case included F. Scott Fitzgerald, T. S. Eliot, and Gertrude Stein, whose early work all appeared in the magazine. Ben's Style section would be a different enterprise for a different era, but its core mission was much the same: to identify the writers and writing that spoke the truth about modern life.

Style unofficially began in early 1966, when Ben hired Nicholas von Hoffman onto the National staff. Von Hoffman was a reporter for the *Chicago Daily News*, specializing in the coverage of civil rights. Before Ben arrived at the *Post* as an editor, the paper had already tried to hire von Hoffman away from the *Daily News*. He had flown to Washington and made the rounds in the newsroom, stopping afterward for a drink with his friend Tom Kendrick, who was a reporter at the *Post* at the time.

"Unless you really need this job," Kendrick told him, "I wouldn't take it. This is an unhappy place. Everybody here is miserable."

"I respected Tom," von Hoffman told me. "I didn't really know anything about the *Post*, and at that time it didn't have any great prestige. I thought, 'I don't need that.' So I went back to Chicago."

But the *Post* stayed interested in him, and after Ben came aboard that interest intensified. As Ben sought to remake the paper, to make it more lively, he occasionally bought von Hoffman's pieces about racial issues from the *Chicago Daily News* service. Though his reporting ran as news coverage, and not as analysis, von Hoffman had a way of injecting a viewpoint into his writing that did more than just convey the news. "Emmett Till was lynched without having his day in court," von Hoffman wrote in 1965, during his coverage of a racially charged trial in Greenville, Mississippi, which the *Post* reprinted. "He was just taken out and murdered. Ever since, his name has stood for the denial of justice to black men in Mississippi."

Von Hoffman had never felt at home in the culture of the *Chicago Daily News*—an editor there had once introduced him to a visiting guest as "our niggerologist"—and in early 1966 he again began to look for other opportunities. An interview at *Newsweek* led to lunch with Ben and Larry Stern, the *Post*'s National editor, and before lunch was over von Hoffman had agreed to come aboard. "I was signing before I was thinking," he told me. "It was clear that Bradlee was a very enthusiastic man. It was obvious that he was up for trying things. And so I went to work."

Week after week, month after month, Ben put von Hoffman's charged writing about civil rights and racial issues on the front page of the paper. In June of 1966, after James Meredith was shot during his "March Against Fear" through the South in support of black voting rights, Ben sent von Hoffman to cover the march, which Dr. Martin Luther King, Jr., had stepped in to save. For three weeks von Hoffman filed from Mississippi, blending eyewitness reportage with ominous detail:

BATESVILLE, Miss., June 11

All the town seemed to be waiting for the Meredith Mississippi freedom marchers. There were white teenagers, sun-burnt blonds in madras shorts, straddling parked Hondas at the street's edge, and elderly ladies in fresh, hot-weather cottons on the front porches.

The Klan was waiting, too.

When he got back, von Hoffman billed Ben and the *Post* for a pair of shoes. ("And we *paid* it," Ben says.)

When Dr. King was murdered in Memphis, Ben sent von Hoffman to cover the funeral. "Every inch of this is going to be covered by every television network in the world," von Hoffman told him, "so we're not going to have any news. I think we have to do it differently." Ben agreed.

On the day of the funeral, von Hoffman filed a story that began, "The Rev. Dr. Martin Luther King Jr. led his last march here today. He was in a cherrywood coffin, carried in an old farm wagon to which were hitched two downhome mules." The story captured a series of vivid impressionistic details, including one college student's wry observation that Dr. King would have been unhappy with his own funeral. "All the poor people are standing so the rich people can sit," he said.

When Ben Gilbert saw von Hoffman's story, he was furious. "This is not going to lead the newspaper," he told National editor Larry Stern. "This is a crummy sidebar and it's going inside." The two of them fought about it so vehemently that Stern threatened to resign if it didn't lead the paper, and they had to call Ben to play referee. They read the story to Ben over the phone, and when they got through, Ben said, "Run it."

"Where?" Stern asked.

"On the front page," Ben said.

This was another example of Ben moving Gilbert out, to be sure, but it was about more than that. What Ben wanted most from his newspaper was a different way of writing about and experiencing the news. Von Hoffman's pieces were full of life and detail; they brought readers into the story in an entirely different way than standard, straight reportage could. Television could bring you the visual images, and the Associated Press could give you the facts. Newspapers, if they were going to do something genuine and interesting, had to try to tell you something that you couldn't get anyplace else.

"Nick expanded all the boundaries of writing at the paper," the reporter, editor, and columnist Jim Hoagland told me. He referred to von Hoffman's hiring, and Ben's unstinting support for what he did, as a "crucial moment" at the paper.

"You saw what Nick could do," Hoagland said, "and you realized what *you* could do. And Ben backed that up."

One of Ben's least favorite sections in the paper had always been the "for and about Women" section, which he found trivial and demeaning. The section was full of recipes and cooking tips and pictures of garden parties hosted by the wives of unimportant generals, the kind of stuff that "bored the ass off of all of us," as Ben likes to say. It treated women as "women," not as people.

Ben replaced Russ Wiggins as executive editor of the paper at the end of September of 1968, and shortly thereafter—not his first order of business, but close—he sent out a memo to Kay Graham and top editors proposing that the "Women's section as it is now constituted be abolished." He tasked David Laventhol, a favored assistant managing editor who had already played a pivotal role in helping Ben redesign and streamline the *Post*'s cluttered front page, with brainstorming ideas for what a different section might look like. "We needed a feature section," Ben told me, "and we needed to treat women as human beings, and we needed great help in organizing the paper." He wanted to try to kill all those birds with one stone.

Two weeks later, on October 11, Ben reviewed a prospectus from Laventhol describing "a new *Washington Post* section devoted to the way people live. . . . People would be stressed rather than events, private lives rather than public affairs":

A number of old departments—women's, food, travel, books, gardens, amusements, TV, shows—would be combined into the new seven-day ongoing operation. The new section would <u>not</u> mean the abandonment of women's news; rather it would expand the horizons of the kind of news women are interested in. It would greatly open up the confined and space-poor "amusement" pages, provide standard everyday locations for key features, develop whole new areas of coverage in the leisure field; and cut across traditional barriers to apply cultural reporting to individual lives.

It's hard to believe that this was a radical idea, but up until then you never knew, looking at the *Post* each morning, where the TV schedule was going to be. You had to figure out its location from the key box on the front page of the newspaper, or else hunt for it. Book reviews appeared in one section one day, and in another section the next, as did theater reviews and the like. One of the most basic functions of any new section was simply to consolidate all of the disparate arts and features coverage in one reliable daily location.

But Ben was after more than organization. He wanted a designated location at the paper where the writers he had hired, von Hoffman and others, could spread their wings. He wanted humor and personality and bold design and new ideas, a section that would provide a mechanism by which the newspaper could express its view of itself, its personality. When we had lunch with a group of White House Fellows in 2007, Ben was asked what was important to him about a newspaper, and he said, "You've got to have some sense that it's got a soul, and it's got a sense of humor. How to get that without making a fool of yourself is one of the goals." The core mission of Style was to push the conception of what a newspaper could be.

The name itself came hard, and took some getting used to.* As Ben began to gear up for the launch of the new section, he called his old friend Myra MacPherson to tell her that he had an offer that she couldn't refuse. MacPherson had been working for *The New York*

---

*K: I don't know who came up with "Style."

 B: I did.

 K: You did?

 B: As a throwback from "Lifestyle."

 K: No wonder it won.

 B: Well . . . as I remember, one of your suggestions was "Treats and Giggles."

 [Eugene Patterson told me that B. J. Phillips, a female reporter who would go on to write the section's first lead story, actually came up with the name, but so many people have claimed credit for it that it's easier just to stick with Ben.]

Times, but she was married to Morris Siegel, who had been a sports reporter at the *Post* in 1948, when Ben arrived.

"We're starting a new section, and it's going to be great, and I want you to be a part of it," Ben told MacPherson when she arrived at his office.

"My kids are two and four," MacPherson said. "You know I can't work full time."

"For Chrissake," Ben said, "the *last* thing those kids need is *you* around the house full time."

MacPherson laughed—then, and as she recounted the story to me. "I said, 'Well gee, what's it going to be called?' He said, 'It's going to be called Style.' No one had ever even *heard* of that as a concept. And I said, 'As opposed to substance?'"

MacPherson signed on, joining the team that would incubate Style, including Laventhol and von Hoffman, who had been named "Culture Editor" but never did much to earn the distinction. In December of 1968, while the formative Style deliberations were still under way, MacPherson published an in-depth three-part series on abortion, which was then illegal, that ran on the front page of "for and about Women." Like von Hoffman, MacPherson took on controversial issues but also took you into the room with people:

> A pretty 17-year-old from North Carolina looked fixedly at a wall while her embarrassed, nervously smiling parents hovered nearby. A young married college student in bell-bottomed pants and vest read magazines along with her school teacher husband. . . .
>
> A man in another room, who runs the two-year-old nonprofit, volunteer clinic . . . says he has felt compelled to help women with unwanted pregnancies ever since he saw a dying woman brought into a New York hospital four years ago—victim of her own attempt at abortion, a coat hanger imbedded in her uterus.

This was striking writing for a family newspaper in December of 1968, and particularly for the "for and about Women" section. It was the direction Ben was pushing in.

On January 6, 1969, with a polyglot editing and reporting team in place, the first edition of the Style section ran in the pages of the *Post*. The lead story, "WANTED BY THE FBI," profiled a female kidnapping suspect and was intended both to attract attention and to announce the section's departure from the old conception of women's news. It wasn't the world's greatest story, but it was different, something that hadn't been done before. Letters poured in from across the country, including from Ben's former opposite number at *Time*, Hugh Sidey, who wrote in to say that he found Style to be "a splendid reading adventure between the Wheaties and the bacon—it's got a lot of the magazine feel which worries me a bit—nevertheless. I like it and tip my hat to the editor."

Ten days into the Style experiment, on January 16, the entire section was devoted to the concept of trains, including a somewhat garish picture of five trains that was supposed to make the reader feel as if the trains were coming at her. "If you wanted to make an announcement that this section is going to be different, the absolute antithesis of the society page, you couldn't have done it any better," von Hoffman told me.

Ben was thrilled; Kay was not.

"Kay hated the idea of the Style section," von Hoffman said. "She fought it every inch of the way. She wanted nothing to do with it." Kay liked the old women's section, and so did her friends. As soon as Style got under way, disgruntled society matrons began bearding Kay at the various parties she attended around town, furious that the *Post* had done away with their section. When the issue with the trains came out, Kay blew her top.

"She had an absolute, total fit about this thing," von Hoffman told me. "First Bradlee goes up there and God knows what transpires between the two of them. Next, Laventhol goes up there and God knows what transpires between the two of them. But he comes down bruised. And finally Bradlee looks at me and says, 'Your turn.' So I go up there and peek around her door, and she looks at me, and I go 'Toot! Toot' [imitating a train]. And she says, 'Get out of here, you son of a bitch!'"

Kay landed on Ben particularly hard. In May of 1969, she wrote
Ben and Eugene Patterson, whom Ben had brought in as his managing editor, a scalding memo:

> [I]f you all think women no longer want women's news—but
> better—there is an information gap. Bill and Don are Nick [von
> Hoffman] readers, but Garfinckel's and Lord and Taylor don't care
> and shouldn't. I do want the Bill, Don and Steve group but I would
> also like the Post still to be here when they grow up. . . .*
>
> I can't see why we have to build ourselves a structure in which [I]
> have to fight and plead and beg to get into the paper (and I have
> never said this before in 5½ years) what I quite frankly want to have
> there. . . .
>
> Enough for now, but could this whole thing please be among top
> priority now that we address ourselves to it with some of this in
> mind? Or am I wrong? I am still listening—sort of—but I hope it's a
> two-way thing.

That she didn't usually intervene so directly meant that Ben had to
take her seriously. He tried to buy time, telling her that the section
was coming along, sending her joking memos signed by "Ben
('Where are you hiding the Women's Section') Bradlee." But even
by her own admission Kay kept coming at Ben like "a dentist drill,"
writing him frequent memos and generally hectoring him about the
direction of the section.

It built and built, until one day when they were together and Kay
was leaning on Ben, in the heat of the moment he turned to her and
snapped, "Get your fucking finger out of my eye." He couldn't do
what he needed to do with her nibbling at him all the time.

The moment has since taken on a kind of legendary status among
the old-timers at the newspaper—in terms of the Style section, but
also in terms of Ben's relationship with Kay and his autonomy as

---

*The "Bill, Don and Steve group" referred to her children, the younger generation who
liked the hipness of the writing.

editor. Most people who know anything about Ben's relationship with Kay can recite that phrase, often without prompting.

In hindsight, Kay was able to admit that she had overstepped. "You have always been patient, wise & deft in your strength," she wrote to Ben privately a couple of years after the debut of Style, "and only once told me to get my finger out of your eye & I did." This was the thing that Ben could do with Kay that nobody else could do, his magic trick. "Get your fucking finger out of my eye": he alone could stand up to her and have her love him for it.

Though Kay hated Style at first, eventually the sheer quality of the writing and reporting in the section began to define the paper in a way that straight news reportage never could have. Writers like von Hoffman and MacPherson and Sally Quinn, who joined Style in June of 1969 and would later become Ben's wife, developed a hard-hitting, freewheeling way of writing stories—particularly political stories and profiles of prominent Washingtonians—that the staid National desk couldn't ever hope to emulate.

As MacPherson put it with me, "We could hit and run." Where the beat reporters had to develop relationships and respect boundaries, Style reporters could parachute into a national primary for two days, interview all the major players, and then write the truth of what they'd seen without fear of repercussions because they'd be on to the next story by the time the previous one had been set in type. National reporters brought home the facts, but Style reporters could capture mood, atmosphere, feeling. After Style took root, nearly every other newspaper in the country would copy it, because it made so much sense. (And yet no paper could truly copy it, because other papers didn't have the center that Style had, which was the political life of the nation's capital.)

In time, the Style section came to rival the front section of the *Post* in prominence and prestige. People would read page one of the paper and then flip to see what was on the front page of Style. When I asked von Hoffman when he knew that Style had arrived, he said, "The day I walked in and Bradlee told me that Art Buchwald wanted to be moved into the section." Buchwald's humor columns had customarily appeared on the op-ed page of the paper, at the back of the front section, but as of August 11, 1970—a year and a half after Style's founding—his column would appear on the front page of the Style section, which more people read.

"On at least one occasion," von Hoffman told me, of his more controversial pieces, "advertisers called up and said, 'We're killing our advertising.' And Ben never mentioned it to me."

Though Sally Quinn and others would create plenty of controversy for Style and for the *Post* in later years, in the early days it really was von Hoffman who got people going. His columns routinely savaged sacred cows in Washington: military wives, whom he wasn't afraid to call "sad and somewhat dumpy," or racial hypocrisy, or duplicity in politics. Often, in the aftermath of a particularly vituperative von Hoffman special, a couple hundred outraged readers would call or write to the *Post* to cancel their subscriptions. Ben loved this; it was proof of von Hoffman's effectiveness. ("And they would all come crying back the next day," Ben told me.)

Kay didn't love it, but she could abide it. Von Hoffman, she would write to complaining readers, "almost alone among American journalists, is telling us what it is in the minds of the vast youthful segment of our nation which we little understand but often greatly resent when its misunderstanding of us threatens the fabric of society." She knew that he was pushing them in the right direction, even if she didn't agree with him most of the time. Kay once threw a shoe at von Hoffman across the newsroom. And when he dared to write a piece about her hairdresser, she told him later, "If you hadn't been kind to him I would have cut your balls off."

But mostly Ben kept Kay at bay.

"People knew that Ben had absolute independence from Kay then," Len Downie told me, of the era after the Style section got up and running, "in part because she complained about it all the time."

Downie has as complete a view of the professional Ben as you can get. He started at the *Post* as an intern in 1964, a year before Ben's return; he was a reporter under Gilbert when the battle for supremacy in the newsroom was waged; he edited Woodward and Bernstein during the tail end of Watergate; and he worked his way up the ladder and eventually replaced Ben as executive editor in 1991. Downie saw it all, from every angle. He's the only other living person who knows what it's like to edit the *Post* and to work so closely with both Grahams.

When I asked him what the most important part of Ben's legacy was to him, he said, "The independence that he established with Kay right from the beginning." He talked about how the role of an independent executive editor is "one of the last great dictatorships in American society." Like Ben, he got used to hearing Kay or Don say, "It's your call" and mean it.

"That's a great freedom and a great responsibility at the same time," Downie told me.

Downie never worked for the Style section, but in early 1969 he had an experience with Ben that echoed von Hoffman's and presaged what was to come for the entire newspaper. He and Jim Hoagland had been working for months on a series about racial discrimination by savings and loan associations in D.C. They called it "Mortgaging the Ghetto," and it ran over ten days, starting on Sunday, January 5, 1969—the day before the Style section premiered:

So one day when I'm hard at work on writing, Ben comes over to me and he says, "What are you doing?" And I started to explain, in my long-winded way, like I am right now, what it was that I was doing. And of course, Ben cut me off after about three sentences— Ben has a short attention span—he didn't want to hear any more. He just said, "Well, these guys were just in my office a little while ago, and they said they represent all the savings and loans in town, and they said if we publish your series, they're going to pull all their advertising from the newspaper."

Well, I think my heart stopped. I just didn't know what to say. I was worried about what Ben was going to say next. Long pause— maybe he did it dramatically for effect—he puts his hand on my shoulder and he says, "Just get it right, kid," and walked away.

We did do the series, we did publish it, and the *Post* lost about a

million dollars in advertising, which was a lot of money back
then . . . and I never heard another word about it.

The whole newsroom knew that Ben was willing to stand by a young
reporter who had put in the work to get something right, regardless
of the business consequences.

"They were both finding themselves," Downie told me, of Ben
and Kay as Style and the paper as a whole really started to fly. "Remember,
it was assumed that she wouldn't run the paper. She's finding
herself. She's trying to figure out how to do this. And she's
putting a lot of faith in Ben. And Ben is finding himself in a way that
he'll never be able to articulate, but could be seen. He's trying things
out.

"So there had to be, whether it was spoken or unspoken between
them," Downie went on, "they had to both understand that they
were experimenting together. And they were both going full blast."

GEMSTONE

This memorandum addresses the matter of how we can maximize the fact of our incumbency in dealing with persons known to be active in their opposition to our Administration. Stated a bit more bluntly—how we can use the available federal machinery to screw our political enemies.

—White House counsel John Dean, August 16, 1971

From the time G. Gordon Liddy was appointed CRP [Committee for the Re-election of the President] General Counsel in December 1971, his principal efforts were devoted to developing, advocating, and implementing a comprehensive political intelligence-gathering program for CRP under the code name "Gemstone."

—Senate Watergate Report, 1974

If you are expecting me to tell you about the elections, only 27 days away, I am going to disappoint you.

I tried that 20 years ago, when I was covering my first national campaign while working for Newsweek magazine.

For some reason that I have conveniently forgotten, I was talking to a group of hotshot businessmen in Detroit at the Economic Club.

After I had talked for a few minutes, there were questions from the audience. They wanted to know who I thought was going to win.

I demurred. Reporters shouldn't predict. I was too green. The election was too close. And on top of all that, I didn't know.

But they insisted. And, finally cornered, I allowed as how, if I had a gun at my head, I thought, maybe, Jack Kennedy would just squeak in.

Afterwards, a stubby little guy—turns out he was a General Motors vice president with a salary of $250,000 a year (and I was making nineteen five)—came up to me and poked a stubby finger hard into my chest, and said:

"Listen, sonny boy, if you want to amount to anything in your business, you just stick close to Dick Nixon."

Which, of course, I did.

—BCB prepared speech text, Wittenberg University,
Springfield, Ohio, October 7, 1980

WE DRIVE ALONG ROUTE 114 from East Hampton to Sag Harbor in two separate cars. When we arrive at the restaurant, we're led to a tight but beautifully set table near the front windows, overlooking Sag Harbor's main drag. My wife shoots me an eyebrow as she takes her seat for the evening, between Bob and Carl.

It's Ben's eighty-ninth birthday, Thursday, August 26, 2010. The big party at Grey Gardens isn't until the weekend, but today is Ben's actual birthday, and Bob has made the announcement that he wants to take the entire house out to celebrate. Given how nice the restaurant is, and how many of us there are—twelve in all—this is not a low-value proposition.

The first bit of wine sets in, and the talk turns to Watergate. Elsa, Bob's wife, leads the discussion, asking people questions and saying she wants to focus on "old times," but the truth is that Bob and Carl and Ben don't seem to need much prodding. Bob and Carl play off each other in their well-worn way, clearly enjoying the opportunity to tell stories about Ben with Ben himself sitting there. Everybody at the table is well aware of my role, and so the stories take on a kind of grandstanding quality, with style points at a premium.

I haven't brought my notebook. I'm there to have fun, not to take notes or make people self-conscious. But as the wine flows and the stories start to spill out I begin to rue my decision. Nobody is saying much that's historically new; it's more about *how* they're saying it than anything else. Sally mentions offhand that I really should have brought my tape recorder, and after a couple of people around the table reiterate that idea I contemplate the possibility of putting the phone in my pocket to inconspicuous use. A night like this won't happen again, at least not for me.

As the phone's recorder cuts in, the conversation has just turned to Martha Mitchell, the wife of John Mitchell, the former attorney general and campaign manager for Nixon who eventually went to prison for his role in the Watergate scandal. Martha was famously gabby and difficult to control, and in the first days after the break-in at the Watergate she enjoyed calling reporters (notably Helen Thomas) to deliver her opinions on developing events. As the story goes, during one of these calls on June 22—five days after the break-in—one or some of the security men around Martha ripped the phone out of the wall while she was still talking. Later, she alleged that she had been "forcibly sedated" when those around her feared she would reveal too much. She was a strange bird, a kind of canary in the coal mine of Watergate, and after her husband left her she took the odd step of inviting Woodward and Bernstein up to her apartment in New York:

BW: She said, "Are you and Mr. . . ."—she always said Mr. Bern-STINE—"busy?" And I said, "Well, what's going on?" And she said, "The son of a bitch finally left me."

CB: Remember, we didn't know what had really happened . . .

BW: And so she said, "He's moved out, and you and Mr. BernSTINE come up here, and you can go into his office. He left all these papers . . ."

CB: She was a well-known drunk by this time. . . . She intimated that there was more to the Watergate story than anybody knew. . . .

B: Did he have a girlfriend? I bet he did.

CB: Well, later—Martha must've been about sixty.

BW: So we call Bradlee, we always observe the chain of command.

CB: Oh yeah.

BW: This is one of the great lessons of this. We call the city editor, we had eight levels of editors between us and Bradlee. So we just said, there's not time. And Martha . . .

CB: This is part of the good cop/bad cop between us.

Elsa: And it was Sunday.

CB: It was always Sunday.

BW: So we call Bradlee, and we say we have this offer to come up and go
through his papers. And so Bradlee says, "We better get the lawyers."

CB: Legal reasons.

[The editors, reporters, and lawyers agree on a theory of "constructive
abandonment" that allows them all to feel that what they're doing is
okay.]

BW: And she greets us at the door, I remember it, and she had a martini
in one hand and the Chinese menu in the other, and she said, "Let's
order."

B: This is Martha?

BW: "I hope you nail the son of a bitch."

CB: [The apartment] had a lot of cabinets. There was this linen closet
that was painted all powder blue. And she said, "I think that he keeps
stuff up in there." So I took my shoes off and went crawling around in
this closet, throwing down [papers].

BW: There were letters in there, one from Elmer Bobst who ran a big
drug company, saying, Dear John, if we give a hundred thousand dollars in the '72 fray, campaign, will you help us with our problems with
the Securities and Exchange Commission? I mean, no one ever writes
letters like that anymore. But they did.

Everybody at the table has heard most of these stories before, but it's
fun to hear Carl and Bob egging each other on, with Ben cracking
wise whenever he sees an opening. Conversation turns to Robert
Redford, and to how boring *All the President's Men* seems to their
kids. Bob retells the story about Pakula and Robards having to find
fifteen different ways to say "Where's the fucking story?" Carl tells an
abbreviated and often interrupted version of the moment in September of 1972 when he and Bob realized that Nixon might well be
impeached.

"That was a word I never used," Ben says, as serious as he's been
the whole night, "and a word that I told you never to use."

As we are having dessert, Bob gives his own toast, in earnest:

BW: One of the fires in my life is Elsa, who—and she lights many fires. And one of the things she's said over recent years is, "Take Ben to lunch. See Ben. Go do this, go do that, with Ben." And we have the saying, in our family, because in our place in Maryland we have sculls and we go out and row, and the saying is, "Any day you row is a good day." And I have, in the last good number of years, realized that any day you get to spend some time with Ben Bradlee is a good day. So thank you.

Quinn [Ben's son]: He also put you on the map, too.

[laughter]

Sally: Or maybe the other way around, they put him on the map.

B: We shared that.

BW: No, no. [To Quinn] Your father had the answer to this. Nixon put us on the map.

CB: He's right.

WOODSTEIN

My perceptions of both of you? You and I have had conversations about this, old buddy. I thought you were a guy who was not always running at top speed but you had extraordinary talents that you didn't always use. And I thought Woodward, who the Christ was Woodward? I had often said that Woodward reminds me of me as a beginner. I thought that you were hopelessly inexperienced to tackle something like this and I probably would have fought tooth and nail if I had known then what I know today to involve either one of you.

—Ben's response to a question from Carl Bernstein in a private interview with Woodward and Bernstein for *All the President's Men*, July 16, 1973

IN THE FALL OF 2008, Bob took Ben out to lunch and, naturally, brought along his tape recorder. Over the course of the lunch, Bob tried to dig down into some of the general principles of Ben's career at the *Post*, to locate or articulate what it was that made Ben tick as an editor. That's an impossible thing to do, as Bob must already have known, but there is one moment that resonates.

"I didn't realize when I came on how important just the people were," Ben said. "It's one thing to say you've got to get the best people, but you've got to get the *right* people. There's a lot of luck in that. *Lot* of luck in that. How the hell did we get you?"

"Yeah, I mean, I was lucky," Bob said.

"You know, how much credit do I deserve for that?"

"But you . . ."

"But I had created an atmosphere that appealed to you."

"Exactly, exactly."

"I understand that," Ben said. "And I understood it even then, I think."

Bob decided that he wanted to be a journalist—a *Washington Post* journalist, to be precise—in August of 1970. After four years at Yale and another four years at sea with the Navy, he had spent his fifth and final year in the service working at the Pentagon, as the watch officer overseeing worldwide Teletype communications. He was a driven, ambitious young man, eager for life experience after having given so much of his youth to the Navy, and he wanted to be where the action was. He had applied to Harvard Law School, but that was the safe choice, an extension of the life he had already led.

Most biographical sketches of Bob include two episodes from his childhood that theoretically primed him for his career in investigative journalism. Both hinge on secrets. The first occurred after Bob's parents divorced, and he and his brother and sister chose to live with their father. Their father remarried, to a woman with children of her own, and at one of their first joint Christmases Bob felt quite acutely that he and his siblings had been given the short end of the stick. He tracked down the prices of all the gifts and then compared the amounts that had been spent on him and his siblings to what had been spent on his stepsiblings. "It was a moment of great emotional distress for me and my father when I confronted him and showed him that the money he'd spent on them and on us was so dramatically out of balance," Bob told an interviewer in the eighties. His response to disorder and distress was to locate and take solace in the facts.

The second episode occurred when Bob went to work as a janitor in his father's law offices in the small, Republican suburb of Wheaton, Illinois, where he grew up. His curiosity about what his dad did led him to nose around in the files, eventually reading whole confidential reports and realizing that people's public fronts often masked more sordid private lives. An esteemed local school official, for instance, might secretly be trying to seduce a female student; what you saw wasn't always what you got. As one of his editors would put it later, "Woodward was very naïve and yet very aware of original sin at an early age."

As the 1970s began, *The Washington Post* was doing to the Pentagon and to the Nixon administration what Bob had done to his own father that Christmas as a boy: holding the authorities accountable for their actions, describing the distance between public statements and the realities they often obscured. Bob saw this all firsthand from his perch at the Pentagon. "You could just see the disparity between the classified message traffic and what was being said publicly," he told me. The *Post* was out to expose the facts, and he admired the paper for it.

In August 1970, his time in the Navy over and his law school plans in the dustbin, Bob walked into the *Post* and asked for a tryout. He had no experience as a reporter, but he talked his way into an interview with Harry Rosenfeld, the Metro editor who would be one of his main overseers during the Watergate story. Rosenfeld had never interviewed a naval intelligence officer for a job before, so he decided to give Bob a chance. "I thought he was worth a tryout," Rosenfeld said to me, still sharp at eighty-two. "But that's all I thought he was worth."

"I failed miserably," Bob told me. "Wrote a lot of stories, none were published."

"You don't know how to do this," Rosenfeld said to Bob, after the tryout was over. "If you're really serious, go get some experience."

Rosenfeld helped him line up a job interview with the editor of the *Montgomery County Sentinel*, a small weekly paper in suburban Maryland. When an editor at the *Sentinel* asked Bob why he should hire him, Bob said, "I want this job so bad I can taste it."

After he was hired, he shone. He had a good nose for controversy, and he worked prodigiously. Within a couple of months he was scooping the *Post* on stories, so much so that Jim Mann, his competitor at the *Post*, started recommending that the paper hire him. Rosenfeld noticed, too. "It began to be embarrassing," he told Kay Graham later.

Rosenfeld had instructed Bob, somewhat loosely, to get a year's experience and then knock on the *Post*'s door again. Bob doesn't do loose. Nine months after he'd left, he started calling Rosenfeld at the office and at home, hoping for a second chance. One hot summer day in 1971, Rosenfeld was on vacation from the paper, painting his basement. He was up on a ladder, "furious with the world," as he put it, when the phone rang. His wife, Annie, called him upstairs, and when he got there and realized that it was Bob he blew his top. "Goddammit, Woodward!" he shouted into the phone. "Call me at the office!"

He slammed the receiver down and turned to his wife. "That asshole is calling me up all the time!"

"Isn't that what you always say is the kind of person you want?" Annie said.

Soon enough Bob was back making the interview rounds at the

Post, and this time he made it all the way to the top, to the final up-or-down interview with Ben.* During their interview, Ben homed in on Bob's time in the Navy, referring to it "as if it were the brotherhood," as Bob remembered it later. This was an Ivy League kid and a Navy veteran, like Ben himself, who had forsaken an ordained slot in the establishment to pursue journalism as a calling and as a career. Just as Ben had been brought in as the low man on the city desk in 1948, Bob was brought in as one of the lowest-paid reporters on the paper, covering night police for the city staff. His first day at the *Post* came precisely 366 days after he'd been sent off to the *Sentinel*.

His first story, about a lawyer who had been disbarred, ran on September 17, 1971, on the third page of the Metro section. Six days and five stories later, Bob made the lower left corner of the front page with a story about a fire that killed five of six children in one family. The next day, he was back up on the front page with a follow-up story, reporting that the mother of the children had been offered a chance to move her family out of their unsafe house but had never answered the letter from the National Capital Housing Authority.

This was a breakneck pace and Bob maintained it. Sometime shortly after Bob was hired, Ben held one of his occasional lunches with new reporters in one of the upstairs dining rooms at the *Post*. Three or four cub reporters sat on either side of the table, and when Ben walked in he went immediately to his place at the head. "Which one of you is Woodward?" he asked as he sat down. Bob raised his hand. "You're all over the paper," Ben said. "Good work." That was the highest praise you were ever going to get.

Ben has always been accused of playing favorites, and he has always responded by saying that the people who were his favorites were the people who produced. Of Bob, he once said, "People have to write stuff that is relevant and that gets in the paper, and wherever you put him that's what happens."

In January of 1972, just four months after he'd been hired, Bob produced ten front page stories (and a host of others) as he zeroed in on low-level police corruption in D.C. In February he had another

*This is the interview Bob describes in his long letter on pages 22–23.

seven front page stories, following the trail all the way up to the former number two man in the metropolitan police department's internal affairs unit.

While Bob was working on the police corruption stories, he had
an experience that everybody in the newsroom longed for. As Bob
was sitting at his typewriter hammering out an early draft, Ben walked
across the newsroom, stopped at Bob's desk, and pulled up a seat next
to him. This was a rarity, a public tactic that everybody noticed and
that Ben used masterfully throughout his career. It scared the hell out
of Bob, that all of a sudden Ben was looking over the shoulder of a
lowly Metro reporter, firing off questions about the story: Where is
this coming from? How sure are you? Ben seemingly grasped every
important detail in the story in less than two minutes, and then he
was gone.

After Ben walked off, Bob felt that he had arrived. "You feel like
you've been authenticated," he told me, of Ben's visit to his desk.
"Like what you're doing is . . . blessed."

"You couldn't keep him out of the paper," Ben told David Halberstam a couple of years later. "You know, you'd give him the real
shit detail, and the next day he'd have it on page one. I was using him
before Watergate as an example of someone who can always get in
the paper. He knew how to crack the code."

Bob himself told Halberstam that when Watergate came around
people thought that he worked so hard on it because he recognized
it for the story it would become—which wasn't true. "It was not that
it was Watergate," Halberstam wrote of Bob in his interview notes,
"he simply was working that hard, he was that driven and he was that
insecure." On the morning of Saturday, June 17, 1972—the same
morning that the five Watergate burglars were arrested and the epic
journey began—Bob had yet another story on the front page, about
a U.S. Civil Service Commission vice chairman who was steering
business to one of his cronies.

"I think [Woodward] engendered some jealousy and resentment
because of his work," Rosenfeld told Kay in their interview years
later. "But it was outstanding. And when Watergate breaks there's no
question in my mind . . . nor in Howard's [Simons, the managing

editor] . . . who's the first person we'll put on the story. There's no question."

"There was no question," Kay agreed.*

Ben put it in his own way many years later, when he was talking about how hard Bob worked and an interviewer had the temerity to ask, "But didn't he cause you problems as an editor?"

"Jesus," Ben said. "Editors should have such problems."

In July of 2009, I went up to New York City to talk to Carl. He had been hard to pin down. I had been trying to get an interview with him for six or seven months, with no success, but this time I had him. I took the train up to meet him for lunch.

We had met in person a couple of times, when I worked for Bob. Carl would call at Q Street every once in a while, and at first I got a kick out of relaying the message: Bernstein for Woodward! Sometimes he stayed in the guest room on the third floor of Bob's house, where we worked, and he would pop his head into my office and ask what I was working on.

In those days, Bob didn't talk about Watergate much unless he was at a public event and the inevitable bore asked him who Deep Throat was. The sheer number of people who did this was staggering. I always thought Bob handled it pretty well, evasive but gracious, never betraying any irritation. If it wasn't a question about Deep Throat, it was a joke about Redford playing Bob in the movie. Bob's line on that was pretty good, too: "You have no idea how many women I've disappointed."

It didn't take much to figure out that, of the famed duo, Bob was the dutiful son and Carl the profligate one. You could tell just by looking at them. Both had held the live wire of Watergate in their

*She may have been snowing Rosenfeld, at least a little bit. "One of the interesting small pieces of the puzzle & one I suspect you don't know," Kay wrote to Ben in 1974, after Watergate was over, "is that I met Bob Woodward—I mean really met him & knew which one he was—at the Pearson Awards lunch." That lunch was in December of 1972. She had bet the paper on two reporters that she couldn't distinguish from each other until after their most important reporting had already been done.

hands at roughly the same age, in their late twenties, but it seemed like Carl had held on a little longer and been burned a little deeper.

In the whole "Woodward and Bernstein" game, Bernstein always comes out on the bottom. I defy anybody to find a substantive piece about Carl Bernstein from the period 1974 to 1990 in which somebody doesn't refer to the fact that Carl was known for borrowing money that he never repaid, or that he smoked cigarettes but rarely had his own supply—and *never* had his own matches (the horror!). These details are meant to reveal his character, his nature, which we are implicitly supposed to question.

And then, of course, he gets crushed by comparison with Bob, who pumps out biennial bestsellers like batches of brownies. It's an unenviable position for anybody to be in, measuring your career next to Bob's. Bernstein fell apart after Watergate, but it's hard to imagine that he could have kept up, even if he'd managed to hold his life together.

I arrived on time for our interview, but Carl had me cool my heels in the lobby of his apartment building for a while. I expected that. When I eventually made it up to the apartment, he opened the door, classical music blasting behind him, and welcomed me in. I walked straight toward the source of the sound, which turned out to be two of the nicest stereo speakers I'd ever seen. We gave them a quick listen and then moved into Carl's office, just off the living room, which was lined with hundreds of vinyl records, mostly symphonic recordings and opera but also a healthy selection of old rock records. There were four different tube amplifiers in the room—only one of which was in use, hooked up to his system via a series of industrial-level electronic connections—two racks of sophisticated audio gear, and two state-of-the-art record players. You could buy a very nice car, maybe even more than one, for the cost of the unused audio equipment in that room.

He wanted to know, right away, what Bob had already told me about Ben. "How much time did he give you?" he asked, before I'd even been able to pull out my tape recorder. He wanted me to know that he and Bob have a "different understanding" about the *Post*, that they talk to each other about it in ways that they wouldn't with anybody else. The sense of competition, of wanting to be seen as Bob's equal and to make an equally weighty contribution to what I was doing, was unmistakable. After some small talk, we agreed to go out for lunch and start the tape recorder there.

We walked around the corner to an Italian place. Carl told me the pastas were great but that he couldn't have any because he'd put on some weight. Then he proceeded to order a salad and an enormous plate of deep-fried seafood that he inhaled as we spoke, including the tails of the shrimp that he initially had cast aside. There was something impulsive and endearingly childlike about him. Whenever he made a point that he thought was particularly important, interesting, or surprising, his eyes would bug out just before he said the capping phrase and then he would deliver it, smile, and wait for my reaction. I remembered what Ben had told me once, that Carl was whip smart but also "the kind of guy who was looking at you while he was talking to you, to see how he was going over."

Carl grew up as a lefty, the son of two communist Jews. He started as a copyboy at the *Washington Evening Star* at the age of sixteen, working three and four days a week during the school year and then summers full time. Later he moved in and out of college, taking classes at the University of Maryland but eventually proving himself to be fundamentally allergic to the idea of doing homework and going to class. "I got thrown out, I quit," Carl told me, as if there were no difference.

After a few years at the *Star*, Carl bumped up against the paper's policy of not hiring reporters who didn't have college degrees. He took a job on the *Daily Journal* in Elizabeth, New Jersey, and moved to Manhattan. He spent a year working on whatever he wanted to in New Jersey—long features, investigative pieces, column work—and ended up winning three state newspaper association awards. When the year was up, in 1966, he wanted out. The *Star* still wouldn't take him without a college degree, so he applied to the *San Francisco Chronicle*, *The New York Times*, *The Washington Post*, and the *Washington Daily News*. The *Daily News* made him an offer, but he didn't want the job there.

"The reason I wanted to go to *The Washington Post* was because of Bradlee," he said.

"Already?" I asked. Ben would only have been back at the *Post* for a year or so by then.

"Absolutely. Because you could see by then that he was turning [the *Post*] into a different kind of newspaper."

He started off in Metro, as nearly all new reporters did, and quickly earned an enduring reputation as a cigarette bummer and money borrower. "Very talented and erratic . . . in my work habits," as he put it to me.

"That's the story line."

"The story line is fairly true. My agenda usually tending toward my own." We laughed. "Partly out of a view of journalism, partly out of my own character."

The Bernstein stories from Carl's early days at the *Post* really are pretty funny. Apparently he used to rent cars on assignment and then leave them parked in random locations only to forget about them, running up enormous tabs with the rental companies. When Carl was covering city hall, the city editor, Steve Isaacs, paid an unannounced visit one day and arrived to find Carl asleep on the couch in the press room. His reputation as an unreliable employee and as a person who spent beyond his own means, and beyond the paper's, was legendary by the time Watergate started. The joke around the newsroom was that Bernstein had spent more money covering the Virginia legislature than Murray Marder, one of the *Post*'s foreign correspondents, had spent covering the Paris peace talks.

Ben's pre-Watergate perception of Carl was that he was "lazy, talented, streetwise"—not an uncharitable description. At one point in 1972, just after the *Post* had moved into its current building on 15th Street, Ben noticed that Bernstein would unthinkingly let his cigarettes burn out on the brand-new floor around his desk. That did not endear him to Ben. "If we'd have had a list of people to get rid of, he would have been very high on it," Ben told Halberstam in the late seventies. "His laziness was almost unparalleled."

Despite the differences in background and temperament, Carl looked up to Ben in much the same way that Bob did. "I ask what he thought about Bradlee," Halberstam wrote privately of his interview with Carl, "and he says, that when he first knew him, 'I was in awe of him and yet I was bothered by the fact that he didn't know how good I was.'" Typical Bernstein bluster, but he would also tell Halberstam that he admired Ben more than any other man he knew besides his own dad.

In the months and years leading up to June of 1972, Carl's main goal—a goal shared by many Metro reporters—was to land a spot on the National staff. That was where all the big-name guys were, the guys whose desks Ben would linger over, punching arms and trading gossip. Those were the highfliers, and Carl was always a highflier in his own estimation. The quickest and most likely path to the National desk lay in convincing Ben to send him to Vietnam, where he could write (or so I imagine) a series of feature stories full of novelistic detail and veiled but trenchant political sentiments and then return to the paper as a hero. Bernstein told me that he asked Ben, repeatedly, to be sent there, and Ben said no every time. When I asked Ben if he ever thought seriously about sending Bernstein to Vietnam, he looked at me like I was crazy.

Some weeks before Watergate, Carl decided that if the *Post* wouldn't give him the bigger opportunities he felt he deserved, he would have to go elsewhere. On a whim he called Jann Wenner at *Rolling Stone* and talked his way into an interview. "Wenner was so fucking long making a decision," Bernstein told me, "that Watergate happened in the interim. But I would have gone in a song. In a second, I'd have been out of the fucking door . . . I was furious. And I was furious at Bradlee."

Good son, bad son, good cop, bad cop—these dynamics started early and stayed in place for the rest of Carl's relationship with Ben and with Bob. In October of 2007, the Society of Professional Journalists invited Bob, Carl, and Ben to sit on a panel commemorating the thirty-fifth anniversary of Watergate. Backstage, before the discussion started, the panelists and moderators were milling around, waiting for the event to start, when Carl called to say that he was going to be late.

"I'm not surprised that Carl's late," Ben said. "I'm *amazed* that he called."

I witnessed Carl's aggrandizing tendencies firsthand when our interview at the restaurant was over, and we were walking back to his apartment. We ran into a woman Carl knew, and after they said hello she looked over at me. "Is this your son?" she asked.

"No," Carl said. Then, out of nowhere: "He's my biographer."

It was a harmless little lie, but he said it right in front of me. The woman said she was looking forward to reading the book when it came out, and then we walked back to his apartment without saying another word about it.*

"The thing that I look back on," Ben said to Kay, in one of the interviews for her memoir in 1990, "[was] how lucky we were . . . I mean how we had Woodward and Bernstein, had an awful lot of Washington Post eggs in that basket and you look at Bernstein now and you wonder . . ."

"Well, I wondered then," Kay said, drolly.

"Well, except the thing was, whatever you said about Bernstein, is that Bernstein made the first key connection of the money," Ben said. This is the core truth of Carl, the seminal piece of Watergate reporting that you can't take away from him and that justly brought him his place in history. To drive it home, almost as if to ward off his own disbelief as much as to persuade Kay, Ben said again: "He found that money."

---

*After William Goldman wrote a first draft of the screenplay for *All the President's Men,* Carl and Bob and most others at the *Post* were unhappy with it. Carl and his then girlfriend, Nora Ephron, decided to take a crack at a rewrite, and apparently in that draft Carl exaggerated his role as "the more swinging member of the Woodstein team," as *Time* magazine put it. "Carl," Robert Redford remonstrated after he'd read it, "Errol Flynn is dead."

BEGINNING

The Weather
Today—Cloudy, high in the low 80s, and low near 70. The chance of rain is 40 per cent today and tonight. Monday—Partly cloudy, high in the low 80s. Temperatures range: Yesterday, 49-70; Today, 72-52. Details C4.

The Washington Post

Times Herald

95th Year · · · No. 196 · · SUNDAY, JUNE 18, 1972 Phone 223-6000 40¢

Both Sides Claim Victory in N. Vietnam Offensive

Diplomats Feel 'Something is Afoot' to End War

By Murray Marder

News Analysis

Analysts Measure Hanoi's Goals and Results

By Laurence Stern

News Analysis

See VIETNAM, A4, Col. 1

See ASSESS, A14, Col. 1

5 Held in Plot to Bug Democrats' Office Here

By Alfred E. Lewis

Sen. George McGovern nibbles, on a Polish sausage while campaigning in a Buffalo market yesterday.

Appeals Court Delays Ruling On Pilot Strike

By Jack Eisen

Nader Blasts Civil Service As Arrogant

By Mike Causey

You know as a journalist, that there is no decision should I go down that road or down that road, there were just thousands of little decisions, get the goddamn story in the paper. And by the time you had done it it was over.

—BCB to Frank Waldrop, former editor of the *Washington Times-Herald*, undated but likely 1990

WHEN THE NEWS OF THE break-in at the Watergate Hotel and Office Building first hit the *Post* newsroom on the morning of Saturday, June 17, 1972, Ben wasn't even in Washington. He was out at his country place in West Virginia, where his phone line was spotty, and didn't fully grasp what was happening until he came home on Sunday night. That day the first stories describing the break-in had run in the paper, and by that night the second day's stories, linking one of the burglars to the Committee for the Re-election of the President (CRP), had already been written.

Howard Simons, the managing editor, had made all the executive decisions about placement and play of the stories up to that point. The specific decision to send Woodward to the courthouse that Saturday, where he would famously hear James McCord, one of the burglars, admit that he worked for the CIA,* had fallen to city editor Barry Sussman. The decision to allow Bernstein to muscle his way into the story, as Bernstein so often did when he sensed that something big was going on, fell to Sussman, too.

That Sunday, Carl and Bob had their first real collaboration, in which Carl surreptitiously took each page of Bob's draft story out of the city desk editor's hands and rewrote it on his own. The story, the first of many to appear under their joint byline, began, "One of the five men arrested early Saturday in the attempt to bug the Democratic National Committee headquarters here is the salaried security coor-

---

*Upon hearing McCord mention the CIA, Bob said "Holy shit" out loud to himself, the first of many.

dinator for President Nixon's re-election committee." Their partnership wouldn't solidify until more than a month later, but it had begun.

Late Sunday night, after the paper had been put to bed, the *Post's* night police reporter called Bob to tell him that the name "Howard E. Hunt" had appeared in two of the burglars' address books, with entries for "W. House" and "W.H." next to Hunt's name.* When he arrived at the office Monday morning, Bob called the White House switchboard and asked to be connected to "Howard Hunt"—having no idea who Hunt was or what his role might be. The operator rang an extension, but nobody answered. When she came back on the line, the operator told Bob casually, "There is one other place he might be. In Mr. Colson's office." Hunt wasn't there, either, but Colson's secretary kindly gave Bob the number of the public relations firm where Hunt also worked.

Later that day, Bob confirmed through the White House personnel office that Howard Hunt was a paid consultant to Charles Colson, special counsel to the president and known widely as Nixon's hatchet man. He reached Hunt directly at the public relations firm and asked him why his name and number were in the address books of two of the burglars. "Good God!" Hunt said, before begging off and saying that he had no further comment.† A call to Robert F. Bennett, the head of the public relations firm (and later a senator from Utah), yielded an unguarded reference to the fact that Hunt had worked for the CIA, something Woodward hadn't known. The next morning a story would run in the paper under the byline of Bob Woodward and E. J. Bachinski, the police reporter who had given Bob the tip, and it included Bob's interaction with the White House switchboard operator, Hunt's "Good God!," and the link to the CIA.

But that morning, Ron Ziegler, Nixon's press secretary, was asked about the Watergate situation. He cautioned that "certain elements may try to stretch this beyond what it is." The incident was nothing

---

*Either the burglars or the reporters had the order of Hunt's name wrong. He was actually E. Howard Hunt, the "E" standing for Everette.

†Bob later told an interviewer that Hunt had an "'I'm packing my bags' quality to his voice that I've never heard before really in my life."

more than a "third-rate burglary attempt" and didn't deserve any additional response from the White House.

Nearly the whole of Watergate is there, three days into the story. You couldn't prove anything from a name in an address book or a switchboard operator's easy fluency with where Howard Hunt might have been, but in retrospect you can deduce the rest of what happened from these details alone. If Charles Colson knew what Howard Hunt was up to, you could bet pretty safely that President Nixon knew, too. And Ziegler's characterization of the break-in as a third-rate burglary—a phrase now legendary for its calculated understatement—typified the White House's response to Watergate for much of 1972.

At the *Post*, you had Woodward and Bernstein nosing around the story and figuring out how to work with each other, not yet a team but becoming one. They were overseen by Sussman and Rosenfeld and Simons, but not yet Bradlee. He hadn't even been there for the first few days, which is meaningless as a detail but important in terms of understanding how a newspaper works. Executive editors don't usually dig their hands into stories that small; there isn't time. And stories that small don't get bigger unless the reporters and the city editor and the Metro editor and even the managing editor, all of whom were more involved in Watergate than Ben was at first, have the resourcefulness and determination to make it so.

One of the oddities of Ben's memoir is its singularly unsatisfying Watergate chapter. It's by far the longest chapter in the book, and also the least revealing. Most of the material is cribbed from *All the President's Men* and a couple of other key texts.* It reads as if Ben

---

*All the President's Men has supplied the basic narrative structure of the *Post*'s involvement in Watergate ever since it was published in 1974. I can't fault Ben too much, given that I have also relied heavily on that book—in large part because Ben, Bob, and Carl all referred me to it when they couldn't remember things. In the endnotes that accompany this book online, I have been careful to cite every specific instance in which I've quoted from *All the President's Men*, but in some ways it's impossible to cite the determinative role that that book has played in nearly every account of Watergate since its publication.

scanned those other books, put all of the important events in chron-
ological order, and then just left it at that. You get no sense of what
it felt like to live through Watergate as the executive editor of *The
Washington Post*, which is the one thing most readers might reasonably have hoped for. Ben doesn't do soul searching. But why couldn't
he tell us something that we didn't already know?

I cycled through a lot of different answers to that question as we
spent more and more time together, but I think the right answer is
this: if you dig around in the archives of an executive editor, you can't
help but realize just how difficult and all-encompassing the job is.
While Woodward and Bernstein were out in the newsroom writing
down every quote from every source and obsessively working over
the small details of the story with Sussman and Simons, Ben was
holding editorial meetings on other topics and worrying about the
play of the stories on the next morning's front page and what he was
going to do about the budget for next year and who was going to
cover the antiwar rally that half of the reporters' and editors' wives
were marching in. There were larger stories like the Vietnam War and
the presidential campaign of 1972 to deal with, in addition to pressing
internal issues. Three months before the break-in, the *Post* had been
sued by seven black reporters for racial discrimination in employment
practices. In June, as Watergate bloomed, Ben and the rest of the
editorial and business staff were still figuring out how to respond. He
had other things to think about.

Ben has also never been known for his ability to retain small daily
details, from "forgetting" about some of Kay Graham's less inspired
requests to meeting reporters on his own paper numerous times and
having them never be quite sure that he knew what their name was, or
where they reported from. Even in July of 1973, while the Watergate
story was still unfolding, he didn't remember much about the beginnings of the story, other than an (admittedly powerful) general feeling:

Woodstein interview, July 16, 1973:

B: . . . I'd love to claim such prescience in late June that we knew where
  this thing was going, but that's a lot of shit. We didn't.

BW: What was your reaction when you first heard about it?

B: I was probably, you know, fun and games. Hell of a good story . . . you knew once they'd been arrested they had no real defense and it would be a fun story, in terms of it was going to hang around, that it was going to make a lot of people embarrassed. . . .

I will not be able to remember the individual decision-making things but [two weeks into the story] I sure as hell was beginning to realize that the reputation of the *Post* was going to hang out there publicly, whereas I was ready to back you guys up, I wasn't as ready as I became later. . . .

CB: When did you first start—

B: What painted the scene was a gradual and not so fucking gradual in terms of all that time but a steadily and slowly increasing awareness that we were going to play the hardest ball that we had ever played. I mean not to put too fine a point on it and I might suggest to you that I don't believe I trailed either one of you by very far.

BW: That's right.

B: I mean, you were fucking around with another police story and then one more thing would come up and the look of incredulity on both of your faces I will remember until I die.

That's most of what Ben remembers about Watergate. By nature, he thinks about the things that are in front of him. If he's not looking at you or talking to you, odds are he isn't thinking about you. Watergate to him was *what happened*. He doesn't deal much with larger implications. That's for other people with more time on their hands.

If you really want to know what Ben thought about Watergate, and what he learned from it, you're better off focusing on how he behaved during the Janet Cooke scandal in 1981, which I'll get to later. The simpler and perhaps more fruitful question to ask about Watergate is this: What did Ben *do*? What does an executive editor really *do*? How do you lead an entire newspaper—a frightened owner, a turf-wary staff, an unlikely pair of young reporters—through the greatest newspaper story of the twentieth century?

———

First, some basics. Watergate began early in the morning on Saturday, June 17, 1972, when a security guard named Frank Wills (who plays himself in the movie) discovered that the lock on a stairwell door in the garage of the Watergate complex* had been taped. He removed the tape and continued on his rounds. When he returned to that same stairwell some time later, he discovered that the door had again been taped—a woefully incautious move on the part of the burglars†—and called the police.

Scout 249, the closest marked police unit to the scene, was low on gas, so the call at the Watergate fell to Cruiser 727, a set of plainclothes cops. A few minutes later they arrived at the Watergate and went inside. The spotter who was part of the criminal operation saw this from his post at the Howard Johnson motel across the street, but he didn't realize at first that the plainclothes cops were police. It wasn't until they were upstairs and turning the lights on in the offices of the Democratic National Committee headquarters with their guns drawn that the spotter realized what had happened, and by then it was too late.

At 2:30 that morning, the intruders were arrested. The police had been expecting a bunch of kids looking for dope money, not five men in business suits and rubber gloves who were as scared as they were. In the burglars' possession were a walkie-talkie, two cameras and forty rolls of unexposed film, lock-picks, bugging devices, tiny tear-gas guns, and roughly $2,300 in cash, most of it in sequential $100 bills. This was not your average break-in.

As the first details about the case seeped out in the *Post* and other papers, it was clear from the CIA connections that it was a story but it wasn't at all clear just how far up the chain it would go. At the time, Nixon was well ahead in the polls and he and the men around him were seen as reputable, competent people who couldn't possibly have

*The Watergate complex is a set of five modernist buildings in downtown Washington, D.C., overlooking the Potomac River. There are three apartment buildings, an office building, and a joint hotel/office building. The DNC headquarters were on the sixth floor of the joint hotel/office building; the burglars stayed at the hotel.

†This was so colossally stupid that the FBI, according to Acting Director L. Patrick Gray, suspected that there had been double agents involved—i.e., that somebody within the bugging team itself might have wanted the team to get caught.

been involved in such an inept and low-yield operation. Even Bernstein didn't think it went all the way to Nixon yet.

Day by day, week by week, Bob and Carl and the other reporters on the staff kept digging up little pieces of information: before Watergate, Howard Hunt had "showed a special interest" in Teddy Kennedy;* Bernard Barker, one of the burglars, had tried to acquire the plans for the Miami Beach convention hall where the Democratic convention was to be held later that year. The *Post,* like other papers, referred to the whole situation as the "Watergate caper," connoting frivolity and harmlessness, nothing more than political fun and games. Everybody was pecking around the edges, following the scent of possible dirty tricks, but nobody knew what the whole story was. Toward the end of July, Woodward went on vacation, and Bernstein went back to covering the Virginia legislature.

Two developments got everybody going again. The first was that *Newsday,* an afternoon paper on Long Island, reported that G. Gordon Liddy, a finance lawyer for CRP, had been fired by campaign manager (and former attorney general) John Mitchell in June for having refused to answer questions from the FBI about Watergate. Liddy would eventually be indicted for his role in the Watergate burglary; this was the first shoe dropping. The second development was that Walter Rugaber of *The New York Times* wrote two stories that opened up the money trail. On July 25, he reported that Miami telephones listed under the name of Bernard Barker had placed at least fifteen phone calls to CRP, more than half of which had been placed between March and June.

Howard Simons had been following all of this closely, and when he saw the *Times* story he was upset. He marched across the newsroom to Barry Sussman's desk with the *Times* in his hand and asked

---

*Woodstein's story initially alleged that "Howard Hunt conducted an investigation" into Kennedy; Ben, in his famous walk across the newsroom that introduces him in the film version of *All the President's Men,* forced them to change it to "showed a special interest." As it turned out, their story was correct, and Ben had toned it down and knocked it off page one out of what Bernstein perceived to be loyalty to the Kennedys. When they reminded Ben of this fact after their reporting had been proven to be correct, he admitted, "You bastards have got me now."

him, point-blank, "Why didn't we have that?" He wanted Sussman to put two reporters on the case, full time, a small Watergate desk. Woodward was an obvious choice; Bernstein, less so. Later that day, when Sussman told Simons that he wanted to assign Bernstein as the other reporter, Simons is reported to have screamed.

After some digging on the phone, Carl discovered that the Dade County state's attorney had subpoenaed some of the burglars' Miami records as part of his own investigation to see if any state laws had been broken. The prosecutor referred Bernstein to his chief investigator, who said that in addition to the telephone logs he also had some of Barker's bank records. Bernstein made a date to come down a few days later to look at them. Before he could get there, Rugaber got there, and on July 31 *The New York Times* reported that four cashier's checks issued from the Banco Internacional in Mexico City had been deposited in Barker's account in April, the same account from which the burglars had drawn their serially consecutive $100 bills. Rugaber didn't know what it meant, other than that perhaps the Nixon campaign had been laundering money through Mexico to conceal the identity of some of its contributors.

Bernstein was already on his way down to Miami the day that Rugaber's second story ran in the *Times*. He read it on the airplane. When he landed, figuring the *Times* had them beat, he called Sussman and asked if he should stay in Miami or go on to Mexico City. Sussman told him to stay, arguably the most important decision made by any *Post* editor during the initial phase of Watergate. Bernstein's scheduled visit with the investigator later that afternoon uncovered a $25,000 check from a man named Kenneth H. Dahlberg that had also found its way into Barker's account. (Rugaber had seen that check but hadn't known what to make of it; the Mexican angle seemed the more promising one.)

Bernstein called the details of Dahlberg's check in to Woodward, and Woodward did some sleuthing. The *Post* librarian found a picture of a man named Kenneth H. Dahlberg standing next to Hubert Humphrey, the former vice president and senator from Minnesota, so on a chance Woodward contacted directory assistance in Minneapolis and asked for a number for Kenneth H. Dahlberg. When he received one he called it, and Dahlberg himself answered. After a few quick questions, Bob asked about the check.

"I turn all my money over to the committee," Dahlberg told Bob, in reference to CRP. "I'm a proper citizen, what I do is proper." Dahlberg hung up and then called back through the *Post*'s main switchboard, just to make sure Woodward was actually a *Post* reporter, and then he revealed that he served as the Midwest campaign finance chairman for Nixon. At a meeting in Washington, Dahlberg had personally turned the check over to the treasurer of the committee, Hugh Sloan, or to Maurice Stans, the committee's finance chairman.

That night, Bob wrote the story for the front page. "Bug Suspect Got Campaign Funds," the headline read on August 1, with this lede: "A $25,000 cashier's check, apparently earmarked for the campaign chest of President Nixon, was deposited in April in a bank account of one of the five men arrested in the break-in and alleged bugging attempt at Democratic National Committee headquarters here June 17."

Bernstein had found the money.

The August 1 story was a turning point. It's also the best concrete example of the *Post*'s direct influence on the machinery of government and the inquiries that would lead to Nixon's resignation. Critics of the *Post* often claim that the paper didn't do anything but print leaked details of the investigation, but that isn't true. In some instances the *Post*'s reporting was the impetus for the investigation itself—no small feat—and this August 1 story is a prime example. On the day the story ran, Philip Hughes, the director of the Federal Elections Division of the General Accounting Office, declared that the GAO was going to conduct a full audit of CRP's finances. He explicitly cited the *Post*'s reporting as the basis for his audit request.

On August 2, Woodward wrote a follow-up story about the GAO on his own but decided to put Carl's byline on the story alongside his. The story noted, with some satisfaction, that the GAO audit had been undertaken "because of an article in yesterday's Washington Post." Up until then, the two reporters had been jealously protecting their own information and suspiciously eyeing the other guy, wondering if he would try to run off with the story. As of August 1, that was over, at least in a formal sense. Nearly every Watergate story that either man worked on for the rest of the paper's coverage of the scandal would carry the names of both men.

The difficulty with Watergate from the start—in terms of reporting, but also in terms of making the story understandable and compelling to an average reader—was how complex it was. That's a big part of why it played out the way it did, how it could stay on the back burner for weeks and then, as the pieces fell into place, suddenly boil over. You can see why, particularly in August and September of 1972, Carl and Bob had the story mostly to themselves.

Take that August 1 story. It had the general outlines, but you couldn't prove causal relationships. As it happened, Dahlberg's check hadn't actually directly funded Watergate. His check had been converted to cash because the CRP finance people were trying to avoid a new April 7 reporting deadline on campaign contributions and were simply using Barker as a conduit. On August 9, Bob and Carl ran a story on the front page of the *Post*, "Stans Denies GOP Money Funded Watergate Break-In," providing this very explanation. The August 1 story had been right and wrong at the same time, right on the substance but wrong on the implication. These kinds of things happened all the time.

On August 12, Carl and Bob ran a standard process story about the civil suit that the Democratic National Committee had filed against the burglars for invasion of privacy—yet another confusing aspect of Watergate. The civil suit was brought by Lawrence O'Brien, the chairman of the DNC, and sought $1 million in monetary damages for invasion of privacy as a result of the bugging. The discovery process for that case was public at first, except as it pertained to the criminal investigation . . . which was essentially impossible to determine.* The deeper point is that there were parallel investigations,

---

*On August 22, Judge Charles Richey decided to seal all pretrial testimony in the civil case, to protect the rights of people who might later be charged in the criminal case; Edward Bennett Williams represented Lawrence O'Brien and the DNC. "I don't remember a conversation I had with Williams in which I didn't thank him for the deposition that he just sent over," Ben once said of the period after the depositions were sealed. "I said, 'We're missing page seventy-eight on the Mitchell deposition.' Always said that. He'd say, 'Fuck you.'"

criminal and civil, which meant that there were a number of people digging around who were occasionally willing to share tidbits with inquisitive reporters. The August 12 story was otherwise unremarkable except for one significant feature: up until then, all of the jumps for the Watergate stories had been labeled either "Bugging" or "Incident." ("See INCIDENT, A8.") That morning, a new jump appeared, and would appear for the duration: "See WATERGATE, A7, Col. 1." The scandal had a name.

The rest of August was a slow, steady drip. On August 22, Woodstein reported that the GAO had discovered violations in the handling of nearly $500,000 in campaign contributions and expenditures at CRP. The story was notable because it was the first appearance of the term "slush funds," which would become so important in September and October. That same day, the Republican Party nominated Richard Nixon for a second term as president of the United States.

A week later, on August 29, Nixon held a press conference at the Western White House (his home in San Clemente, California), where he rejected requests from Democrats for a special prosecutor. He referred to an internal (nonexistent) investigation run by White House counsel John Dean and claimed, "I can say categorically that his investigation indicates that no one in the White House staff, no one in this administration presently employed, was involved in this very bizarre incident." He was lying through his teeth. "What really hurts in matters of this sort," he went on, "is not the fact that they occur, because overzealous people in campaigns do things that are wrong. What really hurts is if you try to cover it up."

GO

So there came a time when it seems to me, not to be conceited about
it, but where I made all the decisions. And that wasn't initially, but
there came a time, and why or when, I don't know, I'd have to reflect
on it.

—BCB memoir interview, May 16, 1990

BEN HAS SOMETIMES CLAIMED THAT he was "hooked" on the Watergate story as early as June 20, when he heard about Hunt's "Good God!" and the switchboard operator. But it wasn't until Carl found Ken Dahlberg's check in Miami that Ben really started to clue in to how big the Watergate story could be. (Still: Ben wasn't in the office when the big August 1 story ran. He was on a three-week vacation at his country place in West Virginia and wouldn't return to the paper until the middle of August.)

As the story grew, Ben naturally began to take more of an interest in the reporting. The National staff of the paper, where all the hotshots worked—people like Haynes Johnson, David Broder, Dick Harwood, Jim Hoagland, and Bill Greider—was Ben's bailiwick. Those were the people he cultivated, the group he had worked so hard to build when he first came over to the paper, and he saw them as an extension of himself. As a rule Ben didn't spend much time attending to the Metro staff. "They were the lords of the manor," Metro editor Harry Rosenfeld told me, of the National staff, "and we were the field hands."

"You never know when you make a decision what you know when you're going to sit back and reflect [on it]," Ben told Bob and Carl in their private interview in the summer of 1973. "I suspect if I had known on July 17, or June 17, the play of this story . . . you guys would have been lucky to have a hunk of it. And I would have been wrong, but there is no way I could have made any other decision."

One of the great accidents of luck and timing with regard to the Watergate story, from an internal *Post* perspective, is that Ben stayed out of the direct management of the coverage for as long as he did. Had he come in earlier, he would no doubt have insisted on putting one of his heavy hitters on the story. But nobody on the National staff was willing to work as hard, and with the same desperation, as Carl and Bob were. It's always silly to play "'If' history," as Bob calls it, but Watergate could never have happened the way it did if Ben had gotten deeply involved earlier. By the time the story reached Ben's front burner Carl and Bob had claimed it as their own.

On September 15, 1972, the Watergate grand jury indicted G. Gordon Liddy, Howard Hunt, and the five burglars who had been caught in the act. Only two days before, Woodstein had reported that Maurice Stans, the finance chairman of the reelection campaign, had "personally approved the secret—and perhaps illegal—transfer of campaign funds through Mexico." A suitcase full of cash, as much as $700,000, had been flown in to Washington by an oil executive and delivered to CRP headquarters on April 5, just two days before the new disclosure deadline. Yet the grand jury, and the prosecutors running the criminal investigation, decided to indict only those lowest to the ground and closest to the break-in at the Watergate itself.

After the indictments were handed up, a Justice Department official described the investigation as "in a state of repose." The entire Watergate story might well have died there. A criminal case against anybody other than the people who had been caught red-handed seemed highly unlikely, if not impossible.

But Carl and Bob weren't about it to let it die there, and neither was anybody else at the *Post*. Two days later, on September 17, Woodstein published one of their most important stories to date as the off-lead in the paper.* Headed "Spy Funds Linked to GOP Aides," this was the lede graf:

---

*The lead story is the right-most story above the fold in a newspaper, and theoretically is weighted as the heaviest and most important news story; the off-lead is the left-most story above the fold and second in importance, though depending on the makeup of the page these things can take slightly different forms.

Funds for the Watergate espionage operation were controlled by
several principal assistants of John N. Mitchell, the former manager
of President Nixon's campaign, and were kept in a special account at
the Committee for the Re-election of the President, The
Washington Post has learned.

This was a significant advance, linking the campaign manager's office
at CRP and the Watergate burglary more explicitly and with harder
evidence than the reporters had managed before. More striking even
than the content is the story's tone. Often Carl and Bob would base
a story on a paragraph or two of new information and then spend the
rest of the article making their case about the entire burglary again,
retelling the story with the same old details. The September 17 story
is written authoritatively, strongly, with minimal hedging on facts.
It's hard to read the story now as anything other than a declarative
statement by Woodstein and by the *Post* that, low-level indictments
notwithstanding, this thing wasn't over.

A story the next day named Jeb Magruder, the deputy director of
CRP, and Herbert L. (Bart) Porter, the scheduling director, as two of
the people who withdrew more than $50,000 from a "secret fund"
that financed intelligence-gathering activities against the Democrats.
"There is no indication that the money allegedly withdrawn by Porter and Magruder was used directly to finance the Watergate bugging," the story conceded, but the noose was tightening.

A big September 20 story reported that two other top campaign
officials, Robert Mardian and Fred LaRue, had "directed a massive
'house-cleaning' in which financial records were destroyed and staff
members were told to 'close ranks' in preparing a public response to
the [Watergate] incident." These are the first public traces of the
cover-up, which was what would ultimately ensnare the Nixon
White House. The authority of the reporting is on a completely different level from the reporting of a week or two before.

The "slush fund" was proving to be the key to the entire operation. A CRP spokesman, by way of response to the September 20
story, would say only that the *Post*'s sources were a "fountain of misinformation." This was one of the nondenial denials that everybody

at the *Post* was starting to get used to, and in a certain sense it only egged them on. In *All the President's Men*, Woodward and Bernstein refer to this story as a dangerous one. The *Post* was going deeper than the grand jury had.

On the morning of September 28, Carl and Bob rode out to see Hugh Sloan, the former treasurer of CRP, at his home in suburban Virginia. He had become a willing source, in large part because he was protective of his direct boss, Maurice Stans, the finance director at CRP. As the reporters pressed him, Sloan revealed that Stans had been one of five people with "authorizing authority" over the slush fund. That didn't mean that Stans knew what each batch of money was being spent on, Sloan insisted, only that he could approve the outlays. Sloan then revealed that John Mitchell, the former attorney general of the United States and the former director of CRP, had been the first person in charge of the secret fund, beginning in 1971, while he was still serving as attorney general. Woodstein knew this was big—Mitchell had likely broken the law while serving as the ultimate arbiter of it—but they desperately wanted all five names. Sloan would confirm only that Stans, Mitchell, and Magruder had been three of the five, and when he wouldn't budge Woodstein returned to the *Post* to meet with their editors.

This is the first meeting in Ben's office in the book version of *All the President's Men*, which isn't an accident. Bob and Carl use this meeting as an opportunity to introduce who Ben is, "an alluring combination of aristocrat and commoner," a man who could curse at a reporter and then slip into perfect French, or put out his cigarette "in a demitasse cup at a formal dinner party . . . and leave the hostess saying how charming he was."*

In the meeting, the reporters presented what they knew, and then what they thought they knew and would be able to prove with more

---

*The hostess in this particular story, often told by Howard Simons, was actually Kay Graham herself. "Howard still can't get over the fact that Ben put out a cigarette in a cup of coffee at Mrs. Graham's house and got away with it," Haynes Johnson told Alan Pakula.

digging—namely, that H. R. (Bob) Haldeman, Nixon's chief of staff, was probably one of the five people in control of the fund. If they could get all five names, they'd be able to write the definitive version of events. As they rambled on about the possibilities for the story, Ben interrupted them.

"Listen, fellas, are you certain on Mitchell?" he asked.* "Absolutely certain? Can you write it now?" When they said yes, he stood up and said, "Well then, let's do it."

"The reporters understood Bradlee's philosophy," Woodstein wrote later. "A daily newspaper can't wait for the definitive account of events."

Before dispatching the reporters to write the story, Ben reminded them that they were now taking a step into the big leagues. Everybody in the room knew what that meant. And then, Ben said simply, "Go."

Years later Bob and Carl would tell Ben that the thing they remembered best about that meeting was "Go." That fits with the iconic, ballsy image of Ben. But from an editorial perspective the more illuminating aspect of their conversation is Ben's identification that the Mitchell component was news, and that they should break it off and run it as a separate story. "He was right and we didn't even realize it," Carl would say later. Instead of thinking about their larger theories and waiting for all of the pieces to fall into place, they should go with what they had and keep the story moving. This really was "Bradlee's philosophy," as Carl and Bob understood it, and as I do, too. If you know it and you can prove it, you use it before somebody else does.

Later that night, after the story had already been sent to the composing room to be set in type, Bernstein called Mitchell to give him a chance to respond. It was about 11:30, and Mitchell was woozy— maybe drunk, maybe just groggy. Carl read him the lede of the story: "John N. Mitchell, while serving as U.S. Attorney General, personally controlled a secret Republican fund that was used to gather in-

---

*The dialogue in this scene is quoted from *All the President's Men*.

formation about the Democrats, according to sources involved in the Watergate investigation. Beginning in the spring of 1971, almost a year before he left the Justice Department to become President Nixon's campaign manager on March 1, Mitchell personally approved withdrawals from the fund, several reliable sources have told the *Washington Post*." Mitchell's initial response was, "Jeeeeeeesus," and when Bernstein kept reading Mitchell just kept saying "Jesus." Then it got more colorful from there, as Woodstein's interview with Ben revealed a year later:

BW: The one maybe you'll specifically remember is [that] Mitchell controlled the secret fund, that Katie Graham is going to get her tit caught in the wringer.

B: Yes, I remember that very well. I remember being called at twelve o'clock at night by you—

CB: Saying use it but take "tit" out.

B: Yeah. I remember that vividly.

BW: Let's get this specifically.

B: Well, I remember you calling me saying that you had reached Mitchell, and let me see if I can, "You're going to run that crap? It's all been denied. If you run that Katie Graham is going to get her tit [caught] in a big wringer . . ."

CB: "Fat wringer."

B: "Fat wringer."* And I debated calling Mrs. Graham [Woodward laughs] to see how she felt about her arrangements being in the Washington newspaper, then I asked you, "Was he drunk?" I think. And I think you replied that he might have been, and then I asked you several questions in my charming, inimitable manner as to whether you

---

*The quotation, as it ran in the next morning's paper: "All that crap, you're putting in the paper? It's all been denied. Katie Graham's gonna get caught in a big fat wringer if that's published. Good Christ! That's the most sickening thing I ever heard." Years later, Art Buchwald, Ben's great friend, had a gold tit made as a gift for Kay. ("Can't you imagine Buchwald going in there and ordering it?" Ben said to her years later.) And a dentist from Anaheim, California, sent her a wringer. When she wore them both together, Ben would routinely beg her to take them off.

were taking notes, whether you didn't make it up. Then I remember
deciding to run it, and I think I got you to reread it several times and
it seemed to be that Katie Graham was going to get caught in or get—

BW: Leaving "tit" out.

B: Leaving "tit" out. We just felt that the publisher's arrangements—it
was my decision to leave her arrangements out.

When Ben got the call from Bernstein he was in bed with Tony, and
he remembers being stunned by what Mitchell had said and pillow-
talking with Tony about it. "I did think it was funny," he said later,
"and I thought it was ballsy to go ahead and run it." Even this late in
the story, Ben wasn't quite sure that he entirely trusted Bernstein. On
the phone Ben made Carl read his notes back twice to see if any of
his wording changed.

The story, with Mitchell's censored quotation appearing in the
seventh graf, ran the next morning. This was one of the shortest of
the major stories during Watergate, probably because Ben had given
them so little time to think about it and execute it. Instead of piling
on facts to make their case, Carl and Bob got straight to the point.

After it ran, Ben began to let the reporters know that he was interested and, more important, that he wanted to win. When the *Los
Angeles Times* scooped everybody the next week with a firsthand account of the bugging from Alfred Baldwin, the lookout on the night
of the burglary, Ben made it clear that he wasn't overly pleased. "I
would like to have had that one," he told them. It used to be Simons*
or Rosenfeld or Sussman who would bust their balls if they got
scooped. Now, increasingly, it was Ben.

"Mitchell kind of intrigued him," Bob told David Halberstam a
few years later. "And you have a sense of Bradlee, when he's interested in a story, he's prowling around, you know, do it for him. It gets
very personal."

---

*A number of editors at the *Post* claimed that Simons basically "explained" the Watergate
story to Ben in the early stages, that Ben (like most readers) had a hard time tracking all of
the details. By October of 1972, he no longer required any explanations.

In late September, Bernstein had received a tip about a man named Donald Segretti, a young California lawyer and Army veteran who had been hired by the Nixon campaign to disrupt Democratic political activities across the country. One of their bright ideas was to infiltrate Democratic campaigns by offering to spy on one Democratic candidate on behalf of another—while reporting to the Republicans the whole time. The thinking went that if they disrupted the Democratic primary enough, and created enough infighting, no candidate would be able to regroup in time to be able to mount a real challenge to Nixon.

Bernstein eventually confirmed, through a Justice Department source, that the Watergate investigators were aware of Segretti as a political saboteur. The term that the official had heard for Segretti's activities was "ratfucking." Another Justice Department official said that political sabotage of the type that Segretti had coordinated was "basic strategy that goes all the way to the top." Once he had confirmation, Bernstein wanted to write the story right away, but Bob wanted to check it with someone first.

Few figures have loomed larger in recent journalistic history than Deep Throat, Bob's famed secret source. He is a huge part of the mystique of Woodward and Bernstein, the *Post*, and Watergate, and for more than thirty years his identity was the best-kept secret in Washington. Until 2005, when Mark Felt, the former assistant director of the FBI, stepped forward, nobody at *The Washington Post* knew his identity except for Bob, Carl, and Ben—and Ben didn't find out until after Nixon resigned. In 1972, Bob identified Throat to his bosses only as somebody high up in the Justice Department, and when Throat's information checked out the *Post*'s editors learned to trust him. (Howard Simons came up with the name, which honored Bob's "deep background" ground rules with Felt* and made an ir-

---

*Journalistic rules can be a bit hard to follow, and interpretations vary. Generally speaking: "On the record" means you can quote a source, by name; "on background" means that you

resistible connection to a pornographic movie of the same name that
had come out earlier that year. Simons also dubbed Woodward and
Bernstein "Woodstein.")

Because of Felt's high position at the FBI, he was reluctant to talk
on the phone or meet in person at any obvious location. According
to Bob's descriptions of their relationship, he and Felt worked out a
system by which they would signal each other during the day and
then meet that night in a deserted parking garage in Rosslyn, Virginia, just across the Potomac River from downtown D.C. If Felt
wanted to talk, he would mark a page of Bob's *New York Times* (delivered to Bob's apartment house lobby each morning) with the appointed hour. If Bob wanted to talk to Throat, he would move a
flowerpot with a red flag in it to the rear of his apartment balcony.
Other arrangements obtained at times, but this was the main way
they signaled for meetings with each other.

On October 8, Bob and Deep Throat would have one of their
most important meetings in all of Watergate. After hearing Carl's
information about Segretti, Bob didn't think there were enough specifics for a story and wanted to check with Throat. There wasn't time
to put out the flowerpot—Bob was returning from New York City
too late in the day for that—so by a different prearranged signal Bob
called Throat at home and (without saying who he was) asked for a
garage meeting that night.

Throat didn't know anything about Segretti specifically. "I don't
know about Segretti—I just don't know. I can't tell you anyway," he
said, according to Bob's confidential memo written up the next
morning. But Throat did confirm—and even went beyond confirming to explain, something he didn't usually do—that there was a massive political sabotage operation run out of the White House during
the 1972 presidential campaign. More than fifty people had been involved. Segretti would have been just a piece of it.

---

can quote the source without naming them (e.g., "a close friend says," or "a high government official revealed"); "on deep background" means that you cannot quote the source at
all and cannot name or identify them either, but you can use the general information provided to deepen your reporting; and "off the record" means that you can't use the information at all, in any way, unless you can somehow get other sources to confirm it.

As Bob put it to me later, the Segretti material alone was a five or a six on the Richter scale, but the extra dimension of a massive political sabotage operation brought it straight up to a ten. At the end of their meeting, when Bob said that he needed specifics if he was going to put this all in a story, he asked Deep Throat about something called the Canuck letter. Throat told him it had been a "White House operation" from top to bottom.

The Canuck letter was a different piece of the puzzle, and an important one. Ed Muskie, the senator from Maine, had been one of the leading candidates for the Democratic presidential nomination in early 1972. As the Senate Watergate Report would later reveal, the Republican political saboteurs ran riot on Muskie's campaign and effectively knocked him out of the race. Some disruptions were relatively small—sending huge batches of unordered pizzas to Muskie campaign events, that kind of thing—but the Canuck letter was big.*
In late February of 1972, as Muskie was preparing to campaign in New Hampshire, the *Manchester Union Leader* (a right-wing newspaper run, coincidentally, by the man who bought Ben's old paper, *The New Hampshire Sunday Times*) printed a forged, poorly spelled letter claiming that Muskie had made a derogatory remark—"Canucks," but spelled "Cannocks"—about "Franco-Americans." The following day, the *Union Leader* reprinted a derogatory story about the drinking and smoking habits of Muskie's wife, Jane. The day after that, as David Broder noted on the front page of the *Post*, Muskie broke:

> With tears streaming down his face and his voice choked with emotion, Sen. Edmund S. Muskie (D-Maine) stood in the snow outside The Manchester Union Leader this morning and accused its publisher of making vicious attacks on him and his wife, Jane.
>
> The Democratic presidential candidate called publisher William Loeb "a gutless coward" for involving Mrs. Muskie in the campaign

---

*The Nixon men had code names for the various operations against Muskie. "Ruby I" and "Ruby II" involved installing spies in Muskie's campaign, while "Sedan Chair I" and "Sedan Chair II" involved hiring people to pull political pranks at Muskie's campaign appearances.

and said four times that Loeb had lied in charging that Muskie had condoned a slur on Americans of French-Canadian descent.

In defending his wife, Muskie broke down three times in as many minutes. . . .

Now they had what they thought were three stories: Segretti, which Bernstein would write; White House involvement in the Canuck letter, which Bob would write; and a more sweeping story about the "basic strategy" of ratfucking, written by both of them.

A chance encounter in the newsroom that morning changed things yet again. A National reporter named Marilyn Berger walked up to Carl as he was taking a break from writing and asked him if he and Bob knew about the Canuck letter. They did, but they'd just found out about the White House's possible involvement in it that morning from Deep Throat. Why was she asking? Because Ken Clawson had told her that he had written it, Berger said.

Ken Clawson had been a reporter at the *Post* for four years before leaving to join the Nixon administration as a deputy director of communications in early 1972. Ben knew him well, though Carl and Bob didn't. Clawson had wanted to be National editor, and when the job went to Dick Harwood, as Ben once put it, Clawson "gave up" and took the job at the White House.

Berger said that two weeks before, at the end of September, she and Clawson had been having a drink in her apartment and that Clawson had told her personally that he'd written the Canuck letter. "He really practically blurted [it] out," she would say later. When she asked him why, according to the memo she made after their conversation, he replied that Nixon's campaign was most afraid of Muskie as a candidate, and that they wanted him out of the race.*

In a private interview with Kay Graham long after Watergate, Berger said that she hadn't told Ben right away because she was scared of him. "I really was," she said. "I was afraid of his building up the

---

*The thing most people don't realize is that the dirty tricks operation *worked*. The Republicans feared Muskie and Teddy Kennedy the most, and wanted explicitly to run against McGovern, whom Nixon summarily defeated in a landslide.

story to more than I was ready to." She had wanted to discuss Clawson's admission with David Broder first, but Broder had been out of town on a political trip. As soon as Broder got back to the office, Berger told him about what Clawson had said, and he urged her to share it with "the boys." That was what had brought her across the newsroom to Carl.

After Berger delivered the news, Woodstein and Broder sat down with her to ask precisely what had happened.

"Why did he tell you?" Bob asked.

"You know why he told her," Carl said.

"Why did he tell you that?" Bob asked again.

"He was trying to impress me," Berger admitted. "He wanted me to go to bed with him."

"What did you think?" Carl asked, wondering why Bob had persisted.

"I just wanted her to say it," Bob said.

From there, the reporters took the story to Ben. He was upset that Berger hadn't told them all sooner, but he also admired her for eventually coming clean, given that the incident had taken place in her apartment, with a married man, and alcohol was involved. "It was not an easy story for her to tell," he said a year later. "I remember putting her through a really kind of rough course of sprouts and being absolutely convinced that Clawson said it but not being convinced that Clawson did it." (The running sexist joke in the newsroom was that "it only sounds like 'I wrote the letter' if you're on your back.")

Berger was uncomfortable with her name being used in the story that Bob and Carl were drafting. "Do you have to use my name as a source?" she remembered asking Ben. "If [Clawson] had told Haynes Johnson, would you have said, 'told Haynes Johnson'?"

"No," Ben said. "And if it were Haynes Johnson he wouldn't have waited two weeks to tell us about it."

At Ben's suggestion, Berger asked Clawson out to lunch at the Sans Souci, a favored French haunt for people at the *Post*. At lunch, Clawson told her that he wished that she hadn't told Woodstein about it, that he would deny it "on a stack of Bibles over his mother's grave," according to Berger's recollection. When Woodward called Clawson later that day, Clawson claimed that Berger had misunderstood him, that he had never admitted writing it in the first place. Then Clawson called Berger back, saying that he'd be ruined if the details of the story came out. It would not look good if his late-night drinks with a comely reporter ended up on the front page of *The Washington Post*.

After he hung up with Berger, Clawson called Ben. This was something that Ben could get excited about. Not only was it a big Watergate story, but it involved the personal sexual escapades (or at least attempted escapades) of a former employee who had forsaken the *Post* for the belly of the beast. Ben knew that he had the advantage, even without the late-night-drink aspect: "Clawson, given a certain amount of booze," Ben once said, ". . . will tell you that I was his hero."

The location of Clawson's conversation with Berger wasn't relevant to the story, but that didn't prevent Ben from letting Clawson twist awhile on the phone, as he begged Ben not to put it in. It's a great scene in the movie, one that Robards plays with raised-eyebrow perfection. Bernstein later said privately that Ben was "so excited," once he'd talked to Clawson, "because [he] knew finally this day that he had everybody. And he was showing a kind of kid-like gleeful thing at various times." Ben spent most of the afternoon out in the newsroom, near Berger's desk, or near Woodward's or Bernstein's, roaming around, trying to figure out what people knew.

That night, around 6:00, the reporters and editors gathered in Ben's office for a final meeting. The three story ideas had been whittled down to two, and after reading through the initial copies of each of those stories Ben made the decision that only he could make: instead of two partial stories, they would go with "one big ball-breaker" that incorporated everything that they had found out over the previous few days. As Bob later remembered it in an interview with Alan Pakula, Ben had said, "This is one story, fellas. You've got one story. Put it all together."

"It wasn't his opinion," Bob told Pakula. "It was an instruction."

Ben went over to his typewriter and wrote two long paragraphs about the Canuck letter, and then watched over Bernstein's shoulder as Bernstein sat at his own desk and typed out the lede of the story, two paragraphs that (miraculously) no editors changed:

> FBI agents have established that the Watergate bugging incident stemmed from a massive campaign of political spying and sabotage conducted on behalf of President Nixon's re-election and directed by officials of the White House and the Committee for the Re-election of the President.
>
> The activities, according to information in FBI and Department of Justice Files, were aimed at all the major Democratic presidential contenders and—since 1971—represented a basic strategy of the Nixon re-election effort.

"This was a declaration of war on the White House," Bob told me. "Essentially saying, 'You have a secret campaign to fuck with democracy . . . to decide who the Democrats are going to nominate.'" More broadly, Bob told me that the moment this story became one story was the moment where "We understood Watergate." Ben would later describe the October 10 story as the "seminal work" of the entire *Post* effort; Carl called it "the most important story." It was the first time where they pulled the camera back and took in the bigger picture. They had spent so much time on the particulars—this fund, that fund, who wrote what check—that they hadn't put all the pieces together in the most basic way, to say outright: This is what these people were up to. This is how nefarious it really was, and is.

And this is what we're up against.

The first few grafs are also interesting purely as an example of how meticulously Woodstein used language. As they described it later, nobody had actually told them that what they were about to report "represented the stated conclusions of the federal investigators." They knew only, by putting various puzzle pieces together, that FBI and Justice had uncovered enough information to substantiate the story's claims. "We were hanging by threads sometimes," Bob told me.

And so if you look at even just the first four words of the story— "FBI agents have established"—you see how thoughtful the choice of "established" is. All it means is that FBI agents have information in their files that could lead them to that conclusion; they've established it, in other words, whether they know it or not. But it went in the newspaper just the same, one of the bigger reportorial and analytical leaps that they had made.*

The ball breaker went out over the wires at 7:00 P.M. on October 9, which gave newspapers that subscribed to the *Washington Post– Los Angeles Times* news service a chance to run the story. This was an option that most regional papers had routinely neglected to exercise during much of the summer and fall. The *Post* was usually, or at least mostly, on its own in its Watergate coverage. Not so this time. After seeing the *Post*'s story, *The New York Times* put together its own version for the front page, "largely quoting the *Post*," as Ben noted in his memoir. "There are many, many rewards in the newspaper business, but one of the finest comes with reading the competition quoting your paper on its front page." These were the moments Ben lived for.

Both reporters would tell Alan Pakula, in preparation for the movie, that Ben had been particularly brilliant that day, first with Clawson and then later with the decision to turn the two stories into one. "He made two quick, great decisions," Bernstein said. It was now clear to everybody at the paper that this was going to be the most important series of stories that *The Washington Post* had ever run, and that the major decisions were going to be made in Ben's office from there on out. Howard Simons had played a major role, probably *the* major role, up to that point, but now even he acknowledged that they would all be waiting for the final nod from Ben.

The next morning, after the story ran in the paper and all hell had broken loose at the White House, Ben approached Bob at his desk and told him that they needed to have a chat. Carl was out of town,

---

*According to his book, *In Nixon's Web,* acting FBI director L. Patrick Gray III received a copy of Woodstein's October 10 story and wrote "Have we?" next to the lede. Beside at least two other claims about the FBI in the story, Gray wrote, "Did we?" Clearly the man at the top hadn't come to the same conclusions as Bob and Carl had. A memo Gray commissioned to look into his questions concluded that Woodstein's opening sentence was "pure conjecture on the part of the news reporters," and that several other statements were "absolutely false." Gray ridicules much of Woodstein's reporting in his book.

so Ben and Bob went alone over to the Montpelier Room at the Madison Hotel, just across 15th Street from the *Post*. They sat at a corner table, and Ben grilled Bob on where the stories were coming from, who the sources were (though not to the point of revealing names), poking every which way. He hadn't known the details up to this point, but now that he was betting the paper on them he wanted to know what he could.

This lunch was the genesis of the lasting impression of Ben that Woodstein captured in their book, as Bob later told Pakula:

> He turned to the waiter and ordered sort of, "I'll have this and I'll have that," this and that, in French, very quickly, and then just turned around and said, "By the way our cocks are on the chopping block." And he is able to traffic and to think in those two worlds. If you wanted to say that those two worlds are on one end and the other, and he travels in all the ones in between.

The mythic, omnivorous beast of Bradlee. But the larger point was true: his cock *was* on the chopping block now, and so Ben was going to drill down in ways that he never had before. After they'd talked for about an hour, with Ben at least marginally satisfied with how well Bob and Carl were handling their sources and the information that those sources were providing, Ben asked the question that defines, perhaps more than any other, who he was as an editor and as a person. As they were wrapping up, he turned to Bob and said, "Now what have you guys got for tomorrow?"

FALL

Tuesday story in Post "cast a pall over entire committee."
"I keep thinking it's over, and then you guys call w. something else."
He said that if we make any error then they will jump on us. "That's the way the game is played."

—Bernstein's memo of an interview with
confidential CRP source, October 12, 1972

ON THE MORNING OF OCTOBER 10, at the White House, press secretary Ron Ziegler didn't know quite what to do. The press corps was after him about the *Post* story that morning, and all he had to offer was, "I have nothing further to say to you about the story that ran," or some variation. He referred reporters to Ken Clawson's denial and CRP's denial, which had been included in the story. The official statement from CRP, in its entirety: "The *Post* story is not only fiction but a collection of absurdities."

"May we film you denying these stories or saying you have nothing further to add to this?" one reporter asked.

"No," Ziegler said.

Later: "I am not leaving anything open. I am just telling you I have no further statements or comments or information to provide you on the story that ran in The Washington Post this morning."

Toward the end, Ziegler brought out the first in what would become a legendary series of verbal acrobatics in the press room. A reporter asked, "Has anyone in the White House, since publication of the story in The Washington Post, Mr. Dean or otherwise, talked to Mr. Clawson to find out whether this story is true or not, whether he did this or did not do this?"

"I would just conclude this by saying, giving you my final comment on the subject, that Mr. Clawson has already issued a statement on the subject."

"That is not my question," the reporter shot back. "I wondered whether anybody at the White House checked with him."

"The matter was denied by Mr. Clawson and that stands on the record," Ziegler said.

"Is that a White House denial?"

"It is a denial by the individual involved."

"Is it a denial by the White House?"

"It is a denial by Mr. Clawson and one with which I do not disassociate myself."

The next major story ran that following Sunday, October 15. Ben had been on Bob and Carl for something big, something to show that the *Post* wasn't going to back down after staking its new claim on the 10th. The Sunday story was big. The three-column story, "Key Nixon Aide Named as 'Sabotage' Contact," led the paper and named Dwight Chapin, Nixon's appointments secretary, as Segretti's contact in the spying and sabotage operation against the Democrats. For the first time, Woodstein had followed the trail of breadcrumbs through the gates of the White House itself, to one of Bob Haldeman's key aides.*

That same Sunday, *Time* magazine—one of the *Post*'s only real competitors on Watergate—reported that Chapin hadn't just been the "contact": Chapin had *hired* Segretti, and the president's personal lawyer, Herbert W. Kalmbach, had paid Segretti for his services. Since the *Post* had a rule that they wouldn't print information from another publication unless they could verify it themselves, Bob quickly confirmed through other sources that Kalmbach had paid Segretti, and that Kalmbach had also been one of the five people with control over the slush fund. They now had four of the five. The

---

*In June they had reported that Howard Hunt's name had appeared in the burglars' address books, along with the notation "W. House," but Hunt was only a consultant and had already been cut loose. This was the first link to a high-ranking member of the permanent staff.

next morning, October 16, "Lawyer for Nixon Said to Have Used GOP's Spy Fund" was the off-lead of the *Post*'s front page.

If the October 10 story had been a declaration of war, the stories from the *Post* and *Time* on the 15th and the 16th were the battle cry, one that was joined in turn by the White House and Nixon's campaign staff. The *Post*'s reporting had been hitting closer and closer to home, and finally the White House struck back.

First up was Ziegler. At a press briefing on the morning of the 16th, when asked whether the president was concerned about the recent reports about Chapin, Ziegler said, "The president is concerned about the techniques being applied by the opposition in the stories themselves. . . . The opposition has been making charges which are not substantiated; stories are being written which have not been substantiated." When asked who the opposition was, he said that he thought the opposition was clear—unmistakably referring to the *Post*. He could have gone after *Time,* too, but everybody knew whom he meant.

"I will not dignify with comment stories based on hearsay, character assassination, innuendo, or guilt by association," he said, phrases that other Republican spokesmen would echo throughout the day. "That is the White House position; that is my position." Later he added, "It goes without saying that this administration does not condone sabotage or espionage or surveillance of individuals." (Note what a nondenial even this is: "condone" is such a curious word to choose. Sometimes we don't condone our own behavior, but that doesn't mean that we don't do it.)

Senator Bob Dole, who doubled as the chairman of the Republican National Committee, went on the attack that afternoon in a speech before an audience of black Republicans at a hotel in downtown Washington. "Given the present straits in which the McGovern campaign finds itself," Dole said, "Mr. McGovern appears to have turned over the franchise for his media attack campaign to the editors of *The Washington Post*." He insisted that, thus far, there had been "enormous headlines about political disruption and very little proof." The *Post* was in league with "the desperate politicians whose fortunes they seek to save," and had become McGovern's "partner in mudslinging."

Later that same day, Clark MacGregor—the director of CRP and Nixon's campaign manager—held a "press conference" in which he read a prepared statement that had been given to him by the White House: "The *Post* has maliciously sought to give the appearance of a direct connection between the White House and the Watergate—a charge the *Post* knows—and half a dozen investigations have found—to be false." After finishing with his statement, which also accused the *Post* of having a "celebrated double standard [that] is today visible for all to see," MacGregor walked out of the room without answering any questions.

That night, in response to inquiries from media across the country, Ben wrote out his own statement:

> Time will judge between Clark MacGregor's press release and the *Washington Post*'s reporting of the various activities of CRP. For now it is enough to say that not a single fact contained in the investigative reporting by this newspaper about these activities has been successfully challenged. MacGregor and other high administration officials have called these stories "a collection of absurdities" and the *Post* "malicious," but the facts are on the record, unchallenged by contrary evidence.

"I understated it before," Ben told Carl and Bob when he showed them his statement. "This is the hardest hardball that's ever been played in this town."*

Two days later *The New York Times* reported that Segretti's credit card or phone had been used to make several calls to Chapin's home in Bethesda, and also to the White House and to Howard Hunt. This was pretty hard evidence that Segretti had reported to Chapin, or at least kept him informed, and that the White House had been aware of what he was doing. That morning, Ziegler denied that anyone

---

*That day, October 16, the *Post* dedicated its new building at 1150 15th Street, the same building that it occupies today. And so, perhaps coincidentally, the modern physical *Washington Post* came into being on the very same day that its modern reputation was made, standing by its Watergate reporting under a coordinated and withering attack from the White House.

presently employed at the White House had "directed activities of sabotage, spying [or] espionage" against Democratic presidential candidates. When reporters made clear that "direction" and "involvement" were two different things, Ziegler said, "If anyone had been involved in such activity, they would no longer be at the White House because this is activity that we do not condone and do not tolerate." As Peter Osnos noted with sober neutrality in the *Post* the next morning, "Although Ziegler's statement appeared to be the firmest denial yet of reports linking White House aides to the alleged GOP sabotage campaign, it fell short of satisfying questioning reporters."

For the next few days, the Watergate story was mostly quiet on the front page of the *Post*. The Oakland A's won the World Series, talks in Vietnam seemed headed for a truce. Then, on Wednesday, October 25, 1972, the *Post* dropped its biggest bomb yet:

"Of all the quicksand I have been in," Ben wrote to a friend seven years later, "50 percent of it could have been avoided if the headlines had been right." He wasn't referring specifically to the Haldeman story of October 25, 1972, but he could have been. The headline that led the paper that morning, "Testimony Ties Top Nixon Aide to Secret Fund," was wrong, although the bulk of the lede graf was correct:

> H. R. Haldeman, President Nixon's White House chief of staff, was one of five high-ranking presidential associates authorized to approve payments from a secret Nixon campaign cash fund . . .

That was all true. The mistake came only in the final clause of that long first sentence, echoing the headline above:

> . . . according to federal investigators and accounts of sworn testimony before the Watergate grand jury.

The fourth paragraph carried Haldeman's denial, issued through the White House press office: "Your inquiry is based on misinformation because the reference to Bob Haldeman is untrue." Woodstein and their editors included the denial in the story but didn't think much of it; it felt as vague and tossed off as most of the denials that had eventually been repudiated by new developments in the story.

They didn't realize they were wrong until the morning the story ran. Hugh Sloan, their main source and the man whose testimony to the grand jury the headline (and most of the story) hung on, stood beside his lawyer as the lawyer said, "We categorically deny that such a statement was made to the grand jury." Suddenly, in a rapidly disorienting experience that Bob later likened to an automobile accident, air was rushing out all around them.

Woodstein had hunched that Haldeman was the fifth person in control of the fund for a while. It just made sense. The Chapins and the Strachans and the other mid-level functionaries at the White House and CRP were all tied into Haldeman. He had basic and fundamental control over what happened at the White House, from who saw the president to how the president's orders were executed. There was no way that Watergate or any other political espionage campaign could have gone on without his knowledge or authorization, but the reporters had never been able to prove it. They were always sticking insinuating sentences into their stories—"Chapin was the number one assistant to Haldeman"—only to have the editors strike them out.

"I thought we were aiming higher and higher and I suspected that you guys . . . had them in your targets, maybe even before you should have," Ben told Carl and Bob a year later. "Maybe you knew it but you couldn't prove it, and I was determined to keep it out of the paper until you could. Even when I was absolutely convinced in my mind that there was no way that any of this could have happened without Haldeman and Ehrlichman, and Nixon . . . I was going to do everything in my power to be sure that we didn't clip him before we had him."

In the days leading up to the major story of the 25th, Woodstein had worked all of their sources. Bob went to Deep Throat and fished, telling Throat (though it wasn't yet true) that they were going to run a story naming Haldeman as the fifth person in control of the fund. Deep Throat didn't bite. He told Bob, "I won't be a source on a Haldeman story," that he wouldn't and couldn't name Haldeman himself. Bob thought Deep Throat's palpable fear and caginess meant that Haldeman had to be the right name.

A few days later Carl and Bob went out to visit Hugh Sloan. Using one of their familiar tactics—pretending to know something that they didn't actually know, to see if the source would confirm it—Bernstein told Sloan that he knew the fifth person in control of the fund was Haldeman. Like Throat, Sloan refused to be a direct source on a Haldeman story. When the reporters asked him if he had named all five people in control of the fund to the grand jury, Sloan said yes.* By process of elimination—Was it Colson? Was it

---

*Sloan did not intentionally mislead them. In his briefing with the prosecutors before his testimony, Sloan did apparently name all five in control of the fund, including Haldeman,

Ehrlichman?—they ended up right back at Haldeman again. Sloan then told them, somewhat coyly, that he would have "no problems" if they wrote a story suggesting that Haldeman had been one of the five.

From there Bernstein called Angelo Lano, the Watergate case agent in the Washington field office of the FBI. Using more of the same blustering tactics, claiming that he was working on a story about the FBI's ineptitude, Bernstein prodded Lano into confirming (as Bernstein interpreted it, at any rate) that the FBI had encountered Haldeman's name in its own investigation, and that Sloan had named Haldeman to the grand jury. When Bernstein circled back to make sure he was right about Haldeman, Lano said, "Yeah, Haldeman. John Haldeman."

The "German shepherds," as they were known, were Bob Haldeman and John Ehrlichman—easily enough confused, but still. Bernstein had already hung up by the time he realized what had happened, so he called back. According to Bernstein, Lano confirmed that it was Haldeman and said that he always had trouble with first names.

Now they had three sources, or so they thought. In retrospect it's hard to believe that what Deep Throat had told Bob was an actual confirmation of their story. Even Bob himself said to Carl afterward that he thought it was a "yes and no" confirmation, whatever that means. He had asked Throat to warn him off if the Haldeman story was bad and Throat hadn't warned him off; there was room for ambiguity there. Regardless, Throat hadn't said anything (or been asked anything) about grand jury testimony. As Bernstein understood it, Angelo Lano had actively confirmed that Sloan had named Haldeman in front of the grand jury, but then Lano had gotten the name wrong at the end. And Sloan himself said that he had named everybody to the grand jury, hadn't he?

That night Woodward, Bernstein, Sussman, Rosenfeld, Simons,

---

but he didn't then repeat those names in response to questioning before the grand jury. He would have named Haldeman there, too, but the prosecutors never asked.

and Ben all met in Ben's office. Harry Rosenfeld remembers that Ben "start[ed] to cross-examine them very very sharply. And in that cross examination somehow the notes don't quite show what the story shows, and Bradlee's cross examining . . . shows that Sloan doesn't quite say what they're saying, and I'm embarrassed because I've represented the story as being every bit as good as they say it is, and now here's my top editor finding out gaps that I didn't find out."* Barry Sussman writes in his book, *The Great Cover-up*, "Bradlee began asking questions the way a prosecutor would . . . I don't remember any of us aside from Bradlee asking questions, and there was no small talk. When he was done, he asked the rest of us whether we felt we should run the story. We all said yes. 'Okay, go,' Bradlee said."

Simons apparently still had a few doubts. He was known around the paper for saying, "When in doubt, leave it out," and he was a little less prone than Ben to allow excitement about a "holy shit" story to obscure his news judgment. He felt that something was fishy, and he asked Woodstein if they could get another source.

They had only about twenty minutes before the first edition deadline. Bernstein contacted a source in the Justice Department, but the source refused to answer any direct questions. Thinking on his feet, Bernstein told him that they already had it from three sources. All he needed was confirmation, or a heads-up if they needed to hold off. He devised a system, what Ben would later describe as "a gimmick that plowed new—and unholy—ground in the annals of journalism." Bernstein would count to ten, and if the lawyer was still on the phone after Bernstein reached ten it meant that their story was accurate. When Bernstein got to ten and the lawyer was still there†—

---

*Ben found faults in other stories, too. "Once Bradlee and Simons were involved routinely," Rosenfeld told me, "Sussman would bring me the story, I would go over it, bust his chops, and then when I was satisfied I would take it to Bradlee and Simons. Frequently, to my chagrin, they would find things I had not found. This was a process that helped make the stories as solid as they were."

†Apparently Bernstein screwed up the instructions. "Carl got his signals screwed up," the source told Barry Sussman later. "I didn't give him the 'confirm' signal, I gave him the

this is the famous scene in the movie, where Dustin Hoffman goes sprinting through the newsroom to intercept Jason Robards just as the elevator door closes—the story was sent down to the composing room.

What happens next is one of the better scenes in the film, and certainly Robards's best scene. In a sense the movie presents the stakes for Ben in the aftermath of their mistake better than any of the books or interviews.

It's the next day, the day the Haldeman story runs and the denials start to pour in, and all of a sudden Robards appears in the newsroom. The camera zooms uncomfortably close on his face, there's a beat, and then he bellows "Woodstein!" The two reporters scurry across the newsroom and into his office. As the television plays Sloan's lawyer's denial of their story, their huge brass ring of a story, Robards glares at each of them. We hear the television coverage shift to Ron Ziegler at the White House, but the camera stays with Robards.

"Why is the *Post* trying to do it?" we hear Ziegler ask rhetorically in the background.

Robards's eyes are glued to Woodward, who is off camera.

"You have a man who's the editor of the *Washington Post* . . ."

Robards blinks slowly, masterfully, knowing what's about to happen before it does, and then coolly switches his gaze to the television, where Ziegler continues, ". . . by the name of Ben Bradlee. I think anyone who would want to honestly assess what his political persuasions are would, I think, come to the conclusion quite quickly that he is not a supporter of President Nixon.

"I respect the free press," Ziegler says. "I don't respect the journalism, the shabby journalism, that is being practiced by the *Washington Post*."

Robards never says a word, but his emotion is clear. For all of his ranting and raving and cursing throughout the movie, this is his most

---

'deny.'" "It's amazing," Pakula would later tell Woodward and Bernstein. "In trying to protect yourself from your disaster, each one . . . fucked yourself up more and more."

powerful and revelatory scene. It's the moment where Robards lets
you in, literally in the blink of an eye, to the weight that his character
is under, that Ben was under. The attacks were becoming more personal now. Though it's not in the film, the night before Bob Dole
had launched a personal attack against Ben in a speech in Maryland,
calling him a "Kennedy coat-holder" and "a small-bore McGovern
surrogate," including a nasty threat that "[Ben] and his publication
should expect appropriate treatment—which they will with regular-
ity receive."

Now, the very next day, when the stakes were highest, his two
Metro reporters had let him down. Dole's was just the first salvo in a
series of public attacks against the *Post*, and against Ben, for their
mistake.

"No one can imagine how I felt," Ben wrote in his memoir. "We
had written more than fifty Watergate stories, in the teeth of one of
history's great political cover-ups, and we hadn't made a material
mistake. Not one. We had been supported by the publisher every step
of the way, and she had withstood enormous pressure to stand by our
side. Pressures from her friends as well as her enemies. And now
this . . .

"It was a jackass scheme," he concluded, "and I should have caught
it. All along, we had wanted to 'win' without knowing what winning
might turn out to be. But all along, we knew we could not afford *any*
mistakes. And now we had made one."

ROSENFELD/SIMONS/BRADLEE
/BERNSTEIN/WOODWARD/DOWNIE

FROM SUSSMAN

Following is a recap of the charges made against us Tuesday night
and Wednesday by Ziegler, MacGregor and Dole. I am not dealing
with the ad hominem attacks but rather only with the specific
instances in which they say we are wrong in fact. My conclusions are
that we appear to have made one definite error and perhaps a

second: a) Sloan did <u>not</u> name Haldeman to the FBI, b) Haldeman
was not interviewed by the FBI. Beyond that I feel there is no
indication from what Ziegler, MacGregor and Dole said that we
have made any other mistakes. That is, I feel at this point that we are
right on Haldeman.

By the evening of the 25th, all involved had come to the conclusion
that Sussman describes. Haldeman had in fact been the fifth person
in charge of the fund, but Sloan hadn't named him to the grand jury,
and the FBI hadn't interviewed Haldeman. Sloan's lawyer, who had
no idea that his own client was the source of the story, told Bob that
the *Post* had been wrong about the grand jury but that they didn't
owe Haldeman any apologies. As Sloan would later put it, his denial
was strictly limited to the way that the story had been written. So
they were in the uncomfortable position of being essentially right on
Haldeman but unable to prove it or to counter the denials coming
from the White House and other Republican surrogates.

Kay Graham was clearly getting an earful, too. She sent the following down to Ben's office, written by hand, with a copy of the Haldeman story attached to it:

Ben—

I have now heard from a mutual acquaintance that the lead paragraphs
in this story is what is bothering the White House most—I must say—I
have a problem with them—one—that it says Haldeman had access to
the fund 2—the fund financed a spying & bugging campaign—a basic
element of the Nixon re-election strategy was conceived by high
presidential aides—

   Haldeman is a high presidential aide (unspoken assumption that
Haldeman conceived <u>spying & bugging</u>)—we say—"all we said
was Haldeman had access to the fund." But if that *is* all we said—
we certainly implied much more—This really troubles me—not
you?

                                                              Kay

The squeeze was on. She didn't normally reach down like that. During Watergate Ben would often reach up, to reassure her that there was a team of editors overseeing every story; he often asked Edward Bennett Williams to talk to her, too. "We must keep her strong," Ben would say to his pal, and because Williams was instrumental in the civil case Kay trusted him when he confirmed the direction of Woodstein's reporting.* Largely this strategy worked. But, as Ben would say later of the Haldeman mistake, "That's the one where Katharine's sphincter tightened just a little bit."

Oddly enough, this was the day that Bob and Carl had scheduled a lunch meeting with Dick Snyder, the head of Simon and Schuster, to discuss a possible book deal based on their reporting. They sat through lunch thinking instead that they might have to resign from the *Post*.

After lunch, the reporters went looking for Angelo Lano, the FBI agent they felt had led them astray. When they found him, he told them that he would deny having spoken to them. When they saw one of Lano's colleagues in the hallway—FBI memos declassified in 1980 suggest that this was assistant U.S. prosecutor Earl Silbert—they decided to gamble. Woodstein confronted Silbert and told him that Lano had been their source. In so doing, they were betraying Lano's confidence and violating their own ethical standards, but they were desperate to know where they had gone wrong. Silbert gave them nothing.†

When they got back to the office, they were beside themselves. Ben, less so:

---

*Ben would later say that, throughout the fall of 1972, Williams was a constant source of reassurance for him, too. "The kids have got to be right because [the Nixon people are] lying so much," Williams would tell him. "If they've got nothing to hide, why are they lying so fucking much? And the reason is because you've got them."

†An FBI memo written the day of Woodstein's confrontation with Silbert and Lano holds that it was "an outrageous lie" that Lano had been a source of any kind for Bernstein. Lano swore out an affidavit that he never told Bernstein anything, and that on their phone call on the 24th, Bernstein had been fishing and Lano's use of Haldeman's name had simply been "confirming that he knew what Bernstein was talking about." Could be true, but Lano could also just have been covering his ass.

BW: I remember that Bradlee was very calm . . . there was a certain se-
renity in him . . . a certain power of saying, "Goddamn it, don't panic,
don't fly off the handle."

CB: In both meetings we had, he was very much like that.

BW: And he was willing to take the epistemological step of, "God
damn it, I don't know anything here. Maybe Sloan's not telling the
truth."

At a meeting in his office, Ben made the executive decision that the
paper was not going to name its sources. If they named Lano in the
newspaper, all Lano would do was deny it, and then they'd be in an
unwinnable pissing match. His basic message to the reporters was to
sit tight, to go back to their sources again, to give it some time. The
refusal to rush into some kind of correction or admission of fault
was also an expression of support. By that time Ben knew enough
about their reporting and about the Nixon administration to know
that the reporters weren't going to be far off. Until there was coun-
tervailing evidence and something more than just a denial, you
didn't fold your hand. You held tight and hung tough and protected
the institution.

And so Ben sat down at his typewriter and typed out a one-
sentence statement: "We stand by our story." There are a lot of
other things he could have written. There were parts of the story
that really *were* wrong. But if the Nixon people could outright lie
all over the place, surely Ben could stick to his guns and give his
reporters some cover. He had come too far with Woodstein to
abandon them now. He remembers trying out any number of different statements before finally deciding to say, "Fuck it, let's go
stand by our boys."

If you want Ben as the editor of Watergate in a single sentence,
that sentence is it.

Ben took a similarly defiant approach with angry readers. On the
day that the statement ran, a reader wrote Ben, "I observe from today's issue of your yellow sheet that you 'stand by' your story concerning Haldeman which means that you stand by a lot of damn lies.
I suspect that your father was a bachelor."

Dear [Angry Reader]:

Thank you for your moderate letter and your suspicions about my
father.

    I suspect that your mother was sorry.

Sincerely,

Z

Ben's office, March 23, 2011, 12:10 P.M.

B: Don't feel that you have to protect me.

Me: I appreciate that.

B: You and I have a great relationship, and there's nothing you can do in this book that's going to change it. So just follow your nose.

BEN'S DEFIANCE ASIDE, THE HALDEMAN story was a serious blow. Carl's secret source at CRP had told him that the administration would jump on them if they made a single mistake, that that was "the way the game is played." And now the administration was jumping, with both feet. As Bob put it to me, "We got crushed."

As the *Post* scrambled to respond to the administration's denials, world events also turned in the administration's favor. The October 27 front page of the *Post* carried a two-line banner headline, "Peace 'Within Reach,' U.S. Says; Hanoi Discloses Nine-Point Plan." Realizing that the peace-is-at-hand moment in Vietnam would swallow just about anything else, the Nixon people craftily sent Clark MacGregor out to sit for a televised interview with Elizabeth Drew on PBS, in which MacGregor admitted to the existence of the slush fund and named five people who had either authorized or received payments from it. Much of what MacGregor revealed had been previously denied by the White House, and some of the information corroborated much disputed Woodstein accounts. But Ben refused to put MacGregor's revelations on the front page of the paper, saying that it would look like they were "grinding it in." Bob knew that *The New York Times* had already decided to run the MacGregor story on the front page, and he was angry that Ben wouldn't do the same. He thought it was a political decision, not a journalistic one, and he was probably right. Ben stood by Carl and Bob, but in the wake of their mistake the balance of power had shifted.

A few days later, still desperate for a way to regain their standing, Bob set the flowerpot with the flag in it at the back of his balcony, the signal for a meeting with Deep Throat.

"Well, Haldeman slipped away from you," Deep Throat said when they met that night. He was upset. "From top to bottom, this whole business is a Haldeman operation," Throat whispered. "He ran the money. Insulated himself through those functionaries around him." They had moved on Haldeman too soon, and now nobody around Haldeman would be willing to talk. "Everybody goes chicken after you make a mistake like you guys made," he said.*

Though Throat castigated Bob throughout their meeting, in one stroke he had also finally and explicitly confirmed that Haldeman had been in control of the fund. When Bob got back to the *Post*, he and Carl wanted to write the story immediately, but again Ben was hesitant. Then George McGovern appeared on *Meet the Press* on Sunday, October 29, citing the Haldeman mistake as fact, at which point everybody at the paper realized that they needed to put out some kind of correction or clarification.

A *Time* story out the day of the 29th reported that Chapin had admitted to the FBI that he had hired Segretti, and it gave Woodstein the pretense they needed. Their story, "Magazine Says Nixon Aide Admits Disruption Effort," ran on the front page the next morning. The opportunity to set the record straight about their own reporting came seven grafs in: "*Time*'s account also said 'no hard evidence could be developed to support a charge by The Washington Post that H. R. Haldeman, the White House chief of staff, was one of those with control over a fund that paid for spying and disruption.'" The reporters noted that Sloan had told them that his denial was strictly limited, and that federal sources of theirs had confirmed that although Sloan hadn't named Haldeman to the grand jury, Haldeman had in fact

*Throat's dialogue is quoted from *The Secret Man* (2005), Bob's book about his relationship with Mark Felt.

been authorized to make payments from the fund. "One source went so far as to say 'this is a Haldeman operation,' and that Haldeman had 'insulated' himself, dealing with the fund through an intermediary."

Woodstein knew that they and the *Post* could now stand fully behind their reporting, which was a source of great relief for everybody at the paper but particularly for the two young reporters, who had worried about losing their jobs. But that certainty came at a price: to save their own hides, Woodstein had broken a rule with a source for the second time in five days. Bob's agreement with Deep Throat held that the information Throat provided was on deep background and, therefore, explicitly unquotable.

"I had very bad feelings about quoting [him] so directly," Bob would write years later in *The Secret Man*. "It really was contrary to the rules we had established of deep background. But I was frantic to get a story in the paper correcting our mistake."

Playing a little bit fast and loose with journalistic conventions while taking on a massive governmental cover-up and conspiracy seems like an inevitability in some ways. And the truth is that in *All the President's Men* (and, later, in *The Secret Man*) Bob and Carl fessed up to almost everything questionable that they'd done. They didn't have to, but they did, and it makes them more human and compelling to know that when confronted with the hard questions they didn't always come down on the comfortable side.

The general logic of the reporters' justification of their tactics throughout the book is "No harm, no foul." Sure, they might have lied to some of their sources in order to try to provoke those sources into "confirming" information that the reporters didn't actually have, but it was in the service of exposing a deeper truth and therefore justifiable. The same went for Bernstein's numerous admitted violations of the *Post*'s policy that all reporters had to identify themselves before soliciting information from sources, or Woodward's questionable quotation of Deep Throat. This kind of justification came up against its most severe test toward the end of 1972, when Ben and the rest of his editorial team made an ethical and legal decision that would dwarf all of the other, smaller ones, and nearly land Carl and Bob in jail.

On November 7, 1972, with the *Post*'s Watergate team back on its heels, Richard Nixon was reelected by one of the largest margins in the history of presidential politics, sweeping every state in the union except Massachusetts and the District of Columbia. Outside D.C., the general public still hadn't really caught on to Watergate, despite the *Post*'s front-page treatment of the scandal. Nixon was overwhelmingly popular and there were bigger issues—Vietnam, the economy—than what seemed (to most) to be low-level political hijinks not connected to Nixon himself. Most regional newspapers ignored the *Post*'s stories, and in fact tended to give more coverage and credence to White House denials than to what the *Post* had reported.

In the wake of the mistake on Haldeman and Nixon's overwhelming victory, the *Post*'s trail on Watergate stories officially went cold. Nixon had a new hand, and so did his men. Four days after the election, Chuck Colson went on the attack in a speech to the New England Society of Newspaper Editors in Kennebunkport, Maine. He blasted Ben and the *Post* with renewed vigor, referring to Ben as "[t]he self-appointed leader of what Boston's Teddy White once described as 'that tiny little fringe of arrogant elitists who infect the healthy mainstream of American journalism with their own peculiar view of the world.'" He went on:

> If Bradlee ever left the Georgetown cocktail circuit, where he and his pals dine on third-hand information and gossip and rumor, he might discover out here the real America. And he might learn that all truth and all knowledge and all superior wisdom just doesn't emanate exclusively from that small little clique in Georgetown, and that the rest of the country isn't just sitting out here waiting to be told what they're supposed to think.

As Ben said later, "That's some pretty personal shit." Of all the low moments, this was a pretty low one. The *Post* wouldn't break another major story about Watergate until December 8, four and a half weeks after the election. Bob always likes to say of this period that Ben threatened to "hold our heads in a pail of water" until they came up with a story.

In their desperation for something—anything—that they could use, the Watergate team at the *Post* made the decision to allow Woodstein to approach the grand jurors in the criminal case, to see if they could peel one off. The grand jury had already heard all of the government's evidence, and the trial of the five burglars and Hunt and Liddy was scheduled to begin in January. This was a dubious enterprise, no matter how you slice it. Whether it was illegal for the reporters to approach the grand jurors or not, it was definitely illegal for grand jurors to leak information to reporters.

In advance of the decision, Ben called his lawyers, Joe Califano and Edward Bennett Williams, to get their advice. (After leaving the Johnson administration, where he and Ben had squared off on Walter Washington and the Kerner Commission, Califano had joined Williams's law firm and now helped represent the *Post*.) "The toughest questions we had with Ben," Califano told me, had been "can they talk to grand jury members. And we kept telling him no. I'll tell you, from my point of view and Ed's point of view, after a while, anytime Ben would call either of us, we'd go right to the other guy's office. Because we figured if he were getting the no answer from one of us, he'd just try the other one." Califano laughed. "Or he'd rephrase the question."

Ben's recollection is slightly different. "I recall asking them if there was a law against going to the grand jury," he told Evan Thomas for his book *The Man to See*, a biography of Williams. "They said it violated no law, but they didn't say go ahead and do it, either. My guess is that Ed blurred it, and I blurred it." When I asked Ben if this was how he still remembered it, he said yes.

Ben okayed a preliminary sortie with the aunt of a *Post* editor's neighbor. She was rumored to be on the grand jury, but it turned out to be a different grand jury. A few days later, Bob went to the courthouse and talked one of the clerks into showing him the grand jury list, although the clerk wouldn't allow him to take notes. So, bit by bit, Bob memorized the list, excusing himself every few minutes via one pretext or another and then going to the bathroom to write out the names, addresses, ages, occupations, and telephone numbers of the grand jury members in his notebook. (Ben loves this part of the story, Bob's tenacity and resourcefulness.)

After a long meeting at the *Post*, Ben and the rest of the Watergate editors decided to allow Bob and Carl to try to contact the grand jurors, with the admonition that they identify themselves as *Post* reporters and not attempt to strong-arm anybody. Woodstein spent the first weekend of December of 1972 ringing the doorbells of the grand jurors who appeared, from the basic information that Bob had memorized and copied down, to be the most susceptible targets. According to their book, they struck out.

That would have been it, the end of the story, if one of the grand jurors hadn't informed the prosecutors on Monday morning that a *Post* reporter had made contact. Judge John Sirica wasn't pleased, and Williams intervened to try to steady the situation. (They were old friends; Williams was godfather to one of Sirica's kids.) The next morning, Williams summoned Carl and Bob to his office, where he told them that Sirica was angry and that he had barely been able to keep them out of jail.*

Two weeks later, on December 19, Sirica called the reporters into his courtroom. "I was ready to take them to task for their tampering," Sirica would write in 1979, in his memoir *To Set the Record Straight*:

> But the prosecutors urged me not to punish the reporters. They pointed out that the grand juror who was contacted had been faithful to his oath not to discuss the case and had turned the reporter away without saying anything. . . . I settled on a stiff lecture in open court, reminding everyone present that to approach a grand juror and solicit information about a case being investigated was to ask for a citation of contempt. I praised the grand jurors for their

---

*Williams didn't like any suggestion of a backroom deal with Sirica and objected to its publication in *All the President's Men;* just before the book came out he appealed to Simon and Schuster to have it eliminated from the manuscript. When it made it into the final draft, Williams refused to talk to Woodward for two years.

refusal to cooperate and recessed the proceeding to let the message sink in.

Carl and Bob were in the clear, but their consciences weren't.* As they would write in their book, they hadn't done anything explicitly illegal but they had "chosen expediency over principle" and had "dodged, evaded, misrepresented, suggested and intimidated, even if they had not lied outright."

"I agree," Sirica wrote, of the reporters' own uneasy assessment of themselves. "Had they actually obtained information from that grand juror, they would have gone to jail."

Ben made no apologies. "I remember figuring, after being told that it was not illegal and after insisting that *we* tell no lies and identify ourselves, that it was worth a shot," he wrote of the grand jury episode in his memoir. "In the same circumstances, I'd do it again. The stakes were too high."

On March 3, 2011, I asked Bob about his and Carl's tactics directly. I laid out the long list of questionable stuff that they had done, including the visits to the grand jurors.

He smiled. "I wouldn't be too literal-minded about that," he said. "I mean, it was a dicey, high-wire thing to do. But that's what we did. That's what the whole enterprise was."

Twelve days later, Bob gave a talk at the Poynter Institute in St. Petersburg, Florida, to a crowd of nearly two hundred. He was asked about James O'Keefe, the young provocateur who had recently and surreptitiously filmed high executives at National Public Radio speaking ill of Republicans and Muslims.† "I don't think [what O'Keefe did] is the highest form of journalism, and I wouldn't do it," Bob said. "There are laws against entrapment, and I think there's

---

*Later that same day, December 19, Sirica held the *Los Angeles Times* D.C. bureau chief, John Lawrence, in contempt of court for failing to turn over audiotapes of the paper's interview with Alfred Baldwin, the lookout on the night of the break-in. Lawrence was jailed, without a chance even to say goodbye to his wife, while Woodstein walked free.

†The veracity of O'Keefe's videotape recording has since been challenged, but hadn't yet been at this time.

not only a legal basis for that but a moral basis that you want to represent who you are and get it clean.

"In the Watergate investigation, Carl Bernstein and I went to talk to grand jurors," Bob said, by way of explanation. "We had legal advice saying we could do it. It was very risky. It's something I'm not sure I'd do all the time, but when you're convinced the system of justice has collapsed, I think you have to be very aggressive. But we didn't say we were from the U.S. attorney's office. We identified ourselves as *Washington Post* reporters—and we got nothing from the grand jurors."

Ben's Watergate files weren't the most organized part of his archive. There were bits here, other pieces there—much like the story itself. It took me a long time to put everything together, to align the dates on the memos with contemporaneous developments in the news. Memos that at first hadn't seemed all that interesting began to make more sense as I considered them in context.

One of the more tantalizing of these memos, from the start, was a dense seven-page document with two initials and a date at its top. It was hard to read, a faint copy of a typewritten document, and all over the map in terms of substance. In my notes from the first time I read it through, I had written to myself, "Seems to be some kind of juror," but there was no year in the date and I had no concept of what that might have meant. The memo had more than one hundred data points in it, short statements that Carl had taken down in seemingly rapid-fire style. (The author identifies himself as "CB" in the memo, Carl's usual MO, and by comparison with other memos this one clearly came from Carl's typewriter.) I slotted it in my "Bernstein" file as a good example of Carl's thoroughness, Woodstein's hunger for the story.

In February of 2011, I realized that in order to write believably about Watergate I was going to have to understand the story in a way that I hadn't up until then. I was going to have to spend as long as it took to read every single one of the newspaper stories and all of the relevant books. In order to know what I had, and what to say about

Ben's role in all of it, I couldn't just focus on the major episodes that everybody has already written about a thousand times.

And so I read through all the newspaper stories from 1972 and the first half of 1973, up to the point where Haldeman and Ehrlichman have resigned and the *Post* has won the Pulitzer and Nixon's presidency has begun to hang visibly in the balance. After that, I went back to read the appropriate chapters in all the various books, and then I reread the Watergate memos I had found in Ben's files. Then, and only then, I read *All the President's Men* start to finish for the fourth time. If there was anything in it that I didn't understand, which had always been the case before, I wasn't going to put the book down until I understood it.

Everything went smoothly until I reached the book's accounting of the grand jury episode. After the meeting with Williams, where Williams warned the reporters that Sirica was pissed and that they'd better cease all contact with grand jurors immediately, Woodstein wrote that, chastened, they "returned to more conventional sources." Bernstein visited an unnamed woman at an apartment who wouldn't talk to him in person but slipped her number under the door. "Your articles have been excellent," she told him. She was "in a position to have considerable knowledge of the secret activities of the White House and CRP," they wrote. Apparently Bernstein had tried to interview her before, but she had rebuffed him.

Now he had her number, and she was willing to talk. He returned to the *Post* and placed the call. "I'm forced to agree 100 percent with Ben Bradlee; the truth hasn't been told," the woman said. Carl began taking notes, identifying the woman only as "Z". She told him to read their own reporting carefully. "There is more truth in there than you must have realized," she said. She told him that she wouldn't cooperate in the way that a normal source might, answering only some questions and then only vaguely. "Your perseverance has been admirable," she told Bernstein. "Apply it to what I say." She sounded, he thought, "like some kind of mystic."

In the back of my mind, alarm bells started to go off. This all sounded a lot like that memo I had put into Bernstein's file, the one with the data points and the vague reference to a juror. I slid over to my Watergate box and pulled it out. Six grafs down, after some of the "major conclusions" from the interview at the top, lay Carl's description of his contact with the source:

> CB arrived at her home about 7:45 p.m. identified myself through a closed door and she immediately responded, "Your articles have been excellent." adding something about admiring our work, and then asking how we'd got her name. I said I'd like to talk and I'd explain how we got her name and [she] asked: "Are you contacting all the people?"
>
> She then said she'd give me her non-listed number and CB could call and said he couldn't come in and slipped piece of paper w. number under door (this checked w. grand jury list number). I slipped my phone numbers under door, and told her I would call from office and she said that would be fine.
>
> Upon calling her she immediately began: "I've read your articles, the articles have been fantastic, incredible. Your persistence has been admirable."

It was late at night. I was sitting in a remote farmhouse in Rapidan, Virginia, and as it dawned on me I couldn't help myself: like Woodward at the courthouse, only much, much louder, I screamed "Holy shit!" I scanned the rest of the memo to check the quotes from the book against the quotes in the memo, and every single one was a match. In a couple of places, Bernstein had changed some of the words in minor ways, but these seemed more like the inevitable journalistic errors of somebody writing against a deadline than anything else. All of the substance was there. There was no question that this was the same source.

Z was no "mystic." She was a grand juror in disguise. This, too, is obvious from the memo, and not just from the single detail of her number matching up with the grand jury list. Carl, in accordance with the instructions of their editors, was oblique about how he had come across her information: "told her it had come from a source along w. a few other names and this source had 100 per cent right. on previous tips. further I told her that source had said she had exhaustive infor [*sic*] on case but in no way involved. She said 'of course, I was on the grand jury.'" Later: "I tried specific questions and she said she couldn't answer because they 'leading and I took an oath.'" Later still: "she said that her first time in court and she had no idea about what jury duty was like. 'a liberal education.' 'I cared about the case more than most people on the jury.'" Toward the end she tells him, "If we'd learned all there was to learn, we'd have been there six more months."

The date on the memo was December 4, with no year specified. A quick date check revealed that December 4, 1972, was a Monday. In *All the President's Men*, Carl and Bob specify that the visits to the grand jurors took place on the first weekend in December of 1972. Shortly thereafter, I located a list of the grand jurors from the Watergate grand jury, empaneled on June 5, 1972. One woman had initials that matched the initials at the top of Bernstein's memo.*

All these years, Carl and Bob and Ben have described the grand jury episode as a case of flying too close to the sun but escaping before any real damage was done. That is not the truth. The damage *was* done. Carl and Bob, with Ben's explicit permission, lured a grand juror over the line of illegality and exposed her to serious risk. Z would certainly have been kicked off the grand jury had Sirica found out what she had done, and the judge could have imprisoned her without trial for as much as six months for contempt of court. He could also have upended the trial itself. (Z covered her tracks. She either lied directly to the prosecutors when they asked if any other grand jurors had been contacted, or she lied indirectly, by withholding that information and allowing Judge Sirica to act on the assumption that only one grand juror had been contacted and that nothing had leaked.)

So what did Woodstein actually learn from the grand juror? Under the heading of "major conclusions" at the top of the memo, Bernstein lays out the key points from their conversation:

*I know her name but won't reveal anything else about her.

Haldeman, Ehrlichman, Colson and Mardian all figure in the disclosure of wiretap information. A group by itself—apparently no others.

David Packard very involved ("you missed a big one") supervisory, not payments as are Kalmbach and apparently Morton B. Jackson.

John Dean very involved and not just from point of view of doing investigation.

Key names from grand jury pt. of view: Mitchell, Stans, the four above, Kalmbach, (Very important), Porter, (grouped w. Magruder), (sort of a separate entity), Magruder ("extremely interesting"), Odle, ("a dumb errand boy").

Also figuring: Baldwin, Diego, apparently Young, Nov. group ("Magruder is definitely the key"). . . .

Aside from the major conclusions, data throughout the seven-page memo would resurface later in the Watergate coverage: the slush fund, Haldeman's role, the importance of Dean (which wouldn't surface until April of the following year), the existence of a cover-up, the Plumbers, Colson's involvement, the disclosure of wiretap information from the Watergate bug job to people as high up as Haldeman and Ehrlichman.

How important was this information to Woodstein? If their own book is to be believed: crucial. In January of 1973, Senator Sam Ervin, who would run the Senate Watergate Committee, called and requested a meeting with Bob. Bob knew Ervin would seek information about his sources, and the senator didn't waste much time. Here's how Bob thought through his response, according to the book: "Information from Deep Throat and Z and some other bits and pieces might help the investigation, conceivably could even send it on its way," he remembered thinking, but he wasn't at liberty to divulge his sources and so he kept his counsel vague.

Asked by Senator Sam Ervin for his best and most important leads, Bob put Z's information on the same level as Deep Throat's. That's a pretty high level. Either Z's information was formative to their thinking about Watergate in an ongoing way, or from a narrative perspective Woodstein were hyping the import of what Z had told them in order to heighten the mystery and power of their anonymous sources. This comports with Carl's characterization of Z as a "mystic," and is of a piece with the deeply mysterious Throat. Either reason is revealing in and of itself. References to "the riddles of Z" and "Z's statements" continue for much of the rest of the book.

"This was no Batman and Robin trip," Carl confessed to Pakula a few years later, "and this is not some simple thing about simple truths and the good guys and the bad guys. [We faced] tremendous ethical problems . . . some of which we dealt with successfully and some of which we didn't." Watergate was never a fair fight. On one hand, Woodstein's successful penetration of the grand jury is a stunning reporting coup. They didn't coerce Z; she clearly wanted to cooperate. She chose civil disobedience in the face of an unprecedented cover-up and a grand jury investigation that had stopped well short of the truth, and there is honor in that.

On the other hand, Woodstein's repeated proclamations that they "never got anything out of the grand jurors," and the faux hand-wringing in the book, do raise basic questions about ethics and truthfulness. It's one thing to get information from a grand juror and then be coy about where it came from. It's quite another thing to make a public point of honor about never having gotten it in the first place. You can argue about good lies and bad lies, about ends justifying means, but maybe the moral of the story is that nobody gets to come out of the great mud bath of Watergate with his hands entirely clean.

A couple of weeks after I rediscovered the grand juror memo, I laid out the evidence for Ben in his office during one of our regular interviews. I showed him a couple of the quotes, and the descriptions of Z in *All the President's Men*, and how they matched. And then I asked him if he knew.

"It doesn't ring a huge bell," he said. It was hard to tell if he really didn't remember or if he was just telling me that.

"I think it's very likely that you didn't know," I told him. "But I found the memo in your files." He understood what that meant.

Who knew if he'd read it, but he had it, and that meant he might well have known.*

"You can say that Bradlee can't remember, right?"

"Easily. That's all I need to say."

"I mean, knowing that that's the truth," he said. "I'm not ducking it."

"I don't ever feel like you're ducking anything. But because of how strongly Bob reacted to all of this other stuff, I'm going to wait on this one. I don't want to launch World War II again." We laughed.

"I don't ever remember probing whether they had talked to a grand juror," he said. "Maybe because I was scared that they had. I mean, I don't remember holding back, I don't remember being scared about it. But if you told me that they had, it doesn't shock me."

That was as good an answer as I was going to get, as far as Z and Ben go. As for what "World War II" was, I have to start from the beginning.

---

*Before my interview with Ben I had spent a day in Pakula's archives in Los Angeles. Barry Sussman, to Pakula: "Some of their writing is not true . . . that they never got something from a Grand Jury member. Barry thinks that's wrong. They did get information from one person and Carl planned to meet with that person again." This doesn't mean that Ben knew for sure, but it means that they didn't keep it completely to themselves, either. And it meant that I had found what I knew I had found.

DOUBT
(PART ONE)

IN APRIL OF 2010, CAROL, Ben's secretary, called to tell me that somebody had yet again located a couple of stray Bradlee boxes at the *Post*'s storage facility. In one of the boxes were two of the interviews that Ben had done with Barbara Feinman for his memoir in 1990. Like me, Barbara had worked for Bob before working for Ben, and she had been roughly my age when she and Ben sat down for their interviews. Unlike me, she caught Ben while he was still the editor of the paper, and much of the material that surfaced during those interviews—and nearly all of the good stuff—went wholesale into Ben's memoir.

The first of the two interviews was dated May 16, 1990, slugged "Watergate for memoirs." From the first question on, it sizzles:

BF: Did you read the transcript?
  [of his interview with Woodward and Bernstein in 1973 for *All the President's Men*]

B: I read it but I haven't read it as thoroughly as I should. But I mean it's almost better to talk about it from my own point of view rather than from Woodward's and Bernstein's. Well, you know, Watergate in retrospect, it's hard to believe that people were that dumb, were that insane to do that. And it's achieved a prominence in history and in my life that it doesn't really deserve. . . .

  I mean the crime itself was really not a great deal. Had it not been for the Nixon resignation it would be really a blip in history. The Iran-Contra hearing was a much more significant violation of the democratic ethic than anything in Watergate. Watergate really was dirty tricks and arrogance and people thinking that they were all-powerful and could ride roughshod over civil liberties, but it wasn't dealing in smuggled arms and buying foreign nations and shit like that.

I wish I had gotten the chance to interview *that* Ben.

Later I came across a longer section that told me more about what it felt like to be Ben during Watergate than anything else I'd seen:

B: None of the recreations that I've seen do justice to the absolute passion this city had for that story. I mean, every night before you went home, before Williams and Califano for instance, or before Clark Clifford, or before Katharine or before Oz Elliott in New York went home from work they would call up and say, "What have you got?" They had to have a fix, they could not go out to dinner. Kay would drop down on the way home and say something, "Jesus, what have we got tomorrow?" "Jesus, you sure you're right?" The interest in the community and in the newspaper community around the country was extraordinary, just extraordinary.

BF: Was that what was always on your mind during that time?

B: . . . [A]fter the Pentagon Papers was out of the way, until I met Sally, I don't consider I did anything but Watergate. And after that, after meeting Sally, I mean that was another year or so before Watergate was over. Anyway, dealing with Woodward and Bernstein became—as they became more skilled in subterfuge, as they became more skilled in double meanings and triple meanings and quadruple, it became quite hard to deal with. They probably put us all a little bit on the defensive. Their great habit was to come around about seven thirty at night to say they had a helluva story.

BF: Did they do that on purpose?

B: Of course they did it on purpose. Because they thought the guard would be down and they could slip it into the paper without the usual sort of grilling.

BF: That's pretty ballsy.

B: Yeah. And it ruined a lot of dinners and nights because the first few times we said okay, stopped, unpacked and went back to work and would stay there until we got it that we could print it or we didn't print it or waited a day, but at least we—and it was we—Simons and myself and Harry Rosenfeld, Sussman, looked at it, worked it over, made decisions. And then finally we just said, "To hell with it, don't [come] around here at quarter of eight or seven thirty, if you can't explain what you're doing, if you can't do it—terrific that you're doing it, but let's do it in an orderly fashion."

BF: Were they scared of you at all?

B: They say they were but I'm not sure.

The interview continued along that track, branching off in a few different directions but then returning to the movie. At a recent panel discussion, facing questioning about Deep Throat, Ben had said that he didn't want to be held to a Hollywood portrayal of Woodward's secret garage meetings with his source.

"You know I have a little problem with Deep Throat," Ben told Barbara.

B: I know who they identify as—Bob identifies as Deep Throat. Did that potted palm incident ever happen? That seems like a dumb (inaudible) to me. And meeting in some garage. One meeting in the garage? Fifty meetings in the garage? I don't know how many meetings in the garage.

BF: And you haven't pressed him because it's irrelevant?

B: There came a time when I pressed him for his name. But I had a long conversation with Bob in the middle of it as to the source and I said at that time that I didn't have to know the name of the person but if I didn't know the name I had to know everything about him—age, sex, place of work, high, low, what kind of access, who he knew. I suppose after that conversation if I had—

BF: When did you find out?

B: I don't know exactly, some years later.

BF: Do you get sick of it, the Deep Throat part of it, people always asking you who it is?

B: I mean they always sort of, "Who's Deep Throat," that's sort of a standard. No, I can say this to you, there's a residual fear in my soul that that isn't quite straight.

BF: And do you think that's partially because of the Janet Cooke thing? I mean I know that you trust them but do you think that that fear—

B: You can't argue with success. I mean, one way or another they were right. Whether they've embellished that or not.

I read it over a few times, just to see if it meant what I thought it did. Later, unprompted, Ben amplified it:

B: I mean, the movie Deep Throat was out and it was just too perfect to have some sort of porn movie figure to describe some role in the Nixon thing was just wonderful.

But whether—I just find the flower in the window difficult to believe and the garage scenes . . . I mean, I can see that would be a terrific place to meet—once—but you know, I just don't know. But

I have a feeling that that's a fight still to be fought. If they could prove that Deep Throat never existed—they—the fuckers out there, if they could prove that, that would be a devastating blow to Woodward and to the Post, never mind that Nixon resigned but it's the Post's version would be called into account. It would be devastating, devastating.

In any case, you know, I'm a great believer in playing the cards that you're dealt, and I'd been dealt that hand and I gotta play. Time and time and time again the reports that they brought back were proved right. Over the long haul you can't argue with that. Most of them from Woodward.

The interview took place in 1990, long after history had vindicated the facts of Woodstein's reporting. Ben has always stood so firmly behind Woodward that the doubts—the residual fear—surprised me. He makes no mention of them in his memoir, or anyplace else.

The first thing I had to do was ask Ben about it. That was going to be tricky. By that time I was comfortable asking him tough questions, but he was quite good at identifying shaky branches and could rarely be lured into stepping out onto one of them. In that interview in 1990 he had been speaking to Barbara knowing that she was a trusted friend, that she wouldn't (couldn't) repeat a word of what he was telling her. I wasn't bound by those ground rules, but I wanted to handle the subject with care.

It took me a couple of months to find a good moment. One day in early October, just before his son Quinn's wedding, I finally felt like he might be in the right mood. After twenty minutes of talk about Bob and Watergate, I edged my way there. "The only other question I have about it is a little bit of a trickier question," I opened, and then I just laid it all out for him. I wanted to be sure that it was real, I said. Did he still have those doubts?

"Well, I mean, if you would ask me, do I think that he embellished, I would say no," Ben said. "But was he—he did nothing to . . . to play down the drama of all of this. I mean, whether, what was it, flowers in the . . ."

"A flag in the flowerpot and all of that."

"You know, I'm sure they had a signal, and I'm sure it was that way, but whether it was roses or something else, I don't . . . who knows."

He wasn't going to go any deeper, but he hadn't backed away from it, either.

One of the things you learn as a reporter is that you always get your best information at the end. You put all the pieces together, and then you go back to your sources. The more information you have, the more power you have. And so I sat on Ben's doubt about Deep Throat, because I didn't know how Bob would react to it and I didn't want to upset him before I needed to. There would be other questions that I would need his help with first.

But then the grand jury discovery occurred, and suddenly I found myself chasing two strands of the Watergate story, strands that had unexpectedly led me toward bigger questions than I had ever thought I would ask. Of the two, the Deep Throat piece felt like significantly smaller beans. The grand jury episode involved decades of dissimulation and possible illegality. Ben's doubts about a small piece of Deep Throat's spycraft seemed to me to pale in comparison. I wrote Bob to set up what I described to him as a "final interview," hoping this wouldn't be the case but fearing that it might be. Two days later, I went over to Q Street for the interview.

We spent the first forty-five minutes or so on Watergate. I had just undertaken my story-by-story analysis of it, and Bob's memory is like a trap, so he was able to discuss the details of each story and give me bits of color about many of them. I could tell that he was mildly amused by the small-bore nature of my questions, but he humored me.

When I was through with my prepared questions, I slid the three relevant pages of Ben's interview with Barbara across the table toward Bob, with two pages from my follow-up interview with Ben stapled to the back. Bob asked for the date of Ben's interview with Barbara, and then he read silently for a while.

When he got to the second page he spoke for the first time.

"Where he's saying, 'There's a residual fear in my soul that that isn't quite straight,' what's . . ." He trailed off. He knew the news peg as soon as he saw it.

"That's what I was curious about," I said.

"Yeah. And, you know, was there one meeting in the garage, were there fifty meetings in the garage . . ."

"I ask him to clarify," I said, pointing to my follow-up interview. "You'll see where I . . ."

Bob lapsed back into silence and continued reading. "He's mixing up some things here, even," Bob said. I could see, already, his mind trying to find the escape hatch. Ben was confused, Ben was just kidding around. Then he read silently for a while longer.

Seven minutes after he'd started reading, he put the pages down and looked up at me. He was visibly shaken. It was not a look I was accustomed to seeing from him. "I'm not sure what . . ." he said, all vigor drained from his voice. Then, quietly: "What's the question?"

"There is no question," I said, uncertainly. "When I read it, I was surprised. I thought it was a little strange, and I wondered whether you had ever had a conversation with him about it. Whether he'd ever conveyed any of this to you."

"Well, you know, what you need to—I mean, I don't find this, I mean he's saying at some point, he's talking about flowerpots and garage meetings and so forth . . . and 'there's a residual fear in my soul that *that isn't quite straight.*'"

He paused. "You know, I can understand," he began. "He wasn't there. I mean, the whole thing has a . . . you know, as we now know, the whole thing is kind of, a series of accidents and persistent pressure by *me*. You know, that's one thing . . . I was the asshole that kept, you know, showing up and nudging [Deep Throat] and so forth. So, you know, I think that's a strength that he would have a residual fear about what he doesn't know about."

"But that the information was always good," I countered. "To me, it's a real indication of what a newspaper editor does, in a fundamental way. And I thought he clarified it in the interview with me by saying, 'I don't think he embellished, I think they did nothing to play down the drama of it.' And my sense is, that's his basic—"

"Yeah, but this is 2010," Bob interrupted, referring to my interview with Ben. Ben's doubts as the editor of the *Post* in 1990 meant more than any doubts he might have now, as an eighty-nine-year-old man. I conceded the point.

"Look, he's got to be—you've got to understand his strength as a skeptic," Bob said. "And that he would say, 'There's a residual fear in my soul that that isn't quite straight,' and then, you know, 'You can't argue with success.'" He laughed. "I mean, that's Ben. That's—it was right, it worked, but 'There's a residual fear in my soul that that isn't quite straight.'" I could tell from the repetition of that one phrase that Bob wasn't quite convincing himself.

He acknowledged that a lot of what happened in Watergate *was* implausible at first. "That, you know, 'H. Hunt, W. House,' I mean . . . is that possible? You know, so, I mean I kind of like the line. 'There's a residual fear in my soul that that isn't quite straight.' . . . [I]t's kind of Ben's skepticism." I thought this was a smart route to take, and also the truth. A few moments later he said, "You know, the residual fear in his soul that something isn't quite straight, I would embrace that thought."

> BW: You know, what don't you have a residual fear about? You have a residual fear that you hear it wrong. You know, I've told the story about when Tenet said the WMD, "It's a slam dunk," that, you know, maybe he said "slim dick".*
>
> [laughter]
>
> BW: Right? Maybe I didn't hear it right. And so you have . . . a process—you know this—of vetting. Did we get this right, do we have the context right? . . . [Ben] was always kind of nudging me a little about it . . . but, you know, and this again is this, that there was a zone of interaction between a reporter and a source where there is, you know it's kind of hallowed ground, and you don't step in there.

---

*In Bob's book *Plan of Attack,* which described the run-up to the Iraq war, he quoted CIA director George Tenet as having told President George W. Bush that it was a "slam dunk" case that Saddam Hussein was in possession of weapons of mass destruction.

Q: Right.

BW: Isn't that right?

Q: Absolutely.

There *is* a zone between a reporter and a source that editors cannot tread in without breaking the terms of the compact. That really is what Ben had been talking about, in one sense. If you trust somebody, as Ben trusted Bob, you have to take some things on faith, even if you wouldn't swear to them yourself.

We talked a little bit more about Deep Throat, and how he had hidden in plain sight:

Q: People have put so much pressure on it over the years. And the Deep Throat thing just magnifies the mystery of it in this way in people's minds. And I think that pressure—I mean, I remember when I worked for you . . . I was here when you went and saw him. It was February of 2000. I remember coming into the office and you said to me, "So have you figured out who it is yet?"

BW: Yeah.

Q: And I said, no. And I think you were just fucking with me.

BW: Yeah.

Q: I said something like, "I'm not sure I want to know, I'm not sure I would trust myself with that kind of secret." And you said, "Well, I just saw him." No—you said, "I just talked to him on the phone last week" or something. It was before you saw him. I maybe didn't know you saw him. But you said, "I just talked to him on the phone last week, I may go see him," or something like that. And I had forgotten about that until *The Secret Man* came out, and then I remembered, because I was here.

BW: That was very indiscreet of me.

Q: No, but it wasn't . . . I think you were trying to say, "It's a real person" . . .

BW: But the, here's the question . . . that "the residual fear in my soul that that isn't quite straight," what is the natural transaction between an editor and a reporter? Hmm? When he questioned, you know,

"What'd they say?" "What were the words?" "What were, the exact language?" There's doubt that we're getting it right or that we're, you know, the whole Haldeman thing.

Q: Or Bernstein on the phone with his source, you have to hang up in ten seconds and all of that.

BW: Yeah, all of that nonsense. And so I think that's a state of . . . I think that applies, doesn't that, to any . . .

Q: To any interaction you have.

BW: You know, look, when you worked, when we worked together, I trusted you.

Q: Right.

BW: No question about it.

Q: But I could screw something up.

BW: You could . . .

I reminded Bob of our interview three and a half years earlier, when he had said that with Ben, as with one's father, "you never close the deal." In *The Secret Man*, Bob makes the same point about Deep Throat. By the time Bob wanted to air everything out with Mark Felt, to understand why Felt had cooperated in the way that he had, Felt had lost his memory of the events in question. Bob never got any solid answers about Felt's motivation, or even how he executed some of the spy tradecraft—checking Bob's balcony for the flag in the flowerpot, or accessing Bob's copy of *The New York Times* in order to draw a clock face inside of it—that people over the years had called into question.

Bob said that many reviewers of that book had felt that it was "incomplete," that it didn't resolve anything. "You don't get a window into somebody's motives," he said. "You know, what was Nixon's motive?"

Toward the end, Bob pulled the transcripts I'd brought toward him and said, "Let me keep this. I'll put it in my Bradlee file." I told him that was no problem.

"Whatever you make of this . . ." he said, portentously.

"I'm interested to hear your reaction, because that's essentially my reaction," I said, wanting to reassure.

"How could he . . ."

"How do you operate in a realm of doubt and lack of 100 percent certainty? That's the newspaper business. His philosophy is always you don't get the full story any day. You take a piece and you take a piece and you take a piece. So you're not going to be 100 percent certain that it's an authoritative account in any story, really."

"On anything," Bob said.

A minute later we turned the tape recorder off, and Bob asked if I wanted to stay for lunch. Rosa Criollo, Bob's cook, brought out a perfect tomato soup and sandwiches while the two of us shot the shit for a while. It was a fun, pleasant lunch. Bob didn't seem agitated at all, and I figured that the evolution he'd gone through in the interview—from being stunned by Ben's doubt to absorbing it and even appreciating it—was the perfect trajectory. It would make for an interesting byway in the book, nothing more.

When I got home later that day and listened to the recording of the interview, my heart sank. I hadn't fully realized that Bob had repeated that one phrase—"There is a residual fear in my soul that that isn't quite straight"—fifteen times in twenty minutes. I had a bad feeling. When my wife got home and asked me about it, I said it had gone well but that I suspected I hadn't heard the last of it.

DOUBT
(PART TWO)

BB: There came a time when I pressed him for his name. But I had a long conversation with Bob in the middle of it as to the source and I said at that
time that I didn't have to know the name of the person but if I didn't know
the name I had to know everything about him -- age, sex, place of work, high,
low, what kind of access, who he knew, I suppose after that conversation if I
had--

bf: When did you find out?

BB: I don't know exactly, some years later.

bf: Do you get sick of it, the Deep Throat part of it, people always asking
you who it is?

BB: I mean they always sort of who's Deep Throat, that's sort of a standard.
No, I can say this to you, there's a residual fear in my soul that that isn't
quite straight. ──────── [INTERESTING] ─[USE]

TWO DAYS LATER, AT 11:26 on Saturday morning, an email from
Bob arrived. It was pleasant but direct: what was the date of Barbara's
interview with Ben, where was the tape of that interview, and what
did Barbara have to say about it?

I knew Bob well enough to know that this was the beginning of a
process, not the end of one. I thought back to something I'd said in
passing at the end of our interview the previous Thursday and instantly regretted it. We were talking about "slam dunk" vs. "slim
dick," and how one can never be sure that you hear things right, or
that somebody else heard things right. I mentioned that I was relying
on transcripts for interviews that I hadn't conducted, and that one
could always doubt work that somebody else had done. I shouldn't
have said it.

I know Barbara Feinman, and I never for one second doubted that
her transcription of her interview with Ben was anything less than
100 percent accurate. But now Bob was on the hunt, which caused

me to question things I hadn't questioned before. I called Barbara, and she told me that she didn't remember that interview in particular but that it sounded like Ben. She said she had given all of the interview tapes back to Ben when she left his employ. I knew some tapes were at Ben's house and some were in his archives down at the *Post*, which were in the process of being readied for sale.

Ben and Sally were down at Porto Bello, so I called Sally there to tell her that I'd had an interview with Bob and he was concerned about a certain tape. I asked if I could come by the house on Monday morning to see if it was among the tapes in Ben's home office. We made plans to meet at N Street around ten on Monday morning. I did not discuss those plans with Bob.

On Sunday night, at 10:45, another email came in, this one from Sally. Bob had come over to N Street that night to discuss the situation, and he was agitated. She said Bob would be there the next morning when I came to look for the tape, and that Ben had warned her to "stay out of it."

This was unnerving. I barely slept that night as various scenarios unfolded in my mind. Would Bob try to bring Ben down on me? Would he attack the verity of the transcript, or go after the tape before I could get there? Had he already? In my email back to him, I hadn't told him the precise date of the interview for just that reason.

In the morning I called my dad, who doubles as my lawyer. I laid it all out for him, and he listened. When I finished I asked him, in all seriousness, if he thought I should wear a wire to the meeting. He laughed, but I could hear his mind spinning on the other end of the line. No, he said. Nor should I bring my tape recorder, because the legal merits of taping anything surreptitiously weren't something I wanted to have to parse down the road. He suggested I speak as though I were being tape-recorded, to watch my mouth and to make no commitments. If there were any other lawyers there when I arrived, I should turn around and leave. (I realize this might all sound preposterous, maybe even paranoid, but Bob is a powerful man.)

Around 8:30 I called over to N Street. Sally picked up and told me what had happened. When she and Ben had gotten home from dinner the night before, there had been an urgent message from Bob on their machine. She called him back, and he ended up coming over around nine and staying for nearly two hours. As soon as he arrived, it was clear that he was deeply worried about what was in the documents I had given to him at our interview. He gave them to Ben to read, and apparently after Ben read them he told Bob that he didn't see what the big deal was.

She said that at that point Ben got "defensive," angry with her and angry at Bob. I kept asking why Ben had been angry, but I couldn't get a clear answer. Sally hinted that Ben had been irritated with her because she was interjecting too much, which wasn't hard to imagine, but the Bob part was more mysterious. Bob's baseline contention had been that the publication of some of the quotations from Ben's interview with Barbara would undermine his own legacy, Ben's legacy, and the legacy of the *Post* on Watergate. That it would be on the front page of *The New York Times*: "Bradlee Doubted Deep Throat." That the tape of the interview, in the wrong hands, could end up on *60 Minutes*. Sally said Bob had really gotten Ben "worked up" about it, and that he had told Ben flat out that I shouldn't use the material, and that Ben shouldn't allow me to use it. I asked her what I should expect when I got over there, and she said that I should expect for Bob to make a loyalty argument—to him, to Ben, to the paper.

I asked her if I could come by a little early to look for the tape, and she said sure. "You've got a tough decision to make," she said. "I just want you to know that whatever decision you make, I'll respect it."

She asked if I wanted her to be there for the meeting, and because I still didn't know Ben's state of mind I told her that I'd be more comfortable if she were in the house somewhere. The only situation I wasn't sure I could handle, I told her, was if both Bob and Ben were to turn on me together.

One of the maids let me in a little after 9:30. Ben was in the dining room. "Woodward, is that you?" he called out when he heard the front door close.

Here we go, I thought to myself. I walked into the dining room and put on my bravest smile and said, "No, it's just me." He was finishing his breakfast, and I saw that he had a marked-up copy of the documents I had given to Bob in his right hand. I took a seat to his left.

"So I guess I've really stirred the hornet's nest here with Bob," I said.

"It sure seems that way," he said. He flipped through the documents quickly, then put them down on the table. He asked me what I thought of them. I told him that I didn't think they were all that bad in their entirety, but that I wanted to hear Bob out about it. Then he asked me what about them I thought had upset Bob the most.

This was the moment of truth. I told him I was starting to believe that this had struck such a deep chord with Bob because maybe there was some portion of the Deep Throat story, as presented in the book and in the movie, that wasn't quite straight. Maybe it was some of the flowerpot and garage stuff that had always struck me—struck everybody I knew—as implausible. Who knew. But, like Ben, I had never doubted the big stuff, and so you go along with some of the more questionable details because everything else about the story turned out to be true.

Ben's face registered no reaction until I finished talking. Then he smiled and shrugged his shoulders. "That's all I was saying," he said.

My worry fell away in a great rush, and as it left I felt a very deep connection between Ben and me, more powerful than any moment I have ever had with him, before or since. With his whole body, even more than with his words, he was telling me that I had nothing to be afraid of, that he was with me. People who know Ben well talk about these moments of telescopic intimacy with him, where he makes you feel that you're standing at the center of the world and he's right there with you. I had never felt it for myself, until now.

After a few minutes Sally came in, and with time growing short I asked if I could go upstairs to look for the interview tapes. Barbara had told me that they would be microcassettes, probably grouped together. Sally and I went up to Ben's den and looked around, but they weren't there. After some minutes of fruitless searching, we started to head back down the stairs. As we reached the landing be-

tween the second and third floors, we heard the front door open and
Bob coming in. I waited on the landing with Sally, figuring it would
be better for Bob to have time to greet Ben without me sitting there
watching. I was not unmindful of the fact that I would be appearing
at the meeting from inside the house, that I had been the first one
there. After a couple of beats I walked downstairs and joined them in
the dining room.

Bob didn't look like he'd slept a lot. There was something frantic
about him, something off. We shook hands but only in the most
perfunctory way. He was there to get down to business, so I prepared
to do the same.

Within a minute or so we had taken our places at the table in Ben's
dining room. Ben sat at the head, with his back to the fireplace; Bob
sat to Ben's right, with his back to the front windows; and I sat to
Ben's left, facing Bob across the table. We were going to have it out.
Two of the most legendary journalists in the history of the country,
with a lot on the line . . . and me. What am I *doing* here? I thought
to myself, not for the first time.

There was no small talk. Bob had brought a thick manila folder with
him, which he set down heavily on the table in a way that he meant
for us to notice. When Ben asked what it was, Bob said, "Data."
Then he asked Ben what he thought of the whole situation.*

"I've known this young man for some years now," Ben said, meaning me, "and I trust his skills and his intent." Then he looked down
at the transcript of his interview with Barbara, shrugged, and said,
"Nothing in here really bothers me, but I know there's something in
here that bothers you. What's in here that bothers you?"

Bob went into his pitch, which he repeated over the course of the
forty-five-minute meeting. He would read the "residual fear in my

---

*No ground rules were ever established for this meeting, which means that I am free to
report what was said. I did not record it, but immediately after the meeting I wrote out a
six-thousand-word memo of everything that occurred. All of the information in this section
comes from that memo; as a result, a word or two in the quotations might be inexact, but
the substance is correct.

soul" line out loud, and then say to Ben that he couldn't figure out why Ben would still have had doubts about any aspect of his reporting in 1990, sixteen years after Nixon had resigned. This was the unresolvable crux of the problem, and one that they circled for the duration of the meeting: how could Ben have doubted the flowerpots and the garage meetings, when the rest of Woodward and Bernstein's reporting had turned out to be true? Bob thought this was inconsistent, and hurtful. Ben didn't. Bob tried everything to get Ben to disavow what he had said, or at least tell me I couldn't use it. Ben wouldn't do either of those things. After Bob had made his pitch four or five times, Ben said, "Bob, you've made your point. Quit while you're ahead."

Bob turned to me. You know me and the world we live in, he said. People who don't like me and don't like the *Post* are going to seize on these comments as a way to knock me and all of Watergate. In his interview with Barbara, Ben had spoken of "the fuckers out there" who have always wanted to prove that Deep Throat never existed: "If they could prove that," Ben had said, "that would be a devastating blow to Woodward and to the Post, never mind that Nixon resigned but it's the Post's version would be called into account. It would be devastating, devastating."

"Don't give fodder to the fuckers," Bob said to me, and once he lit on this phrase he repeated it a couple of times. The quotes from the interview with Barbara were nothing more than outtakes from Ben's book, Bob said. Ben hadn't used them in his book, and so I shouldn't use them in mine, either.

That argument didn't make sense, and I said so. I told Bob I would think about what he had said, but I couldn't promise him anything. He told me it was his "strong recommendation" that I not use the quotes, then that it was his "emphatic recommendation." Then, when that got no truck, he tried a direct command: "Don't use the quotes, Jeff."

"So you think this is the big story for your book, huh?" he said at one point.

"I think it's interesting," I said.

"Come on," he said. *"Come on."* He wasn't buying it. My editors must be thrilled, he said. I told him the truth: from the moment I had

come across them I had known that Ben's doubts about Deep Throat
were interesting; *of course* they were interesting. You'd have to be a
fool not to acknowledge that.

As I defended myself, I turned to look at Ben, wondering what he
was making of all of this. He was sitting back in his chair, smiling
at me.

Bob closed by making a personal appeal to Ben. "You're this legend," he said. "You're the *editor.*" Ben's doubts in 1990, sixteen years
after Nixon had resigned, were going to mean something to people.
Bob would have to answer old questions that, with Mark Felt's confession in 2005, had begun to feel like settled history. Ben did his
aw-shucks routine, trying to downplay what his doubt might mean,
but he knew what Bob was saying was true. He had clearly made the
basic calculation that Nixon's resignation, and the reporting that had
contributed to it, weren't contingent on whether Deep Throat had
watched Bob's balcony for flowerpot updates, or on how many times
they had whispered to each other in a deserted parking garage. That
was on Bob and Carl, not on Ben or on the *Post.*

At the end of the meeting, when Bob asked Ben for his final opinion, Ben turned to him and said, "I'm okay with it, and I think I'm
going to come out of it fine. So you two work it out."

Without Ben's intervention there would be no way to work it out,
and Bob knew it. When we got up from the table, he hugged Ben
and then walked out.

Two days after the meeting I went down to Ben's office to talk it over
with him. "So I went on my sleuthing efforts to try to put some
resolution on this Woodward thing," I said as I walked in.

"Why has Woodward got his bowels in an uproar?" Ben growled.

"I think it's very strange, I have to be honest with you. But you
want to know something strange?"

"What?"

"This was one of those interviews you did with Barbara, right? For
your book, of which there are maybe twelve or thirteen."

"Yeah."

"I just went down and looked in the tapes. Every single one of them is there but this one." I had gone with Carol to the seventh floor, where Ben's papers were being vetted for sale. I wanted her as my witness so nobody would think anything fishy had gone on. She was as surprised as I was when the one I was looking for was the only one that was missing.

"What does that mean?" Ben asked.

"I don't know."

"Tell me your suspicions. Do you think Woodward's got it?"

"Maybe," I said. He laughed, and then I laughed. The Watergate parallels were a little much. "I mean, I don't think that's crazy. His reaction to this thing was off the charts."

"*Off* the *charts!*" Ben sang. "It suggests that he's really worried. That it might be true."

"I mean, I have to tell you, Ben, that's not what my book's about. My book's about you. I'm not trying to unearth some . . . you know?"

"I know that."

"But his response was so out of proportion to what was there." All Ben had ever called into question in the interview with Barbara were some of the Hollywood aspects of the Deep Throat relationship. He never said that he had doubts about the *information* Deep Throat provided, or about the stories Bob and Carl had written. We were both a bit mystified.

The most important thing to me was to thank Ben for his support before, during, and after the meeting. I had said it to him that day, but I wanted to say it again because it had been my lifeline since.

"Well, I was also being very true to myself," he said. "I mean, I wasn't taking sides except that I was telling the truth as I knew it."

"Right. What Bob wanted you to say was that you never had doubts. He was there to try to get you to say that and there was no way you were going to say that."

"That's ridiculous," Ben said. "I mean, it's ridiculous. If he could prove that I had no doubts, he'd prove that I was a jerk."

I wanted to be crystal clear about it, so I just went ahead and asked him. "You said what you said in 1990, and there's a record of it . . ."

"Yeah."

"And you don't retract it?"

"I don't."

In the wake of the meeting with Bob, I had spent two full days reading all the conspiracy theories about Deep Throat, from the marginally credible to the patently absurd. Even in the wake of the revelation in 2005 that Mark Felt, the number two man at the FBI, had been Deep Throat, questions remain.

Bob and Carl have always maintained, when they first started reporting on Watergate, that the fear on the part of the CRP employees they visited had convinced them that they were on to something. Bob's histaminic reaction to Ben's doubt, the palpable fear, had aroused my suspicions. So had the fact that I already knew that Bob and Carl had disguised a grand juror as somebody else in *All the President's Men*. If they were willing to dress Z up, might they not have hung something extra on Deep Throat, too? It was an idea that could be thought, as Ben would say. I can't say they did. But I also won't say they didn't. Any prospect for proof beyond doubt died when Mark Felt lost his memory.

I played out a couple of theories for Ben but it didn't feel right. "That's not the book I'm writing," I said, and he agreed. "I know you were just standing up for the truth, and I do feel I'm on the side of the truth."

"Well, I appreciate your saying that," he said. "But that's the way I am. I wouldn't—it's inconceivable to me that in his preparation for all of this, to strengthen his case, he didn't neaten things up a little. We all do that! Jesus Christ!"

"If something was coming from here, coming from there, to put it all into one thing that's basically right . . ."

"He thinks that it is a critical and fatal attack on his integrity," Ben said. "And I don't think it is. . . .You should, I think—well, I'm not going to tell you what to do."

"No, but I hear you. I know what you mean."

"Just do it in passing. It's just a little fact."

"Right. But the problem is that his reaction has made it more than something that's in passing, you see?"

We went back and forth again, but th
something clear: "There's nothing in it," mean
Barbara in 1990, "that attacks the verity of his rese

"Zero."

"It's just a little . . ."

"A few of the bells and whistles. Were all the bells and wh
those *exact* bells and whistles?"

"Where he had 90 percent," Ben said, "he was going for 100 percent, and it's that last lunge that drubs you."

We joked around for a minute or two and then walked out front to Carol's desk. After some small talk there he dispatched me as he always does, with a backslap and his standard admonition to "keep the faith."

The admonition rang particularly true that day. My faith in what I was doing, and in who Ben really was, was different now. When Ben told me to follow my nose, he meant it. When he told me he wouldn't interfere with what I was doing, he meant that, too. That hadn't been lip service, even when following my nose struck close to home. Ben wasn't going to back down, and he didn't expect me to back down, either.

I was reminded of the final moment of Ben's interview with Mike Wallace on *60 Minutes* in August of 1974, right before Nixon resigned. Wallace tells Ben that people are going to come after the press if Nixon resigns.

"And what can the press do about it, if anything?" Wallace asks.

"Hunker down," Ben says.* "Hunker down and go about our business, which is not to be loved but to go after the truth."

* "HUNK-uh."

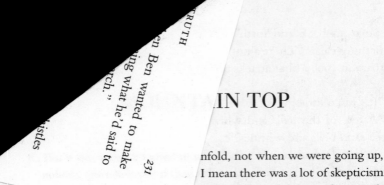

IN TOP

nfold, not when we were going up,
I mean there was a lot of skepticism
nted to believe, and people weren't
that convinced ... until it started to unfold. And then
euphoria, I mean we were all on a high all the time. . . .

B: We had staff meetings about overt expressions of joy. And we had a staff meeting about gloating. And a staff meeting that castration would occur if anybody mentioned impeachment.

K: When we did it the strain we were in—it really in fact wasn't out to get him, or gloat, it was the fact that our reporting was turning out to be visibly accurate. So I mean in fact it was not—we were, obviously we were having a great deal of satisfaction, shall we say, but . . .

B: We were having a good time.

K: Yes, yes.

—Ben and Kay, September 20, 1990

ON JANUARY 30, 1973, G. Gordon Liddy and James McCord, the lone remaining defendants in the Watergate criminal case, were found guilty after a sixteen-day trial and ninety minutes of jury deliberation. (Hunt had already pled guilty, as had the four other burglars—who, as it turned out, were being paid by CRP to remain silent.) Though Woodstein and Seymour Hersh, of *The New York Times*, had reported the payoffs to the four burglars more than two weeks in advance of the verdict, the trial had come and gone without implicating anybody at the White House. The cover-up was becoming visible, but it was still working.

What turned the tide, for the *Post* and for the public's understanding of the case, was the confirmation hearings of acting FBI director L. Patrick Gray III for the position of permanent director. Those hearings began on February 28, and on March 5 Gray submitted a batch of supplemental paperwork to the Senate Judiciary Committee. Included in those documents was an FBI summary of the first month of its Watergate investigation, which included allegations that officials at CRP had attempted to hinder the FBI's investigation from the start. Whenever CRP employees were interviewed by the FBI, lawyers representing the committee had insisted on being present as well. CRP employees later revealed that they had been afraid, under those circumstances, to tell the truth.

Also in the FBI summary, which Woodstein described in a *Post* story on March 6, was an acknowledgment that Hunt and Liddy had traveled around the country, "contacting former CIA employees for the purpose of setting up a security organization for the Republican Party dealing with political espionage." As Woodstein couldn't help but note:

> On Oct. 10, The Washington Post reported that the Watergate bugging stemmed from an extensive undercover campaign of espionage and sabotage directed against the Democrats and conceived in the White House. The White House declined to comment on the Oct. 10 report, which described Hunt's role in the undercover campaign, and Nixon re-election committee [*sic*] said the Post story was "not only fiction but a collection of absurdities."

The FBI had known privately what Woodstein had reported publicly and been slammed for.

An even larger vindication for the *Post* came the next day. In order to answer certain complicated questions from senators on the Judiciary Committee, Gray had crafted a typewritten statement. In that statement, which Gray provided to the committee on March 7, he affirmed that Herbert Kalmbach, Nixon's personal lawyer, had admitted to the FBI that he and Dwight Chapin, Nixon's former appointments secretary, had arranged for the payment of more than $30,000 in campaign funds to Segretti.

This confirmed the stories that had run in the *Post* immediately after the Segretti story on October 10. Now it was no longer a matter of the *Post*'s word versus the White House's, as it had been since September of the previous year. Bob and Carl and Ben and everybody else at the paper might always have known they were right, but now with the help of Pat Gray they could prove it. By all accounts Ben was over the moon that day, roaming around the newsroom and declaring that Pay Gray had saved the free press.

That morning at the White House the questioning of Ron Ziegler took a decidedly different turn. A wire service reporter asked Ziegler whether he was ready to apologize to the *Post* for the previous year's denials on the stories about Kalmbach and Chapin.

"My comments stand," Ziegler said.

"Are you not commenting because the White House finds this embarrassing?" a reporter asked a bit later.

"I'm not going to characterize or give a definition for the reason I'm not commenting further," Ziegler said. Most of the other questions Ziegler was asked that morning were of a similar cast.

In the coming days, Gray's testimony would deeply implicate White House counsel John Dean, who according to Gray had personally requested and received FBI reports on the investigation and lied to federal investigators. Gray's confirmation hearings became a referendum on Dean's role, which in turn dragged Nixon in, insisting Dean wouldn't testify because of executive privilege. The slow dance of administration officials turning on each other had begun, and nobody would do more eventual damage to Nixon than John Dean.

But even still, the lid might have stayed on were it not for James McCord and the letter that he wrote to Judge John Sirica on March 19, 1973, delivered to Sirica the next day and read in open court on Friday, March 23:

The Weather

The Washington Post

Times Herald

96th Year ··· No. 109   SATURDAY, MARCH 24, 1973   Phone 223-6000   10c

Watergate Perjury, Pressure Charged

McCord Ties Others to Plot; Liddy Jailed

By Lawrence Meyer
Washington Post Staff Writer

A tight-lipped James W. McCord leaves Pennsylvania Avenue throng after his court appearance yesterday.

E. HOWARD HUNT JR.
... pleads in court for mercy

G. GORDON LIDDY
... "the leader with the money"

Oil Import Quota Cut Second Time

By Thomas O'Toole
Washington Post Staff Writer

Hanoi Pledges to Release Its U.S. POWs by Deadline

Physicist Will Head Research at Pentagon

By Michael Getler
Washington Post Staff Writer

Prime Rates Vary After U.S. Action

By Philip Greer
Washington Post Staff Writer

McCord Arrest Sparked Mrs. Mitchell's Outburst

By Bob Woodward
and Carl Bernstein

MARTHA MITCHELL
... she found out

McCord, found guilty in the criminal trial, was awaiting sentencing in jail. In writing to the judge, he was breaking a silence he had maintained for nine months, ever since the break-in itself. He wrote that he couldn't "feel confident" talking to the FBI or with prosecutors who "work for the Department of Justice." Several members of his family had expressed fear for his life if he told the truth, but he didn't want to receive the severest possible sentence and so he was willing to talk.

In his letter, McCord wrote:

1. There was political pressure applied to the defendants to plead guilty and remain silent.

2. Perjury occurred during the trial in matters highly material to the

very structure, orientation and impact of the government's case,
and to the motivation and intent of the defendants.
3. Others involved in the Watergate operation were not identified
during the trial, when they could have been by those testifying.

"For the first time, really, I felt in my guts that we were going to
win," Ben wrote later of the moment that McCord's letter became
public. "And winning would mean all the truth. Every bit. I had no
idea still how it would all come out, but I no longer believed Watergate would end in a tie."

McCord's letter marks the end of the *Post*'s singular contribution to
the unraveling of the Watergate scandal. Since Sy Hersh's January
scoop about payments to the burglars, the *Times* had gotten into the
game in a more major way, but with the revelations in Gray's testimony and McCord's letter, Watergate became an unabating national
story for the following year and a half. Television crews staked out the
houses of high presidential aides; there were reporters everywhere.
Though things still happened in the shadows, and Woodstein were
often quite good at penetrating those shadows to reveal bits and pieces
here and there, the tectonics of governmental inquiry took over. At
the end of March, McCord testified under oath to the Senate Watergate Committee that John Mitchell had personally approved plans to
bug the Democrats' headquarters. Woodstein were able to report that
closed-door testimony the day after it happened, in a splashy front page
story, but it was the testimony, not the reporting, that mattered now.

In mid-April of 1973, as the daily drumbeat of revelations suggested
that the president's men were going to take a woeful beating, the
Pulitzer Prize board met in New York City to determine the winners
of the prize for 1972. Prizewinners are determined by different juries
for each category, but the board has the power to ratify, overrule, or
suspend any of those decisions.

Ben had been on the Pulitzer board since 1969. When he arrived
in New York, he was happy to discover that *Post* reporters had won
three Pulitzers for 1972: David Broder, for his political column; Bob

Kaiser and Dan Morgan, for foreign reporting; and Bill Claiborne, for "local spot news," a single story written on deadline. But no Woodward, no Bernstein. And the *Post* itself had been shut out from the public service category, for which entire newspapers could be nominated.

When the jurors had voted, McCord's letter still hadn't come out, and the *Post*'s reporting hadn't been fully vindicated yet. The public service jury had been headed by a man named Arthur Deck, whom Ben describes as "the great sort of newspaper establishment ASNE* hack." Deck was based in Salt Lake City, and Ben figured he didn't understand Watergate and likely didn't care about it. "Probably pro-Nixon, certainly pro-Mormon, just was out of it," Ben says. But now, mid-April, the *Post*'s contribution couldn't be denied. As Ben's version of events goes, Scotty Reston of the *Times* and Newbold Noyes of *The Washington Star* told Ben, right when he arrived at the meeting, that the board should use its power to overrule the public service jury and give the award to the *Post* instead.

"I was thrilled," he says, "and so naïve that I didn't see that they would punish me for that."

In the horse-trading that goes on in situations of that nature—horse-trading always denied by those who participate in it—the *Post*'s public service prize would come with a cost: as the day wore on, the board also overruled two of the prizes that the *Post* had already won. Broder remained, but Dan Morgan, Bob Kaiser, and Bill Claiborne all lost out.

"I was just furious. I mean I was so fucking mad I could hardly stand it," Ben says. "And yet I couldn't complain because there I had just won big casino, we had just won big casino." The citation of the public service award was usually made to the newspaper itself, "for the work of" the reporters who worked on the story, instead of to the reporters directly. That's how the board, with Ben's approval, chose to do it in this instance, too. The board included an explana-

---

*The American Society of Newspaper Editors—and all the "alphabets," as Ben calls them—was not Ben's kind of crowd. He thought they were mostly small-time and resentful of people like him. Eugene Patterson remembered going to one ASNE convention with Ben and having Ben turn to him and say, "There's probably not a guy in this room I'd hire." "There's probably not an editor here who'd hire *you*, Ben," Patterson replied.

tory statement that singled out Bob, Carl, editorial writer Roger
Wilkins, and the cartoonist Herblock, but also made reference to the
"total effort" of the paper.

Word about the Pulitzers arrived at the *Post* on or about April 12,
1973.* Shortly thereafter, Bob and Carl made their way into Ben's
office to have a little chat. They had heard a version slightly different
from Ben's. What they had heard was that Ben hadn't nominated
them for the prize in National Reporting, but had instead "maneu-
vered it" so that the prize went to the paper instead of to Woodward
and Bernstein as individuals. Bob was apparently angrier about it
than Carl. As Halberstam noted later in a private memo, Carl "says it
was really the only time he'd seen Woodward angry at Bradlee." Bob
acknowledged this in his interview with Halberstam as well:

> [Ben] was wearing that black navy turtleneck sweater, and he looked
> like Kirk Douglas as a submarine commander. He was very much
> the naval commander, and he says, "It's a good thing you've come
> in, we've been stalling each other on this." And we told him we
> thought we were getting screwed by it. And we said there was a way
> to put it in for both of us, you know, that we would get it and the
> paper would get it as well. It was, says Woodward, self promotion.
> We wanted our candy too and we wanted our names on it.
>
> We talked about loyalty to us, then Bradlee talked about loyalty and
> he said it, "The paper had its cock on the chopping block," and he
> talked about the economic pressures on the paper. "You don't even
> know what was going on, you don't know what the stakes were," and
> he talked about loyalty and the paper had been good to us and what a
> great thing this was, and he was just . . . Bradlee at his best, absolutely
> seductive, convincing you away from what you want to what he
> wants. You had a sense that he could really move you and change you.
>
> And you also knew that this meant a lot to him to get it for the
> paper, that this was getting even with the Times. The Pentagon
> Papers to him had had blood on every word, that had been his
> phrase and that's what he meant. And then he said to us, you know,

---

*The prizes wouldn't be announced publicly until May 7.

no one will ever forget who wrote those stories, your names are engraved and . . . I mean, he made us feel a little shabby about what we were doing. He made us feel like we were being a little bit gross, and at the same time we knew he was screwing with us.

Ben's version of that meeting: "I said to them, in the last analysis, if it had not been for the guts of the Grahams you guys would be pumping gas somewhere."

On April 17, the *Los Angeles Times* broke a front page story reporting that "The White House will make a dramatic admission within several days that one or more high level officials bear some responsibility for Watergate-type political espionage." That same day, Jim Fallows, then a twenty-three-year-old staff editor at *Washington Monthly*, wrote to Ben to inquire about why he hadn't chosen to run that same story on the front page of the *Post*:

Dear Mr. Bradlee:

I don't know whether to be astonished or amused by your decision to run the LA Times story on page 16 of today's paper. If your own correspondents had produced it, you presumably would have considered it as important as any of the other Watergate stories you have consistently run on page 1. Why the boondocks for this one? Does rivalry among papers (in this case, one whose readership does not overlap yours) overcome news judgment?

Ben's response, three days later:

Dear Mr. Fallows:

I would hope there is room for reaction somewhere between amusement and astonishment.

We considered that story very carefully. It had <u>no</u> details of what major development, or how it would happen. <u>No</u> names. We had already printed that things were coming to one hell of a head, fast. We simply felt it took us very little further.

Other newspapers apparently disagreed, because they had not printed anything like this. We had. The page 16 is accidental. That was the jump page for all Watergate stories. It could just as well have been page 4.

In the Watergate case, I'm just plain damned if The Washington Post is the paper to be asked whether rivalry among newspapers overcomes news judgment.

I showed this exchange to Bob, and he chuckled. He summarized Ben's letter thus: "Fuck you, Jim."

But the *Los Angeles Times* had it right: the story really was about to change dramatically. That same day, the 17th, President Nixon announced that there had been "major developments" in the Watergate case. In a reversal of his earlier position, he was going to allow his aides to testify under oath before the Ervin committee. He had previously said publicly that no members of the White House staff had been involved in Watergate, but on the 17th he changed his mind, as Woodward and Bernstein reported in a front page story on the 18th:

"If any person in the executive branch or in the government is indicted by the grand jury, my policy will be to immediately suspend him. If he is convicted, he will of course, be automatically discharged."

The President's statement was in sharp contrast to 10 months of White House denials of involvement of presidential aides in the Watergate bugging and other political espionage and sabotage activities.

Following Mr. Nixon's brief talk, presidential press secretary Ronald L. Ziegler met with reporters and said that all previous White House statements about the bugging were "inoperative." Ziegler emphasized: "The President's statement today is the operative statement."

That about summed it up.

The next day the story blew wide open, leading into two of the most remarkable weeks in the history of American journalism:

The Washington Post

The Weather
Today—Partly cloudy, high in the middle 70s, low tonight near 58. There is a 20 per cent. chance of rain today. Friday—Fair, high in the 70s. Temp. range: Yesterday, 77-58; Today, 72-58. Details, Page C7.

FINAL

96th Year ···· No. 135   THURSDAY, APRIL 19, 1973   Phone 223-6000   10c

Mitchell, Dean Approved Watergate, Payoffs, Magruder Reportedly Says

By Bob Woodward and Carl Bernstein
Washington Post Staff Writers

JOHN N. MITCHELL
... tied in key meeting

JOHN W. DEAN III
... resignation believed imminent

JEB STUART MAGRUDER
... faces jury today

See WATERGATE, A17, Col. 1

The Washington Post

The Weather
Today—Partly cloudy, high near 80, low to mid 50s. Chance of precipitation 20 per cent today and tonight. Saturday—Fair, high in low 70s. Temperature range: Today, 79-56; Yesterday 78-57. Details, Page C8.

FINAL

96th Year ···· No. 136   FRIDAY, APRIL 20, 1973   Phone 223-6000   10c

U.S. Halts Clearing Of Mines

Stops Talks, Presses Hanoi On Cease-Fire

By Murray Marder and Michael Getler
Washington Post Staff Writers

Lisa Hernandez, left, and her brother yesterday was 79, 15 degrees above nor-

Dean Vows He Won't Be 'Scapegoat'

By Carl Bernstein and Bob Woodward
Washington Post Staff Writers

JOHN W. DEAN III
... preliminary hint

The Washington Post
Times Herald

The Weather
Today—Partly cloudy, high in the low 70s, low around 50. The chance of rain is 10 per cent through tonight. Sunday—Cloudy, high in upper 70s. Temp. range: Friday, 70-51; Yesterday, 75-51. Details on 27.

FINAL

96th Year — No. 137   **SATURDAY, APRIL 21, 1973**   Phone 223-6000   10c

Photo Flights Resumed
Cease-Fire Violations by Hanoi Blamed

By Michael Getler
Washington Post Staff Writer

The United States has resumed aerial reconnaissance flights over North Vietnam for the first time since the Jan. 27 cease-fire, Pentagon sources said yesterday.

Cambodian government troops approach a building destroyed in fighting Thursday in the market town. Timm Klemm

No Proof N. Viets Fighting in Cambodia
Embassy, Pentagon Views Differ   *'Selective' Cease-Fire Breaches*

By H.D.S. Greenway

By Murrey Marder

Mitchell Claims Payments Went For Trial of 7

Denies Fund Was to Buy Bug Silence

By Bob Woodward and Carl Bernstein
Washington Post Staff Writers

Former Attorney General John N. Mitchell told a federal grand jury yesterday that he approved payments out of President Nixon's campaign funds to the seven Watergate conspirators.

After talking to grand jury, John Mitchell meets media.

Nixon Vows Tough Watergate Probe

The Washington Post
Times Herald

The Weather
Today—Mostly sunny, high around 80, low in upper 50s. Chance of rain is 10 per cent today and 20 per cent tonight. Monday—Cloudy, high in the low 80s. Temp. range: Today, 80-58. Yesterday, 74-55. Details, D3.

Index

96th Year — No. 138   **SUNDAY, APRIL 22, 1973**   Phone 223-6000   40c

Watergate: A Crisis of Authority for President Nixon

By David S. Broder
Washington Post Staff Writer

This weekend, for the first time, Richard Nixon confronts the possibility that Watergate may become his "seventh crisis," a crisis of presidential authority.

News Analysis

Haldeman Fund Link For Payoffs Is Probed

By Bob Woodward and Carl Bernstein
Washington Post Staff Writers

Lon Nol Reported To Yield
Seen Letting 3 Opponents Share Power

PHNOM PENH, April 21

Israel Censured At U.N.
Vote Also Hits All Recent Acts Of Violence

By Anthony Astrachan
Washington Post Foreign Service

UNITED NATIONS, April 21—The U.N. Security Council today adopted a resolution condemning Israeli attacks on Lebanon.

The Weather

Today—Cloudy, high in the 80s, low in the 50s. The chance of rain is 30 per cent today and 50 per cent tonight. Tuesday—Fair, high in the 70s. Temp. range: Today, 83-56. Yesterday, 86-66. Details on Page C2.

The Washington Post
Times Herald

FINAL

96th Year — No. 139 MONDAY, APRIL 23, 1973 Phone 223-6000 10c

U.S. and Iran: Oil Romance

Shah Exploits Energy Crisis To Build Power in Gulf

By Jim Hoagland
Washington Post Foreign Service

TEHRAN—Disrupted by Russia politically and economically, the shah of Iran appears to be abandoning previous efforts to achieve a more balanced policy toward Moscow and Washington.

Iran's steady strong lean to the United States have been significantly reinforced in recent months, as

MOHAMED REZA PAHLEVI . . . increases oil output

RICHARD HELMS . . . "believes Nixon's interest"

President Nixon chats with the Rev. John Huffman after Easter services at the Key Biscayne Presbyterian church.

Nixon Staff Is Losing Faith
And the 'After-Haldeman' Speculation Flourishes

By Lou Cannon
Washington Post Staff Writer

KEY BISCAYNE, Fla.—

Nixon Hears An Easter Admonition

By Lou Cannon
Washington Post Staff Writer

Nixon Alerted To Cover-Up In December

By Carl Bernstein and Bob Woodward
Washington Post Staff Writers

As early as last December, President Nixon was warned by members of his own staff that presidential aides were deeply involved in the Watergate bugging and subsequent cover-up, according to highly placed sources in the executive branch.

CHARLES W. COLSON . . . warned President

JOHN N. MITCHELL . . . involvement reported

The Weather

Today—Rain, 'slah around 60, low in the 40s. The chance of rain is 80 per cent today and 50 per cent tonight. Saturday—Cloudy, high in the 60s. Temp. range: Yesterday, 57-53; Today, 96-61. Details, Page D3.

The Washington Post
Times Herald

FINAL

96th Year — No. 143 FRIDAY, APRIL 27, 1973 Phone 223-6000 10c

Gray Destroyed Hunt's Kennedy File After Parley With Ehrlichman, Dean

Magruder Resigns U.S. Job

First Among Watergate Figures to Quit

By George Lardner Jr. and Carroll Kilpatrick
Washington Post Staff Writers

Jeb Stuart Magruder, a former White House aide who served as President Nixon's 1972 campaign director, resigned abruptly from the Commerce Department yesterday.

JOHN D. EHRLICHMAN . . . confirms meeting

JOHN W. DEAN III . . . began talking

By Bob Woodward and Carl Bernstein
Washington Post Staff Writers

Acting FBI Director L. Patrick Gray III last year destroyed documents belonging to Watergate conspirator E. Howard Hunt Jr. after being told by presidential aides John Ehrlichman and John W. Dean III that the documents should "never see the light of day," FBI and other sources said last night.

York Daily News, and subsequently verified by The Washington Post and other newspapers.

Dean Seen Asking Full Bug Disclosure

Bush Warns White House On Watergate Harm to GOP

L. Patrick Gray: reportedly cautious in loyalty.

The Weather
Today—Sunny, high in the 60s, low around 40. The chance of rain is near zero today and tonight. Monday—Partly cloudy, high in the 60s. Temp. range: Today, 58-61; Yesterday, 55-68. Details on Page 38.

The Washington Post
Times Herald

96th Year ··· No. 145   ©1973, The Washington Post Co.   SUNDAY, APRIL 29, 1973   Phone 223-6000   40c

AMMUNITION TRAIN EXPLODES—A huge fireball rises from an exploding bomber as a string of railroad cars loaded with fragmentation bombs and propane gas wreaks havoc in a 18-mile area around Roseville, Calif. Story, A3.

3 Top Nixon Aides
Tied to Cover-Up

Kalmbach Hush Fund Link Probed

By John Hanrahan
Washington Post Staff Writer

Herbert W. Kalmbach, President Nixon's personal attorney, is being investigated by the Watergate grand jury here on allegations that he obstructed justice by providing money used by others to buy the silence of the seven defendants in the Watergate bugging case.

Kalmbach, according to a government source, passed the money on, either directly or indirectly, to the defendants from a secret fund.

Sources from the Committee for the Re-election of the President said yesterday that between $350,000 and $1 million left over from President Nixon's 1968 campaign provided

Dean Cites Haldeman, Ehrlichman

By Carl Bernstein and Bob Woodward
Washington Post Staff Writers

At least two high-level White House officials have concluded that the cover-up in the Watergate bugging case was supervised by President Nixon's principal deputies, H. R. Haldeman and John Ehrlichman.

A third White House official, presidential counsel John W. Dean III, intends to come under oath that he gave regular reports on the progress of the cover-up to Haldeman and Ehrlichman at their direction, reliable sources reported yesterday.

According to one high-level White House source, the President and his top advisers are

H. R. HALDEMAN   JOHN D. EHRLICHMAN
. . . new "revealed leaks on their fates"

Senate Won't Cry
Over 'Those Two'

New Army: Magnet for Poor | D.C. Mayor

The Weather
Today—Cloudy, high around 70, low in the 40s. The chance of rain is 30 per cent today and 20 per cent tonight. Tuesday—Cloudy, high in the 70s. Temp. Range: Yesterday 57-61; Today, 49-63. Details, Page C26.

The Washington Post
Times Herald

FINAL
20 Pages—4 Sections

96th Year ··· No. 146   ©1973, The Washington Post Co.   MONDAY, APRIL 30, 1973   Phone 223-6000   10c

Cambodia Bombing Resumes

Raids Near Capital End 1-Day Pause

From News Dispatches

U.S. jet fighters resumed raids on the east bank of the Mekong River across from Phnom Penh Sunday after a one-day suspension of the bombing.

The Thailand-based F4 Phantom jets dropped napalm and bombs on suspected rebel positions within two miles of the Cambodian capital.

Sources at the U.S. embassy in Phnom Penh said there were no raids Saturday because of the concentration of civilians in the area.

Resumption of Cambodian bombing comes on the heels of the river Sunday to watch the American jets scream down on their targets from their cross and add drink vendors did a brisk trade during the one hour of bombard.

Military spokesmen in

Aides Say Colson
Approved Bugging

Wanted It Expedited, They Claim

By Carl Bernstein and Bob Woodward
Washington Post Staff Writers

Charles W. Colson, former special counsel to President Nixon, knew of the Watergate bugging plan before they were executed and urged that the illegal electronic surveillance be expedited, federal prosecutors have been told by two top officials of President Nixon's re-election campaign.

The two officials, former White House aides Jeb Stuart Magruder and Frederick C. LaRue, have told prosecutors in the Watergate case that Colson made a telephone call to Magruder in early 1972 expressing dissatisfaction that the bugging had not

Sens. Percy, left, and Weicker discuss developments in the Watergate case.

And then the biggest of them all:

Though there was certainly a degree of satisfaction in the *Post* newsroom when word of the resignations of Haldeman, Ehrlichman, and Dean reached Carl and Bob and Ben and the other people who had devoted so much of their lives to the Watergate story, the sweetest vindication would come the next morning, in the White House press room. Adam Clymer, a reporter for *The Baltimore Sun*,* asked whether Nixon was prepared to apologize to the *Post* for the administration's attacks on the paper and its credibility.

"We would all have to say that mistakes were made in terms of comments," Ziegler said. "I was overly enthusiastic in my comments about the *Post,* particularly if you look at them in the context of developments that have taken place. . . . I would apologize to the *Post* and to Mr. Woodward and Mr. Bernstein." They had pursued the story and deserved credit for their work. "When we are wrong, we are wrong," Ziegler said, "as we were in that case." As he finished, he tried to interject a qualifying "But . . . ," but the word was barely out of his mouth before he was cut off by another reporter who said, "Now, don't take it back, Ron."

Nixon got Nixon, Bob and Carl and Ben always insist, not *The Washington Post*. He was his own worst enemy. And it was the series of governmental inquiries, more than any newspaper coverage, that would eventually force Nixon from office. But as Ziegler's apology demonstrates, nobody could deny that Woodstein and the *Post* had played a singular role in keeping the spotlight on, particularly when the story seemed like it might fizzle. As Bob likes to say, the two most important readers of *The Washington Post* were John Sirica and Sam Ervin, and it is fair to say that neither man would have done what he did had the *Post* not kept the pressure on.

"My feeling generally . . . after being interviewed a hundred times by journalists trying to make us glamorous, [is that] there was no magic moment," Ben would say later. "There was no fail-safe, there was no point of no return, there was no moment in which everybody on the paper quaked like hell and called a board of directors meeting and said, 'Fellas, we've got this and should we go or shouldn't we go.' " If there had been any moment like that it had been the Haldeman story of October 25, 1972, the moment when they'd made their

---

*In September of 2000, while standing on a podium in Naperville, Illinois, presidential candidate George W. Bush would famously refer to Clymer, then a reporter for *The New York Times*, as a "major-league asshole."

only serious mistake. More than anything in Watergate they had done the daily and uncertain work of newspapering, getting the story in the paper day after day, using the methodology of journalism as a way to try to understand and explain something that still defies understanding or explanation.

The magic moment for me occurred during my interview with Carl, when he told me a story he would later repeat at Ben's eighty-ninth birthday dinner in Sag Harbor. In September of 1972, when he and Bob discovered that John Mitchell had been among the people who controlled the slush fund at CRP, they had retreated to a vending machine area just off the newsroom to take a break and talk things over.

"I put the dime in the coffee machine, and I literally felt a chill go down my back," Carl told me. "And I turned to Woodward and I said, 'Oh my God.' And he said, 'What?' And I said, 'This president's going to be impeached.' And he said, 'Oh my God, you're right. And we can never use that word in this newsroom anywhere.'

"And we never did," Carl went on. "Lest they think that we had an agenda in the newsroom. We didn't want *Ben* to think that we had an agenda."

But from that moment on Carl knew where it was headed, just the same. "I have no idea to this day where that came from, but I just knew," he told me. He laughed, and then he looked away and thought for a moment. As much to himself as to me, he said, with a shake of his head, "Two twenty-eight-year-old kids standing in front of a vending machine."

CODA

THE FIRST BUZZ LETS US into the photo archives, which my guide Eddy Palanzo duly calls "the morgue." A second buzz deposits us in a musty and poorly lit room farther back, where the *Post* keeps old copies of itself. A decrepit microfilm machine idles off to one side, abutting a couple of rows of freestanding bookshelves. One row holds all the books that used to sit on the shelves in Kay Graham's office, arrayed just as they were before she died, as if preserved in amber. Lining the back wall is a set of cabinets that hold the microfilm, and atop those cabinets rest piles of long rectangular boxes filled with yellowing newspapers.

I'm here because of a sentence that Ben probably never thought much about, buried as it was in the middle of a short letter to his old boss, Russ Wiggins, in 1996. Ben had written to tell Wiggins that he would happily submit to an interview with a woman who was writing a biography of the old *Post* editor, and he promised Wiggins that he would give her the goods. It's an unremarkable letter, except for the kernel that arrives in the middle without any fanfare and departs without any further explication: "I have found," Ben wrote, "that daily journals and diaries aren't as important in recreating the life of a newspaperman as the newspapers themselves."

Eddy shows me how everything works, and then we pull out a couple of the boxes that I've come for. Scrawled on the sides are designations of what's inside: "JFK Assassination," "Pentagon Papers," "Nixon 1" and "Nixon 2." None of them is as complete as the labeling would have you believe, but it's a start. Most of the big Pentagon Papers stories are missing, and a number of the papers in the Nixon/Watergate boxes don't seem like they belong there.

Then I open the box labeled "Nixon 2," and find myself suddenly knocked back. Sitting on the very top of the pile is the final edition of *The Washington Post* from August 9, 1974, with its banner headline in type so large that they had to take a picture of the largest typeface they had, blow it up, space it out, and then reset it: "NIXON RE-SIGNS." The biggest two-word headline ever to run in the *Post*, in every sense. On the wall in his office Ben keeps a copy of the famous picture, where he's leaning over the page form for this historic front page, with the headline in reverse below him.

I pick the paper up gently and hold it like a relic, certain I'm setting off some kind of silent alarm just by touching it. From its weight I can tell that it isn't only the front section. A quick flip reveals that I have in my hands the entire final edition of the newspaper that day—Style, Metro, Sports, the works. Up to now I've read all the newspapers in microfilm or as PDFs online, which give a sense of what the papers looked like but can't compare to holding the real thing in your hands:

The Weather
Today—Rain, high in the low to mid 80s, low in the mid to upper 60s. Chance of rain is 60 per cent today to per cent tonight. Saturday — mostly cloudy, high around 80. Yesterday's temp. range, 77-68. Details, Page D18.

The Washington Post

FINAL

97th Year — No. 247   © 1974, The Washington Post Co.   **FRIDAY, AUGUST 9, 1974**   Phone: (202) 223-6000   15c

Nixon Resigns

By Carroll Kilpatrick
Washington Post Staff Writer

Richard Milhous Nixon announced last night that he will resign as the 37th President of the United States at noon today.

Vice President Gerald R. Ford of Michigan will take the oath as the new President at noon to complete the remaining 2½ years of Mr. Nixon's term.

After two years of bitter public debate over the Watergate scandals, President Nixon bowed to pressures from the public and leaders of his party to become the first President in American history to resign.

"By taking this action," he said in a subdued yet dramatic television address from the Oval Office, "I will have hastened the start of the process of healing which is so desperately needed in America."

Vice President Ford, who spoke a short time later in

front of his Alexandria home, announced that Secretary of State Henry A. Kissinger will remain in his Cabinet.

The President-to-be praised Mr. Nixon's sacrifice for the country and called it "one of the very saddest incidents that I've ever witnessed."

Mr. Nixon said he decided he must resign when he concluded that he no longer had "a strong enough political base" in the Congress" to make it possible for him to complete his term of office.

Declaring that he has never been a quitter, Mr. Nixon said that to leave office before the end of his term "is abhorrent to every instinct in my body."

"But," he continued, "as President, I must put the interests of America first."

While the President acknowledged that some of his judgments "were wrong," he made no admission of the "high crimes and misdemeanors" with which the House

Judiciary Committee charged him in its bill of impeachment.

Ford Assumes Presidency Today

By John W. Finney
Washington Post Staff Writer

Gerald Rudolph Ford Jr., a Grand Rapids, Mich., lawyer who never aspired to national office but had a thrust upon him as a result of two of the greatest political upsets in American history, will become the 38th President of the United States at noon today.

He will be the first American President not elected to national office by the people, having been nominated Vice President by President Nixon last Oct. 12 under provisions of the new 25th Amendment to the Constitution.

President Nixon and daughter Julie embracing Wednesday after the President's decision to resign.

The Washington Post THE NIXON YEARS
A 24-page special section on the Nixon presidency—inside today.

Era of Good Feeling
Congress Expects Harmony

By Spencer Rich and Richard L. Lyons
Washington Post Staff Writers

A Solemn Change
Power Is Passed Quietly

By Richard Harwood and Haynes Johnson
Washington Post Staff Writers

Without even reading a word, you can feel Ben on the uncluttered front page.* This wasn't a typical news day, of course, but still the decision to run only four stories on the front was a bold one. The news spoke for itself. That morning *The New York Times* ran the same headline but in much smaller type; above the fold in the *Times* there are headlines and text for some six different stories. The simplicity of the *Post*'s layout is striking.

As I flip past the front page, I hear an ominous cracking sound. Stray bits of newsprint fall out of the paper and onto the table. Maybe this newspaper is too old to be read. I wait for the bell to go off, but after a few seconds I realize that if anybody cared this paper wouldn't have been rotting away in a disorganized box in a disorganized room. I resolve to be as gentle as I can with it and keep moving.

The first few inside pages hold the kind of national news that everybody that morning in 1974 no doubt skipped over as quickly as I do, run-of-the-mill stories about farm and factory price increases and six consecutive life sentences for a man who had hacked a bunch of people to pieces in Texas. The Watergate coverage picks up again on A6, with a long story by Lou Cannon, the presidential reporter, and then runs uninterrupted through to A23 before spilling over onto the editorial and opinion pages.

Opposite Cannon's piece is the jump from "A Solemn Change," the analysis and reaction piece from Dick Harwood and Haynes Johnson on page one. Harwood and Johnson were the star news writers on the paper. As George Solomon, the former sports editor, once told me, "There were two guys he'd bring out and put on the white horse, Haynes Johnson and Harwood. And those two guys took it up a notch." He likened having them write a piece about Nixon resigning to having your ace pitcher ready to throw Game Seven of the World Series.

---

*Notice that the final edition front page is different from the first edition front page, which Ben reviews in the famous picture; between 7:30 P.M. and sometime much later that night, the editorial team decided to replace the picture of a haggard-looking Nixon with a more tender picture of him hugging his daughter.

"Inside the White House, there were no last minute theatrics, no public relations gimmicks, no coyness about what was to happen and no rancorous remarks about enemies," Harwood and Johnson wrote. "It was an orderly thing, this passing of power." They appreciated the irony that Nixon's resignation speech had preempted three previously scheduled programs on broadcast television with the titles *The Taste of Ashes* (NBC), *The Nature of Evil* (ABC), and *The Last Man* (CBS).

Last Monday, Aug. 5, saw the final blow. He released three more transcripts. They contained the final seeds of his destruction. He conceded he had withheld critical evidence from his lawyer, his aides and staunchest supporters—and that he had personally approved plans for the Watergate cover-up only six days after the break-in on June 17, 1972. All his previous public statements about his role were demolished by his own words.

Ben's *Post* has every conceivable angle covered. There are reaction stories from Grand Rapids, where Vice President (and soon-to-be President) Gerald Ford was from, and from Whittier, California, where Nixon graduated from high school and college, and from outside the White House, and from the rest of America, and from area politicians, and from Congress, and from Ron Ziegler, and from conservatives already voicing support for Goldwater over "Rocky" (Nelson Rockefeller) for the now vacant vice president's job. The Ziegler story shows how far even Ziegler had come since his apology to Woodstein in May of the previous year. The lede graf, a quotation from Ziegler himself: "I think I take away from this job a deep sense of respect for the country's freedom of expression and the strength of a free press."

On the editorial page, Herblock sums it up better than all of the writers:

Opposite the cartoon ran the lead editorial, "The Resignation of a President":

> Maybe too much has already been written—and written too
> sentimentally—about the marvels of the system and how it
> "worked." But it did. And it is important to be precise about *how* it
> worked. . . . It was the conscience and pride and responsibility of
> innumerable people and numerous institutions that combined to
> assert that 1) there was (and is) a norm of official behavior that is
> recognized and respected by all Americans and 2) the President's
> departure from this norm was sufficiently gross and calculated to
> require an extraordinary and unprecedented remedy.

The reference to the working of the system is as close as anybody in the entire A Section of the *Post* that morning came to mentioning the *Post*'s own part in the drama.

Below Herblock's cartoon, David Broder weighed in with "The Country He Leaves Behind":

> Now that it is over, now that the long ordeal has ended for the man and the nation, now that the angry emotions have been vented into the vacuum created by his departure, what one can feel is compassion for Richard Nixon and renewed confidence in the country he left behind.
>
> He wanted so much to be President. The office tantalized and terrified him for 13 years before it came into his possession. And like any passion too long nurtured before it was fulfilled, it turned into something monstrous, something he could not control.

The general theme of most of the paper's coverage that morning—including a long supplemental section, "The Nixon Years"—was not that Nixon had been inordinately evil, only that he had succumbed to certain temptations that most men in power must face. There was an active effort not to demonize him, and much quotation of Shakespeare to set him in context. More than one person wondered at the standard that Americans had now established: if we got rid of Nixon for this, what do we do the next time? The shades of Clintonian perjuries hover just offstage.

I read the rest of the paper, too, just to feel the other contours of that 1974 world. In Sports, Muhammad Ali coined the phrase that has described his upcoming bout with George Foreman in Kinshasa, Zaire, ever since: "We're going to rumble in the jungle." On the Business and Finance front page, a youngish and bespectacled Alan Greenspan looks out from a photograph next to a story about whether his nomination to be chairman of the Council of Economic Advisors would be held up. (It wouldn't.) In Style, Faye Dunaway got married to Peter Wolf, the lead singer of the J. Geils

Band. And in Metro you could find the usual lottery winners, shoot-
ings, and ex-policemen sentenced for their crimes. All of the business of the world still ongoing, even the funny pages, even on a day
like that day.

If the newspapers tell the story of who a newspaperman is, the
Post's Watergate coverage—and, specifically, the August 9, 1974, final
edition of the paper—tells us who Ben is. From the front page on
down, this was the capstone to a monumental undertaking, where
Woodward and Bernstein and the editors and Kay Graham had put
everything on the line in a way that makes the Pentagon Papers look
quaint by comparison. All of the reporters who made the newspaper
great, who defined its political coverage, are represented in this one
newspaper—the older stars and a couple of newer ones, all weighing
in on an event that they hadn't created but in which they had played
an undeniable and at times even central role.

From this one newspaper, you can feel the sheer size of Ben's job,
the magnitude of the undertaking that is the production of a daily
newspaper, measured alongside the odds they were up against with
Watergate and the success they achieved. The simple fact of that ac-
complishment. Ben was in charge of all of those people, and responsible for them, too. He stood behind all of them. And his was the
final word in the creation of the document itself, that incredibly
complex and various document, meant to be read only for a day but
now, in this one instance, for at least a little while longer.

My favorite of all of the pieces in the newspaper was written
by Sally, who was sitting in the press room that day. She wrote a
kind of meta-piece, covering the media covering the story. By this
point Ben and Sally were living together—in the Watergate, of all
places*—but her writing distinguishes her for its quality alone. She
was already widely known for her insouciance and her ability to
distill whole stories from the essence of one well-chosen quote. In
this instance, she took everybody in the entire press room on. The
lede:

---

*"Bob Dole was living there, too," Sally told me. "Blasting the *Post* every day on TV, then
being really friendly to Ben and me in the elevator."

"The air was fraught with tension," dictated several reporters from
the White House press room. "An atmosphere of gloom
pervades" . . . "One has the feeling of being in a cancer ward,
waiting for a patient to die" . . . "one has the feeling of watching
sharks closing in on a victim" . . . "one has the feeling . . . of waiting
for the guillotine to fall. . . one has the feeling . . ."

　　The air was fraught with clichés.

She described the changing atmosphere in the press room as various
developments occurred throughout the day, nailing Ziegler's mood
better than any of the news stories had: "He looked stricken. He was
sweating when he stepped up to the podium, his hands were shaking
and he moved them rapidly from his pocket to his papers to his chest,
a muscle in his cheek was twitching and his voice cracked as he
spoke." She made it personal. To add to her roster of clichés, hers was
the only story in the paper that morning that made me feel like I was
there.

　　She also noted the surreality of the whole situation, when the reporters realized that they weren't going to be able to cover the president's resignation speech and were going to have to watch it on
television, like the rest of America. As the reporters gathered around
the TV, Sally wrote, "[t]he photographers took pictures of the press
watching the President." In the picture of this moment that accom-
panies the article, Sally is sitting on the floor just left of the middle of
the frame, wearing her distinctive oversize seventies glasses, notepad
in her lap.

　　The piece is playful, but the point hits home. The press had stepped
out of the wings and onto the stage during Watergate. Bob and Carl
and Ben and, increasingly, Sally—they had all become part of the
story, actors in the drama itself. The book *All the President's Men* had
come out in June of 1974, making them all folk heroes, as Ben likes
to say. The movie, which would do far more, was already in the
works. Their heightened profiles would beget increased scrutiny and
resentment, something that all of them were aware of but maybe
weren't quite ready for.

　　After Nixon's resignation speech, a pall fell over the press room:

One hundred or so Americans became reporters again. "Well," said someone cynically, "it probably played in Peoria." And another remarked, "I wonder if my paper will send me to San Clemente tomorrow. I guess so. He's probably a good story for at least 10 more days."

But another shook his head in a quiet kind of daze and said, "It's a funny feeling. I've been covering this guy for so many years. And now I'll probably never slug another story 'Nixon' again."

That was it, at its core. Nobody knew what to do next. Though somewhere, in the newsroom or in story conference at some point that very afternoon, I can just imagine Ben turning to some unsuspecting editor or reporter and saying, with zero irony, "So whaddaya got for tomorrow?"

———————

Harry Rosenfeld, September 26, 2011:

We can talk about this endlessly, but the sun sets. Watergate was a piece of gold. It told the truth. If it wasn't right in every last detail, it was right in more detail than any story I have ever dealt with, certainly with that kind of tenure. It was brass solid. And you can argue about this and you can argue about that, but the truth: the truth is, great wrongdoing was revealed, at great odds, that shook up the country and affects it to this day. The paradigm was set by our Watergate investigation. Everybody earned his stripes. Everybody. The fact that they weren't perfect human beings, the fact that they didn't make perfect judgments every time, I don't think gainsays that.

Kay to Ben, Christmas 1974:

The first thing you and I have to do is separate myth from reality because after this year the myth will start to grow and reality will start to diminish even in <u>our</u> minds.

The reality is so much less pretentious but so apparently

impossible to describe. And it really is much nicer because it's human—You are now supposed to be a hero and I a heroine by many and the opposite by many—I think heroes and heroines are both vulgar and boring and usually lead that kind of lives. But when you tell people you were just doing your own thing in an admittedly escalated situation, they say, Ah, yes, etc.

So what are the realities?

They are so complicated of course because we have known each other and our lives have impinged on each other with almost Proustian coincidence, both closer and more distant than they'd think. Closer because I am thinking of the shared Walter and Helen Lippmann type memories—the first tour at the Post, Phil and me seeing you and Jean in Paris, leading up obviously to the drama of Newsweek, followed by the horror years viewed so differently at the time and then Phil's death. You have to remember at that time we hardly knew each other and certainly not in reality or very favorably either—

How could the rest have happened? It couldn't ever again. We were still small enough as a company, still private, and so the impossible happened. . . . I with nothing more than a family feeling, a passion for newspapers and for this newspaper in particular, (not the slightest clue about business, broadcasting or Newsweek—only negative vibes about the latter which was associated only with madness in my mind) took over this peculiar & charismatic entity.

Two years later [meaning 1965] you knocked—typically, brashly, intuitively, humorously, rudely, perceptively, farsightedly, ballsily, and pushy as Hell—And because this was a not unfamiliar syndrome to me—and one whose merits—& drawbacks I knew—I nodded a feeble assent (I guess that's slightly exaggerated I say hastily for all those future fucking Columbia Journalism Review stories.) But there's a kind of core truth to the scene.

Then came another—the years of learning, of stumbling, of fun, of some achievement, progress, mixed with big smelly eggs on the floor—laid and cleaned up or just shoved under the rug until the stain soaked through. The fascinating thing—and the thing to remember is that if you have enough going for you in the way of

momentum and luck, everyone looks at the developing pattern on
the rug whether it's an Oriental design or the stain from the egg,
and says, "What a beautiful rug." And pretty soon we're telling
ourselves—"It's a hell of a rug we've made"—and even funnier, it is.
But let's always remember the stains, the unfinished work, with the
total effect & the fun—my God, the fun. It's unfair, who else has
fun? And that's my Christmas thanks to you, kid—more than even
the Watergates, although that, too—

The things that people don't know—that I know—are style,
generosity, class & decency, as well as understanding of other
people's weaknesses. If I had to name the toughest time for you in
retrospect & the worst time for me in retrospect were the post-Style
years during which you coined a famous phrase—"Take your finger
out of my eye"—

It was out of all these many things that Watergate evolved for you
& for me & for the way it works.

If there was one thing I thought of at the time it was a high wire
over a canyon in which I almost couldn't pull at your coat tails & say
"are we alright because if we're not look below"—It was sort of like
trying to talk to the pilot during a hairy landing. Not that I didn't. . . .

And maybe one of the things it's easy to forget in 1974, is that the
answer was, we were not all right—we were righteous but mercifully
stupid. We were only saved from extinction by someone mad
enough not only to tape himself but to tape himself talking about
how to conceal it. Well, who could have counted on that? Not you
and not me.

Thank God for the reality, it will never be in any book or any
cruddy movie. It's much too good for that.

BCB, April 19, 1985:

Dear Mr. Yanoff and Mather High students:

First, I want you to know I think your interest in writing the principals
who had something to do with Watergate is terrific. I suspect you're
lucky to have a teacher who gives that much of a damn.

The thing about Watergate that made it a major event in our nation's history was the resignation of Richard Nixon, the first President to be forced out of office in the history of our great country. If he had not resigned, it probably would not have been fair to call it a major event. But he did resign, and the only reason he resigned was that he was going to be impeached if he didn't. The way I see it, I have to call that a major event.

Will its importance diminish with time? Sure. Everything diminishes with time. The Civil War, the Depression, World War II, Vietnam. Even the Hagler-Hearns fight seems slightly less important to me this morning than it did on Monday night.

Did we as a country learn anything from Watergate? I wish I were sure that we had. I wish our government officials had learned more than that it is simply better not to be caught. I wish people saw clearly that the real lesson of Watergate is that a bunch of arrogant people cannot pervert the laws of this land to their own benefit without running the risk of shame and scorn.

I know it's popular now to say that Watergate was exaggerated by the press, especially by The Washington Post. But remember this: Dozens of people went to jail, including the Attorney General of the United States. And they were sent to jail by their peers, by jurors, not by journalists.

Good luck to all of you.

JEWEL THIEF

QUEENS

IN "THE LAST DANGEROUS EDITOR," his review of Ben's memoir in *The New Yorker* in September of 1995, former *Post* reporter David Remnick captured Ben's book, and Ben's nature, as well as anybody can in so short a space—with one important exception. Sally is nowhere to be found.

Shortly after the piece was published, Remnick felt compelled to write Ben to explain what had happened. He hadn't set out to write a full personal profile; when others alerted him to the fact that he had failed to mention Sally, he sought but had been unable to find a good place to work her in. He hoped Ben would relay to Sally that he had not purposefully excluded her from the piece, for any reason.

An item in the December issue of *Esquire* magazine made it quite clear that, despite Remnick's efforts at diplomacy, Sally was insulted by the omission. "Hell hath no fury like a power blond scorned," the magazine reported, noting that Sally was "fit to be tied" that she hadn't been mentioned. An anonymously sourced friend of Sally's suspected that Tina Brown, the editor of *The New Yorker* and a woman with whom Sally had feuded publicly in the past, had been responsible for the exclusion. Remnick tried again to defuse the situation: "I know that Sally was baffled that she wasn't in it and said as much to some friends," he told *Esquire*. "As you see it in the magazine is how I wrote it."

"I felt bad about it," Remnick told me when I interviewed him in his office at *The New Yorker*, where he is now the editor in chief, in the fall of 2009. I reminded him of his letter to Ben, in which he explained that he had tried to splice a reference to Sally into the pre-existing piece, but that it hadn't felt right to him.

"I'm a professional," he said. "I could have gotten it in. I was wrong. I was wrong. Not that I owed it to anybody, but I was wrong. Because she is a big deal in Ben's life, God only knows."

That there could be this amount of wrangling over an article that neglects to mention Sally opens a small window onto the long shadow she casts. I suspected, though he didn't admit it to me, that Remnick had concluded that the safest way to deal with Sally in his piece was not to deal with her at all—and even then he paid for it.

I first understood Sally on a sunny summer Friday afternoon in 2009. We were driving over the Key Bridge, Sally at the wheel, Ben in the passenger seat, me in back, headed to a party for Quinn and then down to Porto Bello for the weekend. Somehow the conversation drifted to Gloria Steinem.

"The problem with her was she thought she was sexy," Ben said. "She wasn't, but she *thought* she was." Open and closed, as far as Ben was concerned.

Sally's take was more complicated. She told a long, involved story about how at one point Steinem, the ultrafeminist, had been perceived to be throwing herself at Mort Zuckerman, the real estate magnate. Sally said that Steinem would sit captivated at Zuckerman's feet at public events, mooning over him.

"So I wrote a piece calling her a hypocrite," she said, catching my eye in the rearview mirror. "You know, just to stir things up."

It was a casual moment, but I knew instantly that that *was* Sally, that that was the real person I had just seen. The essence of Sally is that she loves to stir things up. She always does, and always has. Regard her or disregard her, it's at your peril either way.

When Sally came through the doors of *The Washington Post* in 1967, she was a twenty-six-year-old graduate of Smith College who had bounced around through a variety of odd jobs, looking for a way in. She was an Army brat, Southern by birth and sensibility despite having traveled throughout the United States and Europe for much of her childhood, enduring twenty-two different schools before college. Her dad was General William Quinn, an intelligence officer during World War II who helped transform the OSS into the CIA, and later the commander of the 17th Infantry Regiment, 7th Division, in Korea, where he became known as "Buffalo Bill." Her mother was Sara Bette Williams, born in Savannah, Georgia, a bona fide Southern belle who smoked cigarettes through a long holder and threw raucous parties before unpacking the boxes at each new house the Army moved the Quinns into. (Word on the street is that Bette had an affair with Barry Goldwater, one of the general's best friends. She also, apparently, had a crush on Woodward. At one holiday dinner, after a series of strokes had damaged her memory, she turned to Bob and asked, matter-of-factly, "Did we fuck?")

Sally had wanted to be an actress, but she floated around town for a while, working as a social secretary for the Algerian ambassador, among other jobs. After meeting some reporters and taking a liking to journalism, she applied for an entry-level position at the *Post*.

The job was to serve as the secretary to Phil Geyelin, the editorial page editor. He was smooth, urbane, slicked-back hair, familiar with cocktails. After one interview, he told her that she was hired, to start the following Monday. Then he took her to see Ben.

She'd heard of Ben, but she'd never met him before. He hooked her good. "I just remember looking at Ben and being completely dazzled," Sally told me. Ben later revealed that after Sally left, he turned to Geyelin and said, "Phil, you can't hire her because she'll break up your marriage. Don't do it."

Geyelin called over the weekend and told Sally that she wasn't right for the job, that she was "overqualified." She drifted around for a few months, spending some of the summer of 1968 working for Bobby Kennedy's campaign, which turned into a role as an assistant for CBS's coverage of the 1968 political conventions. Eventually she returned to Washington, and early in 1969, desperate to make some waves, she borrowed money from her parents and threw a huge party for her friend, the newly elected congressman Barry Goldwater, Jr. She was well connected from her work with the embassies and through her parents' social universe, so she invited every big name she knew.

The next day, after Sally's party made the social pages, Ben called her up himself. As she remembers it, he said, "Sally, you don't know me, but I'm Ben Bradlee and I would like to talk to you about a job at *The Washington Post*. Would you be interested?" They made plans for her to come in the following morning.

"I still remember exactly what I was wearing," she says. "I had white gloves. Ladies wore white gloves." It was definitely not the seventies yet. "I had a little silk blue dress on and white stockings and cream-colored shoes and a cream-colored bag and white gloves. I mean, it was like the old Hepburn days."

The Style section was still getting under way at that time, and Ben needed a new party reporter. Sally was young and smart and well connected and attractive. Would she want to give it a shot? When she said she would, Ben offered her a six-month tryout. All she needed to do was leave some of her written work behind with him for the editors to review.

"I've never written anything," she told him.

When Ben mentioned this to Geyelin, Geyelin famously responded, "Well, nobody's perfect." (Later versions always put these words in Ben's mouth, but both Ben and Sally insist it was Geyelin who actually said it.) She was hired.

"In those days, you took risks," Sally told me. "You could do things that you can't do anymore." It was different, perhaps, from how Ward Just or Haynes Johnson or David Broder or Carl or Bob came to the paper, but it was arguably as important a moment. And what bound her to all those other people, despite their differences, was that she had come to the *Post* because of Ben.

Over the course of the next three years, Sally would make her name on the party beat and then move on to write profiles of Washington players large and small. The "Sally Quinn profile" became a thing in and of itself, a huge draw at the paper. She always managed to get people to say strange, quotable things, and when they did she pounced.

At a party in October of 1969, she approached Henry Kissinger, who was standing alone by himself.

"What's the matter?" she asked him. "Don't you like parties? Aren't you a swinger?"

"Well," he said, with a grin, "I'm really a secret swinger."

"That was it for Henry," Sally wrote later. "By the end of the week he was 'The Secret Swinger' in *Time* and *Newsweek* and *Life* and newspapers around the world." Kissinger would later joke that while pieces by Maxine Cheshire, one of the *Post*'s society reporters, made you want to commit murder, Sally's pieces made you want to commit suicide.

She once did a series of interviews with George Wallace and his family during the Democratic primary of 1972, before Wallace was shot. Wallace's mother-in-law, a woman named Big Ruby, described Wallace's diminutive stature to Sally in a memorable way: "Shooooooooot, honey, he ain't even titty high."

All of Sally's pieces had verve and personality. She had a particular penchant for sticking it to people she felt were social climbers, sometimes in ways that could feel catty and vindictive. But even her detractors admitted that she nailed her subjects more often than not.

In August of 1972, the Style editors decided to send Sally down to Miami to cover the Republican convention. The National desk had sent their A-team of political reporters, but Style occupied a different perch and would necessarily have its own take. When she got to the gate at the airport, she noticed that Ben was on her flight; as they took their seats, they realized that they were sitting together. They were the only two *Post* people on the plane.

"We fell in love with each other on the plane ride," Sally told me. "Two hours."

Sally is prone to dramatic statements, so I checked this with Ben. He laughed. I asked if he remembered it that way, and he said, "I sure do."

"I wasn't in love with him before then," she says. "I was dazzled by him, but he was so far out of my reach, you know. He had three million children and he's married to the legendary Antoinette Pinchot, Jack Kennedy, blah blah blah. It was just so far away . . . and he was twenty years older. But there we were on the plane, and it was just *shazzam*." It helped that the flight was a particularly turbulent one, and as a Southern belle Sally was quite distressed by the turbulence and simply *had* to put her hand on Ben's thigh to steady herself.

Ben was supposed to have dinner that night with David Brinkley and his wife, Susan, and he invited Sally to join them. But when he got to his hotel, he discovered that Howard Simons had already booked a dinner that night with the National staff. He called Sally, who was staying at a separate hotel, to tell her.

"I was so disappointed," she says. "And I could tell he was, too." Ben invited her to the dinner, but Howard had done the seating and she was stuck at the other end of the table. They shared a few wistful glances but never got a chance to talk.*

*The one story Sally remembers from that night was when Richard Cohen told Dick Harwood that he'd met Harwood's daughter, Helen. Cohen and Harwood were of different cultures, Cohen the young bearded lefty Jew and Harwood the more conservative marine who initially doubted that Woodward and Bernstein's Watergate reporting could even be true. "Cohen, Helen is a dead fuck," Harwood said. "Do you know what that means?" No, Cohen said. "It means you fuck her and you're dead," Harwood said.

The next day, after Sally had left the convention floor and was hailing a taxi, she heard Ben's distinctive voice calling for a taxi behind her. She turned, and they decided to share a cab. Ben was going back to his hotel, did she want to join him for a drink? When they arrived, Phil Geyelin was somehow standing right there, as if he'd been waiting for them. Everybody from the *Post* was already at the bar, he said, and Ben and Sally had to join them. The opportunity had flown. Had Geyelin not intercepted them, the outcome might likely have been different. As it was, Sally returned to her hotel alone.

"So I came back," she told me, "madly in love with him. I had always sort of worshipped him from afar, but in this kind of untouchable way. And he, at that point, was in love with me. I mean, it happened in two hours on the plane."

A word about Ben's love life. It's easy to be flip about Ben being a ladies' man, or women always loving Ben, because most of them do and it's not hard to see why. But even if you believe that Sally and Ben didn't consummate until June of 1973, a year after their flirtation in Miami, even then Ben was still officially married.*

In 1995, Charlie Rose asked Ben, toward the end of their televised interview, "Any great regret?"

"Well, I wish . . . if I hurt Tony Bradlee, I would regret that," Ben said. "If I hurt Jean Bradlee, I would regret that."

"Former wives," Rose said.

"Yeah." Ben looks down and away, caught for a moment by an emotion. "But I still maintain very good relationships with them." He shifts his gaze skyward for a while. "I don't know," he finally says. "I don't regret much. Je ne regrette rien." It's a great end to the interview, and a textbook example of Ben's attitude. He knows that

---

*Sally has insisted to me on numerous occasions that she and Ben didn't get together physically until after she had left the paper for a job at CBS in the summer of 1973. Evgenia Peretz reported in *Vanity Fair* in 2010 that Sally told friends that she had been sleeping with Ben during Watergate and had to be told to stop. I believe Sally, but there are those who don't.

he's hurt some people, but in the grand scheme he doesn't let it slow him down all that much.

Ben's first wife, Jean, is a ghost to me, and seems to be so to Ben, too. Ben has said, on numerous occasions, that they barely knew each other. They got married when he was twenty, on the same August day in 1942 that he graduated from Harvard and was commissioned as an ensign in the United States Navy. "If I had been able or willing at that time to describe a 'trophy wife,' I would probably have described Jean—pretty, sure to be a good mother, fine family and all of that," Ben writes in *A Good Life*. There's something desultory about the description, even as he's trying to be charitable. Jean was from a good family, the Saltonstalls of New England,* and a suitable mate. But he was about to spend four years in the war.

"I don't know why I did it. I don't know today," Ben told me when I asked him why he married Jean. Had there been peer pressure to get married? Was that the box to check before heading off to war? He said no. A friend of theirs from the social set in Boston had already been killed overseas by the time Ben and Jean got married, and it had scared everybody Ben knew. "I would have thought that would have been enough," he told me, "to say, 'Why do we do this now?'"

In some of Ben's letters to his parents from his destroyer in the Pacific, you can feel how much he wants to say the right thing about Jean but somehow can't bring himself to do it in a convincing way:

August 1, 1943

[Jean] has been a marvelous correspondent telling me everything that has happened, and including all her multitudinous philosophies and beliefs, which never cease to amaze me. I think that perhaps is a side of your daughter-in-law that you do not know very well, her amazing

---

*Ben said later, "The Saltonstall family still had a U.S. senator or a governor or whatever the hell it was . . . but the fact of the matter was it was watered out. . . . No Saltonstall male or female had done a goddamn thing for years."

insight into human nature and her controlled ambitions and desires for us both.

December 19, 1943

My wonderful wife has sent me the most beautiful pictures, which I suppose you have seen. I hadn't really forgotten what she looked like, but I had forgotten she was as lovely as all that, I must confess. I am so terribly interested in her, so very confident of her potentialities, so very proud of having the privilege of fighting for her, and so very excited about the prospects of working for what I have fought for—these are all my waking thoughts.

Certainly the ardor of youth is present here, but there's a hollowness, too. "So very confident of her potentialities" doesn't sound like love.

Happily, there is more than just Ben's word to go on in all of this.* In 1949, shortly after Ben had started at the *Post*, a Grant Study interviewer came down to interview Ben and Jean at their home in Chevy Chase, Maryland. In her report, the Grant Study researcher described her first impressions of the couple in this way:

Mrs. Bradlee has blonde hair, worn in a page-boy style. She has well-proportioned features and is attractive, with nothing especially noticeable in her appearance. She is feminine but not plump. She has the style and manner of an undergraduate college girl. She was wearing [a] plain sweater with skirt, with no ornaments. Bradlee, who appeared slightly underweight, wore a brown tweed jacket and slacks. His shirt collar was open, but later before going to work, he put on a tie which he tied loosely. His hair had a crew cut and an unruly appearance, tending to stick out at different angles here and there. He had a very vigorous manner, and both he and his wife talked rapidly and easily. . . .

---

*Jean passed away in July of 2011 but had been suffering from dementia for some years before; Tony Bradlee passed away just four months later.

Bradlee had traveled 500 miles to vote for Truman, then he shrugged, saying, "My wife finally voted for Dewey, so we canceled each other's vote." He showed a little disgust and irritation.

As Ben put it with George Vaillant in 1990, "There was no risk-taking in Jean. I felt like I had to blast her out of Boston and blast her out of Manchester [where Ben worked on the newspaper] and blast her out of Washington and blast her to Paris. There was no sense of adventure in her at all." Jean was a WASP and expected a standard WASP life. Ben didn't become Ben until he'd been through the war, and when he got back he didn't want all that anymore, if he'd ever wanted it at all.

When Ben and Jean moved to Paris in 1952, they were doomed—and in his heart, according to his Grant Study questionnaire from a few years later, Ben already knew it:

Grant Study, June 27, 1955

"As you look back on the years following World War II can you recall particular periods when you were under special pressures from your work or your life: Please specify."

Now, when I am forced after 13 years of marriage to admit that it not only doesn't work, but hasn't worked for at least half of that time, when I am forced to start a new personal life.

In 1967, after Ben had been married to Tony for nearly ten years, the Grant Study questionnaire asked him to rank his happiest and his unhappiest times. "Explanatory remarks would be especially appreciated," the authors of the survey wrote. For his unhappiest period, Ben checked the ages 27–35, the end of his first marriage. "Marriage disintegrating," he wrote in a black marker scrawl next to his check mark. For happiest, he checked 35–42 and 42–49. Next to those checks, he wrote simply, "Rebirth."

Ben fell in love with Tony, really truly in love. There were other women in Paris, but Tony brought out a different side in Ben right away:

B: This was a courtship. I mean, there was a question of whether she would agree to marry me.

    . . . She really was extraordinarily vital and lots of the things that she isn't now, or that she didn't become. I mean my friends were just enchanted with her, would stay up all night and we'd prowl these—I really knew every joint in Paris, and I knew where the underground nightclubs were and she spoke a little French, and we traveled all over the country, to little obscure places, you know, very romantic, get picnics, go up in the fields, we'd paint.

Q: Paint?

B: You don't think of me as a painter, do you?

Q: Pictures or houses?

B: Paintings.

Q: Were they good?

B: No.

Their marriage was mostly a happy one. Even in 1969, after Ben had been at the paper for four years, he would report to Vaillant that things were as good as they ever had been:

He said, "our marriage has a rhythm to it. I know no other marriage like it." He said it burned "terribly brightly, almost too close. We are almost too dependent," and that when this happened, "we back off slightly, not in hostility or enmity" but from an awareness that "the fire is too bright." He said there was a "fantastic closeness." He said when they met, he was separated and she was married, but "when we fell in love, it was a hell of an ambitious project, to break up two marriages to build one." . . . He said sometimes their own closeness led them to ignore the kids more than they should.

One family friend told me that most nights Tony dressed up for Ben's return home from work. As Ben puts it, they were "in business" for a long time.

In the early seventies, Ben and Tony drifted apart—on both sides. They had lost JFK and then Tony's sister, Mary, in a little less than a year, and over the course of the next several years Tony gradually withdrew from social life, which had been so sustaining for both of them. She plunged deeper into her art, and into the spiritual teachings of the Russian mystic George Gurdjieff and his program for self-awareness and discovery, "The Work." Even in 1969, when Ben was still so happy with Tony, he told Vaillant that most nights they were in bed at 9:30 and that they rarely socialized. That might have worked for a while, but that couldn't have lasted forever for somebody like Ben.

In 1990, when an interviewer asked Ben what had happened, why he and Tony had drifted, he said, "I don't know. You see, I really don't still know." But in 1979, with the Grant Study, he gave a different answer:

My second wife and I separated in June of 1973. We are friends now, and agree each of us was replaced in the other's heart and mind. I was replaced by Tony's increasing involvement in something called "The Work", a small group of people dedicated to the life and teachings of Gurdjieff and Ouspensky. I never was sure of exactly what they believed, since they are not supposed to talk about it, but generally they believed that through meditation and self-discipline they could raise their consciousness gradually to levels of total understanding and awareness. There was less and less, and finally no, place for me in this pursuit. Tony was replaced in my heart and mind, by my job, I guess, by the process of getting on top of it, and then by the truly endless, challenging task of using the newspaper for the general welfare. I think we both underestimated the impact each of our non-marital interests would have on the other. The impacts were fatal.

From 1965 on, Ben's life had been *The Washington Post*. And Tony, though she enjoyed some of the people, never had an overriding interest in the *Post* in particular or in newspaper journalism in general. She rarely read the *Post*. As Art Buchwald, Ben's old friend, once put it, "Bradlee's totality of investment in the paper" cost him his marriage. He had given all of himself to something else. That was one of the many reasons, aside from her youth and attractiveness and the chemistry between them, that Sally made so much sense for Ben. She loved the newspaper as much as he did.

In what Sally calls the "agonizing year" before she and Ben officially got together, Ben made a few more than the routine number of trips back to the Style section. Once Sally was talking with Larry Stern, an old *Post* hand and one of Ben's closest friends, and Ben came over and put his leg up on the desk, one of Ben's famous poses, and she and he started sparring. Stern was still there, but he might as well not have been. Ben and Sally went back and forth for ten or fifteen minutes and then Ben walked off.

"Larry turned to me, he had this kind of smirk, and he said, 'That was probably the single most sexual scene I've ever seen in my entire life,'" Sally told me.

In June of 1973, Gordon Manning, an old friend of Ben's who worked at CBS News, offered Sally an opportunity to host the *CBS Morning News*, a program that the network was rejiggering to try to make a run at the *Today* show's audience share. (Some things never

change.) She would be one of the first female news anchorwomen in
history, behind Barbara Walters. She loved her job at the *Post*, but this
was a huge opportunity.

Ben didn't want her to leave, not only because of the frisson of
whatever it was between them but because she was one of the paper's
biggest assets. A memo from Ben to John Prescott, the president and
general manager of the *Post*, from right at this time:

> This will alert you to a larger-than-usual merit raise coming your
> way, and to explain the background.
>
> It involves Sally Quinn, perhaps the hottest property on the paper
> today, if Woodward and Bernstein aren't.
>
> Sally was hired—for peanuts and without experience—maybe
> three years ago. She turned pro but fast. We gave her a $50 a week
> merit raise in May 1971, and have been unable to give her another
> since, because of wage controls. We certainly would have given her
> 50 in May 1972, and another 50 in May 1973. She is that good.
>
> NYTimes has offered her the moon. Ditto NBC and CBS. Ditto
> [Kay Graham]'s friend [Clay] Felker of New York magazine. And
> I've even heard that Oz Elliott has made a move.
>
> I want to bring her to $400 a week, from $338.

It was too late. Sally took the job* and moved to New York, where
she started at CBS on August 6.

In the interim, Larry Stern threw a farewell party for her at the
Post. Sally flew down from New York and asked Ben if he would take
her to lunch that day. He did, and that's when she told him she was
in love with him, that that was the real reason she was leaving. She
knew he hadn't really understood why she had wanted to move to
CBS, and she wanted him to know the truth. She thought he would
say something like, "There, there, dear girl, I've got a family," that

---

*At one lunch where Manning was trying to woo Sally away from the *Post,* he was paged
and had to get up from the table to take a call. When he got back to the table, Sally asked
who it had been, and Manning said it had been Ben. "What'd he say?" Sally asked. " 'Fuck
you,' " Manning said.

kind of thing. But he didn't. As he confessed in his memoir, he had secretly been hoping that she felt exactly as she did. "And so we agreed to meet that night at my apartment," Sally says.

Back at the paper, at about five in the afternoon, Woodward and Bernstein came up with another big breaking story. Ben jogged over to Sally in the newsroom and said, "I know I said I'd meet you at 7:30, how about 8:00?"

"I said, 'How about never?'" Sally told me. "And he said, 'I'll be there at 7:30.'" She smiled. "And he was. I don't know who edited their story, but it wasn't Ben."

Richard Cohen lived in California House, the same apartment building that Sally lived in, and later that evening he was leaving for work when he saw Ben coming in.

"It was like Jimmy Olsen," Cohen told me. "I said, 'Hi Mr. Bradlee.' He looked at me and said, 'Cohen, huh?' I said, 'Yeah. What are you doing here?' I was so surprised. And he said, 'Well, it's Sally's last day, and I promised the kid I'd have a pop with her.'"

Cohen had no idea that Ben was there to seal a much anticipated deal. Mostly he just wondered why he wasn't invited to the party. "I went off and I thought, 'Isn't that nice of him,' you know? 'He's such a thoughtful man.'"

They managed to keep it under wraps for much of the summer and fall of 1973, with Ben making occasional surreptitious afternoon trips to New York but returning to the paper in time for the evening story conference. On one of these trips in the fall, they decided to go out and have lunch at the Tavern on the Green, in Central Park. They didn't want to be spotted, so they took a seat out on the terrace, alone except for a couple of women across the way who were minding their own business.

That afternoon, when Ben got back to the *Post*, Metro editor Harry Rosenfeld sidled into his office and shut the door. "I have it on very reliable sources that you and Quinn—" he started.

"How do you know!" Ben shouted, clearly caught off guard. "How do you know that?"

"I'll never tell you," Rosenfeld said, tongue-in-cheek. "I will never reveal my sources." When Ben incorrectly identified the per-

son who might have ratted him out, Rosenfeld revealed that his own
wife and mother-in-law had been the two ladies out on the patio at
the Tavern on the Green. (When I asked whether he enjoyed this
moment, Rosenfeld told me that he hadn't relished it too much but
felt obliged to give Ben shit, "just to keep the franchise.")

Sally's experiment at CBS would be brief and difficult. She and
morning television were not a match made in heaven; in one particularly uncomfortable moment, she tried to soften a story on exploitive
child labor practices by noting blithely that it reminded her of when
her parents made her clean up her room. Within a couple of months,
she had washed out of morning television and had set her sights on a
return to newspaper journalism, and to the *Post*. Now that their relationship was public Ben couldn't hire her or supervise her, so Howard Simons controlled the process and brought her back to the paper
for good.

There was only one real obstacle during this period: Kay. Because
of her experience with Phil, Kay was never very high on *Post* men
leaving their wives for younger women, and she wasn't keen on
newsroom romances, either. This was both.

"There came a time when I had to tell Katharine Graham about
it, about Sally and I, in her office," Ben told me. "I said, I've got to
tell you that I have—I forgot how I said it, but in effect was saying
that I have started a relationship with someone in the paper. And she
said, 'Oh God, not Sally Quinn.'

"I always interpreted it as saying, who the hell else in the office was
he going to have a relationship with? It wasn't going to be Mary
McGrory," he said, referring to a well-respected but somewhat ma-
tronly columnist who didn't even join the *Post* until 1981. Surely that
had been some part of Kay's reaction, but I thought I detected something deeper and said as much.

"She loved Sally by the end, but she didn't at the beginning," he
conceded.*

---

*In the late seventies, Edward Bennett Williams would tell Halberstam that Kay was "very
pissed" about Sally, "that she was very unhappy when it happened, but she is living with it."

Bradlee,

No one deserves an annonymous [*sic*] letter but until I get securely jobbed elsewhere, this will go unsigned. A couple of years ago any one of us could have walked in and said this to you personally. But, not anymore.

I'm talking about the Sally Quinn deal. Not only do you look like an aging, menopausal Hearst who is turning his newspaper kingdom upside down to flaunt a ten cent canary but the newsroom morale is so polluted now, it is hurting the performance of this newspaper.

The other night at Mary Lou's party bets were being taken on who would be the first to go when your woman comes aboard. You know the ill will Quinn generates around here. . . .

Bringing your bedroom into the newsroom was a bad move. None of us are prudes, Ben, but you've made the Post the brunt of every sick sex joke in town. And, considering what you did to Ben Bagdikian, you should have been smarter. But you don't seem to give a damn about anything anymore. You would be well advised to arrest the rumor that you're going to make your mistress a columnist. That and the reported $42,500 you are paying her is causing ugly vibrations around here, especially since you promised your next employment efforts would be directed to minorities.

Your word is not worth a damn anymore. But you've got all the chips right now. But, that's about all you've got.

Pretty tough, and evidence that Ben started taking shit about Sally right from the start. It hasn't ever let up, not to this day.

Shortly thereafter, another letter came in, from Ben Bagdikian, former *Post* National editor, and his wife, Betty Medsger, a former *Post* reporter. Bagdikian had left his previous wife and taken up with Medsger in 1971, and both felt they had been pushed out of the paper as a result. That letter, dated March 15, 1974:

Dear Ben—

Today we received a copy of an anonymous letter apparently sent to you. Because Bagdikian was mentioned in it we felt compelled to let you know how we feel about it.

The attack on you for your relationship with Sally is stupid and brutal. It has no place in a colleague's professional judgment of either of you. We know how sick that kind of self-righteous condemnation is. When people, including some from the Post, have said similar things we have been disgusted and told them so.

But we would be less than honest if we didn't say that both of us felt the irony of that anonymous letter, given what the Post did to us because of our relationship. . . . Betty, because of this, was pushed out of her job. . . . Afterward, when Betty applied for jobs, highly placed people in the trade knew the story, knew about our relationship and knew, as one put it, "that Katharine Graham didn't like it."

We think of the irony of your being a party to all that cruelty and now having the same thing being done to you and Sally. We think it's ironic but we take no pleasure in it. We're not inspired by what you permitted to happen to us, but we still believe that private lives are no one else's professional business, and we mean no one.

The anonymous letter writer had been on the money: Ben did have all the chips. Different rules applied to him than to other people at the paper, particularly with regard to Kay. Bagdikian would later repeat a tale he had been told, that when somebody mentioned Ben and Sally Quinn with Kay at around this time, she had said, "Well, as Grant needed his liquor, I guess Ben needs his Sally."

Once Ben and Sally became a public couple—and particularly after the movie version of *All the President's Men* came out in April of 1976—they became the target of gossip and public discussion in a way that few people outside politics ever had been. In 1975, *The Washington Star* started a gossip column called "The Ear," run by a woman named Diana McLellan. Though it covered all kinds of D.C. intrigue, "The Ear" reserved a special place in its heart for dirty tidbits out of the O.P. (short for Other Paper), as it called the *Post*—and particularly about Ben and Sally, whom McLellan dubbed the "Fun Couple." Seemingly everywhere the Fun Couple went, every restaurant, every movie, somebody would call the tip in to "The Ear" and it would show up in the newspaper. Sally was often described as Ben's "live-in girlfriend," which felt like a dig at both of them.

This wasn't paparazzi-type coverage, but for mid-seventies Washington it came pretty close. When Sally says that for a time they were like Brad Pitt and Angelina Jolie, it's one of those borderline-crazy-sounding Sally statements that actually turn out to be true.* It got to the point where they didn't want to go out for dinner in public anymore, because of the head turning and whispering and the inevitable gossip item about what one of them had reportedly said at dinner. In his profile of Ben in *Esquire* in 1976, Jim Fallows noted that Ben had been "portrayed in print and on the silver screen as a hero of the nation. On his arm for all to see was one of the certified bitch goddesses of the country." (Sally *loves* that description.) People said and wrote things like that about her, and about them, all the time.

In 1977, "The Ear" reported that a writer trying to sell a piece to *Washingtonian* had "trash-napped" Ben and Sally. Instead of simply reporting that fact, though, "The Ear" went on to list the contents of the "hideously detailed inventory," including ant and roach killer, a get-well card, "a slightly oiled gun-cleaning patch," and "heaven knows what-all, including all *sorts* of odd notes."

Ben hammered out a response to Jim Bellows, the *Star*'s editor, who was a well-respected journalist but also acutely aware of the *Star*'s status as the second paper in town. He had created "The Ear" and enjoyed ribbing Ben, and the *Post*, as much as anybody did. "Printing shit about my garbage is contemptible," Ben wrote, but then he crossed it out. "Poring over anyone's garbage is contemptible enough," he began again, "but your printing shit about the sickie

---

*For readers of a certain age, former *Post* columnist and current ESPN host Tony Kornheiser gave me a more apropos comparison: "When they walked arm in arm, it was like the way people must've felt in a different venue with Richard Burton and Elizabeth Taylor. Everybody knew them. This was well before the Internet. Well before twenty-four-hours television of every stripe. They couldn't walk down the street. Everybody knew Ben Bradlee and Sally Quinn."

who went through mine is a new low—even for you." Ben cc'd Joe
Allbritton, the owner of the *Star*, but then he didn't send it. At the
bottom, he wrote in, by hand, "<u>Not</u> sent, chicken." Somewhat uncharacteristically, he decided to hold his fire.

Jerry Rafshoon, President Carter's communications director at the
White House, told me a story that brought home just how high
Ben's public profile was in the mid- to late seventies. Carter had run
as a man of the people, the clichéd humble peanut farmer, and he was
determined to resist some of the trappings of the "Imperial Presidency." Along those lines, he instructed the military band not to play
"Hail to the Chief" whenever he walked into the room. Rafshoon
thought this was shortsighted. He prevailed upon Carter that "Hail
to the Chief" was an important part of the presidential mystique, that
even if he didn't like it people wanted it and needed it. Eventually,
Carter relented.

Shortly after "Hail to the Chief" made its return to Carter's public
appearances, a reporter asked Carter why the band had started playing it again. As Rafshoon remembers it, Carter pretended to be surprised, feigning ignorance both of its temporary disappearance and of
any private debate about the matter. Instead of answering the question, Carter responded with a quip: "As I understand it, the only time
they play 'Hail to the Chief' in this town is when Ben Bradlee walks
into the newsroom of the *Washington Post*."

Ben had hit it about as big as you can hit it, and Sally only added
to his allure. As Carl put it to me, in the late seventies Ben was "the
most important guy in town outside of the president. Truly. And
with flash and panache that the presidents didn't have, and with a
stability that they didn't have." Carl spent a lot of time with Ben during this period, particularly once Carl's relationship with Sally's friend
Nora Ephron got under way. "Let me tell you," he said to me, "at the
beginning of that relationship [with Sally], I could see Ben become a
whole person in a way that obviously he wanted to and hadn't been."

"Sally is part of the stability," Carl said. "And the stability didn't
exist until those two events, Sally and Watergate. There's a lot of hindsight involved in that; I would never have thought that at the time."

FAME

BENJAMIN CROWNINSHIELD BRADLEE: He is the executive
editor of the Washington <u>Post</u>—a charismatic man of about 50, tough
and bright. An alluring combination of aristocrat and commoner—
Boston Brahmin, Harvard University, WWII Navy, and police-beat
reporter—Ben was once described as looking like an international
jewel thief. Sporting a rooster tatoo [*sic*] on his left arm, he delights in
displaying his street savvy one moment, then rising to greet a visiting
dignitary in flawless French—complete with a peck on each cheek.
He scares everybody with whom he comes in contact, but he does
not mean to. He is courageous in the face of a crisis and is, above all,
a decision maker. His tenacity in pressing his subordinates and the two
reporters, Woodward and Bernstein, was directly responsible for the
ultimate cracking of the Watergate case. 14 pages 13 scenes.

—Casting description from the second draft of the screenplay for *All
the President's Men*, Wildwood Enterprises, September 25, 1974

A COUPLE OF WEEKS BEFORE the official premiere of *All the President's Men* at the Kennedy Center in April of 1976, Robert Redford
held an advance screening for the *Post* brass at the Motion Picture
Association of America, in downtown D.C. Ben and Kay and Bob
and Carl and the rest of the editors sat staggered in the MPAA's private theater, a safe distance from each other. Nobody knew what to
expect. "It was like a fairy tale," Ben told me, "watching a movie
about *you*."

About an hour and a half in, there's a scene in Ben's office where
Robards-as-Ben blows his stack at Woodstein for the umpteenth

time. In the screening room, Kay Graham happened to look over at Ben as that scene began. Robards is leaning back in his chair with his hands behind his head as he receives his briefing from the two reporters. It was a relatively common pose for Ben, and clearly something that Robards (or Pakula) had picked up on and decided to use. As Kay looked over at Ben, she realized that he was sitting in exactly the same position as Robards was, hands on the back of his neck, elbows in the air, leaning back. As she realized it, so did Ben. In a rare moment of self-consciousness, sitting alone in the dark, Ben dropped his hands.

When he arrived at the gala premiere of the film at the Kennedy Center, what amounted to paparazzi at that time lay in wait to take his picture. *The Washington Star*, the *Post*'s main competitor, snapped one of him coming in with Sally. Unaccustomed to this particular kind of spotlight, Ben tried unsuccessfully to hide his face with his hands.

After the movie was over, he could feel the press pushing him toward Robards for the obligatory picture of the two of them together. Ben had prepared some snappy responses ahead of time—he doesn't always just come up with things off the cuff—but as he was being pushed toward Robards he felt suddenly how public his life had become, and how dangerous that could be for a newspaper editor. "This isn't what I do for a living," he remembers thinking. He has always located that precise instant as the beginning of the celebrification of Ben Bradlee, the moment when he realized that they were all going to be bigger than they had ever imagined.

"It is people putting a spotlight on you," Ben told an interviewer in 1991, "and then very soon afterwards, that spotlight is not to illuminate, but it's to fix you and to start examining your flaws . . . to attribute other things to you."

"Did Robards do a good job?"

"Compared to what?"

"The way you feel about yourself."

"Considering two and a half years condensed into an hour and forty minutes, yeah. He didn't do anything that made my flesh crawl," Ben said. Then: "The whole thing made my flesh crawl."

If you ask people in my generation who Ben Bradlee is, many people know. But some will stare at you blankly until you say, "Jason Robards from *All the President's Men*," and then the recognition usually comes pretty quickly. Few Hollywood portrayals of real people have had as lasting an impact, or formed as lasting an association, as *All the President's Men* did with Ben and Jason Robards. Ben knows it as well as anybody else. In a speech in October of 1991, just after he retired from the *Post*, he put Robards on a level of importance to his own life that only one other man shared:

> Think of it, for a minute. All because of two men: Richard Nixon, and Jason Robards. Without them—in this age where celebrities have replaced heroes—it might have been Geraldo Rivera telling you about his sexual conquests. Without them, it wouldn't have been Bradlee.

Ben's original joke was that Redford should play *him* instead of Woodward—true enough—but the casting of Robards proved to be particularly fortuitous, in a way that Ben and even Pakula himself didn't foresee. Pakula initially worried that Robards had played too many losers too convincingly, that he couldn't carry Ben's easy elegance and command authority. Ben initially recommended George C. Scott for the role,* and he was somewhat unimpressed when Robards showed up at the *Post* for a part of one day to spend time with Ben and develop a feel for the newsroom. Hoffman had spent weeks at the paper, shadowing Bernstein, and Redford had been in and out with relative frequency; all Robards had to give was a day. Ben made only one request of Robards in advance of the shoot: "Just don't make me look like an asshole."

---

*Others who were considered: Karl Malden, Hal Holbrook (who would play Deep Throat), John Forsythe, Henry Fonda, Leslie Nielsen, Richard Widmark, Christopher Plummer, Anthony Quinn, Gene Hackman, Burt Lancaster, Robert Stack, Robert Mitchum, and Telly Savalas(!).

He needn't have worried. In May of 1976, after the movie had premiered and the critical raves for Robards-as-Bradlee were in, Robards sat down with Dinah Shore for a televised interview. Right at the top, she told him that the film critic at her station "felt that you stole the picture. I thought you'd like to know that."

"Not true," Robards said.

"You gon' be modest?" Shore asked, all Southern flirt. Then:

DS: The editor in the motion picture is a gentleman, a very dynamic man called Benjamin Bradlee, who is played by my friend Jason Robards here. And I read somewhere that he'd like to get away from the glamour, he'd like to get away from being Jason Robards and go back to being Ben Bradlee for a change. [laughing]

JR: I suppose so. Running a big national daily like that, they have to keep their credibility in a way. They don't want to be thought of as some movie hero or something, and actually we didn't hype this at all. We didn't try any of that. I think they were very pleased about that. But he is a celebrity whether he likes to be or not, you know. He can't help it.

DS: Did you spend a lot of time with Bradlee? Did you get to know him?

JR: No. I had known him, I used to hang around with newspapermen years ago and I had met him in New York a few times at parties, but I never got inside of him or knew him in that way at all. In fact I knew him better after I finished the film—and I still don't know him that well, because his life—he works about eighteen hours a day. You can't get to him. He's always jumping around on all kinds of things all the time.

DS: They really never stop.

JR: No, they never stop . . .

DS: Bradlee was happy with the way you portrayed him, I'm sure.

JR: I guess. He never mentioned a word to me about it. I could tell by his attitude, though. He introduced me to all of his family. Now, I know that it was okay.

DS: But you know there is a resemblance, in the carriage and the attitude . . .

JR: We never strived for it.

Whether he strived for it or not, his resemblance in the film to the essential Ben is uncanny, all editorial flint and casual cool, with the slightest tinge of menace when Bernstein starts to run his mouth. Nobody
else on the screen holds a candle to him, even though Hoffman is
fantastic and all of the minor characters are flawless. The famous statis-
tic is that Robards is on screen for less than ten minutes, but still it was
enough to win him the Academy Award for best supporting actor.*

Robards nailed a basic element of Ben's character—that an operative part of Ben's persona consists of the public performance of
Ben's persona. "We wanted to illustrate how different Bradlee was
from normal editors," Redford once said of Ben's opening scene in
the film, where Robards strides across the newsroom and callously
shoots down one of Woodstein's early Watergate stories. "His self-
confidence, his kind of abrasive gamesman style, his sense of joyful
competitive instinct, but tough. He also liked to perform the toughness, which most people liked." Larry Stern, the zany genius of an
editor and a reporter, put it this way: "When Jason Robards arrived
to play him, you realized he'd been playing himself the whole time.
And later you wondered if Ben was playing Jason Robards playing
Ben Bradlee, or what."

After the movie, whenever Ben strode across the newsroom, it
wasn't just Ben's walk across the newsroom anymore. He'd been
doing it for years, but now even other reporters and editors couldn't
help but experience it in part as Ben's "Jason Robards walk across the
newsroom," as the reporter Scott Armstrong put it to me. People
thought about it.

"It was in their minds," Ben told me, "but I hadn't changed."

Robards's performance also benefited from the fact that the conventions of Hollywood make the story of Watergate easier to tell.
You can convey the powerful core truths without concern for the
prickly edges of facts that don't quite fit. The movie compresses

---

*There was one element of Ben that Robards couldn't quite capture. As Ben's friend, the
writer Peter Stone, put it at Ben's retirement party at Porto Bello in September of 1991, "It
was the first time in the history of film that the real person had more sex appeal than the
actor playing him."

time, elides events, omits important characters—Kay Graham and city editor Barry Sussman most prominent among them—and inflates the roles of others. Not surprisingly, Ben, as Robards portrays him and as the filmmakers conceived of him, comes in for particularly hagiographic treatment: he's essentially God with a blue streak. The game of journalism, as presented in the film, can well be described as learning Robards's standards, discussing Robards's standards, trying to live up to Robards's standards, and then feeling terrible when you fall short of Robards's standards.

"The movie gave everything to Ben," Kay Graham wrote in her memoir, "largely because that made for a simpler story line and because he was played by Jason Robards, but of course that wasn't Ben's fault." It's easy enough to see why the filmmakers, and the film, would gravitate toward Ben. Even before Watergate he was already a star in the journalism world, the outsized personality at the helm of the *Post*. Print pieces referred to him routinely as "the most powerful newspaper editor in the world," and *The Wall Street Journal* had long since run its now legendary and constantly regurgitated description of Ben as "the Hollywood version of an international jewel thief."

When Hollywood actually came calling, he was ready. He spent days with Pakula, and I can only imagine the pixie dust amalgam of dirty jokes and sudden, intense honesty that Ben must have rained down on that unsuspecting man. Pakula got to know the other higher-ups, but the power in the paper was clearly with Ben and Pakula sensed that immediately.

Whenever I think of how the movie turned out, I think of two minor incidents that Ben mentions in passing in his memoir. Twice in his life, once in college and once in the war, casual gambling games with friends turned suddenly serious, with Ben's friends ending up many hundreds of dollars in the hole to him, well beyond their ability to pay. Ultimately, with some prodding from his father and his captain, he forgave the debts. But it is a hallmark of Ben's personality that he won, and that he never lost track of the stakes. With little overt effort Ben always seems to have won competitions that other people didn't realize, or realized only too late, that they were in.

One of the main tensions that the movie and its aftermath magnified at the *Post* was how difficult it was to serve as Ben's number two, as the managing editor of the paper. Though the movie's distortions would have the most wrenching impact on Howard Simons, the truth is that even before the movie came out Ben's subordinates struggled to find roles for themselves within a universe that Ben dominated so completely.

These issues arose as soon as Ben got the top job, in 1968, when he hired Eugene Patterson, the former executive editor of *The Atlanta Constitution*, to serve as his first managing editor. Patterson had been a tank platoon commander with General George Patton's Third Army during World War II, but he had also won a Pulitzer Prize, in 1967, for a series of thoughtful editorials aimed at pushing Southern whites to accept racial equality. He was a top-tier and courageous journalist but, as he put it to me, he "never gained traction" at the *Post*. He was well-liked, and he did his best to make the trains run on time, but eventually he tired of the internal power struggles and realized that a subset of his talents wouldn't ever see the light of day. He left in 1971, spending a year at Duke before moving down to St. Petersburg, Florida, where he had a long and successful run as the executive editor of the *St. Petersburg Times*.

In the late seventies, Patterson sat down with David Halberstam for a series of in-depth interviews for *The Powers That Be*. He saw Ben up close but left before the reputation jockeying that the aftermath of Watergate wrought, and so his critique of Ben rings with a kind of purity that later criticisms don't:

> Says Patterson, I have come in my years to believe finally that every person's strengths in fact bring his weaknesses, and that Bradlee is so strong a figure, so dominates the paper, he wants to have impact, he's so powerful a figure that in effect everybody becomes a kind of minor Bradlee-like creature, everyone plays to him. You know, he is such an absolute chief, that editors under him play to him, rather

than to their own instincts . . . because you want to get points on his
board, and that's the only board that counts there. . . .

He will not lose his temper, but he will never talk in moral terms;
he's exactly like Jack Kennedy in that way, if there's a moral
undercoating he's loath to show it.

He is one of the most sensitive men I've ever met, he has
extraordinary radar, and he has very real humanity. But says
Patterson, he controls his humanity ruthlessly, you know, he protects
himself rigorously against himself. . . .

It is very easy to underestimate Bradlee. When I first [got] there I
thought he was kind of a clever dilettante, but he is ruthless and he
is tough and he is smart and able and very much in charge of the
paper. I made the mistake of thinking that he needed me, and he did
not.

Patterson's famous response, upon being asked why he was leaving
the *Post*, was that "Bradlee needs a managing editor like a boar needs
tits."

Pat Tyler was a reporter under Patterson at the *St. Petersburg Times*
before coming up to the *Post* in 1979, so he knew both Patterson and
Ben pretty well. "Ben was a competitive shark in those days, and you
can't soften that, though we all love him and think of him as a big
cuddly teddy bear today," Tyler told me. "Ben was a mako shark as a
manager, as a newsman, as a person. Tough guy. And he defeated
Gene, drove him off, didn't want him."

When I played this back to Ben, Ben said, "Patterson was very
deceptive. He was like a major, and he barked and was small and
therefore like many people who are small he threw his weight
around a little bit. Totally different from Howard. And they didn't
get along at all." Tyler had told me that Patterson was the kind of
guy who would rally the troops in martial terms, "We're going to
take this hill!" that sort of thing. Ben agreed. "And that doesn't
work at *The Washington Post*," he said. "He didn't have the support,
that hard-to-define support that makes people want to work for
you."

Unmentioned was the fact that Ben hadn't given him that support himself.

After Patterson left the *Post*, he and Ben maintained a high regard for each other. In 1995, as part of his national book tour to promote *A Good Life,* Ben made a stop at Eckerd College in St. Petersburg. Patterson introduced him. "He ran the paper," Patterson said, "and he was pretty good at it. I was a paper pusher, basically, and I was pretty punk at that. I had a nice title. But would YOU like to manage the Yankees under George Steinbrenner? . . .

"This is not a modest man we have here," Patterson went on. "He is not one to shrink from glory. But as Dizzy Dean reminded us, 'It ain't braggin' if you done it.'"

Where Patterson had been perhaps too much like Ben to succeed, Howard Simons was, until the movie tore them apart, the perfect complement to Ben. Temperamentally and culturally he couldn't have been more different—reflective, intellectual, Jewish, born of humble origins in Albany, paid his way through Union College by washing dishes at a fraternity house. He started at the *Post* as a science reporter but quickly worked his way up into becoming an editor, and he was famous at the paper for conceiving of, and then running, what was known as the SMERSH team: Science, Medicine, Education, Religion, and all that SHit. All the stuff, basically, that Ben had no interest in.

After Patterson resigned and Ben pulled Simons into his orbit, the two of them clicked. "We didn't have to finish each other's sentences," Ben once said. "I mean, I knew how he felt. It was extraordinary. And he me. I knew what he was going to say. I literally did." They became so close that each volunteered to serve as the guardian to the other's children should anything befall either of them.

"Ben sucks the flowers dry and Howard waters them back to life" is how Kay Graham once put it. "Howard flushes out the rat and Bradlee swoops down and pounces" is how Pakula characterized it to himself in his own notes. Whatever metaphor you want to use, the paper couldn't have been what it was at its peak without both of them. Ben allowed Simons to run the story conference, ceding most of the daily responsibility for the newspaper to Howard and concerning himself with the bigger picture of running the *Post*, which meant worrying more about next month's newspaper than the next morning's.

It was Simons who received the call on Saturday, June 17, 1972, from Joe Califano, mentioning something about a break-in at the Watergate. It was Simons who approached Barry Sussman in July of 1972 with the *New York Times*'s scoop in his hand and said, "Why didn't we have that?" It was Simons who, according to Haynes Johnson, *explained* Watergate to Ben at first—why it mattered, how it all worked. He was the highest-ranking editor to take an abiding interest in Watergate for much of the story's development, often dropping by Woodstein's desks first thing in the morning to encourage them, pester them, and keep them moving.

None of this makes it into the movie, though Simons does get credit for coming up with "Deep Throat" as the interoffice handle for Bob's secret source. Rosenfeld gets most of the inspirational stuff, the badgering, and most of the doubt gets consolidated in the godhead of Robards. Martin Balsam–as–Simons functions mostly as a kind of schlubby henchman for Robards, not as a force in his own right. He can't seem to do anything without checking with Robards first. But what rankled Simons the most, and the people who knew him well, was that in his first important scene, he listens to Rosenfeld describing the White House connection to the bugging attempt and then says, "Harry, this isn't a police story anymore. This is national, we need a top political writer on it."

Those two sentences were the hammer blow that undid Simons, the step too far into Hollywood oversimplification that ruined his relationship with Ben for the rest of his life. Ben would say later, publicly and privately, that he never thought seriously about taking the story away from "the boys," but it's apparent that at various points he at least entertained the idea. Certainly his surrogate, National editor Dick Harwood, entertained the idea. At one point Harwood and Len Downie, then a Metro editor, had a shouting match about it on the newsroom floor. Harry Rosenfeld told me that he remembers quite clearly a day in October of 1972, as the Watergate story was taking off, when Ben called him into his office and insisted that National run the story from there on out.

There's no paper trail in which Simons argues strenuously for letting Woodstein keep the story, so all I have to go on is the outrage that others expressed after the fact. Simons himself told Halberstam in the late seventies, "There were a couple of times when Bradlee said he would take the story away from the kids and go national. And he felt they were not quite big enough, I mean he had hitters like Harwood, Broder, and Johnson. And I said in effect, 'Over my dead body.'"

"[Howard] is a victim of Watergate," Richard Cohen would say later. "In the movie, for instance, it's Ben Bradlee who says 'Let the kids stay on the story.' In real life it was Howard."

As Barry Sussman put it in his own book, *The Great Cover-Up,* "When the time came it was Simons—not Bradlee or the others— who made the crucial early decisions that led to the *Post's* extraordinary coverage of the Watergate scandal, especially the decision to allow the metropolitan staff, which did not normally report on national politics, to pursue the story." Sussman and Simons and others at the *Post* felt that Pakula and Redford had willfully distorted the truth to benefit Robards's character.

"He never forgave me for it," Ben told Kay years later. "Somehow thought it was my problem or I caused it. It ruined our relationship."

I asked Ben if he and Howard ever talked about the movie after it came out, about the way in which Howard felt wronged.

"Well, it's too long ago for me to be sure," Ben told me. "I thought that we did somehow, but not exhaustively, not so that we tore down the problem and went on."

I doubted that they had, given what I'd found in the files—a batch of memos and letters from Ben to Howard that said "not sent" or "never sent" on them. Ben isn't one to hold back. The fact that more than one of these unsent memos existed indicated to me that there were things left unsaid between them.

The first of them was from 1977, a year after the movie came out, a private memo to Don and Kay Graham titled "Secret Thoughts," with "NEVER SENT" written on it in BCB's hand, above the word "<u>CONFIDENTIAL</u>":

> These thoughts are prompted in the immediate instance by your several reports that 1) a morale problem may be developing as a result of some vague Bradlee-Simons complications. . . .
>
> Let me ramble for a minute, first about Bradlee and Simons. We have an extraordinary relationship; we don't have to finish sentences; we think of the same things at the same time without warning. We complement each other uniquely, I think. The executive editor-managing editor system requires this complementing. Two Simonses would not do the job, and two Bradlees would be chaos. All of this said, we do bristle at each other occasionally—always for the same reason: neither of us is willing to be unimportant. If the executive editor really asserts his presence and his authority to "run" the paper, the managing editor becomes a staff assistant implementing decisions of someone else. (Gene [Patterson] and I experienced some of this). If the managing editor really tries to manage and edit, the executive editor becomes ceremonial. (Russ [Wiggins] and I might have experienced this, if he had not been so much older and so preoccupied with the [editorial] page).
>
> So Bradlee and Simons bristle at each other every so rarely. Maybe it bothers some of the extraordinarily sensitive souls we have collected under this roof. But you must remember we are a team, an extraordinary team, I would guess. You can look at the record, as Mr. Casey Stengel used to say. Under this team (and for lots of reasons, to be sure, like luck and unbelievable support from you), the editorial product of this newspaper is more widely respected than any other paper in this country.

David Maraniss, the longtime *Post* reporter and bestselling author, first came to the Metro staff at the paper right around the time that Ben decided not to send this first memo. "I knew nothing about the history of the internal dynamics of the paper," he told me, "but from the moment I got there I could feel a certain tension between Howard and Ben—from Howard's perspective, not Ben's."

I told him a story I'd heard from another reporter, who had referred to Ben as being a kind of "bugaboo" in Howard's mind.

"It's more than a bugaboo," Maraniss said. "I mean, I think that Ben was like Moby Dick to Howard. It was really the dominant frustration of his life, in some ways. . . . He felt Ben was lucky and he wasn't, and Ben was golden and he wasn't, and Ben was all of those things, you know? Ben was Brahmin and he was Jewish. I think every possible way that you could view an insider and an outsider, Howard felt himself as the outsider."

It's clear that some of these resentments had been in place before Watergate, and before the movie, but the movie and its tilt toward Ben pushed Howard into a realm from which he could not return. He had always resented Ben's privilege and untouchability—and he was certainly not alone in that. "I mean, his old man was a schlep insurance agent in Albany, broke all the time," Ben once said, "and here I was with this bent silver spoon. But we were really kindred souls in a good way, and I rescued him from obscurity to make him managing editor . . . and he resented it terribly. Resented the fact that Sally and I were together. Resented the fact that I had known Kennedy and he hadn't. That I had written a book and he hadn't. That I—he just resented it. As a result his life was miserable."

That Howard took some of these resentments out on Sally was commonly known around the paper. He would tell others, after Sally had been rehired in 1973, "She shouldn't be here. Ben made me hire her." As Bernstein put it during the late seventies: "Howard in the last year has shown a real talent for self-destruction. . . . [H]e's taken on as a project the needling of Sally Quinn, which is not something you do." The needling took many forms, from pretending he didn't see her at parties to keeping her off choice assignments and even grounding her once, in the middle of a campaign, when she submitted an expense account form late—a stiff penalty for a relatively common infraction. Simons would not be the first or the last to take out some of his repressed feelings about Ben on Sally.

By 1980, things had progressed to the point where Ben wrote and then decided not to send another memo, this one addressed directly to Simons:

> . . . I would like to have a serious conversation with you about your future, and our relationship. What that relationship has deteriorated to, and how it's going to change when you return.
>
> As far as I can determine, I am going to be here for another five years. During this time, there is a certain amount of shit that I am going to put up with, and there is a definite amount of shit I am not going to put up with.
>
> In the former category, I include a whole series of actions on your part, which appear from where I sit to have the sole purpose of feeding your ego, making you feel more important. I would like to talk to you about these actions, because I want to be sure you know what you are doing.
>
> In the latter category, I include another series of actions on your part, which appear from where I sit to be unforgiveably and inexplicably rude, selectively vindictive, and disloyal. Here, I'd like to know why as well as what.*
>
> I think I know what bugs you, why you are so resentful. I have tried sincerely to accommodate your concerns, by giving you responsibilities which I would much rather have kept. In the first place, I gave you the job, and provoked the departure of the incumbent to do it.† I gave you story conference. I decided against holding my own weekly staff meeting, when you told me that would undermine your influence.

---

*Ben doesn't remember the exact context of the grievances in this memo, but Tom Wilkinson took one look at this particular graf and said, "That's about Sally."

†Gene Patterson told me that Simons began undermining him—"planting knives in me"—as soon as Patterson arrived in 1968, because Simons had wanted to be the managing editor and had been passed over. Animosities mounted to the point where Ben was forced to choose between the two men, and in 1971 he chose Simons. In the eighties, Patterson attended a party at Ben's house in Georgetown. As he remembered it to me, Ben approached him at one point during the evening and said, "You were right about Howie. He turned out to be a real pain in the ass."

If all of that is not enough, we are in trouble.

Let's talk—away from the glass windows, at lunch on the 13th.

Tom Wilkinson, the former head of personnel at the paper, often played referee between Howard and Ben. "For a while, they didn't talk," he told me. "One of the most difficult times I had at the paper was trying to navigate that." Ben would call Wilkinson into his office, and when he saw Simons coming he would shut the door to keep him out. Then Simons would collar Wilkinson later in the day and ask, "What did Ben say? What's going on?" Wilkinson suggested on numerous occasions that the two men rent a room at the Madison, across the street from the *Post*, and have it out with each other, but they never did it.

The final indignity for Howard was the day Kay Graham told him he wouldn't succeed Ben as executive editor of the paper. He had desperately wanted to be next. "My mother for whatever reasons chooses to share this with Howard," Don Graham told me, "probably thinking, 'I'm doing him a favor, better he learns now than after Ben quits.' It destroyed him."

Ben agrees. "He left because he didn't succeed me," he told me.

Simons left the *Post* in 1984 and went to work for the Nieman Foundation at Harvard. In 1989, he was diagnosed with pancreatic cancer, and the prognosis was awful. He didn't have long to live. Pat Tyler was in Cairo, working as a foreign correspondent for the *Post*, when Simons received his diagnosis, and he called Simons to say goodbye.

"We visited for about five minutes on the phone, signing off, you know, for the last time," Tyler told me. "He said, 'Pat, just remember, you wrote to me first.'" Tyler explained that when he had first applied for a job at the *Post* in the seventies, he had sent his résumé to Howard, not to Ben. I couldn't quite believe that Simons would have chosen to mention something so small in a moment so large, but Tyler looked right at me and made it clear. "The thing with Ben was still the thing that drove him into eternity," he said.

When Simons died, Ben was quoted in the *Times* obituary as saying, "He got short-changed by the movie," that Simons had "led the charge" on Watergate. Gracious, if a little late. For Simons's part, even despite all the difficulty that got loaded onto their relationship, he still managed to refer to Ben on multiple occasions as "the classiest human being I've ever known."

And yet his pain about what had happened to him, his perception that life had dealt him a bad hand, was real and enduring. Simons told an interviewer in the late seventies that on the day of the preview screening of *All the President's Men*, Alan Pakula had called him and said, "I hope you understand why we did what we did, I'd love to come back and explain."

Simons responded, "That's all right, Alan. My children know who I am."

Those two sentences break my heart every time I read them.

Though the movie hastened the fatal deterioration of the relationship between Howard and Ben, Pakula sensed the dynamic before he ever shot a frame. From his notes to himself, before shooting began:

Simons always behind Bradlee (sun) Eternally eclipsed.

HIS NIBS

Mr. Bradlee,
Recently on TV there have been film clips of the new movie "All
The President's Men" with Jason Robards playing the part of Ben
Bradlee.

I hope, to be authentic, when the full picture is shown, it shows
Ben Bradlee eating shit, specifically, Kennedy shit which you so
dearly relish. My hope is that you get a malignant cancer in your
gut, and die a slow death, you miserable cock-sucker.

Sincerely,

—Longhand letter from an admirer, April 11, 1976

WHEN NIXON RESIGNED THE PRESIDENCY in the summer of
1974, the natural question for Ben and for the *Post*—if not for the
whole country—was what would come next. Two years of unstinting Watergate reporting had taken its toll on everybody at the paper,
including Ben and Howard. During the summer of 1973, Ben had
developed a problem with his left eye, which began fluttering and
closing. For ten days he underwent a series of neurological tests,
and at one point doctors thought it might be a fatal tumor; it turned
out to be stress. Howard liked to tell the story that the weekend
after Nixon resigned, his wife turned to him and said, "You're really very relaxed today. I want you to know something. You've been
a son of a bitch for two years."

And so, immediately after Nixon resigned, Kay offered Ben and
Howard three months of paid leave. The next weekend, Ben drove
out to his country place in West Virginia and spent roughly three
weeks there by himself. He spent every morning at the typewriter on

the front porch, cranking out pages, and every afternoon in the woods, clearing his mind. When he returned after twenty-three days away, he brought with him forty thousand words that would form the bulk of his first book,* *Conversations with Kennedy*, which was published in June of 1975.

Ben had always maintained that he was never going to write it at all. In 1969, when George Vaillant came down to Washington to interview Ben for the Grant Study, Ben confessed that with the Kennedys he and Tony had "started to protect our friends, and it's bad for a journalist to have too many friends. You can't let friendship interfere with history." He made it quite plain that he had no intention of using his private notes of his visits with Kennedy for personal gain. "I was offered a fortune for the notes," Ben told Vaillant. "I decided I would give them to my child as a patrimony."

In 1990, when he was getting ready to write his memoir, Ben sat down for another extended interview with Vaillant, this time up in Cambridge. Vaillant returned to the same subject, wondering why Ben had changed his mind:

> V: You were going to give that to your kids as a legacy . . . if you were going to give away the store, what made you decide?
> B: I had had it with Nixon. Nixon had dominated my life for three years, '72, '73, '74, and when he quit, when it became obvious that it was going to end, I wanted to do something totally different. Totally, totally different . . . It seemed to me that [writing a book about Kennedy] would be entirely different and immeasurably better.

That's the only reason Ben ever gave me, too—that after Nixon resigned, he wanted to do something different. He hadn't looked at his notes about his various interactions with Kennedy—some 125 separate encounters in all—since before the assassination. With a paid three-month leave in hand, Ben had time to tackle something new.

It's curious that Ben would decide to deliver a book about his

---

*That Special Grace, Ben's prose poem about Kennedy written for *Newsweek*, was issued as a book in 1964 but hadn't been written as one.

closeness to JFK on the heels of three years of opprobrium from the Nixon people casting him as a "Kennedy coatholder" and Democratic partisan. The reaction of Ben's letter-writing admirer ("you miserable cock-sucker"), while extreme, wasn't unique in its savagery. The first sentence of Taylor Branch's review of the book in *Harper's* magazine in October of 1975 reads, "Ben Bradlee, executive editor of the *Washington Post*, recently delivered himself of one of the most pathetic memoirs yet written by an American journalist about his President." Others were similarly uncharitable. Ben's old friend Jim Fallows wrote in *Esquire* in 1976:

> It was not the coziness with Kennedy which offended but the shallowness of the portrayal and Bradlee's seeming obliviousness to how poor a light it cast on him. Bob Woodward, who admired Bradlee as much as anyone in the newsroom, did not read the book because he had heard bad things about it and was afraid they were true.

I asked Bob about that, because it had cropped up in a couple of places.

"I read it, but I read it very late, many years later," he said. He didn't want to go too far. "I certainly didn't read it at the time, and I guess I didn't want to." While Ben was working on *Conversations with Kennedy*, Bob and Carl had already finished *All the President's Men* and were hard at work on *The Final Days*, the follow-up, and also on the movie. Bob had been busy.

"As I recall the book when I did read it," he went on, "is, it's empirical. Here are my notes. He went to the White House this night, Jackie said this, Tony said this . . . it was like raw data." That was the problem that most reviewers had with it, too: it was just data, without much hint of awareness or purpose. "I know he did it real quick . . . and quite frankly, I think, you know, he was the editor during Watergate, he wasn't the reporter. And he's basically a reporter, you realize that." Bob paused, wanting to be sure I understood him. "And so this was kind of his statement, 'Hey, look, I was there, I'm a reporter, too.'"

That made more sense as a motivation than Ben's insistence that he just wanted to do something different. The movie hadn't come out yet; Ben had no idea that Robards would immortalize him. Writing the book, giving the inside dope on Kennedy—that was a way to keep himself out there, to capitalize on Watergate in a personal way.

"What I remember," Bob went on, "is that it showed Jack Kennedy was just a first-class gossip. He really wanted to know about so-and-so, who's doing this, who's shtupping who."

"And Ben is very, they're very similar."

"And that's Ben," Bob said.

Ben doesn't understand the criticism of *Conversations with Kennedy*, for the most part. His rote response is that what went into the book is exactly what he put into his notes—true, but also the source of many of the book's problems. It's hard to separate the critical reaction to *Conversations with Kennedy* from what must surely have been widespread jealousy of Ben after the successes of Watergate. But whether there were axes to grind or not, critics identified real flaws. Taylor Branch, again:

> Bradlee seems resolutely oblivious to the possibility that, to eyes less bedazzled than his own, his portrait might be a betrayal—a betrayal above all of the limited capacity of charm to redeem character. Kennedy is seen as graceful and witty, but he is shown as petty and vindictive. Kennedy is seen as gay and sophisticated, but shown to be grim and resentful. . . .
>
> It is as if [Bradlee] were stricken by some sort of emotional dyslexia, in which he tells stories of dirt and discomfort but sees only race and wit. His book is either a failed tribute or an unwitting catharsis of Bradlee's illusions, and these twisted meanings come hard upon painful journeys to the drawing rooms and living quarters of the New Frontier. The book is, of course, a best-seller.

Tough stuff, but Branch properly identifies the problem at the heart of the book: the book isn't what Ben thinks it is. In it, he's not doing what he thinks he's doing. What he thinks he's doing is presenting an unvarnished version of his interactions with President Kennedy, thereby shedding new light on the casual, fun side of a man he loved. As he wrote of it in his memoir, "The critics would find the book interesting, but too admiring of Kennedy, not critical enough. I had no intention of writing a critical biography. I had wanted simply to tell what the president and his wife were like when they were relaxed and among friends. Someone I admired had once wished aloud for such a book by some friend of Lincoln's."

From the outset Ben can't seem to resolve a fundamental question, one that he poses at the top but then resolutely fails to answer: "What, in fact, was I? A friend, or a journalist?" The honest engagement of that question would have made for an interesting book, but Ben doesn't take it on. Instead he simply lays out the sum total of his interactions with Kennedy, the raw data, and leaves it to the reader to make the inferences for himself.

Of a trip to Hyannisport: "Apparently the cook was under instructions to have an endless supply [of chowder] on hand in case His Nibs wanted a snack. We watched in fascination as he gulped down four large bowls, one after the other. In anyone else it would have been gluttonous." Harmless enough, and certainly a way for Ben to show, early on in the book, that he wasn't too taken in by the Kennedy mystique. But seeing it, I was reminded of something Ben had said to Arthur Schlesinger some years before during his joint interview with Tony:

B: Jack used to really—first he started showing up about 9:30 or after, and then he used to start showing up earlier, calling up earlier and wondering if lunch or dinner was going to be available. That was the first collision with his eating habits, which were just appalling . . .

AB: We used to feed him in the kitchen. We did at least twice.

Q: How do you mean, appalling?

B: Because he wanted steak and baked potatoes and corn and cake. . . . No variation of this was allowed for very long. . . .

He was terribly vain in the Esquire kind of way. And I remember him coming over here, with his own cocktail shaker full of . . . God, that sounds funny for the President, doesn't it? With his own cocktail

shaker full of daiquiris, and very breezily sort of walking through, out
into our garden, shaking with one hand, sort of right out of the pages
of Town and Country, and whoops!—the whole bottom of the cocktail shaker went out onto his pants. And he immediately refused the
offer that we could make him a daiquiri here, but went right back to
his house to change his pants . . .

AB: It wasn't vanity.

Aggression-tinged moments like that abound in *Conversations with
Kennedy*. Ben rarely refuses a chance to stick it to his old friend, on
matters great and small. When Kennedy finds fault with *Newsweek*'s
coverage of Jackie's trip to India—"That wasn't one of your better
efforts," he tells Ben—Ben can't help but note that Kennedy's reaction had been "critical, this time, not just thin-skinned." Poke.

Vanity: "I remarked that he had put on a little weight. Few things
interest him more than a discussion of his own weight."

On a picture of himself that Kennedy doesn't like: " 'It shows the
Fitzgerald breasts,' he said . . . and in fact it did show the future president with some extra mammary protuberance."

On Kennedy's view of *The Washington Star*'s imbalanced coverage
of two separate issues of the day: "A little simplistic, I thought; the
problem is more complicated than that, but it was an interesting
point."

On LBJ: "This seemed a little petty of Kennedy. . . . There are
times—like tonight—when LBJ's simple presence seems to bug him.
It's not very noble to watch, and yet there it is."

His characterization of the Kennedy children is particularly
passive-aggressive. There isn't a mention of John-John in particular
that isn't tinged, somehow, with a kind of genteel horror:

If you throw your head back in mock surprise, John-John roars with
laughter until he drools. Kennedy keeps urging me to pick John-
John up and throw him in the air, because he loves it so, and because
Kennedy himself can't do it because of his back. "He doesn't know
it yet," the president said, "but he's going to carry me before I carry

him." Caroline came into the room with her wretched little dog. (p. 159)

At one point John-John careened into the small table on which the ambassador's drink was sitting, and dumped it smack into his lap. Tony and I were the only ones embarrassed. (p. 169)

Asked by an interviewer in 1975 why he had written the book, Ben gave a different answer from his standard "wanted to do something different" routine, an answer that comes closer to the spirit of the book than what he has said about it since:

If there was a philosophical point to it, it was to debunk the idea of Camelot. I mean, if you want to be pompous and serious, I think America is ill-served by its love for heroes. I think sometimes we're too comfortable with the heroic explanations of men and the things they do. That's not the way things are.

The point of Ben's book, and it succeeds in this, is to show that JFK was human. Yet aside from the details that Ben delivers—Kennedy cursed all the time, was far more infirm than anybody knew, loved gossip, was petty, might have rigged the Illinois presidential election— you really don't get any sense of what one reviewer called "the essential Kennedy." The pointillist accumulation of detail never quite coheres into a whole, unless you switch your frame of reference. Jackie got that part right away. When Ben eventually showed her a copy of the book in advance of publication, the first words she said were, "It tells more about you than it does about him."

You can't put everything you know into a book. You have to decide what story you're telling, which part of "true" you want to stick with. You hope the facts you do include can double as clues for the ones that you don't.

There is a lot left unsaid in Ben's book about Kennedy. The stunner is that Kennedy was screwing Ben's sister-in-law, Mary Meyer, for the last two years of his presidency, a fact Ben never mentions in the book. He claims at the outset of *Conversations with Kennedy* that "I never wrote less than I knew about him," but either he's lying or he's having fun with tenses. Such a statement might have been true in 1963, but it certainly wasn't true in 1974.

His justification for not including Kennedy's affair with Mary Meyer in the book is facile: "I didn't have a conversation with Kennedy about it." But it's also, apparently, true. He and Kennedy never talked about it, and while Kennedy was alive Ben had no knowledge of the affair. In 1974, when Ben sat down to write the book, most of Kennedy's indiscretions were still only rumors, and none of Kennedy's close associates had made on-the-record allegations about his infidelity. "My rule used to be if private behavior didn't interfere with public business, then it stayed private," Ben told an interviewer in 1995. There is a kind of omerta there that a man of Ben's generation would have had a hard time bucking just to sell books. So he left it out.

But he leaves clues:

> And then suddenly: "You haven't got it, Benjy. You're all looking to tag me with some girl, and none of you can do it, because it just isn't there." Jackie just listened with a smile on her face. And that is the closest I ever came to hearing him discuss his reputation as what my father used to call "a fearful girler." (p. 49)

> The conversation ended, as these conversations often ended, with his views on some of the women present—the overall appeal of the daughter of Prince Paul of Yugoslavia and Mary Meyer. "Mary would be rough to live with," Kennedy noted, not for the first time. And I agreed, not for the first time. (p. 54)

> We had met the Kennedys in the upstairs hall, and Jackie had greeted my wife bluntly, saying "Oh, Tony, you look terrific. My bust is bigger than yours, but then so is my waist." The females

> imported from New York for the occasion had been spectacular
> again, and at one point Kennedy had pulled me to one side to
> comment "If you and I could only run wild, Benjy." (p. 147)

It's all there: we never talked about it, Kennedy made an oddly inti-
mate comment about Mary, and Kennedy also kept his eye out for
attractive ladies and wished he could run wild. Ben was leaving bread
crumbs so that when the truth finally emerged he'd have his ass covered.

Ben didn't take that approach purely out of loyalty to his friend.
The entire Mary Meyer saga had taken a macabre turn when she was
murdered in October of 1964—less than a year after the president—
while walking along the towpath of the C&O Canal in Georgetown.
Witnesses fingered a slight black man who was found down an em-
bankment from the scene of the crime, shivering in the water, but he
was eventually acquitted. Given Mary's relationship with Kennedy,
and the fact that her ex-husband, Cord Meyer, had been relatively
high up in the CIA, people have since suspected that the CIA had
something to do with it.

It's one of those conspiracy theories that never quite get off the
ground. But what gives the CIA angle some credence is that, after
the funeral, one of Mary's friends called Tony and told her that Mary
had instructed her to retrieve a diary of hers should anything happen
to her. Mary's friend, Anne Truitt, was in Tokyo, so she asked Tony
to look for it. When Ben and Tony arrived at Mary's house the next
morning, they unlocked the door and walked in only to find that
James Angleton, the CIA's chief of counterintelligence, had already
made his way inside. He was a family friend, and he, too, was looking
for the diary. They all searched together, but nobody found it. Later
that same day, Ben and Tony realized that they ought to search the
converted garage behind their own house, which Mary had been
using as a studio. When they arrived, there was James Angleton again,
trying to pick the lock to the door. "I collared him," Ben said later,
"and said, 'You get the fuck out. In the first place, you're breaking
the law.'"

It's strange enough that Angleton was there. What happens next is even stranger: after finding the diary in Mary's studio, and realizing that it contained references to a love affair with the president of the United States, Ben and Tony decided that they would follow Mary's instructions, which called for the diary's destruction, by giving that diary to *James Jesus Angleton*. Full stop. The two pages that describe this encounter in Ben's memoir are the only two pages that still feel fishy to me. The reason Ben gives: "[H]e promised to destroy it in whatever facilities the Central Intelligence Agency had for the destruction of documents. It was naïve of us, but we figured they were state of the art." A guy who had been snooping around, and who worked for the CIA, and whom you tell to get the fuck out, is the guy you give it to for safekeeping and destruction?*

Apparently the diary was filled with paint swatches—Meyer was a painter—and only a few written passages. Ben says there's no "thrusting and heaving," but Tony did once acknowledge that there were some "JFK's" in it. In Ben's files at the Kennedy Library I uncovered a late draft of *A Good Life* with some of Ben's notations on it. Written in by hand next to Ben's description of the diary, but omitted from the final work, was this sentence: "I remember only one phrase: 'He says I am the only woman he kissed while making love,' or words to that effect."

After *Conversations with Kennedy* came out, Ben heard from Jim Truitt, Anne Truitt's husband. Jim Truitt had been the first editor of the Style section and a close friend of Phil Graham's, but he had left the *Post* in 1969 and in the years since had had a nervous breakdown. He felt that Ben and Kay and others at the paper had done him

---

*Even stranger: Angleton didn't actually destroy the diary. He kept it, and only disclosed that fact years later, when Tony asked him point-blank how he'd destroyed it. Tony retrieved it from him and burned it herself. "You have to think that he didn't do it because he wanted to retain some kind of control over somebody," Ben told Barbara in 1990—but over whom, or for what reason, nobody knows. There are people who have claimed over the years that Ben worked for the CIA, and who see the Angleton episode as supplementary evidence. I don't buy it. (A CIA memo from February 18, 1971, based on internal reports of Ben's years in Paris: "A reliable source described Bradlee as an unscrupulous, ambitious individual who has no sense of security and little sense of discretion. He is in constant personal and financial difficulties, drinks heavily, talks too much and is emotionally unstable.")

wrong during his departure and its aftermath, and apparently he was still bitter.

In September of 1975, he sent Ben a threatening postcard expressing some surprise that Ben had turned away a *National Enquirer* reporter "who just wanted to ask about your sister in law banging JFK, the diary, etc." In February of 1976, Truitt again turned to the *National Enquirer*, and this time the story of Meyer's affair with Kennedy ran, both in the *Enquirer* and the next day in the *Post*. According to the *Enquirer*'s researcher, Truitt had exposed the affair to show Ben up. "Here is this great crusading Watergate editor who claimed to tell everything in his Kennedy book," Truitt is alleged to have said, "but really told nothing."

It's a tangled situation, one that nobody will ever plumb fully. But the existence of Kennedy's relationship with Mary had caused Ben to do some reevaluating of his own, as he told Barbara Feinman privately in the interviews for his memoir:

BF: Were [Tony and Mary] real close?

B: Yes. I think they had sort of overtones of being rivals.

BF: Was one prettier than the other?

B: They were both awfully pretty. I mean Tony Bradlee was a lovely woman. She was spectacular looking and in those days so full of sparkle and energy and dancing on the top of tables. Very romantic. But I think in the old days Mary used to sort of just to keep her hand in used to try to swipe boyfriends. There came a time—Tony and I took forever to get married because I was living in Europe and she was living here and it took two and a half years. And there was a time when I felt that Mary was making a play for me and just for the sheer joy of it. Not for any great love, just thought it would be fun to see if she could break it up. That was in Paris and you know rules seem to be changed . . . anyway, it never happened. And I think that I always thought that Tony obviously had kind of a crush on Kennedy too and that it really sort of rocked her what she had had from a distance, Mary went through the red light and grabbed.

BF: So Tony was angry at her in death?

B: I think so, a little bit. I don't know, it's more complicated than that.

Mary Meyer and Tony Bradlee exiting *Marine One* at Grey Towers, the
Pinchot estate, Milford, Pennsylvania, September 1963

In October of 2008, presidential historian Michael Beschloss appeared on NBC's *Nightly News with Brian Williams* to discuss an interview that Ben and his then colleague at *Newsweek*, Jim Cannon, had
conducted with presidential hopeful John F. Kennedy on January 5,
1960. (Cannon had been working on a book about presidential politics and had asked Ben to line up the interview.) Williams heralded it
as the "audiotape of an extraordinary conversation just discovered
that everyone, including members of the Kennedy family, will be
hearing tonight along with us for the first time." The segment that
Williams aired focused on Kennedy's absorption with politics, and
with the fact that he seemed privately to be more worried about losing the nomination than he did publicly.

"You rewind the tape," Beschloss told Williams, "you go back to
the time before he was president, he wasn't even sure he was going

to get elected. He didn't see himself as a grand historical figure. He had some of the same fears and anxieties that the rest of us do."

Shortly after the broadcast, audio copies of the interview and an official transcript arrived at Ben's office. Having seen the news segment, I read the transcript casually but felt no great sense of urgency about any of it. I figured that Beschloss and Williams had milked out all of the interesting bits.

A couple of months later, I ran into Beschloss at a party at Ben and Sally's. We talked about the Kennedy interview, and then he asked me if I'd listened to the tape.

"I've read the transcript," I offered.

"Listen to the tape," he said.

As soon as I put my headphones on I understood why. As the recording comes up, you hear Cannon saying "Testing, testing," and then Ben's voice, impossibly deep: "Tell 'em about school." Tony's young daughter, Tammy, starts talking about making a calendar but grows shy. Cannon invites Rosamond, another stepdaughter of Ben's, to give it a try. She squeaks out "Writing!" but doesn't have much else to say either. We are transported back to Ben's living room, circa 1960. The tape recorder whooshes into silence, then whooshes back into life—this was a reel-to-reel job—landing hard on the unmistakable voice of JFK: "You can't overestimate the egoism of children, can you?"

It's a wonderful recording, an hour and sixteen minutes, from JFK's dining room at 3307 N. You can hear the ice in the glasses, the silverware clattering on the plates, Tony and Jackie carrying on side conversations and giggling with each other while the men get down to business.

The first thing I noticed was how Ben and Kennedy talked to each other. You can *hear* their closeness. JFK completes Ben's sentences, anticipates Ben's questions, talks about Ben's work and career aspirations in a way that reflects real intimacy. They kid around with each other in the free and easy way of people who spend a fair amount of time together.

I also realized fairly quickly that the official transcript wasn't accurate—or, I should say, not complete. A good deal of the conversation hadn't been transcribed, many of the more human and gossipy bits:

> B: But Jack, you preserve your energy very well. Just noticing you on that one trip, you lasted a hell of a lot better than I did.
>
> [Woman]: [Ben] got more sleep, didn't he?
>
> JFK: Yeah, he did, but he was up drinking all night.

Kennedy is surprisingly dismissive of Jackie. In response to a question about other career paths he might have taken, Kennedy says, "I will say there was never any emphasis on my going into business. Never."

Jackie chimes in, "Which he really would have liked."

"No he *wouldn't* have," Kennedy snaps. "I was completely uninterested in it." There is a moment of confusion, and then he says, with some derision, "Why don't you sit in there," clearly pointing to a different room.

"We like it, Jack!" Jackie pleads.

"We like to be with our men," Tony says. A different era. But Tony is uncowed. A few minutes later: "Could I ask a question?"

"Sure," JFK says. He says it very sweetly, slowly, with none of the impatient scorn he'd shown Jackie.

"Is being president the ultimate of everybody's ambition?"

"I suppose being head of whatever organization you're in, I suppose is that, but most importantly is the fact that the president today is the seat of all power." He takes her question seriously. "I worked for two years on the labor bill. Eisenhower made one fifteen-minute speech on the labor bill and had a decisive effect on the action of the House of Representatives, his speech. His one speech, took fifteen minutes."

I thought I detected something in the tone of Kennedy's voice. "He flirted with Tony," I wrote to myself in my notes. I knew that Kennedy had once referred to Tony as his "ideal woman," but hearing them all talk brought it home. My mind moved to a deeper suspicion. "Maybe that's the big secret?" I wrote.

At a few points, Kennedy throws a couple of shots across Ben's bow. Asked for the hundredth time why he wants to be president, Kennedy says, "Ben would understand. My scope is far greater than Ben's. He works extremely hard on his effort, but my scope is unlimited. His scope is somewhat limited, because he goes to press every week . . . but my scope is really dependent on my judgment now and energy. And tactical and strategic sense. And then the scope is unlimited. Well I mean how the hell can you help but think that that's the most absorbing thing in the world?"

Tony chimes in, in Ben's defense, "It's not so bad being a reporter."

Toward the end of the interview, Ben has clearly taken enough guff from his pal Jack, though he's given some, too.* Ben mentions a man named Josephat Benoit, the former mayor of Manchester, New Hampshire, who had studied at the Sorbonne. "I used to get great exclusive stories out of Josephat by talking to him in French."

"You both have that French Canadian accent," Kennedy says, tweaking Ben.

"Bulllllllllllshit!" Ben sings, in protest. "I had a flawless Tours accent."

JFK isn't having it. "The *raarrrrrrrrrrr* that you put into your 'r's," he says, twisting the knife.

"Yeah, but Joe Benoit studied at the Sorbonne, so he spoke flawless French, and he didn't *speak* that kind of French." Ben's genuine irritation at the affront to his accent is unmistakable.†

JFK diffuses the tension by playing to the room. "Can you see the

---

*For most of the interview, Kennedy has lived on a different level from Cannon and Ben, parrying their questions, always a step ahead of them, demonstrating the quickness that would characterize him as a candidate. The only moment Kennedy goes back on his heels is when Ben tells him that he didn't think a statement Kennedy had made earlier that week had been any good. Kennedy promptly, and with great conviction, blames Pierre Salinger.

†It would surface again later in *Conversations with Kennedy:* "For some reason it bugs Kennedy that I speak French. Kennedy finds it intolerable that he doesn't have the facility for languages that others have, and his pride in Jackie's linguistic talents is tinged with jealousy and bewilderment. His French can only be described as unusual." Fallows, writing for *Esquire* in 1976, of this moment: "Bradlee cannot be as blind to his own one-upmanship as he pretends to be."

future secretary typing all this out?" he jokes, referring to the running tape recorder. Everybody laughs, because Kennedy's busting
Ben's balls, like a big brother almost. They're there to talk about the
presidency, and instead Ben is talking about Josephat Benoit. The
tape recorder gets turned off shortly thereafter, then back on for a
few final questions. I had a little chuckle as I realized that I was that
future secretary, and that Kennedy would never have guessed that I
would actually find that particular moment significant, or why.

In November of 2009, I drove down to Charlottesville to spend an
evening with Rosamond Pittman Casey, the young girl on the tape
now grown into an artist who looks a lot like old pictures of her
mom. We talked for a while about Tony. I told Ros (as she's known)
that I was struggling to get a bead on Tony, that there was something diaphanous and ungraspable about her. She agreed. She said
that she had always had a hard time fixing who her mother was, that
there was always some portion that Tony kept to herself. Just like
Ben.

"Ben was a great stepdad," she told me, though he had taken some
getting used to. The year that they had spent en famille in Paris,
when Ben and Tony were first married, had been miserable. But
eventually she and Ben had become friends. He teased her a lot,
sometimes more roughly than she might have liked, but she understood that that had been his way of reaching out.

I turned the conversation toward Kennedy. I mentioned that I had
listened to the old interview, and that I thought I had heard some
flirtation with Tony on it, something in the character of Kennedy's
voice.

"Ben hasn't told you?" Ros said. Her daughter, Clare, who was
sitting opposite us, looked up with some interest.

"No," I said. "He hasn't."

Together, Ros and Clare and the novelist John Casey, Ros's husband, told me a story and swore, all three of them, that it was true.
Tony had told them all, more than once, about an incident with

Kennedy on a yacht. They had been belowdecks, just the two of them, and Kennedy was forward with her in a way that made her uncomfortable and upset. There was some implication that Kennedy had chased Tony around and tried to push her up against a wall, been quite aggressive with her. Ben had either sensed it or perhaps even walked in on the aftermath, but apparently he could never pry the whole story out of Tony afterward. They maintained that Ben knew about it in a general way, that he'd mentioned it to them before.

I wasn't surprised, but it felt strange to harbor a suspicion for so long and then have it confirmed so abruptly. I repeated what they'd told me, in my own words. "I just want to be certain I have this right, and that I'm not making anything up or exaggerating," I said.

"It happened," Ros said.

Ben has always kept—figuratively, if not literally—what he calls a "Too Hard" file, where you slot the stuff that you know you need to deal with but can't quite bring yourself to confront. The information about Tony and JFK went straight into my Too Hard file, because it felt personal in a way that my questions about Ben's career never did. In July of 2010 I told the story to Sally, and she told me to ask him about it, so I went into his office and told him the story as it had been told to me.

B: I think Tony had a crush on him.

Q: Right, and you've said that before.

B: But I don't—you know, I'd be absolutely stunned if he did anything about it or she did anything about it. I don't think they did.

Q: No implication that anything was done—no implication of that at all. Just that he said (or did) something to her that made her uncomfortable.

B: Tony was really upset when she learned about Kennedy and Mary . . . no question about that.

Q: You already have both in *Conversations with Kennedy*, and more in your memoir, just that Jack said in front of you guys, you know, Jackie said, "You always say that she's your ideal."

B: Yeah.

Q: So it was no secret that he liked both Mary and Tony.

B: Yeah, yeah.

Q: But I felt obligated to ask you, just to chase that down.

B: I know of no overt incident of any kind. Although I am aware that . . . he definitely had that from Mary and did something about it . . . I mean, I can't believe that Tony would've had an affair with him, or vice versa.

Q: No. I never would believe her. I would believe anything about him.

B: Maybe Jack would've given it a shot.

From:	[Rosamond Casey]
Subject:	Re: quick question about ben
Date:	August 3, 2010 11:02:51 PM EDT
To:	[Jeff Himmelman]

Dear Jeff,

You are right, there are two reasons Ben might not remember. Either it is because Mom did not tell him about it, which could speak as much to a guilty attraction to JFK as her wish to protect Ben. Or he has forgotten it / put it out of reach of his memory. I doubt the latter because I know he was proud of the fact that the President had a kind of crush on his wife. He often quoted JFK saying that Tony was his "ideal woman." I personally think he would have enjoyed knowing it had happened.

I checked with two of my siblings and they both remember what I remember: Mom told us (children) at different times some time post Ben, that JFK had chased her around the hold (down below) of a boat (presidential yacht? There are pictures of Ben and Mom with the Kennedys on a small yacht or pleasure boat together. I have always assumed it was the same boat but do not know that for sure).

It was hard to know how uncomfortable this made Mom feel. But I got the feeling at least a little . . .

Ros

In her 2004 book about the Kennedy White House, *Grace and Power*, Sally Bedell Smith recounts an on-the-record conversation with Tony about exactly what had happened, and when.* In May 1963, Jackie threw a forty-sixth birthday party for her husband aboard the *Sequoia*, the presidential yacht. It was a rowdy night, with a lot of drinking and dancing. As Tony made her way to the bathroom late in the evening, she sensed that Kennedy was following her.

"He chased me all around the boat," Tony told Bedell Smith. "A couple of members of the crew were laughing. I was running and laughing as he chased me. He caught up with me in the ladies' room and made a pass. It was a pretty strenuous attack, not as if he pushed me down, but his hands wandered." She said that she was "pretty surprised, but I was kind of flattered, and appalled too." She didn't tell Ben about it at the time but said that she had told him many years later.

"Jack was always so complimentary to me, putting his hands around my waist," Tony told Bedell Smith. "I thought, 'Hmmmm, he likes me.' I think it surprised him I would not succumb. If I hadn't been married maybe I would have." Of Kennedy's relationship with her sister, Tony said, "I always felt he liked me as much as Mary. You could say there was a little rivalry."†

Ben is a hyperaware person. If he didn't know that Kennedy had gone after his wife, he certainly seems to have sensed it subliminally. As with the Mary Meyer episode, he leaves us clues about this in the book, too:

> Somewhere during the conversation, Jackie said to the president
> "Oh, Jack, you know you always say that Tony is your ideal." The

---

*I didn't know of the existence of this book, or of Tony's cooperation with it, until I came across its description in the obituary of Tony Bradlee that ran in the *Post* shortly after her death in November 2011. Ben hadn't mentioned it to me, and had said he knew of "no overt incident," so I had presumed that the whole thing was still somewhat secret.

†On March 15, 1961, just a few months after his inauguration, Kennedy chose the Pinchot sisters as his dinner partners, one on either side, at a White House dinner dance.

president replied "Yes, that's true," and then a second or two later added "You're my ideal, Jacqueline." (p. 187)

[of a trip to Ireland and Europe]
The president immediately asked [Tony] to go with him on his plane, and I just as immediately nixed that as an impropriety. "Jesus, you said that fast," Kennedy said, apparently impressed more by the speed than the morality. (p. 190)

Kennedy renewed his offer to take Tony again on his own plane, and the offer was again refused. (p. 192)

In his book *Journals*, Arthur Schlesinger recounts his reaction in 1974 to the news that Ben was working on a book about Kennedy. "I fear it will be greatly resented by the Kennedys," Schlesinger writes of *Conversations with Kennedy*, "because I am sure it displays JFK in relaxed, gossipy and somewhat irresponsible moods in the evenings." He was right. But then, fascinatingly, he reports what Ben said to him about it, including sentiments that would have made Ben's book significantly more truthful and more interesting:

Ben said to me, "I really don't think that Jack liked me very much. He always thought I was a spiv, in the British sense—a little glib and scheming perhaps. But I think he was rather in love with Tony. He fucked Mary but he was in love with Tony. But I do think I entertained him.

Kennedy kept Ben in a compartment—a compartment that he hoped to get some use out of, one way or another. Ben has been honest about this. But what Ben has never admitted is the feelings of rivalry and resentment that so often bubble over in his book. Ben has always been accustomed to being the insider, the tall pole, the guy with the upper hand. Kennedy deprived him of that advantage and then reminded him of it, one of the very few who could out-Bradlee Bradlee. (Ben was used to having other men's wives develop crushes on him, not the other way around.) When you hear the two men talking on that tape from 1960, you can hear their friendship and their re-spect for each other, but you can also hear Kennedy rubbing Ben's nose in it a little bit. Ben is a competitive person. He wouldn't have liked that much.

And so he wrote a book in 1975, and got paid a lot of money for it, in which he was able to put the mythic Jack Kennedy into a less mythic perspective. I believe his motives for that were deeper and more complicated than he has ever let on. As Ben would learn over the next couple of years, in the wake of the film version of *All the President's Men* and the resentments that it would engender at the *Post*, nobody likes somebody who has always got the upper hand.

Memoir interview with Barbara Feinman, May 31, 1990:

B: I remember [Jackie] started to stiff me, publicly stiff me, and there was a convention in New York and Sally and I were together so it must have been '76, not married, and that was after the book. She called me up a couple of times wanting to see a copy of the book. "I hear everybody's seen a copy but I'd like to see a copy." I said, "Jackie, no one has seen a copy of the book, except the editor." And she said, "Joe Kraft has seen it," which was true, I had shown it to him. And then I said, "I'll send it to you right away." And I sent it to her right away.*

And she called back in about a week and she plainly didn't like it. "It tells more about you than it does about him," and she said, "I showed it to the children and I didn't enjoy showing it to them very much." I suppose because of the language and I said I'm so sorry and it seems to me that it is a eulogy of this man and blah, blah, blah and we hung up. Not screaming mad at each other and she didn't say please don't do it or anything like that, but plainly miserable, unhappy.

The next thing was this time in 1976 that we were going to some-

---

*Ben used even this to his advantage. "Bradlee, who lived on the same block as Kennedy, lets you know that Jackie Onassis is very eager, too eager perhaps, to see what he is writing," Robert Lenzner wrote, in August of 1974, in a massive magazine piece comparing Ben and Abe Rosenthal, the managing editor of *The New York Times*, in *The Boston Globe*.

body's house, [Arthur Schlesinger's] house who was having a party at
the convention and Sally and I were walking up West something street
and I saw her a hundred feet away coming down the steps. I said to
Sally, "Here's Jackie." And she had turned and started walking towards
me before she saw me and I put out my hand and she just walked right
by. Boom—walked right by. Amazing. Even if you were pissed at
somebody you could give them a sort of brittle little hello. And then,
I don't know when, it could have been before that we had been down
together, the same time at this resort in St. Maarten and she was in a
cabin one down from us with John and Caroline. It couldn't have
been more than fifty feet. Once we were getting out of our little cabin
to go upstairs to dinner and the path just yea far from the front door
and I bumped into her again and she just stiffed me again. And I
haven't talked to her, have not talked to her since.

BF: Does that bother you?

B: Yeah. It hurts my feelings a lot. I don't want to be her best friend but
I think this is shit. She can say, I really wish you hadn't written that
book. Probably somebody's fed her some stuff. . . . I've sort of said to
various people I'm really upset by that. I would like it to end, I would
just like to shake her hand, end it right.

Ben never got the chance to end it right with Jackie. In 1992, he
wrote to Caroline Kennedy, "I would just like to say hello sometime
and the same goes for Jackie. We got crossed for reasons that I don't
understand and I would like to uncross our wires." Nothing came of
it. Later, when Ben heard that Jackie had fallen ill in early 1994, he
apparently wrote her a conciliatory letter (no copy of it exists in his
files), but he wasn't sure that it ever reached her. She never responded.
"I know how that must have hurt, but I can understand it," Ben's
friend Eppie Lederer (better known as Ann Landers) wrote to Ben in
1995, of Jackie's repeated rejections. "You knew too much that she
needed to forget."

Jackie might have wanted to forget Ben, but he has never wanted
to forget her. For the last several years, up until he began to prepare
his papers for sale, Ben rented a safety deposit box at the bank across
the street from the *Post*. There he kept, among other things, his

Washington Post stock certificates, two personal letters from President Carter, and two small effects of Jackie's.

The first was the mourning card that Jackie had sent to Ben and Tony in December 1963, just after her husband had been killed. The second was a small White House notecard, filled on its blank side with Tony's handwritten notes from dinner at the White House on August 14, 1961. The men present had all weighed themselves, and Tony had taken the numbers down. But that's not why Ben saved it. The reason he saved it is on the card's flip side: a wide and perfect lipstick kiss from Jackie. It's a memento of her former tenderness, frozen in time, that Ben kept safe, and to himself, for nearly fifty years.

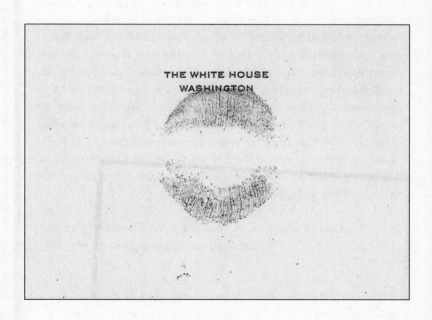

CHRISTMAS AFTERNOON

Then Woodward says . . . I Halberstam, now I have to deal with the question of the Post, whether it is going into a decline, and he says this is very private and to go to no one else, that Kay Graham has talked to him, that she is very disturbed about the Post and what's happened to it. . . . Her feeling is that it has slipped. . . .

She also feels that Bradlee has somehow lost his interest, that post Watergate she feels he is being pulled away in part by Sally Quinn and the life style, that his interest is not in the paper, and that Jim Bellows, she has a feeling. . . . [Jim] Bellows is in the City Room at the Star every day, I have a sense of him right in the middle of that City Room with his sleeves rolled up, I have a feeling that he's right there. And she doesn't have that feeling about Bradlee, and she's very disturbed and she says, you know, she may have to move him out, this is a real concern, that if necessary she will bring someone in like Gene Roberts to edit the paper. And she feels the paper is too much of a club, the national staff is a club . . . herself said of Howard that his job was somehow to wipe up after Ben.

—David Halberstam's memo of a private interview with Bob Woodward, undated but sometime post-1975

IN EARLY 1976, BEN RECEIVED another unsigned memo. Sprawling over nine pages of six-ply paper, it laid out a series of problems at the Style section and then went on to address some of the deeper problems at the paper.

"You've got the best staff of any paper in the country," the author wrote, "but they are floundering. They seem to lack leadership, direction, excitement, and energy." Editors were too scared of each other, too political, and never took responsibility for themselves. "There are so many little things you don't know, that are kept from you by your editors. Without reporters and their energy and enthusiasm and respect you can do nothing." Maybe Ben had been "too nice recently." Maybe now he would "have to kick ass."

> I know you can, and will. I know you've done it for 10 years and you think the challenge is gone. But it isn't. This is the biggest challenge you've ever had. And it should be exciting for you. Just because you won the gold medal and the Olympics once doesn't mean you can't try for it again. You are the only person who is capable of doing it. All you have to do is show them that you mean business, shake things up and it will start to turn things around. But you've got to do it now.
>
> I love you.

It was, of course, from Sally. In the years since Watergate she had watched, along with everybody else, as the paper had struggled to find its way. She once likened Ben's state of mind after Nixon resigned to a postnatal depression. Every part of him had been activated, and then it had all been taken away.

In May of 1973, right after the *Post* had won the Pulitzer Prize for its Watergate reporting, Ben wrote to an admirer that he realized they were all riding high, and that eventually they would have to come down again:

> When this wild self-congratulatory ski-jump is over and we hit solid ground once again, it's the respect of your peers that means a goddam thing, not the TV cables in the city room, not the cover stories, not even the apology of that piss-ant, Ziegler.
>
> The moments I most cherish are those too rare occasions when one is doing just exactly what one was put on this earth to do . . . not practicing psychiatry without a license, not cost accounting without talent . . . and that's what all of us here are doing these days.

At the time of that writing, Ben couldn't have foreseen just how long the wild, self-congratulatory ski jump would be, or how hard it would be to stick the landing. With Nixon's resignation in 1974, the publication of *Conversations with Kennedy* in 1975, and the premiere of *All the President's Men* in 1976, Ben had been flying high for nearly three full years.

In the interim, the newspaper had to come out every morning. What was *The Washington Post* going to be, in the wake of Watergate? As Halberstam wrote, memorably, of Ben, he is "a man by nature geared for big events, not little ones, and the biggest event of all had already come his way." Many on the paper, notably both Carl and Bob, thought that in the wake of Watergate the *Post* should have mounted a challenge to *The New York Times*'s status as the newspaper of record in the United States.

"Ben's job, it seems to me, was to then take the post–Watergate *Washington Post* and determine where it was going to go," Carl told me. "And Bob and I believed it should go national, and I'm sure that Watergate had given it enough of an impetus that it could have done it. Because right then it was a better paper than *The New York Times*. Because the Style section was at its apogee. Because of what had happened with the Watergate reporting, and that lesson carrying over." The paper had missed an opportunity, in large part because it enjoyed a local monopoly in D.C. (having effectively eliminated the *Star* as meaningful competition) and could comfortably occupy its lucrative perch as D.C.'s preeminent paper. "I don't know how much is conscious or unconscious," Carl told me, "but clearly it went back to the local model."

Bob wouldn't give me the same criticism directly. In one of our interviews, he quoted Tom Ross, who was the old D.C. bureau chief for the *Chicago Sun-Times*. One night in the wake of Nixon's resignation—Bob thinks it was in early '75—Bob had dinner with Ross and the reporter Mort Kondracke, who worked with Ross at the *Sun-Times*.

"Tom was one of these people who is a very wise commentator on the press," Bob told me. "And this is all on the record. What he told me, he said, you know, the sadness or the tragedy after Watergate is that the *Post* had an opportunity to become *the* great newspaper. *The New York Times* plus."

"With personality and flair . . ." I said.

"And all the kind of 'cruising speed,' the phrase Ben uses," Bob said. "And it didn't happen. He was very critical of the Grahams and Ben." (Ben often said of *The New York Times* that he admired its "cruising speed," meaning its general and sustained level of excellence. Ben thought that from a standing start the *Post* could compete with the *Times* on any given story, but he also admitted that the *Post* was not as reliable a daily index of what mattered in the world.)

"That's mostly a Graham decision, is it not?" I asked. "I mean, Ben can't make that decision."

"No, no, he could," Bob said. "He could've pushed it. He could've said, 'Let's reevaluate who we are. What's the next big play? What's the next move?' And that's not Ben."

In the wake of Watergate the *Post* certainly could have undertaken a major challenge to the *Times*. At one point in the early seventies, 1,600 people applied for the fifteen available summer internships at the *Post*. There was no problem attracting talent; the problem was figuring out what to do with the talent they already had.

Carl left the paper at the end of 1976, largely for his own reasons but in part because the paper didn't know where to put him. "One of the reasons I left," Carl told me, "was [Ben] wanted to offer me a local column that became [Richard] Cohen's column, and I didn't want to do that. I was like, 'Shit, I've done Watergate, and now I can't go to Vietnam again?' I said, 'What the fuck is going on here?' "

Richard Cohen had been on his way out the door, too.* "I was sick of *The Washington Post*," he told me. With David Broder, he had generated much of the *Post*'s first-rate coverage on Vice President Spiro Agnew, and after writing a quickie book about Agnew he re-

---

*As Cohen tells it, when Ben offered him the column he said, "Make sure you're accurate. Don't make a mistake." Cohen replied, "I get it. So if this thing succeeds, you take credit, and if it fails it's over for me." And Ben said, "You got it."

turned to the *Post*. "They put me on the city desk as a reporter, and they were just giving me a hard time. I don't know why I deserved it. . . The first story they sent me on was a garbage fire. I thought, 'What is this about?' . . .

"Ben could attract such great talent," Cohen said. "But he also didn't know what to do with it half the time." Building the *Post* in the sixties, adding great reporters in bunches, was a far different enterprise from managing them all once they had made it.

Post reporter Jules Witcover told David Halberstam that "Howard Simons and Ben are really out to lunch in the post-Watergate era." After Watergate there had been "a lot of talk about staying up there, really turning it on. But Ben really has been playing at being a celebrity. He claims he doesn't like it but he really does like it, and he liked the kind of glamour that Watergate brought. At the same time he really has no attention span."

Larry Stern, Ben's neighbor and one of his best friends on the paper, put it more simply, and maybe more accurately: "Ben is bored now, and that has become a serious problem at the paper."

These were the knocks on Ben from below, an important constituency but not nearly as important as the one constituency that mattered most: Kay Graham. He served at her pleasure, and by all accounts she was displeased, too. In her memoir, she would describe the period 1976 to 1981 as "the most difficult years I ever lived through," in part because of the malaise that Sally, Bob, Carl, Cohen, and Witcover had described:

> I had some grave concerns about the quality of the paper and of the editing. I felt that the national staff and the metro staff had let down, that we were doing things superficially. Ben didn't agree with me, but Bob Woodward did, putting it succinctly one day: "The paper is going down the shit hole." It is to Ben's great credit that he and I survived the difficult times and all my questioning. . . .
>
> Not listening to me—and to others—was both Ben's strength and his weakness. However, as I wrote him at the time of this disagreement about the quality of the paper, "No superficial

problems either of us may have at any particular moment matter compared to the basic trust and rapport with each other. Because if that's there—and it is there as far as I'm concerned—all else flows from it.

—Clipped comic from Saturday, October 19, 1974, saved in Kay Graham's private files, with her handwriting at the top

There is no relationship that has mattered more to Ben's life than his relationship with Kay Graham. Sally has played a vital role since 1973, but without Kay Graham there is no Sally—first because Kay picked Ben as her editor, and then later, in 1973, because she accepted Sally's role as Ben's partner even though it violated her sense of propriety.

Sally knows this as well as anybody. "I know I've told you this before," she wrote to Kay in December of 1978, shortly after she and Ben were married, "but I want to impress upon you again how grateful I shall always be for the way you received me and us after we got together."

It made so much difference in the way we were accepted not only at the paper but in the community and if anyone is responsible for the fact that our relationship worked out it has to be you—I know how hard it must have been for you and how generous an act it was.

After Kay died in 2001, Sally wrote a column for the Style section. "Kay and Ben had worked so closely together before we were together that she often seemed like a very welcome third person in our marriage," she wrote. "[A] favorite aunt, a wise confidante, a pal. When Ben was invited by President Ford to a White House dinner, he took Kay instead of me, with my approval."

Is there such a thing as a welcome third person in a marriage? I suppose there might be. That Sally could write something like that illustrates what was so transformative about Ben's relationship with Kay, a powerful man working for an even more powerful woman in an era where there wasn't much precedent for that kind of relationship.

"When I put you there and you related to me," Kay told Ben in the interviews for her memoir, "it was a whole different ballgame." All of the editors and businesspeople that she had inherited from the Phil days had been condescending to her, showing her the ropes while never quite believing she could master them. "I don't mean they were really condescending, I guess," she said, "but at the same time they didn't think of me as a boss. And I don't mean you did in any . . ."

"Yes, I did," Ben interrupted her. "I really did."

Kay was always, irrevocably, the boss. That was the only reason Sally would have tolerated anybody else as a "welcome third person" in her marriage. Kay and the Graham family owned the A shares of Washington Post Company stock, the voting portion, and as Ben likes to put it, "one of the lessons I learned in journalism is that you don't argue with the A shares."

Ben has often said that his most important job as editor of the *Post* was "managing the Grahams." For the bigger moments of his career, including the doldrums of 1975–1976 and beyond, that meant managing Kay. She didn't much like the idea that Ben managed her—he largely had her convinced that she was one of the boys—but from their letters to each other it's quite clear that he did.

Just before Christmas in 1968, shortly after he took over as executive editor, Ben sent Kay a letter in place of the holiday flowers that he had sent to her in previous years. "No reasonable quantity can convey my Christmas thoughts to you," he wrote. "And so I wonder if you will settle for a Christmas letter from someone who admires uncommonly your style and sense and commitment and maybe most of all, your company."

"Dear Ben," Kay wrote back the next day, "That's the nicest Christmas present I have—and you are so great throughout the year that I have to send the news right back."

Thus began a tradition of Christmas letters between Ben and Kay, what they would later refer to as their "Mutual Admiration Society." At the end of each year, they both sat down to collect their thoughts about each other, and about the paper, and then they sent them along. Aside from Kay's extraordinary letter at Christmas of 1974, describing her recollections of how Watergate could ever have happened, the letters follow a predictable pattern: a brief reference or two to recent events, followed by encomia to how wonderful it is to work together.

But as the malaise at the *Post* set in, in 1975, the letters begin to change:

Christmas Eve 1975

Katharine –

Another unbelievable year that ends with my love and respect for you enhanced and vigorous.

For Christmas, I want you to understand how valuable and strong and gutsy you have been at a time when the future of this great newspaper hung in the balance. You will never do anything more difficult, and you will never do anything with more grace and courage.

For New Year's, I want the turmoil ended, so that we can return to our task of putting out the best paper in the world without compromise and without menace.

And for all of 1976 you should remember that down here in uncommon delight and constant anticipation sits your friend.

B

Dear Ben,

Thank you for your letter which I love. My delay was due to both the wild rush & a Scrooge-mood.

You have been a wonderful colleague, friend, support & pillar throughout these many years but especially this one. The great thing you do for the paper and for me is to be a critical voice of a gentle kind—an independent spirit but a collaborator extraordinaire, and a serious ear with a relievingly humorous tongue—& a refuge for me in a storm—

I know how hard the last 3 months have been on you. It's not what you are & should be about. It's the contrary. Whereas I have been living most of the hours with people who were all together, you have been living each day with people who were all over the lot but who had to be—for essential reasons—calmed & hand held by you & Howie.

Whereas I have been hoping for 8 years to turn this part of the building around—it's constrained what you've been working to do for 10—& added to the post-Watergate problems too. And yet you've put your very understandable & deep worries aside to help us do this incredibly tough thing.

Ben—I know it's going to be good—better than you think from every point of view. I pray it's over before too long but it would be fatal to try to push it faster than it can go—It was not looked for but was so desperately needed—In an odd sense it's a business side Watergate that fell on our heads but then had to be pursued—

One great thing is we've always believed & trusted each other—no matter how tough the going—& had fun too. So my end of the year letter to you is to thank you for this great gift & to send you my love.

The "business side Watergate" was the pressmen's strike, which began in October of 1975 and didn't end until February of 1976. The strike was an inflection point in the history of the *Post*, and in Kay Graham's ownership of it.* Since taking the Post Company public in 1971, Kay

---

*As I was leafing through the box of Kay Graham's letters at a desk outside Ben's office in the summer of 2010, he happened to walk by. He reached into one of the various piles I

had sought ways to make the operation more self-sufficient, and more profitable. Many in management felt that the craft unions at the *Post*, the people who actually fabricated the paper, stood in the way of those goals. The unions had gotten away with a series of sweetheart deals in the sixties and seventies because they could effectively close the paper down if they refused to work. (When composing-room workers were unhappy, they sometimes slipped phrases like "This paper is edited by rats" into the final edition of the *Post*, which drove Ben up the wall.) While the *Post* was still competing so heavily with the *Star*, the *Post* brass couldn't afford to alienate anybody.

But in the wake of Watergate, Kay and the corporate side of the company had the upper hand, and in essence they crushed the unions. The business side sent news executives and others out to a "scab school" in Oklahoma, where they learned how to run the presses and other basics of newspaper production. When the pressmen eventually walked out, on October 1, 1975—after doing an extensive but much-disputed amount of damage to several of the printing presses—those news executives stepped in and produced the paper themselves. Nearly all of the reporters at the *Post* crossed the picket lines to help put out the paper.

John Hanrahan was a notable exception in all of this, a reporter who refused to cross the picket lines and who eventually left the paper as a result. He thought that the *Post*'s ruthlessness with the unions wasn't merited purely because some pressmen had damaged the printing presses. "I was sympathetic to the pressmen with missing fingers and breathing crap in their lungs all the time," he told me. He bore Ben no ill will, but he thought that most of the people who crossed the picket lines were hypocrites. "It's very easy to take a liberal position when it's happening someplace else," he said. "If this were happening at some other place, all these reporters would be saying, 'Boy, that's terrible.' "

---

had made and blindly withdrew this particular letter; after scanning it for a few moments he humphed and said, "Business side Watergate, you might want to look into that." True to form, he had instinctively picked out three of the most interesting words in that entire box.

During the roughly four months of the strike, everybody on the paper had to work two jobs. People slept in their offices. Management brought in catered food, and Ben and Kay both did stints taking classified advertising requests, with entertaining results:

> K: . . . One day everybody was really busy and this Mercedes dealer called in and he had six cars and therefore he had to go through, I said, listen, I'm new here, so please go slowly. . . . [P]eople weren't aware that we were on strike. And so I didn't wish to point out that I was replacing this person, so I just said, please go slowly because I'm new here and so I kept making him repeat, you know, because it goes a–c–d–c and all this stuff and then there were abbreviations for air conditioning. . . .
>
> I was writing away and he obviously thought I was retarded. And so he said, I think you'd better read that over. And so I read it over very fast and obviously accurately because at least I could take down what he was telling me. So he said, you sound over-qualified. He said, "You could be anybody, you could be Katharine Graham." And I said, well, I mean, I'm so stunned, that I said, "As a matter of fact, I am."

When the strike ended, the Post Company was on significantly more profitable footing. And though the strike had been "crushed with methods and with a severity that are not usually accepted in the third quarter of the Twentieth Century," as Henry Fairlie noted in *The New Republic* in 1977, the paper somehow managed to win the public relations battle, too.

The reason the strike is an inflection point in the history of the paper is less due to the particulars of its handling than to the indication it provided that Kay Graham's mission was changing, her own sense of purpose. They had scaled the journalistic heights, and now—by her own admission—she wanted to scale the corporate heights. The greatest publisher in the world coveted the title of "greatest businesswoman," and so a business side Watergate was just what she had hoped for. The defeat of the unions improved the *Post*'s standing on Wall Street, but it also changed the cast of the company. During some of the *Post*'s formative years, Kay Graham, like her father before her, had been willing to sustain major losses in advertising and a lower profit margin in order to produce the journalism that had changed the course of history.* Now her focus was different, and you can see it in the Christmas letters:

December 1977

Katharine:

This has really been your year—in a way that all your other years have not been. The year when your decisions and your actions and your commitments have come spectacularly together. I think you got your Pulitzer in business at last. . . .

When the real history of this paper is written, I think a definite, post-Watergate dimension will emerge—not doldrums, as we thought, but digestion. Our new notoriety had to be digested, then the strike had to be fought and won, all at the same time. Now, 1977 was the first time that these two processes were completed and life returned to something like normal.

According to the notations of one of her researchers, she kept the original copy of this letter of Ben's in her desk drawer, apart from the others.

As kind as Ben's letter might have been, this was a moment at which there were significant strains on their relationship, and on the paper. These were the tough years that Kay spoke of in her memoir, the years when Ben and Howard and the others were "out to lunch," or at least perceived to be, the years when Kay considered moving Ben out. In her memoir, Kay makes only vague references to her dissatisfactions, but in a confidential memo to Ben in June of 1977, she lays some of them out quite plainly:

---

*During the middle of Watergate, an advertising executive told Kay that automotive advertising was down $3 or $4 million in that particular quarter because the Republican owners of the local car dealerships weren't thrilled with the *Post*'s Watergate coverage. "They don't like what we're doing about Nixon," the man had said. And apparently Kay had looked at him and said, "Well, it's a good thing we can afford it." Told that story in 2008, Ben said, "We ought to just say a silent prayer for her, because they could."

Ben, we all make mistakes in choosing people for promotions, and I am the one who can write a very long book about it. But we have to learn from mistakes, what is wrong with the process which led to them. With the best process you are still going to go wrong at times. . . .

Superb as is your record and your net effect, it has been despite the decision-making process which has led us to things like Bagdikian, Rosenfeld,* Patterson. . . . This is not to discount the many right decisions. . . .

I have to say something personal in closing. When I send down the mail, the complaints, or even my own views when Howard is away, I do not feel that people's views or even my views are truly listened to before being rejected. I do not feel legitimate requests are followed up, or that I get an answer whether it has or whether it hasn't. . . .

You are right that I would never do what Joe Allbritton did—just order something killed or changed. It's not the way to do things most productively for the paper, and obviously you wouldn't work that way from your point of view.

But in order for our system to work, both sides have to listen to each other.

For another thing, if I don't feel I get a hearing, I wonder what people under all of you feel?

That's the ominous dangling end of the memo, reminiscent of Kay's displeasure during the early days of the Style section. In her Christmas letter at the end of that same year, she would refer again to the finger Ben had told her to keep out of his eye:

At times—& recently—I can get in periods where I come on like a dentist drill & am a trial to people around me & to myself I must say. . . .

I have a feeling that this year has been a particularly hard one for you

---

*After Watergate, Ben had promoted Harry Rosenfeld from AME–Metro to AME-National. Every single person I interviewed who mentioned that promotion characterized it as a failure.

& that my finger may have loomed larger or different because of other pressures.

If that is so nothing is more important than for you to know—really to know—how central & how essential you are to this paper, to the people on it all over, not just the 5th floor—& to this person on the 8th.

Ben says that he never for one second had the thought that Kay was going to move him out. But it's clear from the confidential memo, and then from Kay's letter afterward, that she had been upset with some of his management decisions and ultimately felt that she needed to reassure him about his importance to the paper and to her. Most of the other letters have pat references to their closeness, but this letter stands out because the reassurance feels so real, as if Ben actually needed it:

> If the year has been tough on you for whatever reasons, I sure want to help & not be part of the problem. It's what we've always done for each other. That way we've come an incredibly long way & we have a long way to go. The all important thing is to continue to have fun en route. I send you a big hug, a kiss & a goose.

At Kay's funeral in July of 2001, Ben's was the only speech to receive an ovation—spontaneous, long, and loud. In it, he mentioned how Kay had closed this letter to him as evidence of what fun she had been to work with. Ben doesn't tend to remember unimportant things. Though the big hug, the kiss, and the goose were certainly a playful expression of the dynamic that they shared, it seems likely to me that he remembered this letter so favorably because it had come at a time of uncertainty for him—whether he knew it or not.

When you read these letters, you come away with the feeling that there was slightly more to the relationship than either of them lets on. They were both pursuing agendas, each in their own ways. Kay was focused on the growth of the Post Company and seemed intent on finding a way to voice her displeasure about the direction of the

paper without upsetting Ben or pushing him away. And Ben, whatever he says about it, was plainly trying to stay in her good graces. He
has insisted at various points that the reason he survived Kay's capriciousness as an executive was that he wasn't afraid of her, that he was
willing to call her on things, that he didn't kiss ass. True, up to a
point, but it has to be said that Ben really did kiss ass—it's just that
only Kay saw it:

December 21, 1978

Dear Katharine:

Another fabulous and fascinating year needs to be formalized by
another love letter from me to you. And the first thing to say this time
is that there will be a next time, that my next letter will be just as
thankful as this one for your support and your presence and your
kindnesses and your humor. Dammit, we do have fun together, you &
I, and that is one of the particular joys of working in this joint.

This year a particular kindness from you to me needs memorializing:
your treatment of Sister Quinn & her social life. In a real way it was
your acceptance of us that made our life together as OK as it was &
thus as fine as it is. Thank you for that. . . .

There is something so warm and comfortable about the sight of you
striding pridefully across the city room of your paper.

For it really is your paper, Katharine. It bears your mark, as it bears
no other. You were a better publisher than Phil; you know that. And I
suspect better than your father—because you brought less baggage to
the job, less mindset. I don't worry five minutes about Don, but don't
you forget for five minutes that you did all this, you got us here and
gave us such a wonderful time en route.

Remember that, dear friend, if the blahs should rear their ugly head
at some dreary, winter time.

Love

High praise, and an admittedly deserved benediction: 1978 was Kay's
last year as publisher of the *Post*. Earlier that year, she had decided to

step aside and to move Don in to succeed her, starting officially in January of 1979.* But there's still some undeniable ass kissing going on here. Note also that they have covered some distance since the previous year's troubles: "The first thing to say this time is that there will be a next time . . ." He had survived.

"I don't know exactly when," Jim Hoagland told me, "but Kay fell in love with Ben. But it had to be unrequited, and they both understood that." Hoagland was one of Kay's favorites at the paper, and for a time her presumptive choice to succeed Ben as executive editor. Though Kay would write in her memoir that her relationship with Ben "always seemed to be depicted in exaggerated ways," Hoagland did not appear to be exaggerating.

I told him a story about my first trip to Grey Gardens, in the summer of 2007. After too much wine, I had made the mistake of saying in front of Sally and Ben and some friends that I didn't see how Kay could have avoided having a crush on Ben. Sally lit up. "Of *course* she was in love with him!" she cried, and as she launched into her theory about it I glanced over at Ben. He looked visibly uncomfortable for a moment or two, and then he stood up from the table without saying anything and walked upstairs. It was the only time in all my experience with him that anything like this ever happened.

"That is truly odd to me," Hoagland said. "Because, look, Kay developed crushes. This was, I think, probably the most serious one, ever. Except for Phil, and stories I don't know about. So I'm surprised at Ben's reaction."

The record of Ben's life is littered with uncomfortable answers to questions about Kay. "Do you find Kay Graham attractive?" an interviewer once asked him.

Ben was smart enough to realize, and then to respond, "That's a no-win question."

---

*In February of 1977, Ben and Kay had shared a plane ride together, and on an American Airlines boarding pass they predicted their retirement dates. Kay predicted June of 1979, missing by six months. Ben predicted August of 1981, missing by ten years.

"They've gone through about five publishers at *The Washington Post*, endless editors at *Newsweek*, but Ben Bradlee and only Ben Bradlee has survived," Robert Kaiser told David Halberstam in the late seventies:

> And [Kaiser] thinks it is almost sexual. And he says it's very important that Ben was the person who said to Kay about Phil in that traumatic moment—let him have the divorce. A kind of honesty there. And he says of Ben Bradlee, he is the person who brought Kay into the modern world, and literally and figuratively taught her to say "fuck." He was wonderful at playing her, no one could play her better. He plays her perfectly, he plays her yet he seems to be outside her reach.

"Everybody does think she loved you, but that's okay," I said to Ben in his office one afternoon, revisiting the same topic I'd brought up with him so many times before.

"I think she loved me in *the* most platonic way," he said. "We loved each other. It's hard to say it, because people would take that as an admission of all the terrible things that they think."

I told him people had often said things to me about her being in love with him, but I'd never heard anybody allege that he would have or could have reciprocated.

"I've never felt that I had to defend myself in that," he said.

From Ben's perspective I think that even factual statements about Kay's obvious fondness for him demean their relationship, reduce it to its lowest common denominator. To him, and to history, the most important aspect of their relationship isn't whether Kay was always, semisecretly, a little bit in love with him; it's what they were able to accomplish at the newspaper. Those of us who stand on the outside of that relationship naturally have some curiosity about Kay's feelings, and about Ben's, but the truth is that only the two of them really know what kind of bargain they struck. What matters is that it worked.

In 1995, when Ben's memoir came out, Kay threw a book party

for him. In its aftermath, Ben realized that he hadn't thanked her for the party, and also that he hadn't ever given her a "properly dedicated" copy of the book. He wrote her a letter to apologize, and this is how it ends:

```
Katharine, you have been the most important force in my
life.  You have been a joyous partner who makes my heart
leap every time I see you.  There is nothing that can change
that, not even my own clumsiness and momentary selfishness.

The party was such a generous gesture.  Your words were so
graceful and welcome, the way everything about you comes
across to me.


                    Love,



                     Ben
```

That's it, all of it. You can call it whatever you want to.

SUPERNIGGER

April 15, 1981

"Jimmy's World" was in essence a fabrication.
I never encountered or interviewed an 8-year-old
heroin addict. The September 28, 1981, article
in The Washington Post was a serious misrepresentation
which I deeply regret. I apologize to my
newspaper, my profession, the Pulitzer board and
all seekers of the truth. Today, in facing up to
the truth, I have submitted my resignation.

Janet Cooke

God, I wish this shit would finally go away. People do less time for homicide.

—Janet Cooke, via an intermediary, December 4, 2011

October 16, 2007, seventh floor, *The Washington Post*, 3:15 P.M.:

Me: I couldn't make this stuff up if I tried.
  [Ben stands in the doorway of my temporary office, laughs, and then moves off toward his own office. Suddenly he stops, turns halfway back toward me. Over his shoulder:]
B: You *could*. Just don't.

IN JULY OF 2010, I met David Maraniss for lunch at a Mexican restaurant near the National Cathedral. Maraniss is a tall, loping man with a kind face and a gentle Midwestern demeanor that doesn't quite conceal the sharpness underneath. As we looked over our menus, we talked about how he came to the *Post*, and about the relationship between Howard and Ben.

I kept asking questions in their proper order, chronologically, focusing on him, trying to establish a rapport. After about ten minutes, he turned to me and said, "I know you mostly want to talk about Janet Cooke. That's fine." He laughed. I protested a little, but it was true and he knew it.

If Watergate is the great achievement of Ben's career, then Janet Cooke is the great failure. Ben has said on numerous occasions that his nightmare is that the Janet Cooke incident will occupy the second paragraph of his obituary. In his journalistic life, whether he likes it or not, it's the Pentagon Papers and Watergate and then, after the doldrums of the late seventies, it's Janet Cooke.

Cooke was a young reporter at the *Post* who fabricated a story about an eight-year-old heroin addict. Her story, "Jimmy's World," ran on the front page on Sunday, September 28, 1980. Immediately suspicions arose that the piece wasn't fully accurate—inside and outside the newsroom—but for a variety of complicated reasons the *Post* stood by its story. So much so that the editors decided to submit "Jimmy's World" for a Pulitzer Prize. So much so that the piece won the prize for feature writing.

After Cooke's victory was announced in April 1981, the Associated Press and other news outlets began to check the biographical facts that Cooke had submitted as a part of her Pulitzer nomination package. Alarming discrepancies emerged. She said she had studied at the Sorbonne, for instance, but a prior copy of her résumé made no mention of it. She claimed that she had graduated from Vassar, but officials there said they'd only had her for a year. These falsehoods, once discovered, loosed a torrent. Two days after the Pulitzer had been awarded to Janet Cooke, Ben found himself in the unenviable position of returning the prize.

A friend of Ben's once told me that Watergate was a "particularly rich mirror" for who Ben is: his support for his reporters, his ability to stave off criticism, his adrenaline on a good story, his nose for the jugular. That's all true. But the stakes during Watergate were so cosmic, so existential not just for the *Post* but for America's system of government and faith in elected officials and all the rest, that it's hard to isolate Ben's particular piece of it.

Janet Cooke was also an aberration, but a smaller one. The universe of the Cooke story is the universe of the *Post* itself. The currents and processes that Janet Cooke was a product of, and those that she in turn unleashed, mostly played out within the confines of the *Post* building on 15th Street. There are no governmental conspiracies to decode, no complex transactions. Janet Cooke fabricated a story, and she got away with it. Not only did she get away with it, but she won a Pulitzer Prize for it. The incident and its aftermath tell you a lot about Ben, about the newspaper that he ran and the culture he helped create. How "Jimmy's World" happened is the flip side of the great golden coin of Watergate. It's a rich mirror for Ben, for the *Post*, and even, in unexpected and powerful ways, for Watergate itself.

In 2006, Jim Lehrer conducted a series of long interviews with Ben that aired on PBS as a program called *Free Speech*. Lehrer found himself frustrated by Ben's refusal to say much that he hadn't already said before. The way Lehrer put it to me, when I asked him about it, was that Ben "doesn't think in the voice of God. He thinks in the voice of Ben. It's a very different perspective."

There was, though, one moment in the interviews where Ben addressed a difficult subject directly. "One of the reasons the Janet Cooke story got through the system at the Post was that the Post editors and the Post reporters, people who were supposedly supervising her, came from elite or very different backgrounds," Lehrer said. "They didn't live in those neighborhoods or whatever. Is that a problem?"

"Let's say the obvious," Ben said.

"Yeah," Lehrer said, knowing what's coming.

"That Janet Cooke was black," Ben continued. "The people she was writing about were black, and she was writing about blacks who lived in a slum neighborhood. I don't get there often and neither do the people—I mean, that was a very unspoken dimension of that and I don't see why people can't speak about it."

In the wake of the scandal, some of the white people at the *Post* contorted themselves into uncomfortable shapes in order to avoid the impression that Cooke's race had anything to do with what happened. The purpose was honorable—they wanted to prevent a backlash against other black reporters—but, as is often the case when people protest that something obvious had nothing to do with an outcome, one can generally assume that it in fact had *everything* to do with that outcome. Janet Cooke didn't fabricate her story because she was black. But how she got to the *Post*, and how she was treated once she got there, is a different story altogether.

Nobody I've ever come across has called Ben a racist, but certainly by birth and education and opportunity he was born among the white elite and stayed there. His use of racial terminology is reflective of his era, certainly not progressive in any way. In the seventies, Harry Rosenfeld told me, "Political correctness was already setting in, and Ben didn't get the memo." Even in the eighties Ben didn't have much trouble referring to various people as "the hardest-working white man I know." But he was also at least semi-aware of his shortcomings in that regard:

Memoir Interview, slug "War," January 3, 1990:

B: There was a total awakening for me about blacks because I had known
no blacks in my life. There just weren't many blacks in my life. Growing up there were no blacks in my preppie boarding school I went to,
obviously. There were probably three blacks in my class at Harvard of
1100. And the blacks on the destroyer were all mess boys and they were
called mess boys. And they had all been absolutely screwed over by the
recruiters. The recruiters had said join the Navy and you'll be a machine gunner, you'll be a this, you'll be a this, you'll be a that. Whereas
in fact, they did have battle stations on guns, short of action, they were
serving soup, making beds, shining shoes. It was a disaster.

BF: How did you feel about it?

B: I was appalled by it. In the first place I didn't know it until somebody
talked to me about it. They got harassment, I mean I'm sure I didn't
know the half of it. . . .

BF: Was that the first time you thought about race?

B: Surely. Probably. I'm slightly embarrassed I didn't think about it
more.

In a long, uncharacteristically reflective letter to Kay Graham in
1998, long after both of their eras at the paper were over, Ben wrote
that he had never considered himself a racist. "But the point is that
none of us had any personal experience with racism. We literally
didn't know what blacks were talking about when they used the
word, unless they were talking about a lynching, or a Klan cross
burning."

When I got to the Post, I <u>knew</u> that I wasn't a racist—I just knew it—
and therefore I could not get my arms around the concept that
intelligent people thought that I was. And of course from their point of
view, I was. Because of my totally white perspective, because of my
total removal from the black experience, because of my unawareness of
the common denominators of the black experience—like poverty, like
inferior educations, like unequal opportunities. . . . I began, just barely

began, to grasp the fact that there was a white version of the truth and a
black version of the truth, and they had damn little to do with each
other.

During Ben's first stint at the *Post*, in the late forties, one of the assistant city editors monitored the police radio, and when something
occurred in a black neighborhood he would wave his hand dismis-
sively and say, "That's black, don't worry about it." The *Post* employed a pair of photographers known as the Jonas brothers, one of
whom picked up the head of a black man who had been decapi-
tated by a trolley car and asked his brother to snap photos of him
holding it aloft like a trophy, with the Capitol in the background.
And there had been Ben's reportage of the riots over the integration of the pools that Phil Graham had buried after making a backroom deal.

But it wasn't until Ben's tenure as executive editor at the *Post*—Ben
assumed the editorship of the paper five and a half months after Martin Luther King, Jr. was assassinated in Memphis—that race became
a pressing internal issue in his professional life. By June of 1969, trouble was clearly brewing: "I hate very much to have to add up our
black employees," Steve Isaacs, the city editor, wrote to Gene Patterson, the managing editor, in response to a query from above. "We
don't keep statistics on this sort of thing, any more than we keep
statistics on green employees, Jewish employees, employees against
the war, etc." Isaacs noted that over the previous five or six years
editors had made a concerted effort to hire black reporters. "If anything, I suppose, we have discriminated in favor of blacks, hiring
those who seemed to have potential and who could be developed
into first-class newsmen. We have had some success at that."

In November of 1970, a year and a half later, Ben received a letter
from a white reporter indicating that things were getting worse:

I've come up with two broad observations: a few of the blacks
appear to be using race as a crutch for some of their own
shortcomings as journalists; and serious racial problems exist at The

Post. The major issue is how to deal with both without causing a blow-up with the blacks that would certainly hurt The Post and prevent an embryonic white back-lash from burgeoning and damaging the operation of the newsroom.

I encountered this sentiment frequently in behind-the-scenes memo traffic between the (white) editors, many of whom felt that the paper had, in a knee-jerk way, simply hired as many black people as they could, not all of whom belonged there.

Another year later, Ben received a thoughtful but ominous memo from a black reporter named David Hardy. "I have been doing some long and hard thinking about the tone and content of our conversation last Thursday," Hardy wrote to Ben on November 3, 1971. "I was particularly distressed by a couple of things you said, such as 'I have some things I'm trying to do and I don't need anybody putting obstacles in my way.'" He went on:

Mr. Bradlee, not once on the few occasions when I felt it necessary to approach you to discuss internal problems have I done so with the intention of presenting you with any obstacles. (I have been in the newspaper business long enough to know and respect what you have done to make the Washington Post the newspaper that it is.) . . .

I am not an alarmist; but I know trouble when I see it and came to you only so that something could be done before conditions sparked an incident and added to the polarization between the races inside the company.

He made reference to "reactionary white supervisors (who still don't feel blacks are capable of performing certain jobs) and cynical blacks (many of whom are content to sit back and wait for an incident 'so we can get the shit on')."

"You may not want to admit it," Hardy wrote, "but these attitudes among the races are just as pervasive on the fifth floor* as they are in other parts of the paper."

*"The fifth floor" means the newsroom.

I remember encountering Hardy's memo for the first time in Ben's archives, and being surprised by it. It wasn't that Ben only saved things that were favorable to him. He seemed always to relish letters from people who disagreed with him or called him an idiot. But this was different. Hardy had clearly made a reasonable approach and been rebuffed. How could Ben have blown David Hardy off, a man who seemed—on paper, anyway—so eminently reasonable?

Then I flipped the page and saw Ben's reply:

Dear David:

I had so many obstacles thrown in my path last week—everything from anonymous, obscene letters to trouble-making crap leaked to that bible of the newspaper business, Women's Wear Daily—you've got to forgive me, please, if I reached out wrongly to include you as an obstacle. I don't. I value your advice. I think you are now in a position to do this newspaper that I love a great deal of good, and I would like to offer you any help I can. I suspect the most effective help I can offer is to listen to you.

The only obstacle I feel you could put in my path would be to let some relatively minor irritation inflame itself into a major crisis. As you point out, too many people would like that. . . .

I'd also like to know everything you can tell me about the "reactionary white supervisors" on this floor.

Can we talk about all this—and more?

Every year, starting in 1969, Ben invited the top editors at the *Post* to a retreat at his country house on the Cacapon River in West Virginia. They called it, with some irony, "Pugwash," after the nuclear disarmament conferences started by Bertrand Russell in the fifties. It became a yearly and much larger tradition over time. A look at the proceedings from one of the early Pugwashes gives you some sense of what black reporters at the *Post* were up against:

That's Eugene Patterson with his hands folded at his mouth, then Phil Geyelin, then Ben, then the cup, cigarette, and glasses of Howard Simons. Note who's dealing.

During the Pugwash of 1971, one of the major topics that the editors took up was the issue of race at the paper. Thankfully, somebody brought a tape recorder and used it.

"Certainly on the question of blacks Gene and I have been deeply involved and deeply depressed," Ben said at the start of the discussion. "I had a black news aide that the fourth floor ran out because they kept calling him a nigger." A pretty concise description of the problem.

Others had similar experiences. Harry Rosenfeld said simply, "I want to see some white faces doing the menial jobs." Howard Simons: "I also find that we are racist in the sense that we regard the blacks at the Washington Post in a monolithic way. We talk about them as blacks. We don't talk about the whites that way—we talk about the whites as individuals."

Everybody agreed that they needed to offer more and better training for black reporters, and then a debate ensued about newsroom culture. Should reporters be allowed to wear black power necklaces and that kind of thing? "If a guy goes out with a black fist or a button, he's telling people what he thinks, he's taking a position," one editor said. "I don't think he should."

"More than an Afro hairdo and those sharp flared pants?" Ben interjected. "My God."

It sounds like what it is, a bunch of World War II–era white guys talking about black people as if they were Martians. But reading through the whole transcript, I was struck by how genuine and thoughtful the debate was, despite the cultural barriers and some of the paternalistic terminology. *They* weren't saying "nigger," and they were deploring the people who did. They didn't have the answers for the racial problems at the *Post*, but their effort to try to figure it out feels sincere. "We were all trying very hard," Gene Patterson told me, "but we were learning together, and we were learning very slowly."

On Monday, February 7, 1972, seven months after the final triumph of the Pentagon Papers and a little more than four months before the break-in at the Watergate, Ben received a letter signed by nine black Metro reporters. Addressed to "B. Bradlee," the letter laid out twenty questions that the reporters wanted written answers to by that Friday. The first question: "Why in the past has there never been more than one black reporter assigned to the National reporting staff?" The fifth: "Why are there no blacks in top editorial management positions?"

In the wake of the letter, Ben received numerous confidential memos from highly placed white editors saying that many of the reporters who had signed the letter were subpar reporters indistinctive of race. Of one of the signers, an editor wrote, "He is in the wrong business, and we have all told him so." Much later, Ben would write privately of the disgruntled Metro reporters, "The fact that some members of this group were less than able didn't change anything. We made a classic, maybe racist, decision by hiring a multitude of blacks because we felt guilty, rather than hire the best blacks at a time when we couldn't even define what the best black was, or could be."*

---

*It wasn't only the white people who felt this way. Leon Dash, one of the signers of the letter, agreed with Ben in an interview in 1993 that some of the other black reporters didn't

A week after the initial letter, Ben and Howard Simons had their first meeting with the black reporters in a conference room at the *Post*. Ben read his prepared answers to their questions, which boiled down in most instances to this:

> B: You ask why there are no blacks, only one black or only two blacks in various departments. My answer is both simple and complicated: We have not yet been successful in matching our commitment to hire, assign and promote blacks with our commitment to hire, assign and promote the very best journalists we can find to fill the needs we have. This is the cutting edge of the problem that we now face.

He read out the rest of his statement, and then there was silence. One of the reporters said to Ben that they would use Ben's written response to come up with a suggested affirmative action program, to be presented at a later date.

"You don't want to talk anymore?" Ben asked.

"We wanted to hear what you had to say, Ben," one of the reporters said.

"Well, why don't we hang it out?" Ben asked, trying to keep things moving, suspicious that that was all there was to it.

"Everything we had to say was in the questions."

"Was it really? I mean, I don't want to try to deny what you said, but I have the feeling you've got more on your mind than that. An affirmative action program is something that I'd be damned interested in," Ben said. "But I'd like to hear you on the subject of how deep is our problem, what is our problem, how to . . ."

"That's something we'd be better off . . . taking up at another time," another of the reporters said. "What we're suggesting . . . is another meeting."

"Jesus, I got cranked up for nothing!" Ben exclaimed, recognizable across the eons as himself. "I think my door is open to anybody.

---

belong at the paper. When Ben referred to one reporter, with typical lack of political correctness, as somebody who was "selling dope and screwing white girls," Dash chuckled and said, "I'm with you."

Apparently other people don't think so. . . . But I do not feel abused by people coming in to talk to me, and I would like to say that." He also said that he hoped that the reporters wouldn't let their grievance hinder them in getting about their business. "Don't let it interfere with your jobs, please," he pleaded. "Don't be too suspicious of us."

Two weeks later, after some additional back-and-forth, the Metro 9 had become the Metro 8, and they presented Ben with an affirmative action program/quota system that was nearly impossible for the *Post* to achieve. "By one year from enactment of this plan," they wrote, "black employment on the Washington Post newsroom floor should be in the range of 35 to 45 percent in every job category." The current percentage of black newsroom employees was 9.3 percent, 37 out of 396. Out of the 37, only 13 were reporters.

"That was our bargaining position," Leon Dash told Ben in their interview in 1993. "It was put out there to negotiate from."

"Did you have any sense that this was going to be difficult for Bradlee to do?" Ben asked, referring to himself in the third person as he often did. "I mean, because he had to persuade the racist bean counters . . ."

"Whether it was difficult or not, this was our position," Dash said. "You don't achieve anything if there's no blood on the floor. You can't achieve it by sweet talk, or appeals to reason, or appeals to morality. You have to confront the situation."

Right around the time of the Metro 8 proposal, Dash had decided to confront the situation in personal terms, by driving over to Ben's house late one night.

"I was very angry," Dash remembered later.

"Yes, you were," Ben said.

Dash felt that his immediate editor was racist and was trying to drive him out of the newspaper, and he wanted Ben to know about it because he felt Ben had been kept in the dark. He was also drunk, and at Ben's house he proceeded to get drunker. "I was a little bit scared," Ben admitted in 1993. Tony and the kids were upstairs while the two men thundered down below them, Tony listening intently to Dash's voice and deciding that because his intonation dropped at the end of each phrase he wasn't going to do anything physical.

"There was justified anger," Dash said. "You couldn't see the forest through the trees, and it was right in front of you."

"Well, it was true," Ben said. "You were right. That was a seminal moment for me. Because I hadn't been yelled at. I didn't get yelled at all that much by anybody, but I sure as hell hadn't been yelled at by a black, and I hadn't been accused of things that were true."

Dash had resolved to shake Ben's tree, as he once put it, and that evening he did. "That was a key moment in my understanding of this," Ben told him in 1993. "The thing that impressed me about your argument is that we were racist in our lack of sensitivity. We didn't think about it ever. I mean, things that destroyed you just didn't get on our screen."

"At all," Dash agreed.

But Ben's personal appreciation for Dash's position didn't mean that the Metro 8's proposal made sense for the newspaper. As soon as he received it, Ben wrote to Kay Graham and the rest of the legal, editorial, and managerial team with his response:

```
MEMO TO:  John Prescott
          Mrs. Graham
          Simons, Geyelin, Baker
          Mr. Beebe, Mr. Finberg, Mr. Califano


FROM:     Bradlee

RE:       Affirmative Action Program proposed by
          Eight Post Blacks on February 28.



          I believe we should hammer out some
affirmative program -- hopefully without capital
letters.  I believe we should do this with all
feasible speed.

          But I reject out of hand the establishment
of any quota system for The Washington Post.

          We can and should treat blacks with more
sensitivity.  We can and should have more  --- and
more qualified --- blacks on the paper, and in
positions of more responsibility.  We can and should
```

```
do more training of all new employees, black and white.
We can and should do more intelligent recruiting of
black reporters and editors.  The implementation of
these possibilities and desires will be an affirmative
program.

        But the quality of this newspaper is the
only thing in this world that is important here, and
a quota system -- for whites, blacks, males, females,
Jews, WASPs, old, young, Orientals, Chicanos, Ivy
League, Big Ten, North, South -- is simply unthinkable.
```

He would say the exact same thing to the Metro 8 as he had to Kay Graham. "Except for the firmest conviction that the only quota appropriate for this newspaper is a quota on quality," he wrote on February 29, 1972, "I find much of interest in the program proposed in your letter of February 28." He proposed a time to meet, but the terms of the standoff were already clear.

Over the next few weeks, Ben and the rest of the editors came up with a plan that proposed a wide variety of solutions—hiring an equal employment opportunity officer, offering black reporters training at the Columbia School of Journalism, adding a black editor to Metro, creating a mentoring system for young black reporters with older established reporters.

The Metro 8 weren't having it. "We have discussed your proposal of March 10," they wrote on March 15, "and find it an insult to our commitment, vague and totally unacceptable." The memo concluded, "We are here today again to discuss numbers." Ben had hoped to avoid a major flare-up—when Dash handed him the first letter on February 7, Ben had told him "Don't let this go too far"— but it was clear that they were now at an impasse. Eight days later, after another reporter dropped off, seven of the original nine black reporters filed an official complaint against the *Post* with the U.S. Equal Employment Opportunity Commission.

Contrary to the impression that the complaint created, the *Post* actually had a better track record on racial matters than most other mainstream newspapers. Shortly after the complaint was lodged, Bill Raspberry, a black man and a highly respected columnist at the *Post*, put it this way in one of his columns: "The Post, it must be said, has done more than any other white newspaper in the country, both in terms of its editorial policy and in terms of its newsroom hiring practices. And when you do more, more is expected of you." That was evidently the Metro 7's view, and also that of some of the newspaper's readers:

To the Editors:

As a long-time subscriber and former admirer of the Washington Post, I urge you to respond favorably and vigorously to the insistence of your black reporters that there should be many more blacks at all levels of participation and responsibility in handling the news which your paper offers to us, the readers.

I have been shocked and greatly disappointed by the paper's response to the black reporters' protest—shocked because I thought that the Washington Post was far too sophisticated to resort to the irrelevant and obsolete plea "we're doing better than others," and disappointed because I would have expected the Post to recognize immediately not only the justice of the black reporters' position but the importance of black and other viewpoints in the paper's operation.

Ben's response:

Dear Ms. Ware:

On February 7, 1972, The Washington Post had more black reporters, photographers and editors than any other newspaper in America.

On May 30, 1972, The Washington Post had 42% more black reporters, photographers and editors than it did on February 7, 1972.

Racial issues are rarely only about numbers or hires, and so some people slammed Ben for his lack of understanding even as he and the others around him made the only kind of effort that they knew how to make. Roger Wilkins, the black *Post* editorial writer who had been cited by the Pulitzer board for his exemplary work on Watergate, eventually left the paper and would occasionally lob tough memos and letters into Ben's inbox.* ("I understand that you recently said that you're tired of pampering blacks . . . one of the things that makes us tired and gives us the pain that makes us flaky is that we have to pamper arrogant and stupid—at least as they relate to us—white people.") Some of the letters from Wilkins and, later, from Juan Williams, make you wince; they're pretty direct attacks. The implication is that Ben was removed enough and white enough that by definition he was part of the problem.

Ben didn't back down, but he got the message. To Wilkins, years after he had left the paper:

Dear Roger:

I am now recovered from your letter about Sharpton. But it took your wonderful message about the Chris Stern party to do it. I'm used to having you alternate between anger and love by now. I appreciate the love more than the anger but I know you understand my frailties better than most.

Let's eat.

But Ben also wasn't going to apologize for things that he didn't think were his fault. This was Ben's response to a long letter about racism at the *Post* from Richard Prince, one of the Metro 7, in 1979, roughly two years after Prince had left the paper:

---

*When I called Wilkins to try to set up an interview, he told me he wasn't interested in talking to me, because it wouldn't be "truth-telling." "Ben made it this far with all his medals and his reputation intact," Wilkins said, before dismissing me. "I don't want to drop a lot of shit on him."

April 26, 1979

Dear Dick:

      I note your long and accusatory letter of
April 15.

      It seems to me that you have equated your
own failure here and elsewhere with "the pervasive
racism in the American media." I don't.

      I wish you peace and good luck.

               Sincerely,

On July 12, 1979, less than three months after Ben's reply to Richard Prince, Ben received a letter from a young reporter on the *Toledo Blade*, a woman named Janet Cooke. "Dear Mr. Bradlee," it began, "I have been a full-time reporter for The Blade for slightly more than two years, and I believe I am now ready to tackle the challenge of working for a larger newspaper in a major city."

She was black, a Phi Beta Kappa graduate of Vassar in 1976, according to her résumé, and she had excellent clips. "The answer to a modern editor's prayers," Ben wrote of her later. "Female Phi Beta Kappa graduates of Seven Sisters colleges who can write the King's English with style don't grow on trees, white or black, and we were a decade into our commitment to increase the number and quality of minorities and women on the staff." Six months later, she was at a desk in the newsroom.

Everybody who ever knew Janet Cooke agrees that anybody in Ben's position would have snapped her up just as quickly as he and the *Post* did. She wrote beautifully and was beautiful herself; she dressed well, carried herself with style, and made a splash from the

moment she walked into the newsroom on January 3, 1980. You
could almost forgive Ben for having thought, somewhat naively, that
a new era was beginning at the paper, not necessarily post-racial but
one in which gains had been made, consolidated, and kept. He seems
to have hoped so himself, as a letter written two weeks before Cooke
began at the *Post* indicates:

December 21, 1979

Ben Johnson
City Editor
Post-Tribune
Gary, Indiana

. . . Let me tell you this funny story. We gave a lunch for civil leaders
the other day, and Mayor Barry was there. He got up to complain about
The Post's coverage and suggested that instead of assigning Milt
Coleman (who is black) to cover City Hall, we assign a white reporter.

His reasoning was that a white reporter would be liberal and
therefore easy for him to manipulate.

I laughed and told him that we all had come a long way; we had
crossed a lot of bridges to get to this particular place.

They *had* crossed a lot of bridges. Janet Cooke's direct editor at the
District Weekly, a small local section, was Vivian Aplin-Brownlee, a
black woman herself. Milton Coleman would go on to become the
city editor for the daily staff and would be Cooke's direct editor on
the "Jimmy" story. Far from being the only black person for miles,
Janet was surrounded by black people in positions of direct editorial
control. This was surely a sign of progress, wasn't it? Black editors
editing a story by a black reporter about the black community: wasn't
that the right way for this to work, and exactly what the Metro 7
would have wanted?

In her desperation to get out of Toledo, Janet had lied on her résumé to create just the impression that she had created. And though
later people would protest that Janet's race had nothing to do with it,

nobody really believed that—least of all Cooke herself. Seventeen years after she faked her résumé, when asked what her purpose had been when she sat down at her typewriter to create that false, idealized portrait of herself, she made clear that she had harbored no illusions about the nature of the enterprise.

"My goal," she told reporter Mike Sager in 1996, "was to create Supernigger."

JUNKIES

Q: When did you start thinking that you might want to be editor of the paper?

BW: When Ben said, "Become Metro editor."

Q: Which was '79?

BW: Yeah, we were still finishing *The Brethren* . . .

And so I thought—remember, this is all on the record, quotable—Ben was, you know, a journalistic icon and leader, father, godlike figure in the profession. And to be Ben Bradlee's, you know, successor would've been . . .

Q: An honor.

BW: . . . well, more than an honor. I remember people like Dick Harwood took me out to dinner or lunch and said, you'll be the executive editor of the paper someday . . . there was all of that stuff. Until we all discovered that I wasn't any good at it.

Q: Is that really true, or do you just say that?

BW: No, no, that's really true. I just wasn't. And Ben realized it. And Janet Cooke brought it to a head in a way that was—it just brought it to a head of, you know, this guy supposedly has got a good shit detector, and where was it? Fair question.

—Dining room at Grey Gardens, East Hampton,
Long Island, August 28, 2010

I'VE ALWAYS THOUGHT THAT THE term "news junkie" applied in a particularly vivid way to Ben and to Bob—and, in a slightly different way, to Carl, too. Much of the process of addiction is a doomed attempt to recapture the pure rush of the initial high. Ben and Bob and Carl were all doomed. Nothing they could ever do, no matter how distinguished, would be as big as what they'd already done.

Carl rode the fame high for as long as he could, living it up as a literary lion in New York City, dating Bianca Jagger and Elizabeth Taylor, neglecting his work, and then eventually getting sober. He got chewed up and spit out the fastest. When you meet him now, it's Carl 2.0 or even 3.0. It's not the same guy.

Bob is still Bob, digging for that newspaper high, plunging himself back again and again into his reporting. He impressed the entire paper when he returned to the *Post* newsroom in the fall of 1975—after a year's unpaid leave to work on the movie version of *All the President's Men* and on *The Final Days,* his second book with Carl—and started working the phones. He hasn't let up since then, really. I worked for him from 1999 to 2002, and though he was older and richer he hadn't lost any drive or determination. He works at a furious pace, always in pursuit of the next secret, the next scoop, the next scandal, haunted by what he doesn't know but might be able to find out. There is a kind of compulsion to his repeated reenactments of the processes of investigation and discovery. They are the vein that he keeps tapping, over and over, in just the same way, even as the world changes around him.

In 1976, when the movie version of *All the President's Men* came out, Bob was only thirty-three, with ladder still to climb at the *Post* and in his life. He was still, as Ben would say, on the come. Ben was at the top of the ladder and had nowhere else to go. What kept them both going at the *Post* was the search for another story that would quicken the pulse and get everybody in Washington talking. At the *Post*, they called these "holy shit" stories. Bob sitting in the courtroom when James McCord reported that he worked for the CIA is the holy grail of the holy shit story, the high of all highs. After Watergate it was a stated and unstated goal, an expectation that everybody understood at the *Post*, that what got Ben and the rest of the newsroom going was the holy shit stories, the big ones.

In May of 1976, just after the movie premiered, the *Post* broke the news that Congressman Wayne Hays of Ohio had kept Elizabeth

Ray, his mistress, on the federal payroll for two years, at an annual salary of $14,000. It wasn't exactly Watergate, but the *Post* had Hays cold and it was certainly the kind of story that made you say "Holy shit" to yourself as you made your way through your bowl of Wheaties. Ray played the part of kept woman with flair. "I can't type, I can't file, I can't even answer the phone," she told a *Post* reporter.*

Hays denied aspects of the story—thus heightening the stakes—but he didn't realize that *Post* reporters had observed him eating dinner with Ray the week before. Three days after the first story, another ran on the *Post*'s front page: "Hays Reverses Himself, Admits 'Relationship.'" The lede: "After two days of denials, Rep. Wayne L. Hays (D-Ohio) admitted yesterday that he had had a 'personal relationship' with Elizabeth Ray, but denied her charge that he put her on the public payroll to be his mistress." Hays had taken to the House chamber itself to deliver what the *Post* described as a "dramatic confession."

The story made a splash. For starters, it had sex in it—always a plus, in Ben's book. One veteran reporter said that the Hays story was the only time he had seen Ben fully engaged since Nixon had resigned two years before. These were the years of an acknowledged malaise at the *Post*, when people (including Kay) thought Ben was out of touch.

By the late seventies, the *Post* was starting to come back around. When Bob took over as assistant managing editor for Metro on May 1, 1979, he commanded the largest news staff of any of the assistant managing editors—108 reporters, nearly one fourth of the reporters on the entire newspaper. As he told me, this was the moment when he threw his hat in the ring in earnest to succeed Ben as editor of the *Post*. The way to the top was to produce, plain and simple, and Bob knew those rules better than anybody. Where he had thrown all of himself into his own reporting for more than eight years

---

*Right after I started working for Ben back in 2007, I came across a topless picture of Elizabeth Ray somewhere in the files. (At some point after the scandal, she had posed for *Playboy*.) I brought it into his office, where Ben looked at it approvingly for a minute, eyes on her chest, before handing it back to me and saying, "Lungs."

at that point, he now threw himself into the task of prodding the huge Metro staff into coming up with the kinds of holy shit stories that would make page one of the paper.

In November of 1979, six months after he took charge of Metro, Bob and Pat Tyler came up with just such a story. Tyler had uncovered evidence that the head of the Mobil Oil Corporation, a man named William Tavoulareas, had installed his son as a partner in a London-based shipping management firm that had made millions of dollars operating Mobil ships under exclusive, no-bid contracts. Keep in mind that in the summer of 1979 Americans had been forced to endure daylong waits for gas during the oil crisis. Public anger at the oil companies was high.

The story ran on November 30, 1979. Ben, from his memoir:

> If I had known that the 84-inch story would cost the *Post* more than $1,500,000 to run the story, plus thirty lousy days as a defendant on trial in District Court, plus another seven and a half years of appellate litigation, I would have told [Woodward and Tyler] to go piss up a rope.

Tavoulareas was upset with a few words that had appeared in the headline on page one and then in the lede of the story itself: "Sets up Son" and "set up his son." The words seem harmless, and from the context of the story quite obviously true, but Tavoulareas took exception to them and brought suit against the *Post* for libel.

"We got sued because the president of Mobil, in order to say that we were right, would mean that he had deceived his board on how much of a related-party transaction that was," Tyler told me. "That was the issue. He either sued us and blew smoke or told his board he fucked up and fell on his sword. And Tav's not the kind of guy to fall on his sword." Over a long, drawn-out process, the *Post* would spill a good deal of financial blood to defend the story, a process that Ben didn't think was worth it in the end—even though the *Post* eventually won. But the journalism was solid, the kind of reporting Bob was pushing for.

"Of course Woodward is swinging for the fences," Tyler told me, of the Mobil story. "Showing that Metro runs the paper, and that he's the next editor of the paper."

"And, of course, sitting across from me in Metro," Tyler said, "was Janet Cooke."

Cooke had been hired for the staff of the District Weekly, a kind of subsidiary of the Metro section that was distributed every Thursday. It was widely known that if you did well on one of the weeklies—there were sections for Virginia and Maryland as well—you stood a good chance of being promoted to write for the daily newspaper.

Cooke was ambitious, and she worked hard. After six weeks she had her first big cover story in the District Weekly, a long piece about 14th Street and the U Street corridor, which was still burned out from the 1968 riots and had become a haven for drug users and prostitutes. A police officer had been killed in the area, and she rode along with a patrol for an evening to get the pulse of the place. There was a lot of complexity to the story—the dead policeman had a reputation for unwarranted violence, for one thing—and she managed to convey subtlety and atmosphere in a convincing way. The language is vivid: "4:05. Police are called to 14th and Q streets, where an apparent robbery victim has received a deep cut on the neck. He is screaming, blood flowing like burgundy from the open wound."

"It was a fine piece of journalism," her editor, Vivian Aplin-Brownlee, would later tell Bill Green, the man who was tasked with writing the postmortem on Cooke's fabrication of the "Jimmy" story. "She was consumed by blind and raw ambition. It was obvious, but it doesn't deny the talent." Aplin-Brownlee wasn't yet skeptical of Cooke, but others in the newsroom were. One reporter who sat near Cooke's desk didn't believe any of the dialogue in her story; he reached for a red crayon and began to underline every quote that he thought was invented. As he was doing this, he watched as Ben walked over to Cooke's desk, took a seat on it with one foot in the air, and told her, "That's the best story I've read in the paper for a long time."

"I was standing there when it happened," the reporter told me. "And I said, well, I'm not taking [my doubts] to him and telling him. But I had my eye on her after that."

There had also been something in the reporting of the story that presaged what was to come. "She was Gucci and Cardin and Yves St. Laurent," Aplin-Brownlee told Green. "She went out on that 14th Street story in designer jeans and came back to tell me that somebody asked, 'What kind of nigger are you?' She thought it was funny. She had to learn the street." Janet had grown up in a strict and cloistered household in Toledo, drilled in reading and writing by a disciplinarian father and sent off to an elite private school filled with white kids. From there she'd gone on to Vassar, then to the University of Toledo and on to the *Blade*. Very little in her background had prepared her for 14th Street in Washington, D.C., in 1980.

For this reason, among others, Cooke struggled with Aplin-Brownlee from the start. By Aplin-Brownlee's metric, Cooke wasn't black enough. She didn't date black men, didn't have the slang down. Even as Cooke produced story after story for the District Weekly, she never felt that Aplin-Brownlee liked her—and she wasn't wrong. "A whole lot of glamour and flash, as opposed to substance," Aplin-Brownlee told Sager, of Cooke, in 1996. "I would look at her preening at her desk, getting ready to go out in the street and talk to the people. She didn't speak the language. She was hardly useful to me at all." In the years after her fabrication, Cooke would insist that her primary motivation for making up the Jimmy story in the first place had been to get away from Aplin-Brownlee.

In the wake of the police patrol story, which had been such a success, Cooke stayed on the 14th Street drugs-and-poverty beat. In late July of 1980, Aplin-Brownlee had begun to hear rumors about a new strain of powerful heroin in D.C. that ulcerated the skin of the people who used it. She put Cooke on the story, and Cooke spent a month or so digging around. At an interview with the head of a drug abuse program at Howard University, she heard a tantalizing reference to an eight-year-old kid who was apparently being treated at a local residential drug treatment facility.

Aplin-Brownlee was in and out of the office for the month of August, so Milton Coleman, now the city editor on the Metro desk, was overseeing Cooke's reporting. "I talked over Janet's materials with her," Coleman would later tell Bill Green. "She talked about hundreds of people being hooked. And at one point she mentioned an 8-year-old addict. I stopped her and said, 'That's the story. Go after it. It's a front-page story.'"

At any newspaper, the front page reflects an explicit editorial judgment of what's important. At Ben's *Post*, the front page was also where the stars of the National desk shone. Metro stories had to meet a high bar before they'd even be considered for it. Competition for page one at the *Post* was daily, and it was intense—starting from the very beginning of Ben's tenure as executive editor. At *The New York Times*, where decision making was more formalized and less ad hoc, the front-page decisions were often made by the night news editors. People waited in line for their turn. Not so at the *Post*, where Ben and Howard Simons and everybody else spent a lot of time trying to construct the perfect menu of stories for the next day's front. Flashy people and flashy subjects tended to get a far greater hearing, and be pushed for the front page much more consistently, than the kinds of process stories that Ben always called "room-emptiers."

In the wake of Cooke's fabrication, much would be made of the competition in the *Post*'s newsroom. People would call the place a snake pit, a place where everybody was striving to get ahead, where Ben coddled the stars and everybody else tried to become one of them. Cooke's lie was often contextualized in this way. "The allegation is that you 'play favorites' and glory in pitting people against each other," journalism professor George Reedy wrote in 1974, in a study that Ben commissioned to get a bead on dynamics in the newsroom. "In many instances, this may well be nothing but the alibi of the second-rate. But nevertheless, it is a widespread perception."

This notion of pitting reporters against each other—something that Ben claimed he never consciously did—took on a euphemism that shadowed Ben for most of his career: "creative tension." You can't read a contemporaneous account of Ben as executive editor without coming across the phrase.

"Creative tension is real," Len Downie told me. "But not in sort of the clichéd way. What's real is that the whole newsroom was competition. Ben brought in lively, competitive people. We all were competing for the front page."

Harry Rosenfeld was legendary for making histrionic appeals for Metro stories to go out front. He threatened, on a slightly too frequent basis, that Ben was going to "go down in the history books" if he left a certain Metro story off the front page. This routine became so predictable that Larry Stern once hired a Gypsy violinist to wait outside the news conference; once Rosenfeld began his customary spiel, the violinist came waltzing in to provide appropriately dramatic accompaniment.

There is little doubt that, at the twice daily news conferences—and particularly at the earlier of the two—the idea was to get Ben's attention. (He sometimes brought a toy siren into the news conference to shut people up when he found their story pitches boring.) What got Ben's attention was a big story pitched with verve and macho humor and a good punch line. All of the assistant managing editors—the people who ran the various sections, National, Metro, Style, and the like—vied for Ben's and Howard's attention. A story about an eight-year-old addict would certainly have stood out in that crowd.

But whether Janet Cooke and the other reporters were also a part of the "creative tension" bubble is a little less clear. David Maraniss started off as a reporter at the *Post*, and when Cooke made up her story he was an assistant editor on the Metro section. At our lunch, I asked him whether he believed in creative tension, and he said, "It was not there. It's complete bullshit.

"I know it," he went on. "I lived it. I mean, when I got to the paper it was still being sort of bandied about as part of the philosophy of the *Post*, and I never ever felt it. The only tension was really between Ben and Howard. And it didn't affect us, much. But other than that, it was an incredibly good place for a writer. It wasn't because of the tension. It was because of the possibilities. Tension tends to stifle possibilities, and this was the opposite."

When I asked Ben about it, he said that whether he ever intended to create a dynamic of "creative tension" at the paper or not, he gradually came to understand that the perception of it was real. "It may have been unconscious," he said of his own role. He was not a micromanager, and has often described his own style as extremely informal, haphazard, and spontaneous. He couldn't imagine how he would have set about actively implementing a policy of creative tension. "I wouldn't know how to *do* it," he told me. "I don't want to deny that there was that around me. But it's not right that I woke up in the morning and said I've got to really spend some time creating tension today or else I won't be able to do my job. Never."

"Ben hired a lot of people," Jim Hoagland told me, "and not all of 'em made it through. . . . I think Ben had a sense that that would happen. And it was up to you. I mean, this is very much the Bradlee philosophy as I understand it. You had to figure it out. You have to manage your own career. If you're depending on an editor to manage your career, you're dead."

If you take her at her word, Janet Cooke was mostly just trying to manage her own career. When she heard Coleman tell her "it's a front-page story," what she really heard was: this is my chance to get off the District Weekly, to get away from Vivian Aplin-Brownlee, to take a shot at a position working for Woodward and Milton Coleman on the daily Metro staff. She knew intuitively what Hoagland described.

"Everyone has to become an entrepreneur," the Frenchman wrote of the *Post* in the mid-eighties, likening the newsroom more to "a free-jazz orchestra than to a military band." You could make big leaps if you had a chip to play in the game, a hot story, and so you tried to get everything out of it that you could.

The only catch was that Janet didn't have a chip: she had the promise of a chip. In order to have the chip she had to find the boy, which proved impossible. Not because he didn't exist—perhaps there was, in fact, an eight-year-old addict out there somewhere—but because Cooke's sources at various drug treatment facilities refused to divulge any further information. The director of the residential treatment program that had been referred to as the possible location of the eight-year-old addict reported that he had no such patient, and others who had initially been helpful refused to go any further. After nearly eight weeks of reporting and searching, the trail ran cold.

Cooke told her editors this, but the story didn't die there. Coleman checked with Howard Simons and then reported back to Cooke that she could offer her sources complete anonymity. "The jugular of journalism lay exposed," Bill Green would write later, in the most widely quoted sentence of his comprehensive report on Cooke's fabrication, "the faith an editor has to place in a reporter."

A week later, Cooke came back to Coleman and said that she had found the boy. "I kept hearing Milton telling me to offer total anonymity," she said later. "At some point, it dawned on me that I could simply make it all up. I just sat down and wrote it."

What she fabricated at first was a thirteen-and-a-half-page double-spaced memo of an interview that she claimed to have conducted with a boy named Tyrone at his mother's house, somewhere in the Condon Terrace neighborhood of Washington.* It was full of the details that would later make it into the story: the kind of shirts Tyrone wore, the sofas covered in plastic, a rubber tree plant, fake bamboo blinds, a brown shag rug, and on and on. In his memoir Ben would write that "we all saw" this memo of Cooke's, but Woodward told Bill Green he didn't—and that if he had, he might have had some questions about how perfect and complete the quotations were. Coleman saw it for sure, and felt reassured by the presence of Tyrone's name.

"It was a great story," Coleman said later, "and it never occurred to me that she could make it up. There was too much distance between Janet and the streets."

Coleman told her to write up her story based on the memo. He wanted it to read, as he put it, "like John Coltrane's music, strong." After she wrote up a second draft, a *Post* artist was commissioned to illustrate the story—an unusual step in an era of ubiquitous high-

---

*At the time, Condon Terrace was known as one of the roughest neighborhoods in D.C.

quality photographs, but for obvious reasons there couldn't be any photos. The illustration, of a young black boy with sad eyes being injected with a syringe held by a pair of oversize hands, was shocking and powerful. It also borderered on socioeconomic and ethnic caricature. (The cast of the illustration would contribute to the widespread perception in the community, after the story ran, that the *Post* had sought to exploit the story for its own purposes. The oversized hands were supposed to be those of the dealer, "Ron," who routinely injected Tyrone/Jimmy and had threatened Cooke's life, but more than one reader felt that the *Post* was as complicit in the work of those hands as Ron was.)

About a week before the story ran, Bob saw it for the first time. "This story was so well-written and tied together so well that my alarm bells simply didn't go off," he told Bill Green. "My skepticism left me. I was personally negligent." He interviewed Cooke about the story but detected nothing amiss in her description of how she had come by her information. If there was anybody at the newspaper who understood the importance of protecting anonymous sources, it was Bob. Shortly thereafter Ben also read the story, and told Bill Green that at that time he thought it was "a helluva job."

Howard Simons was on vacation the week before the story ran, but he instructed Coleman to tell Cooke one last time that she didn't have to run the story if she didn't want to. "I told her what Simons told me to say," Coleman said later. "I said she had written a story that is certain to be controversial. You have seen a crime and you may be subpoenaed. We don't think so, but you can. You should know that the *Post* will stand behind you 100 percent." She might have to spend time in jail if she refused to identify her sources. "Before the story goes," Coleman continued, "if you don't want to face that, we won't run it."

On the morning of Saturday, September 27, 1980, Cooke told Coleman to release the story. That afternoon, Bob pitched it at the news conference. "Ben was there," he told me. "It had that drawing, and I remember him saying, 'Wow, this is a hell of a story.' And I said, 'Yeah, it really is.'" Front page, they all agreed, though not above the fold. Two of the sharpest and most powerful men at the *Post*—in the recent history of American journalism—had been fooled without ever having had the slightest suspicion about it. That night, at 9:54, the presses for the next day's edition of *The Washington Post* began to roll, eventually churning out 892,220 copies of the newspaper that would make Jimmy a household name in Washington.

"It was kind of Ben and Bob who pushed that story," David Maraniss told me. "Ben wasn't overly involved in it, but it was clear that he loved her, and that story. It was a holy shit story, and he was bored. He's easily bored. Ninety percent of the time he was bored. Nothing was big enough for him."

DEFENSE

JIMMY'S WORLD
8-Year-Old Heroin Addict Lives for a Fix

By Janet Cooke
Washington Post Staff Writer

Jimmy is 8 years old and a third-generation heroin addict, a precocious little boy with sandy hair, velvety brown eyes and needle marks freckling the baby-smooth skin of his thin brown arms.

He nestles in a large, beige reclining chair in the living room of his comfortably furnished home in Southeast Washington. There is an almost cherubic expression on his small, round face as he talks about life—clothes, money, the Baltimore Orioles and heroin. He has been an addict since the age of 5.

His hands are clasped behind his head, fancy running shoes adorn his feet and a striped Izod T-shirt hangs over his thin frame. "Bad, ain't it," he boasts to a reporter visiting recently. "I got me six of these."

Jimmy's is a world of hard drugs, fast money and the good life he believes both can bring. Every day, junkies casually buy heroin from Ron, his mother's live-in lover, in the dining room of Jimmy's home. They "cook" it in the kitchen and "fire up" in the bedrooms. And every day, Ron or someone else fires up Jimmy, plunging a needle into his bony arm, sending the fourth grader into a hypnotic nod.

Jimmy prefers this atmosphere to school, where only one subject seems relevant to fulfilling his dreams. "I want to have me a bad car and dress good and also have me a good place to live," he says. "So, I pretty much pay attention in math because I know I got to keep up when I finally get me something to sell."

Jimmy wants to sell drugs, maybe even on the District's meanest street, Condon Terrace SE, and some day deal heroin, he says, "just like my man Ron."

Ron, 27, and recently up from the South, was the one who first turned Jimmy on. "He'd be buggin' me all the time about what the shots were and what people was doin' and one day he said, 'When can I get off?'" Ron says, leaning against a wall in a narcotic haze, his eyes half closed, yet piercing. "I said, 'Well, s—, you can have some now.' I let him snort a little, and, damn, the little dude really did get off."

Six months later, Jimmy was hooked. "I felt like I was part of what was goin' down," he says. "I can't really tell you how it feel. You never done any? Sort of like them rides at King's Dominion . . . like if you was to go on all of them in one day.

"It be real different from herb (marijuana). That's baby s—. Don't nobody here hardly ever smoke no herb. You can't hardly get none right now, anyway."

Jimmy's mother Andrea accepts her son's habit as a fact of life, although she will not inject the child herself and does not like to see others do it.

"I don't really like to see him fire up," she says. "But, you know, I think he would have got into it one day, anyway. Everybody does. When you live in the ghetto, it's all a matter of survival. If he wants to get away from it when he's older, then that's his thing. But right now, things are better for us than they've ever been . . . . Drugs and black folk been together for a very long time."

See ADDICT, A9, Col. 1

By Michael Gnatek Jr. for The Washington Post

Obviously the occasions when a reporter will witness a so-called natural crime in confidence, and the occasions when he will find it conformable to his own ethical and moral standards to withhold information about such a crime, are bound to be infinitesimally few. It does not strengthen a valid case for the press to claim an absolute privilege and then to say, trust us not to exercise it absolutely. We trust much to benevolent discretion, in public and private sectors, but generally only when countervailed.

—Alexander Bickel, *The Morality of Consent*

Janet Cooke, "Jimmy's World," *The Washington Post*,
September 28, 1980, A1:

[begins:]

Jimmy is 8 years old and a third-generation heroin addict, a
precocious little boy with sandy hair, velvety brown eyes and needle
marks freckling the baby-smooth skin of his thin brown arms.

He nestles in a large, beige reclining chair in the living room of
his comfortably furnished home in Southeast Washington. There is
an almost cherubic expression on his small, round face as he talks
about life—clothes, money, the Baltimore Orioles and heroin. He
has been an addict since the age of 5.

[ends:]

[Ron, adult male] grabs Jimmy's left arm just above the elbow, his
massive hand tightly encircling the child's small limb. The needle
slides into the boy's soft skin like a straw pushed into the center of a
freshly baked cake. Liquid ebbs out of the syringe, replaced by bright
red blood. The blood is then reinjected into the child.

Jimmy has closed his eyes during the whole procedure, but now
he opens them, looking quickly around the room. He climbs into a
rocking chair and sits, his head dipping and snapping upright again,
in what addicts call "the nod."

"Pretty soon, man," Ron says, "you got to learn how to do this
for yourself."

David Maraniss, July 19, 2010:

DM: There were several people who were skeptical of the story after it
ran.

Q: Just right away.

DM: Right away. Not just the city government, which was denying . . . but [black Metro reporter] Courtland Milloy was skeptical,
and I was skeptical. For one smallest of reasons, which was that she
said Jimmy was a Baltimore Orioles fan. No fucking way, inner city
kid in Washington would be an Orioles fan. Baseball even. Maybe a

Redskins fan or a Bullets fan, not an Orioles fan. So I just thought that
was so wrong . . .

Q: Didn't ring true to your ear.

DM: No.

Mike Sager, GQ, 1996:

The story didn't feel right. The dialogue, for instance, sounded like
a white person imitating jive. Blacks in D.C.'s ghettos didn't say, "I
be goin'." They said, "I goin'." And the appointments in the
shooting gallery—matching chrome-and-glass tables? Could Janet,
with her terrible sense of direction, even have found Jimmy's house
at night?

Vivian Aplin-Brownlee to Bill Green, April 1981:

I never believed it, and I told Milton that. I knew her so well and
the depth of her. In her eagerness to make a name she would write
farther than the truth would allow. When challenged on facts on
other stories, Janet would reverse herself, but without dismay or
consternation with herself. I knew she would be tremendously out
of place in a "shooting gallery." I didn't believe she could get access.
No pusher would shoot up a child in her presence.

Bill Green, "Janet's World," The Washington Post, April 19, 1981, A13:

Jimmy's story struck at Washington's heart. The paper had no
sooner reached the streets than The Washington Post's telephone
switchboard lit up like a space launch control room.

Readers were outraged. The story was described as racist and
criminal. The concern was for Jimmy. "What about the boy?" was
the central question. It was repeated for the next four days in as
many versions as the human mind can invent.

By Monday, Washington Police Chief Burtell Jefferson had
launched a mammoth citywide search. He had called on his youth

division to get to work Sunday. Mayor Marion Barry was incensed.
All schools, social services and police contacts were to be asked for
"Jimmy's" whereabouts.

"An Addict at 8," *Washington Post* editorial, September 30,
1980, A18:

In starkly revolting and heart-rending detail, staff writer Janet Cooke
introduced readers of Sunday's editions to "Jimmy's World"—the
story of an 8-year-old, third generation heroin addict in "a world of
hard drugs, fast money and the good life he believes both can
bring." So repugnant, depressing and foreign to most people is this
morally corrupt "world" of one child in the city that it would be a
relief to dismiss this account as an exaggeration or an aberration.

The Washington Post, October 1, 1980, A1:

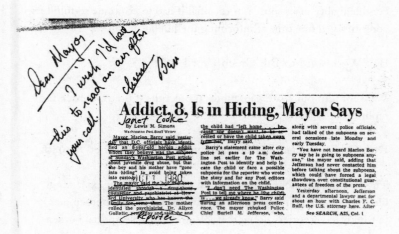

Dear Mayor
I wish I'd had
this to read on air after
your call.
Cheers Ben

Addict, 8, Is in Hiding, Mayor Says

Janet Cooke
By Lewis M. Simons
Washington Post Staff Writer

Mayor Marion Barry said yesterday that D.C. officials have identified an 8-year-old heroin addict whom they believe was the subject of Sunday's Washington Post article about juvenile drug abuse, but that the boy and his mother have "gone into hiding" to avoid being taken into custody.

The mayor said the boy had been identified through a dangerous drugs counselor and psychiatrist at Howard University who has known the family for some time. The mother called the psychiatrist, Dr. Allyce Gullattee, yesterday and said she and *Reporter*

the child had "left home . . . because she doesn't want to get arrested or have the child taken away from me," Barry said.

Barry's statement came after city police let pass a 10 a.m. deadline set earlier for The Washington Post to identify and help locate the child or face a possible subpoena for the reporter who wrote the story and for any Post editors with information on the child.

"I don't need The Washington Post to tell me where he [the child] is . . . we already know," Barry said during an afternoon press conference. The mayor rebuked Police Chief Burtell M. Jefferson, who,

along with several police officials, had talked of the subpoena on several occasions late Monday and early Tuesday.

"You have not heard Marion Barry say he is going to subpoena anyone," the mayor said, adding that Jefferson had never contacted him before talking about the subpoena, which could have forced a legal showdown over constitutional guarantees of freedom of the press.

Yesterday afternoon, Jefferson and a departmental lawyer met for about an hour with Charles F. C. Ruff, the U.S. attorney here. After

See SEARCH, A25, Col. 1

[after the jump:]

The question of whether the newspaper should reveal the name
or location of the boy had become a major issue throughout the city,

as D.C. officials raised concerns that the child's life could be in
increasing danger.

"We're going to do everything we can to get that information
and save that child's life. We'll see how much The Post is willing to
do to protect its First Amendment rights at the expense of that
child's life," police spokesman Gary Hankins told a radio audience
yesterday morning.

The Post's lawyer, John B. Kuhns of Williams & Connolly, said
yesterday, "The enormous public response to this article reflects the
serious concern of the community about drug use, particularly by
our youth. No article about this boy's tragic circumstances would
have been possible if The Post could not protect the confidentiality
of its news sources.

"Although the immediate pressures to reveal sources in a single
case are often intense, such disclosure would gravely jeopardize The
Post's ability to report on this and other issues of vital concern to
the community," Kuhns said. "The Post's decision to protect the
confidentiality of its sources is essential if it is to continue to fulfill its
constitutional function of informing the public."

Bob Woodward to Bill Green, April 1981:

We went into our Watergate mode: protect the source and back the
reporter.

Don Graham personal note to Janet Cooke, October 7, 1980:

The Post has no more important and tougher job than explaining
life in the black community in Washington. A special burden gets
put on black reporters doing that job, and a double-special burden
on black reporters who try to see life through their own eyes instead
of seeing it the way they're told they should. The Post seems to have
many such reporters. You belong very high up among them.

"Mayor Says City Ending Its Search for 'Jimmy,'" *The
Washington Post*, October 16, 1980, C1:

Mayor Marion Barry said yesterday that city officials are giving up on their search for an unidentified 8-year-old heroin addict whose life style, including daily injections of the drug, was the subject of a Washington Post article last month.

"We are kind of giving up on that," Barry said when asked about the comprehensive search for the youth, known only as Jimmy. . . .

Barry said that he and police department officials are convinced that the Post report, including a description of the boy being injected with heroin by his mother's live-in-lover, is at least part fabrication.

"I've been told the story was part myth and part reality," Barry said. He said that after talking to police narcotics officers, and from his own personal knowledge of the drug world from his days as a community organizer, "We all have agreed that we don't believe that the mother or the pusher would allow a reporter to see them shoot up."

Washington Post editors said yesterday that the newspaper stands by its story.

Bill Green, "Janet's World," April 19, 1981:

By the following weekend, Coleman was uneasy. It was a slight feeling, but it was real. "I thought the police would have found him in three days at the outside. I'm not one of those people who believe the police can't do anything right. They could find him. I knew it."

Courtland Milloy was also worried. He and Cooke had gone out to find the second "Jimmy" [for a follow-up story].

"We were supposed to be finding another kid," Milloy said. "But I'll tell you the truth, I wanted to find Jimmy. Hell, that kid needed help. So as we drove around I circled through Condon Terrace, the general area where Janet said he lived.

"It didn't take long to see that she didn't know the area. It's one of the toughest sections in town. I know it well. She said she didn't see the house. I asked her if it was to the right of us, the left of us, or had we passed it. She didn't know."

Ben to Bill Green, April 1981:

Nobody ever came in this room and said, "I have doubts about the story"—before or after publication.

Richard Cohen, October 9, 2007:

Everybody in the office knew that that story was bullshit, but him. And it was a vast, you know, it's one of these vast conspiracies in which nobody said anything. And he's sitting there with his open door policy, as he used to call it, in his glass office, and nobody came in. And afterwards, [National reporter] Walter Pincus and I went to him and said, you know, Ben, you got this open door and a glass office, but nobody came in. You ought to think about that. And he said, "Get the fuck out of here."

Walter Pincus, September 26, 2007:

He had the big glass wall. This was the argument. When we were complaining . . . he said, "My office is open to anybody. Why don't they just walk in and tell me?" And if anybody other than those of us who really knew him did it, they'd be scared shitless. Because he wouldn't even look up.

BCB to Wendy Wick, Ontario Apartments, December 15, 1980:

Dear Ms Wick:

I have been asked by Janet Cooke to write you about her, and I hasten to do so.

Janet Cooke has been a reporter at this newspaper for 11 months. She is a person of extraordinary maturity and responsibility. Her career here has been characterized by commitment, hard work and courage; and, on top of that, she is a nice person.

I commend her to The Ontario without reservation. I consider that you would be fortunate to have her . . . and predict that you will be happy with each other.

If I can answer any questions more specifically, I would be delighted to do so.

Elsa Walsh, August 28, 2010:

[Elsa lived with Cooke at the Ontario from December of 1980 until April of 1981, when the hoax was discovered. She began to date Woodward at the same time.]

Now, looking back on it, I can see that she was just under enormous stress. There were little clues that things weren't quite right to me. I used to play a lot of tennis, and I guess this was just before we moved in and I was staying at her other place, and I was going to go play with Marty Schram, we had this regular kind of tennis time and my tennis stuff was all packed away and I said can I borrow your tennis racket? And she had told me she had been on this top doubles team at Vassar or wherever it was she said she'd gone to college. And she said sure, it's in the closet. And I pulled out the racket and it was kind of like a Walmart racket, and it was not a tennis player's racket. So I thought, that's bizarre. And then all of her checks started bouncing from our landlord at the Ontario, so the landlord said she would only accept the checks from me, not from Janet. . . .

There began to be a lot of rumblings about the story.

Q: But initially you didn't read it and think "Uh-uh."
EW: No . . . but then I asked her about it. I remember sitting in our kitchen once, and she was working on this new story about the hooker,* and she was really complaining about Bob and Milton Cole-

---

*In the wake of the "Jimmy" story, in mid-November of 1980 Cooke told her editors that she had found a fourteen-year-old prostitute. This time Coleman insisted upon meeting the girl in question; after a series of failed or canceled meetings, the story was dropped. Though Woodward and Coleman agreed in hindsight that this should have tipped them off about "Jimmy," it didn't.

man, saying that they wanted to meet the woman. And that, you know, she was really attributing that to them being kind of perverts. And I said, well, you know, other people have said things about Jimmy. What do you think about that? And she said, well, they're just really jealous. And I thought, maybe that's what I am, too, and I dropped it.

PRIZE

Dear Gene and Lee:

No matter what we may think, nor how we may bend current definitions, there is no Pulitzer Prize now offered for feature writing, a category which must represent 30–40% of today's newspapers.

We have the public service gold medal. No room for features in this category.

We have local general or spot news. I'm not sure what general news is, but it is news, not features, and spot news is the opposite of features. . . .

And yet some of the best writing in the press today is being done in this category. Not a paper worth its salt has not started a feature section during the last two decades. Profiles, life-styles, features . . . these are the lifeblood of a newspaper. These are the categories where the fine writers are found. And no Pulitzer to urge them on to greater heights.

I propose that a category be added thusly:

"For a distinguished example of feature writing, a single article or series: One thousand dollars ($1,000)."

—BCB to fellow Pulitzer board members Gene Patterson
and Lee Hills, November 9, 1977

WITHOUT THE PULITZER PRIZE, Janet Cooke's fabrication would probably never have been exposed. There was no way to disprove her, particularly once she invented the fable—after one too many unfruitful attempts to find Jimmy with other reporters and editors—that Jimmy and his mother had moved to Baltimore to avoid further attention. The various doubters in the newsroom would continue to doubt, and editors might attend to later stories of hers with heightened scrutiny, but in essence her secret was safe.

In 1981, Ben was no longer on the Pulitzer advisory board, having ceded his seat in 1979, but prior to his departure he had sought and secured the new feature-writing category. Ben's motivation for creating that category is patently obvious, summed up in a memo from Henry Allen, a *Post* reporter who made a pitch to Ben in 1976:

> You've assembled the greatest bank of feature writers in the
> newspaper business. But every year, at prize time, none of us gets a
> shot at the Pulitzer, unless one of our stories edges into another
> category, such as comment or local reporting. . . .
>   The age of mere color stories and human-interest sidebars ended
> when Style was born. Feature writers get read, get famous, get
> people buying newspapers, and should get their own Pulitzer.

Ben responded by noting that each year he protested the lack of a feature category, but "every year my peers (smile!) impugn my motives, saying that I rise only because of the great collection of feature writers here." He promised Allen he would "give it a new whack," and the next year he did. In 1978, at Ben's continued instigation, the full advisory board voted to create a new category in feature writing, and in 1979 the first Pulitzer Prize in that category was awarded to Jon Franklin, of the Baltimore *Evening Sun*.

Two years later, "Jimmy's World" took the prize.

That Cooke's piece was ever even put up for a Pulitzer in the first place is odd. In all of their various testimonials after the fact, Bob and Ben and Milton Coleman—three editors with direct responsibility for the story—would dwell on the idea that it would have been suspicious for them *not* to have nominated the story. "Not to submit it," Ben told a *New York Times* reporter a few days after the scandal broke, "would have meant something that you didn't want to say, that you didn't believe the story." This is a very strange reason to nominate a newspaper piece for the most prestigious prize in journalism.

"I have used the phrases 'in for a dime, in for a dollar' to describe my overall conclusion about submitting the Cooke story for a Pulitzer or any other prize," Bob said in the wake of the incident. "I believed it, we published it. . . . It would be absurd for me or any other editor to review the authenticity or accuracy of stories that are nominated for prizes. If so, our posture would be as follows: we published the story and said it was true, but now we are going to nominate it for a Pulitzer—now *that's* serious business." They had backed themselves into a situation from which the only perceptible exit was a deeper commitment.

Just before the Pulitzer entries were submitted, David Maraniss reread "Jimmy's World" and didn't believe it. He warned Bob about it, but his warning was compromised by the fact that tensions were high between Maraniss and Coleman. It would have seemed like sour grapes on Maraniss's part to try to quash Cooke's nomination. "A number of people felt strongly that it should not be nominated because it could disgrace us," investigative reporter Jonathan Naumann, who talked it over with Maraniss, would later tell Bill Green. "A couple of dozen people talked about it but we didn't go to top editors. I think we felt it wouldn't be fair to put her on the carpet when we couldn't prove anything."

Despite the doubts, Woodward and Coleman submitted Cooke's story under the "local reporting" category for the Pulitzer Prize. It didn't win. The prize was awarded to the *Longview Daily News* for its coverage of the Mount St. Helens eruption. According to Roger Wilkins, the former *Post* editorial writer who was then working for *The Washington Star* (and who was a member of the board), Warren Phillips, the chairman and chief executive of *The Wall Street Journal*, then proposed that Cooke's story be jumped to the feature writing category. Everybody agreed.

When that category came up for a vote, Phillips moved to have Cooke's story win, bypassing the three finalists that the feature writing jury—who had never even considered Cooke's piece—had voted for. Eugene Patterson, Ben's former number two and now the editor in chief of the *St. Petersburg Times*, didn't like that one bit. As he explained after the scandal broke, "I expressed my opinion that I would not have assigned a reporter to cover a life-and-death story with the pre-condition [Cooke] accepted—namely to refuse to give information that might save the life of the child." As he later told me, he objected for other reasons, too. He had read "Jimmy's World" when it first ran in the *Post*, and "to an oldtime editor's nose the story just didn't smell right."

"My doubts got swept away," he told me, "when Roger Wilkins differed." After Patterson had presented his objections, Roger Wilkins, the only black member of the board present, defended Cooke's article. Wilkins said, among other things, that he thought he could find young heroin addicts within blocks of the Columbia School of Journalism, where the board met. His argument carried the day. "How do you fight that?" Patterson asked me. He abstained from voting because, as he put it, "I was beaten." The rest of the board voted unanimously to present Cooke with the prize.

The board often overruled the juries, so there wasn't anything suspicious about that. But it was yet another twist in the warped world of the "Jimmy" story, that Cooke lost out in the category she'd been nominated in but somehow managed to win in an entirely different category, without that jury ever having read her story. The truth was looking for a way out.

On April 13, the Pulitzer Prizes were publicly announced, and on the 14th the *Post* ran a front page story hailing Cooke's victory. A glamour shot of a windblown Cooke on a rooftop appeared on page six of the Metro section, set above a reprint of the story that had gotten her there.

Ben was sitting in his office on the afternoon of April 14 when the call came in—two calls, actually, one to Howard Simons and one to Ben, at almost precisely the same time. The executive editor of the Associated Press was calling for Simons, and the assistant to the president of Vassar was on the line for Ben. Both were calling with questions about Cooke's credentials, which the *Post* had never checked. Information on the form that Cooke supplied to the Pulitzer committee differed from the information that she had supplied to the

Toledo Blade when she applied for a job there. In fact, the information Cooke submitted to the Pulitzer committee differed substantially from the résumé she had submitted to the *Post* only a year before. The latest iteration was Supernigger Plus, including previously un-mentioned study at the Sorbonne and proficiency in French, Span-ish, Portuguese, and Italian. Vassar's records, Ben was told, showed that Cooke had only studied there for one year—not the four she had claimed when she had been hired.

"My heart sank," Ben told me.

"Did you know right then?"

"You could see ahead where it was going," he said.

Ben has always maintained that the possibility that Cooke had made the whole thing up never occurred to him. "In all my life in the business, there were people who made up scenes—that doesn't seem to me to be preposterous—or who exaggerated things," he said to me. "But to make the whole fucking thing up . . ."

Within a few minutes the top editors at the paper and on the story were assembled in Ben's office. Ben also called Don Graham to tell him about the Vassar problem, and as Graham told me, "We knew immediately what that meant." Even the briefest scan of Cooke's personnel folder revealed the seriousness of the discrepancies, and so Ben and Simons sent Coleman to talk to Cooke, to see if she might come clean. "Take her to the woodshed," Ben said.*

After some grilling, Cooke revealed that she hadn't graduated from Vassar but insisted that Jimmy was real. Later that afternoon they brought her up to an empty eighth floor office, where Ben and Bob prepared to give her the third degree. As they walked in, Cooke was beginning to realize her fate. Crying, she said, to nobody in particu-lar, "You get caught at the stupidest things."

Ben was cordial, but he told her that the lie about Vassar and some of the other issues with her various résumés had caused them to

---

*All dialogue (and most reconstruction of events) from Cooke's interrogation comes from Bill Green's piece that appeared in the *Post* on April 19, 1981. It was written in the days im-mediately after the discovery, when what people had said and done was still fresh in their minds. Nobody has disputed the basic accuracy of Green's account to me.

doubt her. The entire Jimmy story hung on her word, and their trust in her word. If that trust had been abused, they needed to know it now.

"Say two words to me in Portuguese," Ben said.

Cooke admitted that she couldn't.

"Do you have any Italian?" Ben asked.

Again, no.

Then Ben started to ask her some questions in French. Cooke later claimed that she could speak French but hadn't wanted to give in to Ben at that moment; whatever happened, her answers fell far short of the proficiency she had claimed for herself.

"You're like Richard Nixon," Ben told her, perhaps the most loaded words he could use. "You're trying to cover up."

Out of sheer desperation, Cooke concocted a fake name and address for Jimmy, his mother, and her boyfriend. Ben gave her twenty-four hours to prove that the story was true. Coleman went out with Cooke to the address she provided, but they couldn't find the house. "Now, everybody dealing with Cooke believed she was lying," Bill Green wrote a few days later. "But she stuck with her story."

Later that night, around 11:30—long after Ben had gone home—Bob grilled Cooke in a fifth floor conference room, just off the newsroom. The editors had recalled her notes, which had been held for safekeeping at the *Post*'s law firm in case of any legal claim against the paper. Reading through them, Bob saw what he described as "echoes" of the story, but no evidence that she had actually interviewed anybody remotely like Jimmy/Tyrone. Maraniss told me that even from the first bits of her notes he could tell that she'd made the story up.

"It's all over," Bob told her now. "You've got to come clean. The notes show us the story is wrong. We know it. We can show you point by point how you concocted it."

Maraniss, who was friendly with Cooke, played the good cop. "Give up the Pulitzer," he said, "and you can have yourself back."

Eventually, after prolonged questioning but without any admission, Bob and Milt Coleman and Tom Wilkinson, the assistant managing editor for personnel at the *Post*, left Cooke alone with Maraniss.

The two talked for a long time, with Maraniss trying to be as empathetic as he could. Bob and Ben had seemed angry to Cooke, and that had scared her. "Once she was laid that vulnerable," Maraniss told me, "I wasn't angry. So that made it possible for her to tell me what happened."

Slowly, the secret began to unravel. She talked about how scared she had been when she was nominated for the Pulitzer. Eventually, Maraniss told her, "You don't have to say anything to the others, I'll do it for you. What do I tell them?"

"There is no Jimmy and no family," Cooke said. "It was a fabrication. I did so much work on it, but it's a composite. I want to give the prize back."

Just as this was happening, Bob and the other editors outside the conference room reached Ben at home. He told them to stop the interrogation, that maybe it was overkill. But when they walked back in, ready to call things off, Maraniss told them that Cooke had just admitted to the hoax. Bob and Milton Coleman and Tom Wilkinson all hugged her, their fury spent.

"I'm sorry I was such a son-of-a-bitch," Bob said.

"I deserved it," Cooke said.

"Yes, you did," Bob said.

At seven the next morning, Ben called Don Graham and told him that Cooke had confessed. Shortly thereafter the two men met for breakfast at Ben's house, where they discussed what steps the paper would take next. The news had come too late for that morning's paper but certainly wouldn't hold for another full day, so they decided to prepare and release statements of their own. During that breakfast, Maraniss, who was with Cooke at her apartment building, called Ben's house to ask what he should do. Ben told him that Cooke was to produce a resignation letter and a written statement.

"I don't know why Bradlee asked me to get her to write a letter of resignation," Maraniss told me. "I've never quite figured that out."

"Why he didn't just fire her?"

"Yeah. I have no problem with it—either way, she's gone—but he directly asked me to get her to resign."

In his memoir, Ben says, "I can't explain now why I let her resign

rather than fire her on the spot for the grossest negligence." But privately, the motivation was exactly what one suspects it would be. "If
I was really honest with myself I would probably say that if she'd been
white I'd have canned her, because she was black I let her resign,"
Ben told Barbara Feinman in one of the interviews for his memoir.
"You know, I didn't know how that would play racially and I was
concerned about that."*

I ask Bradlee why he thinks Kay chose him and he said that she told
him she respected his ability to spot talent and his ability, if he made
a mistake, to clean it up.

—David Halberstam, interview notes, late seventies

Ben often says that the main thing he learned from his time in the
Navy was damage control. In a speech in Prague in 1990, he talked
about how serving as the assistant damage control officer on the USS
Philip during World War II had shaped him as a newspaperman. "In
that job, one is charged with thinking about trouble and how to
handle trouble before it handles you. I've often thought that ability to
control damage is one of the essential skills of an editor."

In the case of Janet Cooke, Ben made a couple of quick decisions
that helped to minimize the damage. The first was a relatively simple
one: Cooke, and the *Post*, would return the Pulitzer Prize. Early in
the morning of August 15, with Cooke's written admission in hand,
Ben called Joe Pulitzer in St. Louis to inform him of the decision.
Later that morning, he sent this cable to the Pulitzer Prize Foundation in New York:

---

*Even in her resignation letter, Cooke had problems with accuracy, though she was admit-
tedly under duress. She said that her story of September 28, 1981, had been a "serious misrepresentation," when in fact the story had run the previous year. As she told me, through
the reporter Mike Sager, David Maraniss had dictated the letter to her. "I simply signed it,"
she wrote. "Hindsight being what it is, I would handle that quite differently now."

TO MEMBERS OF THE PULTIZER PRIZE FOUNDATION

IT IS WITH GREAT SADNESS AND REGRET THAT I INFORM YOU THAT JANET
COOKE, THE WASHINGTON POST REPORTER AWARDED THE PULITZER PRIZE FOR
FEATURE WRITING MONDAY, HAS DETERMINED THAT SHE CANNOT ACCEPT THE
AWARD.

SHE TOLD POST EDITORS EARLY THIS MORNING THAT HER STORY —— ABOUT
AN EIGHT-YEAR-OLD HEROIN ADDICT —— WAS IN FACT A COMPOSITE, THAT THE
QUOTES ATTRIBUTED TO A CHILD WERE IN FACT FABRICATED, AND THAT
CERTAIN EVENTS DESCRIBED AS EYEWITNESSED DID NOT IN FACT HAPPEN.

JANET COOKE WAS A PARTICULARY PROMISING AND TALENTED YOUNG
REPORTER. SHE REGRETS THESE EVENTS AS MUCH AS THE WASHINGTON POST
REGRETS THEM. SHE HAS OFFERED HER RESIGNATION, AND IT HAS BEEN
ACCEPTED.

SINCERELY,

BENJAMIN C. BRADLEE
EXECUTIVE EDITOR
THE WASHINGTON POST

At two that afternoon, Ben released a statement to the entire newsroom, covering much of the same ground but adding a final optimis-
tic note about the task now facing the paper:

```
      I have also apologized personally to Mayor Barry and
Police Chief Jefferson, who insisted all along that the Jimmy
story was false. And I have also accepted Janet's resignation
with a heavy heart.

      Okay, that's the down side. We've all got to start back
up the hill--together. The credibility of a newspaper is its
most precious asset, and it depends almost entirely on the
integrity of its reporters. When that integrity is questioned
and found wanting, the wounds are grievous and there is nothing
to do but come clean with our readers, apologize to those we
have unintentionally wronged, and begin immediately on the
uphill task of regaining our credibility. This we are doing,
starting right now. This we will do, with your help.
```

BCB.

April 15, 1981

Shortly after releasing the statement, Ben asked Tom Wilkinson to come into his office. Wilkinson was one of Ben's closest confidants at the paper, and he had helped to uncover the fraud on Cooke's résumé the previous day. "Go tell people in the room to gather at the news desk," Ben said, meaning that he wanted to talk to the whole news staff.

Within an hour or so, everybody who was in the building at the time was assembled in the newsroom. Ben walked out of his office and stood near his secretary's desk.

"He said, 'We're giving it back, but goddammit, this is a great place, and we do great work,'" Wilkinson told me. "But as he said it, his voice broke. That was the first time I'd ever seen or heard anything like that. And then he said, 'Let's get back to work.'"

"I remember thinking to myself," Ben told me, of what he felt as he spoke, "are you sure you're going to be here for a long time?" He didn't yet know whether he would keep his job.

Later that afternoon, Ben walked over to the Style section. Jane Amsterdam, an editor of the section at the time, remembers how he looked as he passed through. "It was the first I ever saw sadness in Ben," she told me. "He looked tired."

"You wanna talk, Benjy?" she said, trying to keep things light, to cheer him up. Ben took a stray chair, turned it around backwards— a favorite move of his—and sat straddling the backrest of the chair, facing Amsterdam and Tony Kornheiser and a number of other Style reporters.

"Nobody knows what to say," Kornheiser told me, "and he tells the whole story. He talks for about forty minutes, how he found out and how he talked to her in French and she wouldn't respond. And the crowd grows from me and Jane until there's like thirty people sitting around listening to him. A lot of people might tell you there was sadness. There was *anger*. He was pissed off. This was bullshit. I mean, we were giving back the Pulitzer Prize. You don't ever want to give back the Pulitzer Prize."

"Everybody wanted to be with him," Amsterdam told me. "Everybody just wanted to be together. I think we all realized what was coming, which was what did come, which was you'd go in for a question in an interview for a story and they'd say, 'What does it matter? Just make it up.'"

How to begin to move on from the lowest moment of your professional life? The discovery of a way out hinged on the moment when Ben had turned to Cooke, during his interrogation of her foreign language capabilities, and told her that she was like Nixon, that she was covering up. If there was a lightbulb moment in Ben's career, this was it. Most people agree that Nixon could have avoided resignation had he confessed to the low-level sins of Watergate right away. One of the central lessons of Watergate, which has been hammered home innumerable times since, is that it's always the cover-up that gets you.

And so Ben decided that he and the paper would let it all hang out, that they would tell the truth about the Janet Cooke episode in the pages of *The Washington Post*. Instead of allowing others to gore the ox, they would gore their own.

In making that decision, Ben was helped by an institution that he had put into place at the *Post* shortly after taking over as executive editor. While his creation of the feature writing category at the Pulitzer committee ended up coming back to bite him with Janet Cooke, his support for the creation of an ombudsman position at the *Post* in 1969 would come full circle, too—to save him.

Most major news outlets have an ombudsman on the staff now. Ombudsmen are internal critics, charged to represent the interests of viewers or readers while remaining insulated from regular editorial process and pressure. Freed by that insulation, ombudsmen are expected to speak truth directly back to the organization they work for.

The first American news ombudsman was appointed in 1967, at the Louisville *Courier-Journal*. The original charter for the ombudsman in Louisville was to offer internal criticism to the staff, without printing those observations in the newspaper itself. There wasn't a public component. In November of 1969, Phil Foisie, the longtime foreign editor of the *Post*, proposed that the *Post* create an ombudsman position with the added responsibility of publishing an uncensored column in the newspaper. In essence, he wanted to create a forum for accountability to readers and a way for the paper to air its own dirty laundry. "I realize the risk in this," he wrote to Ben and to Gene Patterson on November 10, 1969. "There could be embarrassment." But, he went on, "There should also be an enormous gain."

This was a serious proposal, and it would cause a good deal of reflection among the higher-ups at the paper. According to Don Graham, Ben wasn't overly thrilled about empowering an ombudsman, but Kay pushed him hard on it because she thought it was a good idea. In 1970, the formal position of ombudsman was created at the *Post*, and Dick Harwood, one of Ben's closest companions and a fiercely fair and independent man, was chosen as the first. At Pugwash the following year, Ben went so far as to call the installation of Harwood a "bold self-destruct step" because of the breadth of the ombudsman's charter and the unpredictability of the outcome. Asked why he wanted to stick with it in the end, Ben said, "Fairness."

The vision of 1969–1970, and the hard work required to make the ombudsman position stick at the *Post*, paid off in the wake of Janet Cooke. There was a great deal of demand inside the *Post* for a thorough account of how the fabrication could have happened; at one point, nearly twenty reporters wanted to staff the story. But Ben didn't need twenty reporters, and he resisted them. ("This was no time for the inmates to take over the institution," he wrote later.) The reason he could resist them was that he had an ombudsman by the name of Bill Green.

Green wasn't a career journalist. He worked in the administration at Duke University and served only for a year as the ombudsman at the *Post* before returning to Duke. He was at the *Post* for the publication of Cooke's story, and he was there when it all fell apart. On the day that the *Post* announced its return of the Pulitzer, Ben approached Green about putting something together about Cooke, and Green accepted. "I wrote this story of 'Jimmy's World' after being invited to do so by The Washington Post's executive editor, Ben Bradlee," Green wrote in his story, four days later. "It is important to understand the verb, 'invited,' because if I had been assigned to do it, that would have violated the relationship The Post has maintained with its ombudsmen for over a decade. The central idea is autonomy for the person who sits in this chair. Without it, the ombudsman would be a fake, like 'Jimmy.' With it, the *Post* takes its chances, as it should."

Ben was willing to take his chances, and he gave the order from on high that everybody was to cooperate with Green's inquiry. He also ordered that Green be given as much space in the paper as he wanted, no restrictions. With the blessing of Ben and Don Graham, Green interviewed everybody involved in the story—all the editors, other reporters who had doubts, everybody—except for Cooke herself, who wouldn't cooperate.* On Sunday, April 19, just four days after the *Post* had discovered the fraud, Green ran a comprehensive

---

*The only public comments Cooke has ever made about the "Jimmy's World" scandal were in an appearance on Phil Donahue's talk show in 1982 and in a mini-PR blitz around the publication of Mike Sager's article about her in GQ in June 1996. She cooperated with that article, which she and Sager then shopped for a movie deal. TriStar pictures bid $1.6 million, paying the two $750,000 up front and promising an additional $850,000 if the movie were ever made, which it hasn't been. Since then, her silence has continued; through Sager, she provided one comment about her resignation letter but otherwise rejected my requests for an interview.

fourteen-thousand-word piece about how "Jimmy's World" had ever come to be. The story, "Janet's World," ran as the off-lead on the front page and then jumped to four complete pages inside.

"It is *the* classic work of ombudsmanship, still to this day," Mike Getler told me. His opinion matters more than most. At the time of our interview Getler was the ombudsman for PBS, but before that he had been a longtime *Post* reporter, editor, and ombudsman himself. "It was sensational. Thorough and excellent, no punches pulled."

Green's report is the reason that most of the facts of the story are known today. He gives the full blow-by-blow, and nobody comes out looking perfect. Woodward is full of self-blame, as is Milton Coleman. Ben is presented not as negligent but as removed, too insulated to have heard the doubts. Though nobody questioned the basic facts in Green's report, some would fault him for being too positive about the *Post* generally, largely because of his "conclusions" section in which he made the basic point that the Janet Cooke episode had been an "aberration that grew in fertile ground."

"To believe that this mistake, big as it was, challenges the honesty of any other story in The Post or any other newspaper, is over-reaching. It won't wash. There is no evidence whatsoever that this kind of thing is tolerated at this paper. To over-reach the other way, if this experience tightens discipline in the news process, it may have done some good," he wrote. His final sentence: "The Post is one of the very few great enterprises in journalism, and everybody associated with it ought to be proud of it."

That conclusion rubbed some people the wrong way,* but for the people who worked at the *Post* it offered a kind of public redemption: Janet Cooke couldn't and wouldn't taint them forever. As one reporter told me, Green's piece "in a way exonerated us, because we

---

*"Here then, after zillions of hard-hitting interviews with some of the finest friends and co-workers it has ever been my privilege to know, are all the facts, every single one, about the scandal that has rocked the known universe to its very core," Michael Kinsley wrote in a parody of Green in *The New Republic*. Under a mock "conclusions" section, Kinsley urged that "2) Bob Woodward should continue to be quoted in *The Washington Post* every day expressing appealing sentiments of self-effacement and modesty. 3) *The Washington Post* should remain a triumphant vindication of the First Amendment."

were a very serious newsroom, very dedicated to truth, and that came through shiningly."

"There is only one damage control, and that's the truth," Ben told Charlie Rose in 1995. "And *you* get it out. And I must say, in that dark, dark moment, I was very proud of that."

Green delivered his report on the morning of Saturday, April 18, and Ben read it shortly thereafter. Years later Green wrote to Ben about that moment, surely one of the most potentially uncomfortable in the history of the *Post*:

> No compliment can rival the one you delivered on that Saturday morning when you came in from your place in West Virginia to see my Janet Cooke piece. It had been punched into the system by Bill Greider because I wrote it on a manual typewriter. After reading it through, you emerged from your office and said precisely this, in a voice that could be heard all the way to the sports desk: "Green, you ungrateful son-of-a-bitch, I salute you!"
>
> That was one for the ages. It ranks high among my private treasures.

At a conference on ombudsmanship in the nineties, Ben would say that they could never have gotten out of the Janet Cooke mess without Bill Green. "I could have talked myself blue in the face and been on every radio station and television station and written a piece for 'Outlook,' and the critics and skeptics would have said, 'Sure, sure.'" Green had written a definitive account that the public could believe—and that was all that he needed to do.

One questioner wanted to know if Ben ever thought that any of the *Post*'s ombudsmen, including Green, had criticized the paper unfairly.

"I sure did," Ben said.

"What did you do in that case?"

"I ate it."

FALLOUT

One of the reasons why the Cooke thing was such a crashing blow was that everybody felt, well, look at the *Post*, they've stepped on it. Look at those guys, walking with their noses in the air, stepped on it. That was number one.

—Peter Osnos, October 9, 2008

[It was] a very big injury, and I can only imagine that Ben took it really very hard, even though, in the aftermath, they behaved in an exemplary way. But you shouldn't underestimate the power of the blow and the level of the embarrassment. It wasn't just a piece that had been made up by somebody that was pernicious. It was made up, they were told it was made up by the mayor of the city, and by a lot of other people, there was suspicion of the piece inside. And then it won the Pulitzer Prize. It's like a Soupy Sales pie to the face. . . . And it came on the heels of the biggest journalistic triumph imaginable.

—David Remnick, October 26, 2009

READERS OF THE *Bulletin of the American Society of Newspaper Editors* for March of 1981 were treated, toward the back of the bulletin, to "Ben Bradlee's Convention Preview." Ben had been dragooned by his friend Tom Winship, the editor of *The Boston Globe*, into serving as the program chairman of the annual ASNE convention, which was to be held in Washington in late April of 1981. The title of Ben's preview, written before the curtain fell on Janet Cooke, was "We're Lookin' Good." "With lots of irons still in the fire," the budding event coordinator wrote, "we have the beginnings of something pretty good, although much of the program is still to come."

Prophetic words. The conference was held in Washington the week after the Cooke scandal hit the papers, and now all eyes were trained on Ben—for all the wrong reasons. At the reception that kicked off the convention, Winship told Ben that he thought they ought to have some kind of organized discussion of the Cooke episode. "There's an awful lot of interest," he told Ben, with a good deal of understatement.

And so an early morning session that was coincidentally supposed to be devoted to ombudsmen—"one of those early bird meetings normally attended by a dozen editors with insomnia," as Ben put it in a letter to a friend—became the Janet Cooke session. According to Ben, seven hundred fifty people and five television cameras showed up. As Al JaCoby, the ombudsman of the *San Diego Union*, put it after the fact, "Everybody here today came looking for red meat."

BCB with Barbara Feinman, May 24, 1990:

BF: How'd you feel?

B: I felt terrible. I felt so terrible. You know, I had to do it. I was performing. It's always been, I've always understood that when I perform I perform. I know that I'm on, and it has been ingrained in me somehow not to fuck up: to be prepared, you can make it look casual if you can get away with it but you've got to do it and you've got to do it right. So I knew all of that and I didn't have the strongest hand. . . .

BF: To say the least.

B: To say the very least. But there were sort of about fifteen or sixteen questions from the floor. I guess Winship was presiding and it was obvious that I had to get up and say my piece, which was essentially that we had acted quickly, I forgot what the hell I said. . . . The fucking television cameras were there. And to their great and everlasting credit [Don] Graham and [Russ] Wiggins were there by my side, never left my side.

In the immediate aftermath of the scandal, Ben had gone to Graham and offered to resign. "If it's the right solution for you, it's the right solution for me," Ben had said. "I'll quit, or you bag me—it doesn't make any difference. I leave."

"I don't think they considered it," Ben told me. "Whether they should have or not is something else. But by that time I was locked into the furniture, for Christ's sake. I was part of the place. And it might have been more costly to them than I thought, or than they thought it was."

"I got all kinds of advice that we should change editors as a result of Janet Cooke, and I didn't consider that a very close call," Don Graham told me. Ben's sixteen years of results as editor far outweighed the one mistake. There were a lot of other people along the line of authority over that story who were equally, if not more, culpable, and Graham didn't fire any of them, either. "I made no change," he told me, "and I'm glad I didn't."

That morning, at the ASNE meeting, the most important thing to Ben—the thing he has always said about it, since—was that Don Graham wrapped his arm around Ben for much of the panel. "Never said a word," Ben would say later of what Don Graham did that morning, "but every time anybody looked, there was the publisher with his arm around his editor."

As the panel began, Ben was sitting in the audience, but all assembled knew that he was the main event. Eventually he stood up and began to take questions from the audience. After a rueful joke about how he'd done more for the conference than any other program chair in history, he tried to modify expectations a little bit. "I haven't had time to collect my thoughts and formulate rules, which I suspect we will do," Ben said. "One conclusion I've reached is that you cannot legislate, you cannot make a rule that is going to prevent, preserve you, save you from a pathological liar.

"Eventually you are going to have to trust somebody," he went on. "If you have a rule that has an editor check every single fact by every reporter, you are not going to put out a daily newspaper, you're going to put out a monthly newspaper."

On the matter of race, Ben said that any suggestion that the Cooke case should call into question the value of affirmative action programs was "just baloney." He was right, though in a certain sense it was a dodge. Janet had been hired in large part because she was black, and everybody knew it. "I think where race came into this question had to do with the white editors," Ben said. This is the part of the racial dynamic that he has always felt most comfortable addressing. "Editors have only a limited number of worlds in which they consider themselves well qualified. In this case, Condon Terrace in Southeast Washington is an area that I do not know anything about. . . .

"The fact that Janet Cooke is black and her immediate editor was black probably made me trust them more, not less," he said.

"Isn't there something wrong with watching a crime being committed?" Al JaCoby, one of the folks who had come looking for red meat, asked a bit later.

This was the main question that people wanted answered, and a fair one. Charlie Seib, who had once been the ombudsman at the *Post*, followed a similar line. When confronted with an eight-year-old being injected with heroin, "Do you wrap yourself in the First Amendment and your traditions and let the child die?" Seib asked. He said that if Ben and Bob and everybody else had "realized that they were dealing with a life and not just a good front page story," they might have tried to find the boy and discovered the hoax before the damage had been done.

"You've got your point," Ben conceded.

Ben Bradlee:
The hoax does not matter—
But why did you not see
what could be done for the
child? If you had you would
have discovered the hoax. your
neat condemned you.

Readers felt the same way Charlie Seib did. Ben could talk all he wanted about press independence and the difficulties posed by journalists who cooperate with law enforcement, but the basic point was that when they'd been challenged on the story they had fallen back on cold, idealized journalistic standards instead of real, human, and empathic ones. Cooke would later tell Phil Donahue that Howard Simons was the only person at the *Post* who ever asked her about Jimmy's well-being or showed any interest in figuring out what the paper could do to help him. Everybody else was just worried about the story.

"It was a moral failure on my part," Bob told me. "The kid was being tortured. An eight-year-old. You should protect children. And so if I'd just been thinking morally, 'We have a responsibility to this kid,' and said to Janet, 'What's the address? We're dropping a dime, I am, personally, to the cops and a doctor, to save the kid, and then we'll do the story,' it would've exposed the fabrication, presumably . . .

"We were so caught up in this kind of muscular, First Amendment, 'Don't fuck with us' [mentality]," he went on. "I kind of liken it to the Haldeman thing. There was almost a Shakespearean element to it. But you don't get to the Haldeman story, you don't get to the 'Jimmy's World' story, unless you're pushing the envelope. If there are ever kind of instructions from Ben, it's push the envelope."

"I don't want to absolve myself in any sense," Ben told me when I asked him about the moral dimension. "I mean, there it is. It happened. And it should never have happened."

If other editors at lesser newspapers were taking a small amount of guilty pleasure in Ben's and Bob's difficulties, so, too, were readers of a certain persuasion. This, from a reader in Goldsboro, North Carolina, April 24, 1981:

Sir:

My, my how the mighty have fallen. Who has the last laugh now? Richard Nixon? At least <u>he</u> wasn't hoodwinked, humiliated and made the laughing stock of the world by a 26 year old black woman!

Or this, from Washington, D.C., a few days later:

> Dear Mr. Bradlee:
>
> I find the Washington Post's agonizing over the Janet Cooke affair both boring and hypocritical. . . . In fact, very few people were shocked by the affair. It was viewed as simply another example of the type of misrepresentation and fraud that one routinely expects from the media. . . .
>
> No one has any respect for journalists anymore. The profession has destroyed itself. Many public figures flatter you, because they know you have the capacity to destroy those with whom you do not agree. But do not confuse fear with admiration or respect. . . .
>
> I expect that Janet Cooke's sense of ethics and integrity is about average for the profession. You should have considered firing Walter Pincus, for example, rather than Janet. At least Janet writes with style.

Ben had given his critics a stick to beat him with. But, Ben being Ben, there was only so much he was going to take. In June of 1981, a Yale student wrote to remind Ben of an answer that he had once given to a question addressed to him at an event on campus. Somebody had asked Ben who holds the media accountable when they make mistakes, and Ben's response had been "our readers." "The brevity of your reply to such an earnest question was amusing to many in your audience, who let you escape to other issues," the student wrote.

> Other members of your audience, however, remained uneasy with that answer, because it is not believable. . . . The American people will not soon forget the Pulitzer hoax at The Washington Post. They will remember it as an early chapter in what may someday be called "Mediagate." Just as important, I hope you will remember this lesson and think a bit longer before answering the next time someone asks you, "Who keeps the press honest?"
>
> Very truly yours,

Ben's response, dated June 22, 1981:

Dear [student with incredibly WASPy sounding name]:

My God, you have gotten pompous at an early age!

Your paraphrased question asks how often do we see the media admit to inaccurate reporting? In the Janet Cooke case, you saw The Washington Post admit to inaccurate reporting. You saw The Washington Post do it before anyone else. You saw The Washington Post do it on the front page. You saw The Washington Post apologize in an editorial. You saw The Washington Post—unasked—return the Pulitzer Prize. There quite literally was no other step I could have taken in the department of autocriticism. Unique in the annals of American journalism. Really.

I am speechless at your injunction that I should remember this lesson and think a bit longer. Before you settle down as a stockbroker or whatever, and join the racquet club or whatever, try to think for yourself, if I may give you a piece of advice.

With the editors at the ASNE and in his correspondence, Ben stuck out his chest and tried to take it like a man. He did the same thing with me. When I asked him how long Janet Cooke hung over his head, he said, "You know me well enough to know that those things don't hang on me very long. It's not that I shrug 'em off, but you can't sit there and moan about it for the rest of your life."

Ben has never been one to moan about anything, to be sure, but I don't think he moved on from it as quickly as he says. Pat Tyler, who was close to Ben at the time, remembers riding over to Ben's house to play tennis in the aftermath of the scandal. "He said that he thought that his career was over," Tyler told me. "He wasn't certain that he was going to recover from it. . . . He really thought that he'd been devastated by Janet."

Memoir interview with BF, May 24, 1990

BF: Were you real depressed?
B: Oh! Terminal.

BF: Really?

B: It sort of convinced me that I'd been flying awful high and been very lucky. I think in effect that I'd—it was a story that I didn't pay enough attention to.

BF: How can you pay attention—

B: You can.

BF: You can?

B: Sure. Early on. I thought Woodward and Maraniss, there were no two better people in the fucking plant that could have done that, passed their standards. It just didn't occur to me that it was going to fail in any way. I didn't see how it could. But you know it was also, you don't quite understand that there were probably seventy-five phone calls a day for a week from people, from reporters all over the country. The determination that you were going to answer every one. That I was going to answer every one. That I wasn't going to slough it off on anybody else, and that I would take the blame, I had to. There was no point in—the first time I would have said well, what I just said to you about Woodward, Woodward was in charge, implying that it was his fault.

BF: Did you ever lose your temper at anybody through this?

B: I don't see what good that does. . . . I was ashamed. I was ashamed vis-à-vis the paper, I had gotten the paper in terrible trouble. I let the Grahams down. The Grahams had been so incredibly supportive.

BF: So you really felt responsible.

B: I was responsible. You can't ride it up and not ride it down. I mean you can't take all the credit for everything . . .

BF: I know but there's a difference between taking the credit and taking the blame and what you really feel and it sounds like you really feel . . .

B: I don't take the credit. But you are the editor of the paper and what happens in the news columns is your fault. . . . I am an extreme pragmatist—I don't spend any time at all on "what if's." None at all . . . I don't need to lay blame anywhere.

BF: That's the mark of a secure person.

B: Well, it's also the mark of a realist. What good does it do when the scars are there?

FULL CIRCLE

FBI Arrests Salvadoran in Murder of 2 Americans — Page A30

The Washington Post

FINAL

Weather

104th Year .... No. 132   THURSDAY, APRIL 16, 1981   20¢

Study Sees 20 Million Losing Some Income Under Reagan's Plan

By Spencer Rich
Washington Post Staff Writer

At least 20 million to 25 million people, most of them living below the poverty line, would have their incomes cut as a result of President Reagan's proposed reductions in welfare, public service jobs, food stamps and the school lunch program, according to a study by the Congressional Budget Office.

The study, prepared at the request of Sen. Edward M. Kennedy (D-Mass.) and Rep. James R. Jones (D-Okla.), shows that changes in those four programs alone would mean cuts for up to one American in 10. Among the hardest hit would be low-income families headed by women, particularly the nonwhite.

The CBO said that even these figures "considerably understate" the real impact of Reagan's budget because his proposals to reduce Social Security, Medicaid, unemployment insurance, fuel aid and assorted other health and social services programs were not included in the study.

The CBO said that because of data limitations, it was able to estimate the impact of only 45.5 billion in fiscal 1982 welfare, public service job and food cuts, and had to leave out the impact of $16.1 billion in other cuts in Social Security, Medicaid and other programs for the poor and near-poor. If these had been included, the affected total would have been significantly higher.

Despite its limitations, the study is the most comprehensive survey yet of the overall effect of the Reagan budget cuts on the poor.

The findings are sure to provide ammunition for Kennedy and others opposed to the Reagan proposals. Reagan and his aides have repeatedly claimed that the Reagan budget cuts wouldn't hurt "the truly needy" but the CBO study clearly shows they would affect tens of millions of people below the poverty line or just above it. Kennedy said yesterday, "It is ironic and tragic that an administration which proclaims itself to be pro-family has given us an anti-family budget which will gut even more pressure on the family structure of those already living at the economic margin.

See CUTS, A4, Col. 1

DR. BENJAMIN AARON
... above gave up on finding shot

Bullet Lodged An Inch From Reagan's Heart

By Victor Cohn
Washington Post Staff Writer

If President Reagan had been taken to the White House rather than to George Washington University Hospital he could have been killed by the bullet that lodged an inch from his heart and aorta, according to the surgeon who operated on him.

Chiefly because the president got prompt and highly skilled modern shock-trauma care was he in no danger of dying, said Dr. Benjamin Aaron, the hospital's director of chest and cardiovascular surgery.

The operation to remove the bullet was more difficult than he had anticipated, and he almost gave up three times trying to find it, Aaron said.

In a three-hour account of the events of March 30, Aaron
See SURGERY, A3, Col. 1

W. Mark Felt, left, and Edward S. Miller after receiving unconditional pardons

President Pardons 2 Ex-FBI Officials Guilty in Break-Ins

By Lou Cannon
and Laura A. Kiernan
Washington Post Staff Writers

President Reagan yesterday pardoned two former top FBI officials convicted of authorizing illegal break-ins, saying that they had served the bureau and the nation "with great distinction."

In a five-paragraph statement issued at the White House, Reagan granted full and unconditional pardons to W. Mark Felt and Edward S. Miller, convicted Nov. 6 of authorizing the break-ins during the Nixon administration's search for radical elements of the Vietnam war.

"I certainly owe the Gipper one," Miller said at a news conference in the crowded downtown office of his lawyer, Thomas A. Kennelly.

The pardons were engineered by Reagan's White House counsel and closest aide, Edwin Meese III, who called Kennelly on Jan. 30 — 10 days after Reagan took office — and invited lawyers for the two former bureau employees, who had met even applied for a formal pardon, to submit memos to the White House outlining the reasons that they should not be punished.

A close friend of the president said that Reagan initiated the action, believing that the agents had not knowingly done anything wrong.

"The president wanted to do it, and he did it," the source said.

Reagan once told an aide that he thought the agents were being penalized unfairly because they believed they were acting according to law. In the pardon statement, the president compared the plight of the two convicted men to that of the draft evaders pardoned by President Carter.

"Four years ago thousands of draft evaders and others who violated the Selective Service laws were unconditionally pardoned by my predecessor," Reagan said. "America was generous to those who refused to serve their country in the Vietnam war. We can be no less generous to two men who acted on high principle to bring an end to terrorism that was threatening our nation."

Felt and Miller were convicted of violating the rights of friends and relatives of the Weather Underground, a radical and sometimes violent organization opposed to the Vietnam war. U.S. District Court Judge William B. Bryant ordered both men pardon sentences, but fined Felt $5,000 and Miller $3,500.

The fines had been stayed pending appeal of their sentences; now they will not have to be paid.

Felt and Miller called the president's action "a very fine thing for the FBI," saying
See PRESIDENT, A8, Col. 3

Post Reporter's Pulitzer Prize Is Withdrawn

By David A. Maraniss
Washington Post Staff Writer

The Pulitzer Prize Committee withdrew its feature-writing prize from Washington Post reporter Janet Cooke yesterday after she admitted that her award-winning story was a fabrication.

Cooke's story, "Jimmy's World," was about an alleged 8-year-old heroin addict in the District of Columbia. It was said to be based on interviews with the boy, his mother and his mother's boyfriend. Cooke now acknowledges that she never met or interviewed any of those people and that she made up the story of Jimmy based on a composite of information about heroin addiction in Washington gleaned from various social workers and other sources.

Her admission followed revelations that certain statements she had made in an autobiographical report to the Pulitzer authorities also were false. Cooke had said that she was a magna cum laude graduate of Vassar College and held a master's degree from the University of Toledo. In fact, she attended Vassar for her freshman year and received a bachelor of arts from the University of Toledo.

Cooke resigned from The Washington Post yesterday.

"It is a tragedy that someone as talented and promising as Janet Cooke, with everything going for her, felt that she had to falsify the facts," said Benjamin C. Bradlee, executive editor of The Washington Post. "The credibility of a newspaper is its most precious asset, and it depends almost entirely on the integrity of its reporters. When that integrity is questioned and found wanting, the wounds are grievous, and there is nothing to do but come clean with our readers, apologize to the Advisory Board of the Pulitzer Prizes and begin immediately on the uphill task of regaining our credibility. This we are doing."

Osborne Elliott, dean of the Columbia School of Journalism, which oversees the Pulitzer awards process, said yesterday afternoon that the Pulitzer board, after being polled by telephone, withdrew Cooke's prize and awarded it to the runner-up, Teresa Carpenter of The Village Voice. "I just think it's a very unfortunate situation to which The Washington Post has responded appropriately."
See PULITZER, A23, Col. 1

ON APRIL 16, 1981, a front page news story by David Maraniss announced to *Post* readers that Janet Cooke had fabricated her story, and that her Pultizer had been withdrawn. That news, as devastating as it was to everybody at the *Post*, wasn't deemed by editors to be the most important story that day; it ran underneath a national lead story, "President Pardons 2 Ex-FBI Officials Guilty in Break-Ins." The lede: "President Reagan yesterday pardoned two former top FBI officials convicted of authorizing illegal break-ins, saying that they had served the bureau and the nation 'with great distinction.'" The two FBI officials are pictured, grinning, at the heart of the front page. The man in the foreground of that picture, the man whose face and smile dominate the entire top half of the newspaper, is Mark Felt, otherwise known as Deep Throat.

It's a stunning juxtaposition. The most famous anonymous source in the history of *The Washington Post*, and perhaps in all of journalism, sits smiling at his own legal exoneration *directly atop* the *Post*'s own admission that a much disputed story based on its second most famous anonymous source had been invented. Felt's secret was still safe, and his smile reads to a modern eye as almost preternaturally smug.

A few days later, Richard Nixon would comment on both the Janet Cooke incident and the pardon of Mark Felt as he toured Monticello, Thomas Jefferson's home, in Charlottesville, Virginia. "This was perhaps as irresponsible an example of journalism as you could find, and I hope the Post does a better job in the future," Nixon told UPI of the Cooke episode. His excitement is clear from the understatement, never mentioning his own tangles with the *Post*, tactfully sensing no personal gain from twisting a knife already so deeply buried in his old nemesis's side. Of Reagan's pardon of Felt and Edward S. Miller for their role in "black bag job" break-ins on members of the Weather Underground in the late sixties, Nixon said it was "a courageous and correct act on the part of the president."

"I know both of these men," Nixon went on. "I testified for both of them, as you may recall, in Washington, and I think for them to have served so long and so well, to have been convicted and then have their citizenship taken away . . . would have been a great miscarriage of justice." According to numerous sources, Nixon sent both Felt and Miller a bottle of champagne, along with a card that read, "Justice ultimately prevails."

Nixon wasn't naive about Mark Felt. As the once secret White House tapes reveal, Haldeman very early on began to suspect that Felt was the source of some of the leaks during Watergate. On October 19, 1972, nine days after the Segretti story ran in the *Post*, Haldeman told Nixon that somebody at the FBI was leaking. "Gray doesn't know who it is, but we do know," Haldeman said. "And it's very high up."

Nixon: "Somebody next to Gray?"

Haldeman: "Mark Felt."

One doubts that Nixon had forgotten this, given that he never forgot slights of any kind, but the dual vindication of the *Post*'s misstep on Janet Cooke and the exoneration of Felt, at whose trial Nixon testified, had perhaps emboldened him.

The coincidence of Cooke and Felt on the front page of the *Post*, unnoticed as it might have been, presaged a larger pattern: the widespread exploitation of the Cooke episode as a vehicle to reexamine Watergate and to voice lingering doubts about Deep Throat. In the May 2, 1981, issue of *The New Republic*, a piece entitled "Deep Throat's Children" argued that "Whatever gods designed the Jimmy fiasco seemed determined to give it the shape of Watergate.

"As a result of the Cooke affair," the piece went on, "there is growing agreement among newspaper people, including the *Post*'s ombudsman, that a confidential source cannot be kept from one's editor. It is not just the reporter who is on the line, but the newspaper he or she works for. This is a sensible rule; but what do you do about Deep Throat? Deep Throat, whoever he may be, is in many ways Jimmy's real father. The mythologizing of how a reporter gets a really good story—meeting mysterious figures in obscure places at great peril—helped Cooke pull off her deception. She assumed the right postures and learned all the gimmicks she hoped would protect her as they had protected sources in the past." The piece argued that Cooke had intuited what her bosses wanted and responded to, whether they told her explicitly or not: a big sexy story, anonymous sources, and the like. "The fabrication was Cooke's, but the myth was the *Post*'s, and Cooke exploited it magnificently."

As with the *Post* of two weeks before, the very next piece in that edition of *The New Republic*, titled "Bag Job Snow Job," concerned Mark Felt's pardon. It's astonishing to see the two pieces contiguous with each other in another publication and to realize it was all right there, bubbling up into the open, but only Bob, Ben, and Carl knew.

When I asked Bob about it, he told me that he didn't remember that this had all happened at the same time, and neither did Ben. When I told Don Graham he just shut his eyes and said, "Wow."

Deep Throat no longer seemed quite so sacred. Critics of the paper voiced doubts that perhaps they might previously have kept to themselves. UPI reported, on April 21, that Senator Sam Ervin called the Jimmy story "an isolated case of evil" that didn't have "any relationship to Watergate." But he did now feel at liberty to say that he thought Deep Throat was a composite. "I think Deep Throat was a symbol that Woodward and Bernstein invented to signify the people who gave them information," Ervin said. "But I think there's a difference between evil and a symbol." The story also noted that Reed Irvine, the head of a group called Accuracy in Media, had gone on record as saying that he thought Deep Throat was a composite and wanted the *Post* to reveal Deep Throat's identity. Ben refused.*

New York Times columnist William Safire went after Ben in a piece called "Bradlee's World" on Monday, April 20, 1981, the day after Bill Green's piece ran. "The irony is that the young Watergate reporter who kept from his colleagues the identity of his all-important confirming source was Bob Woodward, who is The Post's metropolitan editor today—and who did not demand to share the identity of the 'Jimmy's World' source with the convincing liar on his staff." He thought Woodward's admission of culpability was that of a loyalist protecting the man at the top, but ultimately he sided with Ben in keeping Deep Throat's name—and the principle that allowed him to remain secret—sacrosanct: "I have been systematically deceived several times and know how easy it is to be taken in by a skillful liar," Safire wrote. "Journalism need not allow its critics to use one nearly successful hoax as a device to undermine the confidentiality of sources."

---

*Ben had always disliked Irvine. Accuracy in Media fancied itself a media watchdog, and Irvine was a former Federal Reserve Board economist who attacked Ben and the *Post* whenever he got the chance. Years before, Irvine had gotten under Ben's skin by insisting that the *Post* was covering up the genocide in Cambodia. In response, Ben wrote Irvine a letter saying that he was "a miserable, carping, retromingent vigilante," and that he was sick of dealing with him. "Retromingent" means "urinates backwards." Ben has no idea where it came from.

The Deep Throat/Jimmy comparisons stuck around. In 1982, when Cooke went on Phil Donahue's program to explain herself, Donahue made the comparison explicit. Woodward wasn't her immediate editor, Donahue noted, but "the buck stopped at his desk in terms of your story, I think. Can we say that?"

"Exactly," Cooke said.

"He didn't oblige you to tell him the identities . . ."

"No."

". . . of the sources any more than Ben Bradlee obliged him to identify Deep Throat at the time of the Watergate investigations."

"That's correct."

Janet Cooke says more about Ben Bradlee than Watergate does, because she says the exact same thing that Watergate does. That's why all the echoes of Watergate in the Janet Cooke episode matter. In the broad history of journalism, Watergate and Janet Cooke are seen as aberrations, extremes, what's possible in a positive sense and what's possible in a negative sense. But in Ben's life they aren't aberrations at all. They are two very similar examples of who Ben was and how he did his job that happened to have wildly divergent outcomes.

The main point is trust. Newspapers operate on trust, as so much else in the world does, but Ben operated on trust more than most even within the world of newspapers. Alan Pakula, in his copious notes for the movie version of *All the President's Men*, put it this way: "Ben does it not because of lawyers but because he has trust in you. Trust in specific people essence of the *Post*."

That was it. Ben's trust in Carl and Bob and the editors supervising them led directly to Watergate. It was a huge gamble to trust those two young reporters, but Ben stuck with them. Part of that was belief in what they were doing, and part of that was Ben's own intuition about the story of Watergate itself, and where it might lead. Something within him told him to keep going, and he did, and it worked to such brilliant effect that he became a household name.

Ben didn't bet on Janet Cooke in the same way, but what had made Watergate possible made her possible, too. Ben trusted her. He never thought, for one second, that she was making it all up. He also trusted that the editors above her—Coleman, Maraniss, Woodward, Simons—had done their jobs properly, too.

As the executive editor of a newspaper, overseeing every section except for the op-ed page, you have to depend on other people to do the bulk of the work for you. You can't put out a newspaper if you don't. This doesn't absolve Ben of responsibility for what happened, but it does explain how it *could* have happened. On a big story you trusted your team and then went with your gut, with the guts of the people who had been through battle with you. Ben had been through battle with Simons and Woodward before, and they had won.

What makes Janet Cooke more interesting than Watergate, to me, is that Ben picked the wrong horse and it bucked him. What do you do when you play the game in just the same way that you always have, but all of a sudden you find yourself fighting for your life?

On April 24, 1981, nearly ten days after Cooke had confessed, the Howard University journalism faculty filed a suit against the *Post* with the National News Council. The suit alleged that, among other things, Cooke couldn't have come up with the story (or the idea to fabricate the story) herself, that the editors at the *Post* must have been complicit in it.

In June of 1981, the council delivered its opinion on the complaint. "The Council staff canvassed the elements in the Green report and found it to be in truth as comprehensive as it appeared to be," a section titled "Staff Analysis" began. "Nothing discovered in dozens of personal and telephone interviews raised any serious question about the report's basic accuracy."

Then, from the actual opinion:

> Obliged to face the reality that they might have perpetrated a fraud
> on their readers, the editors recognized that their first duty was to
> establish the facts, however embarrassing, and make them public.
> That duty they fulfilled—spectacularly. . . .
>
> A lie perpetrated by Janet Cooke produced a monstrous
> miscarriage of journalism. The Washington Post was negligent in the
> editing process that preceded publication of her false story.

Following publication, it failed to react in any constructive manner to questions from the community and from a few members of its staff regarding the existence of Jimmy.

Once <u>The Post</u> discovered that the story was a fraud, however, the manner in which it reacted was rare in journalism. . . . The massive 18,000 word self-indictment that resulted was an impressive demonstration of a newspaper's acceptance of public accountability.

When you make a mistake, clean it up. It was the reason Kay Graham had hired him.

"Who is Ben Bradlee?" Bob asked me rhetorically when we had finally finished our discussion of the convergence of Mark Felt and Janet Cooke and his life with Ben's, starting with Watergate and continuing into the present day. "He is, 'We do it today, and then we come back and start the next day.' And so here you have Janet Cooke connected to Mark Felt, but only he and I know . . .

"It's riddled with ironies, and you're right—you ought to set those things together. But in the world of Ben Bradlee, you know, you move on. Okay, what's the next story?"

BEN

Mr. B. Bradlee's leadership revisited—The second area of leadership's performance noticed by the news staff is focused on the mission's captain. One straightforward way to understand the rationale behind and the prevailing images of Mr. B. Bradlee's leadership is to compare what reporters believe are the qualities expected of the ideal—Post— reporter and their perceptions of Mr. B. Bradlee. The result is a well-known social phenomena of identification: most reporters provide either identical or similar answers to both questions. Aside from the well publicized stamina traits (high energy level, always at the ready, rarely seeming to run out of steam), the deepest sentiment of reporters is that the Executive Editor's quest is to achieve institutional success rather than a vulgar, personal aggrandizement in wealth and fame. Indeed, Mr. B. Bradlee is viewed as the pure entrepreneur, l'entrepreneur par excellence, dedicated to The Washington Post's mission. This is described by reporters in quasi-religious terms.

—The Frenchman

Tony Kornheiser, June 22, 2011:

I cannot describe to you what I felt, and I'm sure that so many, many others felt, when he walked among us. Ben could have been a king. Ben in that newsroom was King Arthur. I mean, he was.

David Remnick, October 26, 2009:

Most people are filled with illusions about who they are and how
they strike other people. I think Bradlee knows precisely how he
strikes other people. I think he is like that kind of star who is very
aware of the effect he has on other people, and early on learned how
to use that and marshal it to get what he needed in a professional
sense. So that the kid coming in to his office scared, that's a good
thing for him. But then by saying something encouraging or funny
or deflective or uplifting, married to that sense of nervousness. . . .

Somebody in his position all day long is meeting people that, for
the five minutes they meet with him, it's the most important five
minutes of their day. You have to know how to use that to help the
project. The project is maximizing the Washington Post. And there
he was brilliant.

He's in full command of his self. That's his instrument, like an
actor.

David Ignatius, September 27, 2007:

Story conferences are the basic funnel through which all the
information we handle has to pass every day. There are two of them.
Ben used to preside over them. He didn't actually preside; he used to
sit to the left of the managing editor, who would run the meeting,
and he would sit there, kind of leaning back, cracking jokes and
little zingers. If you ever said something stupid, God help you. . . .
I can remember as a young editor walking out of those meetings
sometimes just wiping the tears out of my eyes from laughter,
thinking, "I can't believe they pay me to do this. This is the coolest
thing on earth. God, I'm so lucky. Here I am, and I get to be with
Ben Bradlee. I get to work for the coolest guy on the planet." That
sounds corny, but in a business where you're working too hard,
you're paid too little, that ended up making a huge difference. It was
maybe the most important non-monetary compensation of working
here.

ad 8 BCB

  His secretary Donna Crouch ~~rings~~ **buzzes** in to tell him that
she knows he doesn't want to be interrupted but that Art
Buchwald is on the phone.

  "Arty," he shreiks, "gettin any lately." He pauses.
"Shit, I can't, I already have a lunch. But ~~Tuesday~~ Monday's
not a good day for pussy at the Sans anyway." (The Sans,
pronounced Sanz is short for Sans Souci, Washington's most
recherche restaurant and is only called ~~this~~ "The Sans" by
those who can get a table on a moments notice and who speak
       (Edward Bennet Williams, Washington's
perfect French) "Why dontcha call up Eddie, he wouldn't know most
          guffaws   notorious lawye
it if he fell over it anyway. " He ~~screams~~ with
laughter and slaps his thigh at his good joke on Eddie.
"And Arty, tell Eddie when he's putting his box togdher for
the Skins (Williams owns the Washington Redskins) to weed out
     those
some of ~~them~~ assholes or I'm stayin home." He signs off.

  Before the interview can resume, Simons rushes ~~in to~~
~~say that~~ Don Rumsfeld has just called up to say that Jerry
Ford has threatened to committ suicide if the Post prints
the story that the Shah paid for his swimming ~~pppx~~ pool.
          without a seconds hesitation.
  "Print it," says Bradlee, ~~xithxthexxxxxxxxxxxxxxxxxxx~~
~~xxxxxxxxxxxxxxxxxxxxxx~~ It is then that one~~x~~ can see where
he gets ~~hx~~ his reputation for toughness, for decisiveness,
for coolness under pressure. He turns back to the interviewer
with no sign of the strain his decision must have cost him.

Walt Harrington memo to Bob Kaiser, October 29, 1993:

Nothing compared to the feeling I got the times Ben walked back to
the Magazine to drop a sentence or two about one of my stories,
usually loud enough for everybody to hear. When I heard that he'd
announced that the Bush piece was the best political profile he'd
ever read, my rational side knew enough to discount the remark as
in-house political hyperbole, but I still felt as if God had reached out
and touched me. I even remember being amazed and a little
embarrassed at how good it made me feel.

But looking back, I don't think it was a Great Father and
Obedient Child thing or even that having the boss praise you is
always good, although that was some of it. I think it was much more
that I trusted and shared his judgment. If I could do a piece that got
Ben (1) to read the whole damned thing with his notoriously short
attention span and (2) to get up from his desk and walk over to drop
a quip, I knew I'd accomplished something larger. For me, Ben was
like a medium through which the interests of readers seemed to pass.
If it moved him, I knew it would move them.

The Washington Post

1515 L STREET, N. W.   223-6000
WASHINGTON, D. C. 20005

4 September, 1971

Mr. Bradlee,

When people of power---bureaucrates,
politicans, company excutives--- do something wrong people, myself included, are
fast to attact them. When they do something wright people, again I'm included,
tend to ignore that act and most often
it goes unmentioned.

You gave me your time and attention,
which is uncommon for people of your position.
That was sensitive and good and I could
not allow it to go unmentioned. Even though
I disagree with the final out come, I
do not feel cheated, ignored or unfairly
judged. That feeling is as important as
the job.

Thank you for all the consideration
you gave me.

Wilbur Colom

July 28, 1976

Dear Mr. Chung:

            I agree with you that the Moon Mullins
cartoon was not in good taste, and I am sorry
for that.

            We do not censor comics, and I have
passed your letter on to Mr. Johnson in care
of the syndicate.

                        Sincerely,

July 28, 1976

Dear Bruce:

            Would you get this letter on to Mr.

Johnson, please? The Chinese-Americans have

him by the ying-yangs (if you'll pardon the

expression).

                        Sincerely,

The Washington Post

1150 15ᵀᴴ STREET, N. W.
WASHINGTON, D. C. 20071
(202) 334-6000

BENJAMIN C. BRADLEE
EXECUTIVE EDITOR
(202) 334-7510

July 30, 1986

TO: ROBERT KAISER
        NATIONAL DESK EDITORS

This is Bulletin No. 3 on the subject of "arch" and "ultra."

I have my finger in the dike, trying to prevent "archconservative" or "ultraconservative."

My fallback position remains one "archconservative" or "ultraconservative" for every "archliberal" or "ultraliberal."

Can I have your attention on this, please.

Ben

Grant Study, 1979:

Section VIII: Politics

1. What presidential candidate do you hope will win the 1980
nomination:

Anderson___   Bush X
Baker___   Dole___
Brown___   Haig___
Carter___   Kennedy___
Crane___   Richardson___
Connolly___   Reagan___
                         Ford___

[written in below:]

I suspect Carter will probably be re-elected (12/14/79)

Letter to BCB from John Dougherty, November 29, 1993:

One memory of my time there stays crystal clear. One afternoon, you
stormed into the newsroom carrying a tape deck blasting the theme to
Rocky. Dressed in a white shirt, with sleeves rolled up, you jumped on
top of a desk and announced to a cheering newsroom that the Post was
victorious in a legal battle with Mobil Corp. I remember thinking to
myself, "So that's how to run a newsroom."

Letter from BCB back to John Dougherty, December 3, 1993:

That wasn't the theme from Rocky. That was the overture to Die
Walkyrie from Honus Wagner's great grandfather Richard. I had said
about that trial that it ain't over until the fat lady sings. And that was
the fat lady singing.

Mutual friends are wonderful to have, but they repeat idle thoughts idly. I suspect I thought you had a little asshole in you in your drunkenness at Larry's funeral, but I don't think I've wasted 12 minutes on that subject since that rotten day. I was trying so hard not to cry that day, I suspect that prevented me from similar indiscretions.

Certainly he left his mark on all of us. When I moved from next door to Georgetown it got a little better because I didn't have to speak to him every morning as I left for work and every evening as I came home from work.

Everyone does mourn differently. The way to handle that is to understand that people are mourning, and put the criticism away. Some people say I'm losing my touch, but I find I am less critical as I grow older. Let's forget it.

Your ordeal must have been godawful. And I'm so glad for you and for the biz that it turned out the way it did. I still feel sorry for Westy. Every bone in his body is decent. He just didn't see how he was being used. Then, and now, during the trial.

If I could give you a piece of advice, one which I did not follow after Tavoulareas but which I wish I had followed, it is simply this: Don't gloat; understand this key thought of Albert Camus -- "There is no truth, only truths"; and get on with it.

                         Best,

BCB to Mrs. Arthur Ashe, February 8, 1993:

Dear Mrs. Ashe:

This is a letter to tell you how much Arthur meant to me although we knew each other only slightly and to the world which really revered him.

For almost 30 years he has moved me with his grace and his incredible sense of what is important and what is appropriate.

I would also like to tell you a story that I hope will make you laugh as I think it would have made Arthur laugh if I could have reached him with it.

One afternoon I came in from working in the woods, clearing brush, at our place on the St. Mary's River in southern Maryland. My wife told me Arthur Ashe had called and wondered if I was game for tennis the next day. I found it only a little hard to believe but I wanted to do it so much that I called the number given and spoke to "Arthur" and asked him what he was doing in the area and got an answer that he was trying out a new court. I wanted to play with him so badly, I saw no incongruity in what he said.

That night I told my 10-year-old son that I was going to take him over in the morning to see one of the great tennis players of our time but also one of the bravest and most interesting men I knew. I gave him the whole nine yards—I talked about race relations, achievement, eye on the main chance—it was almost a sermon.

The next morning we drove over to the "new court." We couldn't find anyone immediately. It was a super luxurious home done in incredibly bad taste.

And then my heart sank as I saw someone I knew only barely approach with three racquets under his arm. It was a man named Arthur Esch. I had never considered the possibility that it was he, not Arthur, who wanted to play.

My son looked at me oddly for the rest of the weekend and I didn't get a chance to laugh until I was out of there.

I guess it shows how much I enjoyed Arthur's company and looked forward to seeing him.

The outpouring of love and admiration makes me feel good about my country even though we'll all miss him so much.

With great sympathy,

(s) Ben Bradlee

BCB speech to the Dirks Newspaper Financial Forum,
Atlanta, April 16, 1974:

There are many obstacles on the road between philosophy and
practice. There is rarely such a thing as absolute truth. We can only
print what we think is the truth at the time, what we are told is the
truth at the time. We are writing, in the words of Philip L. Graham,
only "the first rough draft of history." More than any other
profession, we are legitimately subject to the second guess. Unique
among manufactured products, the newspaper is completely different
every 24 hours, and it can't be recalled for mistakes of fact or
judgment. It is produced in an adversary environment where the
goals of the reported inherently conflict with the goals of the
reporter and the reader. It is this daily conflict that gives concrete
importance and meaning to the First Amendment, to freedom of
the press. Without that freedom there is no conflict, and without
that conflict there is no truth.

Interview with Michael Gartner in *American Heritage,*
October/November 1982:

Q: You've just had a son. Will there be newspapers around when he's
ready to enter the real world?

B: I can't help but think so, though maybe I'm beginning to deceive
myself. I think that newspapers may look different, but people will
always want to read hard copy. You can't Xerox television, and you
can't memorize what the radio or television announcer tells you, so
people will always want to study the details and to read the ads. No
question about that. But if a person is looking for a 1972 blue Mustang
with whitewalls, and if he can type that into his computer and come
up with three such Mustangs for sale in the Washington area, that
would scare me if I were running the classified ad department.

Interview with *Harvard Business Review,* September 2010:

Q: Is print journalism a dying industry?

B: Look, when I started in this business, I think there were close to 2,000
daily newspapers in America, which is ridiculous. Some of them
weren't any good. But this country has a handful of papers that are the
best in the world. The reporters are working hard and really, really
searching for the truth. And I guaran-damn-tee you that a lot of the
people putting out the television news and the internet news are getting it from the papers. I don't know what generation you are, but
sometimes I think I can't read without my arms wide open.

1150 15TH STREET, N.W.
WASHINGTON, D.C. 20071
FAX NUMBER (202) 334-5075

BENJAMIN C. BRADLEE
VICE-PRESIDENT At-Large
(202) 334-7510

7/16/92

Dear Ed:

Don't second guess your-
self — and don't look back.
I'm quite sure I'd have made
the same decision you did. It
looked like a bright star.

So it wasn't! Big deal!
Fuck 'em.

Best,

Ben

BEN HAS A NUMBER OF favorite phrases. Among them are "The wisdom of the ages cries out for silence" (when he doesn't want to answer your question), "The caravan moves on" (when he doesn't intend to dwell on something), and "Keep the faith" (when he is ready for you to get out of his office). The one that Sally quotes most frequently is the one she struggles to apply to her own life: whenever she is worried about something, Ben will turn to her and say, "When the history of the world is written, this will not be in it."

By that criterion most of our lives are completely meaningless, but sometimes hearing it helps.

When the history of Ben's life is written, the truth is that most of the eighties, from a pure journalistic perspective, doesn't make the cut. This isn't my judgment alone. In his five-hundred-page memoir, Ben devotes a mere thirty-five pages to the ten years between Janet Cooke and his retirement in 1991. "Historically, the eighties must look not like Ben's glory years," Bob Kaiser told me, with only a slight hint of aspersion. He was just stating a fact.

With the departure of Howard Simons in 1984, Don Graham chose Len Downie as the next managing editor of the paper, and Downie quickly became Ben's heir apparent. The transfer of power was quick and basically painless. Both Downie and Kaiser, who served as Downie's deputy, still remember a particular day in June of 1985, when a TWA flight from Athens to Rome was hijacked and flown instead to Beirut. The hijackers had killed an American serviceman on board and still held several other U.S. citizens as the *Post* went to press. It was a big breaking story and the entire staff was mobilized.

At about 7:45 that night, Ben approached Downie and Kaiser as they stood together in the newsroom, discussing the makeup of the front page and the play of the various hijacking stories. He was wearing his overcoat. "You guys have got this under control," Ben said. "I'm going home."

"Big symbolic moment for all of us," Kaiser told me.

Ben's tenure as executive editor would last another six years, but Len Downie ran the paper from there on out—just as Ben had under Russ Wiggins some twenty years before.

This doesn't mean that nothing happened in the eighties. There were important stories—Iran-contra, the Reagan assassination attempt, and a series of struggles with the CIA and FBI over national security matters (Russian spies and the like) in which Ben played a determinative role. But, increasingly, he was becoming more conservative, and in his own memoir he admits that he had probably begun to lose a step. Downie and Woodward pushed for publication of intelligence-related scoops, and the once hard charging Bradlee found himself pushing back. He didn't want to stick it to people quite as hard as he once had.

But while in the histories of Len Downie or Bob Woodward or even the *Post* itself those might be important stories, they're not overly important to Ben. In 1985 he turned sixty-four years old. His legacy was secure. And though he would often write or call a reporter to tell her that she had done a helluva job on a certain story—thus making that reporter's day—it wasn't Ben's news judgment or his instincts that mattered as much anymore. The stories people tell about Ben from the eighties aren't about what went into the newspaper, for the most part. They are the stories that Ignatius and Kornheiser tell, indicative of the phenomenon that the Frenchman described: in the eighties, Ben's presence in the newsroom meant more to the *Post* on a day-to-day basis than his editorial skills did. What mattered to people was that they worked for Ben Bradlee at a *Washington Post* that still bore his imprint— if not in terms of what went into the paper then at least in terms of how he reflected back what his reporters wanted to see in themselves.

From October of 1972, when the *Post* finished renovations on its newly acquired building on 15th Street, until July 31, 1991, when Ben walked out of the newsroom for the last time as executive editor, he spent most of each working day inside a glass-walled office on the newsroom's northern edge. He had originally wanted his office to be entirely open, no barrier, so he could hear and see everything that was going on, but in the end he was forced to accept a glass partition for security reasons. He could at least see out into the newsroom— and, far more important, the newsroom could see *him*.

The first time you see Robards in *All the President's Men* he is behind a replica of this very glass wall, conferring with other editors in his office. "There is something reassuring about being able to see Bradlee in his office sitting there below his books behind the glass (BIG DADDY)," Pakula wrote in his notes for the film.

Ben intended for the glass wall to convey his openness, his desire to be involved and to know what was going on at all times. But to a large degree Ben's intended symbolism was trumped by a different, deeper symbolism that extended far beyond his physical office: that Ben was the one being observed; that seeing him meant more than being seen by him; that his office, his leadership style, even in a sense his entire career as the editor of the *Post*, were at heart a bravura performance.

I don't mean to suggest that there was anything false about it. I mean only that Ben Bradlee is always on, still to this day. He knows that people are watching him, and he plays it to the hilt. For the last thirty years he has stood almost singlehandedly for a *Washington Post* and a newspaper business that people want to remember. Everybody who knows him takes solace in the fact that Ben will always be Ben, that you can count on him for that. That he achieves this feat as reliably and as gracefully as he does, performance or not, is one of the things that people like best about him.

The book that Sally wanted me to write with Ben was doomed from the start. There really aren't any "lessons" from Ben's life, other than that most people would love to have walked a couple of miles in his shoes. There is very little about him that you can hope to replicate in your own life. "Always tell the truth" or "Be bold" or "Trust your instincts" or some other such formulations would be the closest you could come, but those are bromides and nobody needs them. Only

Ben could do it the way that Ben did it. If you tried any of it, you'd look like an idiot.

Which didn't, evidently, stop people at the *Post* from trying. When the battle to succeed Ben began in earnest—at the level of editors and high national and international correspondents, a plane where creative tension was absolutely and undeniably real—some of the seekers puffed their chests out and offered their own pale facsimiles of Ben's persona. A few went even further. Eleanor Randolph, who was the media reporter at the *Post* in the mid-eighties, asked me what the name brand of Ben's distinctive white-collared striped dress shirts was. When I told her they were from Turnbull & Asser, she laughed. "Turnbull & Asser," she said derisively. "Every once in a while some schmuck would come in wearing one." As another reporter put it to me, "There were at least four or five editors who started wearing glasses with strings around them and talking in incredibly gruff voices, with bold striped shirts. . . . It was hilarious. And very masculine. I mean, the whole thing was like a hilarious boys town."

"A few individuals among the perceived 'high fliers' tend to exhibit some 'over-respect' towards the Executive Editor," wrote the ever reliable Frenchman:

> The posture generates some acerbic remarks from the floor mainly when these "high fliers" desire to interact with subordinates in the same manner as the captain does. On the opposite the most appreciated lieutenants are characters who do not try to replicate the Executive Editor's style but are deeply committed to the same collective values; thus, they strive to implement them according to their distinctive temper.

This was one of the reasons, outside of his clear chemistry with Don Graham, that Len Downie made so much sense as Ben's successor. He was not among the people who thought it wise to wear $100 dress shirts in the newsroom, nor to try to imitate Ben in any way. He was, famously, the son of an Ohio milkman, and he had a different, more workmanlike approach to editing and to management for which he made no apologies.

"Ben was much better with the big stuff than the small stuff," Don Graham told me diplomatically. "I mean, I doubt that Winston Churchill would have been regarded by the people who worked for him as quote 'a good administrator.' Ben wasn't a good administrator, but he had people around him who were."

Ben doesn't deny any of this. In 1991, shortly after his retirement, the dean of the George Washington University School of Business and Public Management wrote to see if Ben would accept an honor from the school. Ben's response:

Dear Dean Burdetsky:

Don Graham has been struck mute at the news that any school of business and management would honor me in any way and as usual I agree with him.

I think that if you just want to fill a hall, then maybe I could help but I feel slightly uncomfortable being honored by you at all.

"People ask me, 'What was your goal for the *Washington Post*, what was your game plan?'" Ben once said. "I really didn't have one. You want to make it better, you know where you're weak, you try to make it strong. And then where you're weak changes and you've got to make it stronger again." Though lofty journalistic principles sound great, this is how most things actually work. Ben's managerial approach was always ad hoc. This is true journalistically, too; there isn't any identifiable record of journalistic principles that he leaves behind in his wake, any rudder for aspiring journalists to steer by, other than always to maintain a healthy skepticism about government and its doings. Ben's greatest contribution was that he made a series of gut calls at crucial moments in a way that inspired confidence in an entire newsroom for an extended period of time.

Outside of hiring the most talented people he could find and then setting them free to compete with one another, perhaps Ben's only other identifiable managerial technique was his twice daily circuit through the newsroom. Nearly every other editor I spoke with mentioned this as one of the primary things they took away from having known Ben. It was a simple act, walking through the newsroom and gossiping with the staff, but as a performer he used these rounds to great effect.

In 1984, Woodward was out drumming up publicity for *Wired,* his book about John Belushi and the Hollywood drug culture. In a morning television interview, Bob said that he had heard an estimate that roughly forty people at the *Post* used cocaine on a regular basis. That afternoon, Ben hammered out a statement: "I don't know what the hell Bob is talking about. None of the editors knows what he is talking about. Cocaine is illegal, and if I hear of anyone using it around here, it's out the door, good-by." The staff didn't know if Ben was pissed, suspicious, or what. Later that afternoon, a reporter in the Magazine section of the paper remembers Ben making his way across the newsroom, pointing at various reporters as he went, shouting, "Thirty-seven! Thirty-eight! Thirty-nine!"

When Ben finished the first draft of his memoir, in 1994, he circulated it to a few trusted readers for feedback. Tom Wilkinson, Ben's old friend at the paper, wrote back with a long list of items that he thought Ben needed to address. At the top of the list: "You have a tendency to overuse the words 'joy' and 'joyous.'" Ben wrote in the margin, "Agree."

Ben had charisma and good looks and wit and great instincts and an interesting backstory and a flair for punch and drama, but without the joy he took in what he did the *Post* could never have become what it was while he was there. Ben loved his job, and he lived for it, and that's mostly how he inspired others to do the same. He loved newspapers and the battle for the news. He loved the process of reporting, the exposure of lies, and particularly the moment when a big breaking story began to make its murmuring way through the newsroom. The height of joy lay in scooping the *Times,* of course, which happened often but never often enough. In 1978, when the *Post* published excerpts of H. R. Haldeman's book before the *Times,* which had paid for the rights, Ben was asked how he felt about it. "Delight," he responded. "Sheer, unadulterated delight."

Joy is often underreported as a reason for why good things happen to some people and not others. In Ben's case, his joy had a great deal to do with how he was able to create an atmosphere in the newsroom that could produce the hard-hitting, vibrant journalism he was after. "That was one of the happiest places I can imagine," he told Shelby Coffey, a former *Post* editor and reporter who had been Len Downie's chief rival to succeed Ben as editor of the paper, in an interview at the Newseum after Ben retired:

> People were doing the best work they could do, and among peers, and they were laughing, and it was a joyous place. It was a joyous place. And, you know, did it ever stop being joyous? I'm sure it did. But I can't remember it. And I remember that the idea of going to work was the most exciting thing in the morning that I could think of. And to create that, you have to believe it.

Ben believed it, and so did most of his staff. People wanted to be there. At the root of Ben's joy was an endless curiosity about what was happening in the world, and why, and what the *Post* might be able to say about it. Woodward and Walter Pincus and several other of Ben's star reporters all describe his curiosity as the base of his drive, personally and for the paper. "What the fuck *happened*?" Ben would ask, sidling over to your desk, and once he put that bee in your bonnet you would do anything to figure out a way to tell him.

"One of the joys of journalism," Ben once said, "is that you don't really run into the same thing over and over again. I come to work and I don't know what the hell I'm going to do in the morning. I mean, we could be interrupted here in the next five seconds by somebody who comes in with news that's going to change the course of the world." Deep down he really is like a shark, driven by an atavistic need to keep moving, to keep driving, always on the hunt for what's next. He claims as his family motto the phrase "Nose down, ass up, and keep pushing forward," a phrase that tells you a lot about him.

The complement to Ben's joy and curiosity, the thing that made him more than just a cheerleader, was his competitiveness. Ben wanted the news first, period. At the daily news conferences, if you were an editor and somebody in your section had been scooped, Ben would pass you a copy of the story with a Post-it note on the top asking simply, "What's this about?" You were expected to have an answer.

During Watergate, Carl and Bob remember distinctly that at certain points Ben would throw a story back at them and exclaim, with undisguised glee, "Eat your heart out, Abe!" Abe was A. M. Rosenthal, the managing editor and then the executive editor of *The New York Times*, a man whom Ben described to me on numerous occasions as his "chief rival." Rosenthal was by all accounts a brilliant (if difficult) man and editor, instrumental in the *Times*'s decision to publish the Pentagon Papers. He was at the wheel from 1969 until 1986, dates that track pretty closely with Ben's. He personified the *Times* in the same way that Ben personified the *Post* for so much of his time there.

For me the competition was over before it started:

From a letter of Ben's, to be read aloud at a roast of Rosenthal in the late eighties:

> Following his legendary nose for news, Abe recently found himself in the Galapagos Islands, 500 miles west of Ecuador deep in the Pacific Ocean. There, he told us in his column, he came face to face with an unafraid iguana, and the iguana spat in his face.
>
> It was inevitable, given the drama inherent in this confrontation that they would make a movie about it. Buddy Hackett will play Abe, and they want Max Frankel* for the iguana.

For his part, Rosenthal was aware of the contrast, too. "I'm back in New York even more tanned and handsome than ever," he wrote to Ben in the late seventies. "My wife has fallen in love with you. Kindly send her a handsome check every week."

These were jokes, but the competition was serious. Rosenthal enjoyed sticking it to Ben just as much as Ben enjoyed sticking it to him. In 1974, Rosenthal told *The Boston Globe*, "I don't want to sound boastful, but I can't help it—we cover the world, and the two papers cannot be compared." This after they'd just had their asses handed to them on Watergate.† Or from *Time* magazine, 1977, in a piece about Kay Graham ("Krusty Kay Tightens Her Grip"):

> Ask A. M. Rosenthal, the *Times*'s executive editor, to name the best American papers and he will tell you. "The Times—space—the

*Frankel was Rosenthal's managing editor, and looked more like Rosenthal than Ben.

†The *Globe* piece was a huge Sunday magazine feature, "The Times, The Post, and Watergate," and it also quoted *Times* publisher Punch Sulzberger saying, "We had to run a long way to catch up, but we've done it." Ben didn't believe this; neither did the piece's author, Robert Lenzner: "No one else interviewed for this comparison of the two most powerful newspaper editors in the nation believes that the Times has made up the ground lost in the first newsbreaks of the Watergate affair. In fact, one Times man calls his paper's performance 'the classic failure of modern American journalism.'"

Washington *Post*—space—and then the others." The *Post*'s executive
editor, brash Ben Bradlee, agrees, although he thinks his own paper
in some ways better. Bradlee envies the *Times* its careful editing, its
good desk work, its "cruising speed." But he also finds the *Times*
"too constipated."

A few years later, the *Times*'s D.C. bureau chief was quoted in the
Washington Journalism Review saying, "What hasn't changed is that the
New York Times sets the news agenda for the television networks and
the other newspapers around the country, including the *Washington
Post*."

"In a pig's ass—and that's on the record!" Ben replied. "The *New
York Times* people wish that were true but it hasn't been since Watergate and they know it."

"I hope you keep trying to accept the *Post* as a truly first rate newspaper," Ben would write to a reader more than ten years later. "We
are not *The New York Times* and do not aspire to be. We are not
pompous. We hope that we are interesting, different. We pray for
readers who won't confuse good writing with arrogance, smugness,
and condescension."

Ben took any attack by Rosenthal or the *Times* as a direct personal
attack. In many ways this was true of his entire career: when Ben
wanted something from you, it became very personal, for him and
for you. The Pentagon Papers were about the *Post* and the *Times*, but
for Ben in a very deep and important way they were also about *him*.
Even when he was in the wrong, when he knew that he'd lost out on
the merits in any given situation, he would make a direct personal
appeal. "Give me this one," he would say, to an editor or a reporter
who had caught him wrong-footed. "Let me have this one, pal."
And more often than not he'd get what he wanted.

As Ben and Rosenthal got older, they developed a kind of fondness for each other—the kind that comes from trading barbs for years
in the press but finally realizing that you're coming to the end of the
road, and that pretensions are silly. In 1986, shortly before his retirement, Rosenthal sent Ben a long, kind letter, full of jokes about his

future role as a columnist and the "lucid instructions" he would be giving the world as such. "Oh, the hell with all this arch stuff," Rosenthal wrote at the end. "You're a good editor and so am I and we have always liked each other, and it's time to say so."

And yet even around that very retirement, the hackles of both men would go up in ways that typified each of them. When Eleanor Randolph went up to New York to interview Rosenthal for her three-part series on his retirement in the *Post*, she asked him what he thought the difference was between the two papers. "I don't always read the *Post*," Rosenthal said. The three-part series, celebrating Rosenthal and wondering about who his successor might be, ran in the *Post* in January of 1986. The stories noted that Rosenthal was being moved out by May of 1987 not because of any lack of fitness for the job but because the *Times* had a mandatory retirement age of sixty-five for its executives.

A few years later, when word started to spread that Ben was thinking of retiring, Rosenthal couldn't resist a cheap shot. "I retire and they do a series about me," he reportedly said of the *Post*. "When Ben retires, we'll probably give him a paragraph." So Ben sat down at his typewriter and crafted a response. "Dear Abe," he began, "Here's your paragraph. Benjamin C. Bradlee, *age 70*, retired today . . ."

On June 20, 1991, Ben sent out a memo to the entire staff of the *Post* announcing his departure. "Tomorrow's newspaper will carry the news that as of Labor Day I will become a vice-president of the newspaper and a director of the *Post* Company," he wrote. "This is a cause for nothing but optimism and excitement about how productively time marches on."

The following morning, longtime *Post* reporter Howard Kurtz broke the news on the front page of the paper: "Bradlee Retiring as Editor of The Post; Managing Editor Downie to Move Up." Inside, on A12, Kurtz had compiled a more complete tribute to Ben: "With Pen and Panache, Bradlee Molded Bolder, Brasher Post." He led with the Walter Washington episode, noting that Ben had built the *Post* from a "small, genteel paper with no national pretensions into what is widely regarded as one of the two or three most influential papers in the country." The size of the newsroom staff had doubled under Ben, from three hundred to six hundred; the news budget increased from $3 million to $60 million; daily circulation had gone from 446,000 to 802,000; and the paper had won twenty-three Pulitzer Prizes. "Even as Bradlee has gradually reduced his role in the newsroom in recent years," Kurtz wrote, "his personality and approach to journalism—hard-hitting, sharp-tongued, and stylish—have remained interchangeable with the paper's public image."*

Ben never had a contract at the *Post*. Nor, that he can remember, did he ever ask for a raise. (His bonus check one year in the eighties was for $198,000, so it's not as if he needed to.) He served, always, at the pleasure of the Grahams, with the clear understanding that once that pleasure had passed so, too, would his tenure as executive editor. "I'm going to retire as soon as somebody with the last name Graham asks me to," he would say when people asked.

But with the birth of his son Quinn in 1982—Quinn had a host of difficulties as a kid, including open heart surgery at just three months of age—Ben had begun to contemplate when he might pass the baton. Once Downie had been chosen as managing editor in 1984, Ben knew that his days were numbered, but he was in no rush to move out and Don Graham was in no rush to move him out. At one of their regular Tuesday breakfasts in 1988, Graham turned to Ben and proposed, "How about working until you hit seventy?" and that was it.

---

*As it turned out, the *Times* ran more than a paragraph. The day after the *Post* broke the news, the *Times* ran a 1,430-word story about Ben's retirement. In addition to recounting Ben's achievements, the piece wondered whether Downie, "the son of an Ohio milkman," could survive, asserted that the *Post* had lost its edge since Ben had taken a step back, aired criticism of Ben from the black community in D.C., and printed a sentiment attributed to former *Times* Washington bureau chief Bill Kovach, who never even worked at the *Post*, describing the leadership atmosphere there by likening Ben to a walnut tree that "puts out a toxin so that other big trees cannot survive nearby." Gracious indeed.

"Currently there's a sort of mythology that the *Post* will change radically if I leave . . . that the bean-counters will take over if Bradlee's not there to keep 'em sort of straight and narrow," Ben told George Vaillant, his old Grant Study interlocutor, the year before he retired. "This is bullshit, it really is . . . because the place, I recognize now, is running just great, and the people who are doing all the work rather than [getting] all the credit are ready to do both. And it's time."

With the announcement of Ben's retirement in June of 1991, the letters began to pour in—from old reporters, old friends, colleagues, competitors. They all said pretty much the same thing. Ben's next door neighbor in D.C. sent in a note about having run into a man named Eddie McGrath, an old Harvard athlete who coached school football in Boston during the 1930s. "Eddie said, 'I coached Ben in the 8th grade,'" the neighbor wrote. "'He was the best quarterback I ever had. He was a cocky little bastard, but he put his heart in every play—and he made the whole team better.'"

The best of the bunch came from Mary McGrory, four days after Ben's announcement to the staff. McGrory had been a legend at the *Star*, and when the *Star* finally fell apart in 1981 McGrory's migration to the *Post* was a shining moment for Ben and also a convenient lever by which to move himself past the agonies of Janet Cooke. McGrory was a perceptive writer and a perceptive person:

> Even with the long buildup, the announcement was a blow. There was a pall over the newsroom. You were our hedge against tedium vitae, in and on the paper. You were our protection against them, whoever they might be. . . .
>
> I will miss you most, not just because I have known you the longest—I've been your friend and fan for 40 years—but because you always had time for me. Some of the terminally self-important around here are too busy to say good morning, but you told me stories and made me laugh. I always loved hearing about your father.
>
> You've had "Scaramouche" quoted to you, I'm sure: "He was born with the gift of laughter and a sense that the world was mad." That's

you, and weren't we lucky that we had you so long and that you made us feel safe and excited at the same time. Thank you.

Love, Mary

On July 31, 1991, Ben's last day in the newsroom, all of the editors showed up at the 2:30 story conference in Turnbull & Asser shirts. ("At almost $100 a shirt, few of them sported the genuine article," Ben couldn't help but note in his memoir, "but the Art Department had provided ersatz white collars for the cheapos.") Several editors pitched bogus stories designed to get a rise out of Ben. He had always been skeptical of science stories in general and in particular of the depletion of the ozone layer as a threat to the health of the planet. One editor pitched a story combining the Big Bang and ozone depletion, just to piss him off. Downie ran the meeting and, in homage to Ben, lobbed gratuitous curses and comments throughout. At the end, the editors balled up their budgets—the roster of stories for the next day's paper—and threw them at Ben, as he characteristically did at the end of each story conference.

Later that afternoon, there was a public sendoff near the north wall of the newsroom, where the entire staff had assembled.

"None of us have really known how to deal with this day, including Ben, including me, because it's a day that we didn't ever really expect to happen or understand how we're gonna get through, or beyond," Len Downie said, starting things off. He talked about how Ben had overseen the renovations of the newsroom in 1972, when the new building was acquired, and also succeeding renovations involving the installation of computerized systems and everything else that came with the transformation of the *Post* into a modern newspaper. "We're in Ben Bradlee's newsroom, quite literally," Downie said. "And, in a more important way, this is Ben Bradlee's newsroom because most of us are Ben Bradlee's people. . . . He gave us room to spread our wings and to fly in a way that nobody else of his genius has been able to do in most other walks of life. Ben created the newspaper that we work for now."

Walter Pincus joked that, in light of Ben's retirement, Robards had given up acting, too. "There have been a whole slew of us who've gone through this place really enjoying every minute of it because we liked each other and because we were working for an extraordinary bunch of people and because the guy running it made it that way," he said.

Meg Greenfield, the longtime editor of the editorial page, came next. She and Ben had had their share of prickly moments. "I don't agree that there will be another Ben," she said. "The Lord made only one Ben Bradlee and editorial writers say, on balance, that was a good decision because what would the other Ben Bradlee do?" Her favorite moment in all of her time with Ben had been when William Rehnquist, then the assistant attorney general (and later the chief justice of the Supreme Court), called to try to prevent the *Post* from continuing to publish the Pentagon Papers after the first day they had run in the paper. As Ben was saying all the right things to Rehnquist over the phone, he was making obscene hand gestures to Greenfield, who was sitting (dying) in his office. This was the posture of the *Post* she remembered, a paper that was "dangerous to people in government."

Tom Wilkinson, the head of personnel, followed Greenfield. The first story he told has always been a kind of legend at the *Post*; a number of different people told me that Ben had said it to them first, and not to Wilkinson. Who knows. As Wilkinson told it, when he became head of personnel, one of the first applicants he saw was "pretty good." "He had a variety of clips—hard news, features, politics, solid experience at a couple of papers, kind of reticent, little soft-spoken, kind of shy, but he interviewed around the newsroom and did pretty well." Ben was the last stop in the process, so Wilkinson sent him in to Ben's office and then went in after the guy left. He hoped for thoughtful analysis of the applicant's strengths and weaknesses, or at least a critique of his clips. Ben's summary: "Nothing clanks when he walks."

"That was the end of the discussion and the end of him," Wilkinson said. "After that, I knew a little bit more about what Ben was looking for."

Woodward got up and told a story on himself. On April Fool's in

1975, an article in the *Post* had run with a composite sketch of a man suspected in the disappearance of a pair of sisters known as the Lyon sisters in Wheaton, Maryland. They had last been seen talking to a man with a tape recorder who loosely matched Ben's physical description. Scott Armstrong and Al Kamen, who were working with Bob on *The Final Days*, were in on the joke, and along with a copy aide at the *Post* they told Bob that Ben was in jail and would only talk to him. "I got dressed, put on my best suit, this was gonna be the interview of the decade, Bradlee in the cell block," Bob said.

Bob immediately began concocting possible explanations for how Ben could have been involved. "I think he's writing a book," Bob told Armstrong and Kamen, thinking out loud about why Ben might have been interviewing young girls with a tape recorder. He was on his way out the door when the phone rang. It was the copy aide calling back to confess that the whole thing had been a joke. "I was willing, as a reporter and as a friend and admirer, to accept any explanation for what you had done to these young girls," Bob said. "And, in an interesting way what was going through my mind: I had forgiven you for the crime that you had not committed. We talk about loyalty and devotion and Bradlee's ability to get people to make strange connections and do things for him that they would do for no one else. Well, that is my best example."

After a few more long speeches, Ben yelled, "When are you gonna put a paper out?"

Haynes Johnson told the story of the impromptu memorial service on the top floor of the *Post* building when longtime *Post* reporter and editor Larry Stern died. After an emotional commemoration at the Quaker meeting house on Florida Avenue, people had returned to the *Post* to drink and to remember Stern, who had dropped dead while jogging on Martha's Vineyard. (Ben was so curious about how it had happened that he requested, and received, the autopsy report concluding that Stern had died of cardiac arrest, most likely as a result of an allergic reaction to a bee sting.) Upstairs in the *Post*'s outdoor courtyard, Ben had been at a loss for words and decided spontaneously to throw his glass against the brick wall of the courtyard. Everybody present had followed suit, and when the bill from the catering company came in for all the broken glasses Ben had it framed and hung in the newsroom next to a picture of his friend Larry.

David Broder followed. I never interviewed him officially for this book, but he would sit with Ben and me in the *Post* cafeteria every so often, eating the humblest slice of pizza you can imagine and telling stories about the old days. The last time I saw him, he told me the same story that he told on the day Ben retired:

> In 1980 at the Republican convention came the moment that really defined him for me. Lou Cannon, our White House reporter, was determined that he was going to beat the world on the choice of Ronald Reagan's running mate for the 1980 campaign . . . and by the third night of the convention, we were pretty convinced that it was going to be George Bush. Lou wrote a story saying, in effect, that the decision had come down for George Bush.
>
> Our neighbors at Newsweek in the next space [literally, right next to them in the convention hall], had had Ford as their lunch guest for an off-the-record exclusive Newsweek lunch that day and at that lunch, Ford had started dropping hints about how he might be interested, and that story built and built and built and the Newsweek people were absolutely riding the hell out of us, saying you guys are wrong, it's not gonna be Bush, it's gonna be Ford.
>
> Finally, late that night . . . Reagan came to the convention bringing Bush with him, saying, "This is my choice." Bradlee got up on the partition between us and Newsweek . . . [Broder claps; when he told me the story, he mimed beating his own chest] "We had it, you didn't," and a few other words besides.
>
> That, to me, was the quintessential Ben Bradlee, outrageous, but why? Because he was so goddamn competitive, so proud of this organization and so goddamned determined that we have it right. I don't think any of us will work for a better editor than that.

When Broder was done, Don Graham stood up. "In a game scheduled for twenty-seven innings, I feel all the excitement of the guy called in to work the top of the twenty-second," he said. Because time was running short, he kept his remarks brief; he didn't tell his favorite Bradlee story, the one that he has told so many times since that it has become a standard part of Bradlee lore. In December 1984, the Reagan administration decided to send off a space shuttle with a military package on it, ostensibly for the first time. In advance of the launch, Caspar Weinberger, Reagan's defense secretary, asked the media not to report on what the package might contain. An Army general threatened to open investigations into any members of the press who dared even to "speculate" about it.

With Ben's prodding, Walter Pincus used mostly open sources to discover the contents of the package, an orbiting "signals intelligence" satellite. After careful consideration, and with no small amount of joy at the prospect of ruffling some feathers, Ben put it in the paper. The next day Weinberger accused the *Post* of "the height of journalistic irresponsibility," braying publicly that the paper had given "aid and comfort to the enemy" and had essentially committed espionage.

A series of uniquely vitriolic letters from readers followed. Addressed to "Ben Bradlee, Kremlin on the Potomac": "If JFK asked you to withhold printing that story, it would have been. You & your paper are traitors and should be tried for treason." Another: "You are unspeakably arrogant and are doing everything in your power to damage the United States. Sir you are a traitor to your country." One took a slightly more oblique tack: "By the way, are you still fucking your mother?"

But the one that got under Ben's skin was from a man named J. C. Turnacliff, dated December 20, 1984:

Ben Bradlee (WASH. POST)
   HOW DO I VIEW THEE? LET ME COUNT THE WAYS.
   (1) DUMB (2) SMART ALECKY (3) IRRESPONSIBLE
   (4) UNAMERICAN (5) A REALLY POOR NEWSPAPERMAN
   (WHAT DID YOU DO DURING WWII?)
   YOUR IRRESPONSIBLE RELEASE OF THE UPCOMING
   SHUTTLE MISSION PROBABLY SET BACK ARMS TALKS
   BY 10 YEARS.

This was Ben's response, dated a week later:

The Washington Post

1150 15ᵀᴴ STREET, N. W.
WASHINGTON, D. C. 20071
(202) 334-6000

BENJAMIN C. BRADLEE
EXECUTIVE EDITOR
(202) 334-7510

December 27, 1984

Dear Asshole:

         I suspect I did more for my country in the war than
you did. I spent four years in destroyers in the Pacific Ocean.
My theater ribbon has 10 battle stars in it.

         That's just for starters.

                              Benjamin C. Bradlee

It's one of the most infamous of all the letters that Ben has ever
written. If I could have gotten away with it, "Dear Asshole" would
have been the title of this book. Kay Graham was said to have loved
that letter more than any other.

But what has always made it interesting to Don Graham was what
happened next. A couple of weeks later, J. C. Turnacliff wrote Ben
back. "Mon Cher Con," he began, "the salutation in your recent
letter (copy enclosed) was vintage Bradlee-eze and I'm glad I have it
for my memoirs. It takes one to know one." He said that he felt compelled to write because he didn't want Ben to think that ten battle

stars meant a whole lot to a Marine Corps combat officer who had participated in landings on Guadalcanal, Bougainville, and Iwo Jima. "I guess we both contributed our share," Turnacliff wrote.

I still think America's interests would have been better served if the press had acquiesced to the Defense Department's request to withhold details of the exact military nature of the January shuttle mission.

I believe in freedom of the press, but I also believe in a responsible press which uses good judgment and places America's security interests above the desire to be the first to blab, whatever the consequences.

Your asshole buddy,

Another week later, Ben returned fire, enclosing a statement from an Army general who said that in his official view the *Post* hadn't violated national security. But this time, Ben began, "Dear Pal." "Do you realize," he wrote at the letter's close, "that I probably took you to Bougainville? I'm glad Weinberger wasn't in your foxhole or my battle station. Keep the faith."

Turnacliff wrote back one last time, saying that he didn't expect a response but wanted to close the loop. "I do . . . hope that your last letter to me made you feel as good as it did me," he wrote. "It's much better being friends than enemies. . . . I must admit that when I saw that large manila envelope containing your reply to my letter I opened it with some trepidation. I thought it might contain an 8x10 glossy photo of you mooning me. Its actual contents were much more satisfying." He had since read both of Ben's books, and said that he felt he knew Ben a bit better. "I hope our paths cross sometime," he wrote. "Two independent thinkers like us can't be all bad."

Don Graham's point, whenever he tells the story, lies less in the obvious Ben-ness of starting a letter with "Dear Asshole" than in the fact that the correspondence grew from there, that the two men ended up as something approximating friends. "One of those nice accidents of Ben's life," as Graham once put it, "but typical." Ben's firebreathing side is more famous than his softer, more forgiving side, but that softer side—particularly with people who showed themselves willing to confess frailty, or to retain an open mind—was always there.

As the celebration in the newsroom drew to a close, Len Downie stood up and read a final testimonial from Nora Boustany, the *Post*'s correspondent in Beirut:

> Whenever I found myself alone on the streets of Beirut, I would just shrug off the shelling, the gunmen and the dark corners, telling myself there is this distinguished eminence up there who really appreciates and understands the true meaning of courage in journalism. I always made it to my destination safely and with the story. I find myself in Beirut again. The streets are a little calmer now, but for me you will always be the grand brave man of the news who watched over me and made me want to give just a little bit more. Thank you for giving us all something so special to believe in. Your fan forever, Nora.

With that, Ben addressed the newsroom one last time. "I was doing great until Boustany's wire," he said. "I am overwhelmed by you, as I have been since the day I met all of you." He didn't want to run too long, but he wanted Downie—"Leonard," as Ben called him—to know that he wanted to bequeath him something.

He went on to tell the story of the ASNE conference in April of 1981, right after the Janet Cooke scandal had unfolded—the meeting of ombudsmen, the 750 people, the television cameras, the works. "What I bequeath you is the loyalty of the publisher," Ben said to Downie. "Because during that day, which was murder for me, it couldn't have been much fun for him, and I can just tell you there was not a picture taken of me that day that did not have Don Graham's arm draped around my shoulder. And that's as meaningful to me today as it was then. So Leonard, you've got that." They embraced. Then, waving to the rest of the newsroom, Ben said, "Thank you all."

As Martha Sherrill, the Style writer tasked with reporting the story of Ben's retirement for the next day's paper, wrote, "Cake waited to be eaten. Bradlee turned to a nearby reporter. 'You're a girl,' he said. 'Cut it.'"

After the farewells and the hugs and the cake, as Ben made his way toward the elevator with Sally, a spontaneous standing ovation broke out across the newsroom. Reporters and editors stood on desks, doing whatever they could to follow Ben as he walked out for the last time as their boss. He paused at the doorway to the elevators and raised his fist in a final salute, and then he put his arm around Sally and walked out for good.

THE MORNING OF SUNDAY, August 30, 2009, broke calm and clear on Long Island, but by noon Grey Gardens was humming. Florists burst in and out of the front door, teams of maids were running up and down the stairs, and the phone was ringing off the hook. Ben had turned eighty-eight a few days before, but tonight was the main event.

At the table in the sun room, Sally and Eden Rafshoon scrutinized the seating charts for the dinner, calling out names, furiously scribbling and then erasing, dishing about who couldn't sit next to whom and why. Ben and I sat in the corner by the television, watching tennis and tangling with a particularly screwy *Times* Sunday crossword. The other houseguests—Maureen Dowd and Eden's husband, Jerry, and an assortment of other D.C. types—lounged and read on the couch or walked on the beach.

The whole thing was like a scene out of a Victorian novel, everybody in the great house preparing for the big party. Grey Gardens itself is a marvel. It was famous before Ben and Sally ever moved in, the subject of an eponymous and classic documentary film from the seventies that later became a fictionalized Broadway show and HBO movie. The house sits at the corner of posh Lily Pond Lane and West End Road, across the street from Steven Spielberg and a healthy stone's throw from the beach. Like Ben and Sally's other two homes it's ritzy and historic and perfectly restored and all of that, but more than anything it's just a beautiful place. The gardens take up an entire acre and are as lush as you can imagine, full of archways and hydrangeas and picturesque seating arrangements that nobody ever uses.

Time spent there is an idyll. You get up whenever you want. Breakfast and lunch are taken outside, under an umbrella on a deck beside the pool. Ben's usually the first to the table, and when you're ready for it Evelyn cooks your breakfast to order. Everybody reads the papers and gossips about whatever happened the night before—in the Hamptons, there is always a party, and Ben and Sally are always invited—until somehow you find that it's after noon, you've been by the pool for two hours, and Ben, baked to a disconcertingly deep shade of red, is pulling himself out of his lounger to make Bloody Marys. A woozy late lunch, a bit more sun with a book, and then you find yourself getting ready for a party, or a catered clambake on the beach, or a gourmet dinner cooked by a private chef. One of Ben's favorite aphorisms, taken from the Jewish elders, is "Love work, hate domination, and steer clear of the ruling class." All true, but a bit hard to wrap your mind around when you're there.

The first guest to arrive was Barbara Walters, mortified to be precisely on time. "I expected traffic," she said to Ben out on the porch, by way of apology for being prompt. "I figured it would take at least another half an hour to get here."

Slowly, in the time-lapse manner of a party getting under way, the back porch began to fill up with guests. Alec Baldwin came next, with cigars "for Jack," who turned out to be Jack Nicholson. Jimmy Buffett and his wife walked in just behind Lorne Michaels. Steven Spielberg and his wife, Kate Capshaw, walked across the street from their house and in through the open front door. Anjelica Huston, the painter John Alexander, Ken Auletta, Richard Cohen, agents and editors from the big publishing houses in New York, editors from *The Washington Post*, almost all boldfaced names in their own right. Soon the place was buzzing, as the first drink settled in.

The dining room was so packed that we had a hard time finding our seats when the dinner bell rang. I had been to some of Sally and Ben's bigger parties in Washington, but I had never been to anything like this before—a fully seated affair with all of the big names, where you were placed next to somebody for a reason and you were expected to figure out what it was. Things got loose pretty fast. My dinner partner to my left, a smart and beguiling woman from New York, asked me toward the end of dinner to tell her who I thought was the most beautiful woman in the room—a trick question if ever there was one. I mentioned one of the older women there, a woman who is classically beautiful in a delicate, porcelain sort of way. A safe bet.

"She's beautiful, okay," my new friend said, placing a piece of duck on her fork and then looking back up at me, "but do you want to *fuck* her?"

It was that kind of party, at least at our table. Paul McCartney stopped by to say hello before dessert, sending a jolt of blushing self-congratulation throughout the room. He, Ben, Lorne Michaels, Alec Baldwin, and a few others all go to yoga together in Amagansett a couple of times a week during the month of August. They call themselves the Yoga Boys, and they all clearly love it.* (The previous night, at a party down the street, Ben had introduced me to McCartney by saying, "Meet a pal of mine. He's working on a book about me." As I fumbled for words, the ever-savvy Macca saved me from myself by saying simply, "It better be good.")

I won't lie. I loved every minute of it. It wasn't until the toasts that something started to feel a little bit off. Sally got up and said that Ben was her role model, her icon, and Ben sawed away on the air violin while the entire room groaned good-naturedly. Ben's son, Quinn, offered up a heartfelt toast about all he had learned from his dad. Others made jokes, and then Ben stood up and said, "Sally, words can't say how much you've meant to me in our thirty-plus years . . ." Before he could finish the sentence, Sally had shouted, "Thirty-six!" Then he called her his "girlfriend," one of his standard laugh lines,

---

*In August of 2011, Baldwin went on *Letterman* to promote *30 Rock* and mentioned the Yoga Boys, prompted by Letterman. "Ben, who just turned ninety years old this year, took the class with us the last couple years," Baldwin said. "What was great was he was the only one who would say what the rest of us were feeling . . . she would say, 'And now we're going to do the lassa shinasana, or whatever the hell it is' . . . and Ben Bradlee literally would go, 'Are you out of your mind? I can't do that. You want me to touch my ankle to my chin? I'm gonna snap my hip in half here.' And we would all cackle laughing, because nobody else would say that."

and sent people on their way. As the crowd stood up to start heading home I realized it was a script that I'd seen before, and that everybody in the room had likely seen it before, too.

The thing about being starstruck is that it wears off. As I looked around the room, a room I had felt such a charge to be in at first, I sensed that on the most basic level Ben didn't give a shit about any of it. This was the fabulous life of Ben Bradlee, the legendary newspaper editor, but I could tell he would have been just as happy watching the Red Sox. The party was about Sally, and about "Ben and Sally," and about re-creating the parties that they'd had during the eighties and nineties, when Lauren Bacall would sit next to Ben and the sexual tension between them could have powered the house. But on this night, as the party broke up, there was something sad about the whole thing, something missing. For one thing, Ben was getting old, and it was starting to show. For another, he has three other children, and none of them was there.

In 2007, when I first started to work with Ben, Carol went on vacation for a week and asked me if I would sit out front and play secretary while she was gone. I had known Ben only for a couple of weeks at that point, and I was still scared to talk to him. I figured that sitting out front might at least up my chances of having a meaningful conversation with him.

Toward the end of the week, one of Ben's kids called on his direct line. They were on the phone for ten or fifteen minutes, and it was a tough conversation. I wasn't eavesdropping; Ben talks loudly and leaves the door to his office open. The conversation had to do with money, and how much of it Ben was willing to part with, and on what time frame. It didn't end well.

The next day, the phone rang again. I don't know if it was the same child or a different one, but the conversation was exactly, eerily, the same. Ben offered a series of reasons for why he had chosen the particular path he had chosen, the same reasons he had offered the day before. Whoever was calling appeared to be trying to wear him down.

The call ended, and as the receiver hit the cradle I heard Ben cry out. It was almost a howl—primal, pained, frustrated. I had a flash of a desire to go into his office and hug him—that's how rough his voice sounded in that moment—but at that point I barely knew him. The little I did know suggested that he wasn't big on expressing vulnerability. I stayed in my chair.

Ben can seem to be so impenetrable at times, always on a different, distant level, at an ironic or irreverent remove. He's bigger than you are, than everybody is, and he knows just how to work it—the right joke, the right phrase, the right stuff to keep you charmed and yet deny you any purchase.

In that one instant, though, the distance collapsed. He was just a regular hurting man sitting twenty feet away from me. It shouldn't have shocked me, I guess, but it did: for all of his success, his wealth, his charm and good cheer, sometimes Ben was as alone as anybody.

I don't want to harp on Ben's family troubles, because most of them are relatively recent and they don't have much bearing on history. The world won't know him for what his sons by previous marriages think about his third wife. But to fail to acknowledge the fallout that a life lived at Ben's velocity leaves in its wake is to commit a lie of omission, and that doesn't feel right, either. Of Ben's three children from his previous marriages—Ben Jr., with Jean, and Dino and Marina, with Tony—only Marina still has a working relationship with Ben and Sally. Dino doesn't talk to either of them anymore, and Ben Jr. talks only to his dad. The problems revolve superficially around money but obviously point toward far deeper issues, too.

It is tempting to blame Sally for much of this. She's a tough woman with strong opinions, and she certainly comes in for her share of it. But even the most cursory reading of Ben's memoir, with its particular disdain for "shrinks," suggests that when it comes time to actually work on emotional issues Ben has never been overly inclined to take things head-on. Long before he began to struggle with his short-term memory, he was capable of hearing about a very difficult problem and then forgetting about it five minutes later. "In my next life, I want to come back as Ben," Sally wishes, because he can say "Je ne regrette rien" and mean it.

Dear Kay:

Thank you for that letter that was so full of feeling.

Things seem to be better for me now—and Dino who was very angry & upset when you saw him at the game is still somewhat so but I don't think he is really too deeply wounded, at least his spirits—and Marina's too—are surprisingly good.

It's been one hell of a summer but I feel as though the time has come to put life back together again.

The note is handwritten, from Tony to Kay, undated but obviously from 1973, the year that Ben left Tony for Sally. I found it in Kay Graham's files, not in Ben's. He's never seen it before, and neither had I—a tangible, real-time expression of what it felt like once the train of Ben Bradlee had left the station.

Whenever I ask Ben about his other marriages and his other children, his pat response is to say that he was "so busy climbing the ladder" of his career that he didn't spend as much time with his kids as he might have liked. This is a true statement, but it's also the sum total of what Ben has to say about it, at least to me. The detachment is real. In fairness to Ben, all his children except for Quinn were born in a very different era, when men worked and women stayed home and men didn't judge other men, or themselves, by how much time they spent with their kids. The definition of a good life has changed. Ben is a loving person, so I have very little doubt that he was good to his kids when he was around. He just wasn't around all that much. For most of his adult life, his ambition didn't allow it.

But even if Ben had been around all the time, still it would have been tough to be his kid. David Ignatius told me about an experience he'd had playing tennis in Ben's backyard in Georgetown during the eighties. "Ben Junior came down from Boston and he was serving, and he double-faulted, and then he double-faulted the next time," Ignatius said. "He was very tight. And Ben said [imitating Ben] 'Suck it up!' And I felt so bad for Ben Junior, you know? Because he's a wonderful guy. And I was thinking, man, I love [Ben], but I'm really happy he's not my father."

In Ben's files I came across a couple of letters to his children, tough letters that indicate how deep the gulf was. "You and I are in pretty sorry shape, to put it mildly, aren't we?" Ben began a letter to one of his children in 1979. "Your mind was seething with 'fuck yous,' while mine was seething with frustration." Later: "Maybe my hang-up about being first and foremost a source of money stems from the feeling I have that the only problems you have that I <u>can</u> solve are money problems. . . .

> This has been a tough letter, but an honest one. One that I should have written you before, because not writing it was somehow not honest of me, because I was feeling all of this.
>
> But I was also feeling great, great love for you. I have felt that from the first minutes of your life when I held you in my arms, and watched you in Mom's arms. And I have felt it through thick and thin, even during those moments when I could have gladly kicked you in the rear end, as I felt last night. Love means help, and a whole lot more, but I want to help realistically. I don't want to help you pull the wool over your own eyes or over anyone else's eyes. I want to help you see the truth, and face the truth . . . about yourself and about others. And I'm ready when you are.

It's not as if "Mom" was perfect, either. In Tony's case, she was the woman who went on a summer-long tour through Europe without her four children, all aged six and under, in 1954. That was how she had met Ben, which blew up her previous marriage. By many accounts, Tony was an absentminded and self-centered mom who had little interest in mothering, sending kids off to school woefully underdressed and underfed on a fairly regular basis. Ben's children, except for Quinn, grew up in tough emotional circumstances after the divorces, despite the privilege.

Much of this predated Sally. Ben alone made the decision to leave Jean for Tony, and to leave Tony for Sally. But Sally is a lightning rod, and she brings controversy with her wherever she goes. She has become the villain among Ben's kids from his former marriages, which is a view one can understand but not entirely countenance. Ben has to sign off on things, too.

"Sally is Ben's secret weapon," one close friend told me, an idea that it took me a long time to understand. "She takes the blame for everything."

When I first set out to interview people about Ben, they would say uniformly flattering things about Sally into my tape recorder—how she kept Ben young and vibrant, how all of the restored houses and parties and social plans were only possible because of her. And then, once I'd switched the tape recorder off, these very same people would launch headlong into whatever the latest family drama was, wondering what I knew, often slipping in a dig or two about Sally in the process. There is always some kind of drama going on with Sally—with a maid, with a child from one of Ben's previous marriages, in her social circle, or with editors at the *Post* who are irritating her. She lives in a roiling universe and everybody who talks to her on a regular basis knows exactly whom she's pissed at.

Publicly, whenever Sally gets into one of her dustups, Ben defends her without fail. In 1986, Sally was angry at Tina Brown because *Vanity Fair*, which Brown ran, had printed a review by Christopher Buckley of Sally's first novel, which Buckley referred to disdainfully as "cliterature." Sally promptly disinvited Brown and her husband, Harold Evans, the esteemed former editor of *The Sunday Times* of London, from Ben's birthday party at Grey Gardens that year. After a couple of additional salvos from both sides, Evans wrote Ben a tough note.

They had known each other long before they'd married their wives, and both Tina and Sally certainly ran their own lives. "But hasn't it all become very unclassy?" Evans wrote.

Ben wrote back that he wanted to answer Evans's note in a "spirit of détente." He defended Sally against Evans's most recent accusations, and then he deployed the insouciant Bradlee charm to try to defuse things:

But as you say, we married strong women, who run their own lives.
Maybe you and I could agree on a resolution and leave it at that. I think
disinvitation was counterproductive—to say the bloody least. I think
"cliterature," and even Buckley, were unfriendly if not cheap shots.

I find hardening of the arteries enormously useful in these matters. It
gets harder and harder to remember what feuds are about. It took me
two days to remember "cliterature."

Anyway, I'm ready when you are. I'll buy you lunch next time
you're in town.

In other contexts, he would make much less effort to be conciliatory.
In October of 2001, "The Reliable Source," the *Post*'s gossip column, noted that Sally had been among a group of "concerned citizens" who had congregated at a restaurant in Georgetown to talk
about what to do in the event of a biological attack. (A few days
before, Sally had written a piece in the *Post* asking for more information about the government's preparedness.) Though the piece, written by Lloyd Grove, was relatively straight for a gossip column, it
ended by noting somewhat patronizingly that one participant had
asked if she might be able to find gas masks for her pets.

To: Len, Steve, Gene
Cc: Grove
From: Bradlee

I would like you all to know that I have taken exactly enough of that
sleazy, smarmy sarcastic shit from Grove & his column about Sally &
what she does.

Next time, I'm going to get his ass! Fair warning.

What I don't understand is how it gets in the paper? Time after time.
You don't ever write about anything positive Sally does, and she does so
much. You wouldn't let any of this shit in the paper if it involved your
wives. And never mind all the help she has given STYLE (and Grove),
even though only 1 out of 10 of her ideas are even considered. . . .

Anyway, I am serious.

Ben.

Gene (Eugene Robinson) wrote to Ben to tell him that it wouldn't happen again; Lloyd Grove didn't apologize, but he did note that he would try to focus on some of Sally's other contributions when he had a chance.

What everybody wonders is what happens privately, when nobody is looking. Doesn't Ben ever get pissed off? Sally herself leaves some hints in that regard. In her first novel, *Regrets Only*, there is a character named Des Shaw, the swashbuckling editor of a weekly newsmagazine who is transparently Ben. When Des falls in love with Allison Sterling,* the rising young star reporter at the *Washington Daily*—and, incidentally, one of the three lead female characters who are all transparently Sally—it doesn't take a whole lot of extrapolation to detect traces of autobiography.

I read the book eagerly, looking for clues about Ben and Sally's relationship that I wouldn't be able to glean from direct questioning. On page 188, I found what I was looking for: Allison and Des are having an argument, which Des ends by turning on the news. "He had to spend a lot of time defending her, which he did willingly and with some ferocity," Sally wrote of Des. "But once they were alone together, his frustrations got the better of him and he lashed out." When I asked Sally later if there were any real-life correlation she demurred, but to me it rings with truth.

In Ben's files, as with Howard Simons and other people with whom Ben had communication problems at times, I discovered a series of unsent letters to Sally, too. In the early eighties, Sally had written Ben a note about needing money for renovations for the N Street house, which she closed by saying that she didn't want to live in a "joyless marriage" and wondered what he was going to do about it. Sally plays hardball.

Tucked into the envelope that Sally had sent to Ben was his response, written by hand, with "not sent" at the top. "Serious talks about money have not been very satisfactory for me," he wrote. "We have them. I give you my feeling that we are spending recklessly, without the slightest evidence that you are listening. And then you

*Sally's middle name.

do what you always wanted to do." It closed: "I guess I'm having trouble understanding what you want from me beyond total acquiescence and endless cash."

Elsewhere in the files I found a handwritten letter of Ben's on yellow lined paper that had been torn in half from top to bottom, right down the middle. There is no address on it, and no addressee, but it's obviously to Sally from sometime in 1978:

I have the feeling <u>that</u> you are always pushing for public recognition as my owner;

- that you feel this makes you a better person, though it changes you nil.
- that you want to be married to be recognized, not to be any closer to me.
- that you want to be cited in Yearbooks, to be recognized, not to be any better.
- you want people to know you buy the suits, the shirts
- you'd rather not get married, than get married quietly & tell no one
- you never fail to say together for 5 years. Must've said it 50 times in Boston.
- Want the world to know your position
- Want to go with me to Marina's school to be seen—not to be step-parented.
- From the very first time you went to the Buchwald Easter Party
- Money, position

BCB Commitment:
(1) I'm yours, publicly, privately, faithfully
(2) I've dealt you in to my life completely, equally, will, social, professional
(3) I've taken risks for you

These are things Ben never says.

In the intervening years, the issues between Sally and Ben's kids have festered, leaving Ben more and more exposed. In February of 2010, Sally wrote an unfortunate column in the *Post* describing the circumstances by which Quinn's wedding to his fiancée, Pary Williamson, had been scheduled for the very same day as the wedding of Greta Bradlee, Ben Jr.'s daughter and Ben's granddaughter. The column made a series of misjudgments about what would be believable to an average reader, including the statement that Sally had received the invitation to Greta's wedding but had given it to Ben to "put the date on his calendar, and he did not." Suffice it to say that at eighty-eight years of age, Ben was not running the Bradlee/Quinn household schedule. That Sally would throw him under the bus in an article about his own children was tough for the people who know them well to stomach. The column immediately caused an uproar, and the comments on the *Post*'s website were so many and so vicious that the paper decided to close them down.

Ben Jr. was outraged. He called the *Post* to complain, and then he composed a vituperative letter to the editor a few days later. He didn't believe for one second that the scheduling of the two weddings on the same date had been an "inadvertent mistake," as Sally had claimed. As he wrote in his letter, he thought it was simply Sally's calculated way of trying to hurt him, both by preventing his father from attending Greta's wedding and by creating a convenient excuse to avoid having to invite him and Dino to Quinn's wedding.

The situation was a mess. Ben Jr. was deterred from submitting his letter for publication only after Ben reached him by phone from St. Maarten, where he and Sally were on vacation, and made a personal appeal. ("Give me this one, pal.") In the wake of that episode, and a *Vanity Fair* piece in July 2010 that recounted many of the family tensions in terms unflattering to everybody, the once fragile family dynamics were in ruins.[*]

All of this to say: Ben isn't perfect, and his life isn't perfect. With his first three kids he was not the world's greatest dad, and from what

[*]After all of the hubbub, Quinn's wedding ended up being postponed until October 2010, so Ben went alone to Greta's wedding that April.

I have seen he really does let Sally roll him most of the time where those kids are concerned. Part of this is a function of his age, but it must be said that part of it isn't. When Sally is on the march, Ben checks out, and then, in the aftermath, he turns on the charm to try to smooth his way through the fallout. He's good at it; it's clearly a kind of survival strategy for him. "Sally has done nothing but enrich his life," a close friend of theirs told me. "But he's had to make some sacrifices for it, which includes accepting some of her more outrageous judgments." That is the truth.

Ben has never spoken to me about the toll that all this has taken on him, but I can see it in small ways. In his office at the *Post*, there are pictures of all of Ben's kids on the walls. In the last few years, as the tensions with Dino have escalated, more and more pictures of Dino have turned up in Ben's office, tacked to Ben's corkboard and taped over other pictures on his wall. It is a quiet demonstration of love, and of some sorrow at the loss, even if Ben never says anything about it out loud.

"My children all know that Sally Quinn has made me enormously happy for thirty-umpteen years," Ben told *Vanity Fair*, "and that is more important to them than anything else, I think." Doubtful. But Ben's commitment to Sally is complete. They love each other, and have loved each other for a long time. You can feel it in Ben's spirited public defenses of her, and also in that agonized unsent letter from 1978—even just in Ben's beau geste of tearing the letter down the middle and then deciding not to send it. I have often felt this intensity when I've been around them, however exasperated they pretend to be with each other at times.

One night at Grey Gardens Ben came down for cocktails with a huge grin on his face. "She smiled at me before I even said anything," he said to me, with genuine enthusiasm, having encountered Sally on his way downstairs. "Tonight could be my lucky night!" As Ben would say, they're still in business.

A few days later we went to dinner in Westhampton. It was nearly an hour's drive, so in Bradlee style the houseguests at Grey Gardens took a limousine. On the way home it was dark and late and quiet, and most people were starting to doze off. Sally was between me and Quinn on one side, and Ben was sitting with friends on the other.

"Why don't you come over here, Sal," Ben said softly. Looking at her, smiling: "I've got a better shoulder than either of those guys."

I've also seen up close what a wonderful dad Ben has been to Quinn. Quinn was born with velo-cardio-facial syndrome (VCFS), a genetic condition that comes with a host of physical and cognitive difficulties. He had open heart surgery at three months, and for most of his childhood one malady followed another. (He wasn't diagnosed with VCFS until he was fourteen.) Once, a trained professional insisted to Ben and Sally that Quinn was retarded and would have to be institutionalized. In those moments Ben's capacity for denial dovetailed with what was best for Quinn: Ben didn't believe it for a second, and so as a family they plowed ahead.

Quinn softened Ben. For one thing, he was born in 1982, which was right when Ben began his slow withdrawal from everyday involvement in the editing of the paper. Ben had time for Quinn in a way that he didn't for his other children. (That, more than the money battles, is what seems to hurt the older kids the most.) But Quinn is so sensitive, and his mind works in such quirky and unpredictable ways, that the only way to understand him is through patience. Ben is not known for his patience, but I have watched him exert it with Quinn over and over and over again.

In November of 2010, I flew up to Boston to go through David Halberstam's archives at the Howard Gotlieb Archival Research Center at Boston University. Jean Halberstam had kindly given me permission to look through her husband's research materials for his seminal book *The Powers That Be*, and I gave myself two days. Five minutes after I arrived, I realized I hadn't left myself enough time.

Halberstam talked to everybody—*everybody*. The transcripts took up two full archival boxes, each capable of holding two stacks of eight-and-a-half by eleven paper six inches high. The interviews made for fascinating reading, and some of the material that Halber-

stam didn't use (and much of what he did) has played an important
role in this book, particularly in my understanding of how others felt
about Ben during Watergate.

Time and again, Halberstam's interviews with *Post* people return
to Ben—his relationship with Kay, his role as editor, his life with
Sally, his presence in the newsroom, even his upbringing. Part of this
is natural. Ben was the boss. It was his ship. But, at a certain point,
Halberstam clearly became smitten, as so many before him have, with
Bradlee as a man and as a character:

> Parenthetical note on Bradlee—this is me talking, not Bernstein.
> It's almost as if he is the Hemingway hero—ideological, not
> ideological, sprung of the moment, grace under pressure, style
> more important than anything else, cool, always charming, there
> but never giving seemingly too much of himself, holding himself
> just in reserve.

"I've only scanned *The Powers That Be*," Eugene Patterson would
write to Ben shortly after the book came out in 1979, "but I see you
mesmerized David."

Part of what makes Halberstam's portrayal of Ben in the book so
interesting—the best of any I've read—is that he includes a good deal
of criticism of Ben. That Ben was superficial, that he didn't care
about the substance of stories but only the impact, that he had no
ideology, that the only thing he believed in was the Washington Redskins. In the interviews there had been a lot of grumbling about this
kind of thing, with people taking shots at Ben for not being a perfect
manager, for having a short attention span, for glory hounding, for
failing to give the paper sufficient intellectual heft. Assessing Ben's
frailties, knocking him down a peg, was clearly a favorite spectator
sport at the *Post* in the late seventies.

I finished the final interview in the stack—Woodward—with
about fifteen minutes left to spare on my second day there. There
were still a couple of boxes that I hadn't done much with. When I
had opened them on the first day, I had encountered row after row

of Halberstam's notebooks, with file cards and loose-leaf paper scattered around them. I figured the transcripts were the best use of my energy.

But now I had fifteen minutes to kill, so I took a quick spin through what was left. The notebooks were mostly indecipherable scrawl, but I found some file cards, bundled together by an old rubber band, that all seemed to pertain to the *Post*. On top of the file cards was a series of pieces of paper with notes written on them, including an old empty envelope from the White House addressed to Halberstam. I wondered what that was, so I flipped it over to look at the back.

Stripped in pencil at the top of the envelope was the word "Bradlee." I couldn't make out much of the rest of the writing at first, but these were clearly notes from a conversation of some kind, written down on whatever piece of paper had been closest at hand when Halberstam took the call. The postmark from the White House was dated May 20, 1977.

I sat back with the envelope in my hand and scanned it, trying to decipher the writing. I had an instinctive feeling that what was written there was going to matter to me.

I stared at the words. Finally, the last phrase on the envelope snapped into focus, simple, direct, conclusive: "Those who wanted him to be more were always disappointed."

Ben is such a legendary figure that it's easy to want him to be perfect, to have him stand for everything that's good instead of the things that he actually stood for. I am as guilty of this as anybody. I decided early on that he had a lock on life, and that if I read his words closely enough and listened to him closely enough and watched him move through the world closely enough he would reveal what he knew to me. That this was futile is obvious to me now, but he is compelling enough that for a long time I believed it.

The secret of Ben is that there is no secret. His nonideology and his passion for great stories were what they were, and nothing more. I have never caught him in a lie. I don't regret a moment spent with him, either in person or in onionskin copy. I would be content if the

picture I have of him grinning and holding my newborn daughter is
the only thing that I keep with me from my time spent working on
this book.

In August 1991, right after Ben stepped down as editor of the *Post*, a
letter arrived at his office from a young woman named Shanon Fagan.
She was a senior at T. C. Roberson High School in Asheville, North
Carolina, and she had recently been named the executive editor of
her school newspaper.

"I have long admired your colorful career in journalism and met
the news of your retirement with sadness," she began. "An era in
newspaper publishing had ended." She praised the "integrity and
extreme dedication" Ben had shown in running the paper. "While
our publication may not rank as a world class journal," she wrote,
with a hint of Bradlee-esque steel, "I intend to run it as if it did.

"In a search to define my position, I write this letter to you. I am
greatly interested in what principles you have followed during your
tenure as executive editor and would be appreciative of any advice
or wisdom you could share with me. I would wish that my small
part in this endeavor could be as honorable and distinguished as
yours."

Fagan's letter arrived at an empty office. After leaving the newsroom on July 31, Ben had departed Washington for a month's vacation on Long Island with Sally and Quinn. He didn't see the letter
until after Labor Day, when he returned to his new digs in the executive suite on the seventh floor of the *Post*, two floors above the
newsroom he had led for more than twenty-five years. There, on
September 5, Ben composed his response:

The Washington Post

1150 15ᵗʰ STREET, N. W.

WASHINGTON, D. C. 20071

FAX NUMBER (202) 334-5075

BENJAMIN C. BRADLEE
VICE PRESIDENT
(202) 334-7510

September 5, 1991

Ms. Shanon C. Fagan
15 Fairhaven Court
Asheville, NC 28803

Dear Shanon Fagan:

I've always had trouble explaining myself and my principles.
I believe in hard work. I believe in fighting all kinds of
domination. I believe in steering clear of the big shots.
I believe in total honesty. I believe in compassion.

Sincerely,

Ben Bradlee

"It's a brave journalist, a brave newsmaker, and therefore a brave reader (or viewer) who can look the world in the eye and say, with authority, 'This is the truth. There is no more,'" Ben said, in a speech in October of 1984. Those words have haunted me as I worked on this book, the bogeymen of historical complexity and my own limitations always taunting me from their perches on my shoulder. But from the day in 2007 when I came across Shanon Fagan's letter until the day that I set these words down, I have always known that I would say, of this exchange, of who Ben is and has been, and of what he has meant to so many people for so long: This is the truth. There is no more.

ACKNOWLEDGMENTS

*Ben Bradlee passed away on October 21, 2014,
surrounded by his family.*

The first people to thank are Ben Bradlee, Sally Quinn, and Quinn Bradlee. How I feel about Ben, and what I owe him, must by now be pretty clear. Less clear is how important both Sally and Quinn were in the formation of this book.

I got to know Quinn first. We spent the better part of a year together, working on his memoir, *A Different Life*, which came out in April 2009. Quinn was so honest with me, so consistently, that at first I found it shocking. The lies that we call etiquette do not register with Quinn. He calls you out. He might struggle with certain conventional aspects of learning, but he has an intuitive sense for people that is as unerring as his father's. He is also one of the gentlest and sweetest people I know. Working with him on his memoir was one of the most satisfying professional and personal experiences I've ever had.

Sally and Ben trusted me because of the work I did with Quinn. When Sally asked me what I wanted to do next, I told her I really wanted to write a book about Ben. Six weeks later, I had an agent and a book contract. I could never have done this without her. Sally is my friend. She has been wildly generous with me, and with my family; she also stood by me at a moment of great professional and personal difficulty, when everything was on the line for me. I knew that by touching certain family circumstances I would likely upset her, but I also knew that if I didn't take them on I would compromise the integrity of the book. Because this book was about Ben, there wasn't enough room for the manifold kindnesses that Sally has shown to me over the last four years. I hope that in mentioning them here I can at least partially repay that debt.

I am also deeply indebted to Bob Woodward. Bob's belief in me when I was a twenty-four-year-old kid changed my life. In the rolling journalism clinic that was everyday life on the third floor of his house on Q Street, Bob taught me to trust my instincts, to write my first thought, and to tell the truth even if I wasn't sure how it was going to go over. His favorite work of mine was always the work that I did the fastest, with the least analysis. (I remember him coming into my office early on and saying, " '*Aforementioned*'? We don't use words like that around here.") He and his wife, Elsa Walsh, and his daughter, Tali, have been friends of mine for a long, long time. Bob gave an impromptu and much-cherished toast at my wedding, and he has always been willing to help me, vouch for me, whatever I needed, since the day I walked in the door.

Now I have repaid him for those kindnesses by including material in this book that I know he didn't want me to include, that he feels will expose him to scrutiny he doesn't deserve. I didn't go looking for the material about Z and Deep Throat, but I found it—and once I found it, I felt I had an obligation to pursue it, and to tell the truth about it. Bob taught me how to do those things, and I could have had no better teacher.

Outside of Ben's direct family, I am also indebted to his extended family at *The Washington Post*. Carol Leggett, Ben's secretary since 1991, has helped me in every conceivable way for the past four years. She has found documents, made phone calls, saved things of interest in a folder marked "Jeff," introduced me to the fried chicken salad (and Steve) at Georgia Brown's, doted on my daughter, and even once ran down to the street to feed coins into a parking meter (without telling me about it) when she noticed that one of my interviews with Ben was running long. Any list falls far short of capturing just how much she has done. She will be my friend long after this book has come and gone.

The entire *Post* organization supported me as I wrote this book, whether they knew it or not. Initially it was the folks on the seventh floor—Eric Lieberman, Caitlin Gibson, and the rest of the legal and executive team—who not only tolerated my presence as I came in every day to work on the boxes but also made me feel welcome. Ev Small and Liz Hylton were both immensely helpful as well. Ev, as I mentioned in the book, found a bunch of additional "Bradlee" boxes that my work would have been worse without. And Liz brought me the box of Kay Graham's correspondence with Ben that opened up an entirely new understanding of that relationship. She also was a great help with photographs.

On the ninth floor, where the big boys sit, I thank Don Graham and Rosemary Kennedy, his right-hand woman. Rosemary never failed to give me a boost, from getting me in to see her boss to making sure I always had what I needed. I never asked Don Graham for permission to write this book, because he never made me feel that I had to.

When it came time for me to secure the permissions for material under the *Post*'s copyright—roughly 90 percent of the material in this book—Bo Jones made it happen. Bo is the former counsel, publisher, and vice chairman of the *Post*, and one of Ben's closest friends; he has also been great to me. (Shortly after we'd drafted the permissions letter, as I was sitting on a couch in Bo's office, he turned to me and said, "I'm just assuming your book is accurate.") Tim Jucovy, an associate counsel at the *Post*, was instrumental in (and quite good-natured about) creating the final permissions letter. And Eddy Palanzo, in News Research, kindly provided me with access to the *Post*'s archives, both physical and online.

Outside of the *Post*, the most important source of research information for me was David Halberstam's invaluable archives, at the Howard Gotlieb Archival Research Center at Boston University. I thank David Remnick, who gave me the idea during our interview in 2009. I also thank Jean Halberstam, who was kind enough to give me permission to visit her husband's archives and then to publish what I found. And I thank Sean Noel, an associate director at the Research Center, for coordinating my visit and then the proper permissions once I'd gone.

Another vital source of information for me, particularly about *All the President's Men*, was Alan Pakula's archive in the Margaret Herrick Library at the Academy of Motion Pictures Arts and Sciences in Beverly Hills, California. I'd like to thank Hannah Pakula, Alan's wife, and Jenny Romero at the library for helping to coordinate my visit, and for picking out everything that I could possibly have wanted to see.

Outside of the *Post* and the various research centers, the greatest resources for me were all of the people who were willing to sit for interviews. I could put a long list of those people here, but nearly every one of their names (along with the fruits of their interviews) appears in the book. I thank everybody who made the time to sit with me and to talk about Ben.

There are a few people to thank in particular. Rosamond Casey, Ben's stepdaughter, fed me dinner in November 2009, but she also did some reporting for me around her mother's relationship with President Kennedy and gave me the permission to use certain of her mother's effects in the book. Ben Bradlee, Jr., Ben's son, graciously provided me with his dad's letters home during World War II. Mike Sager, the former *Post* reporter, never once complained when I asked him leading questions about his friend Janet Cooke, and I am grateful for his efforts with her on my behalf. And Peter Osnos, the founder of PublicAffairs, published Quinn's memoir and has been a friend and sounding board for me ever since.

There would be no book without Esther Newberg, my agent at ICM. She scared me when it was time to scare me and then stood with me when it was time to stand with me. I am lucky to have her in my corner, as an advocate and as a friend. She and Kari Stuart, her close associate, have done everything they could to support me from the start.

At Random House, I have first to thank Susan Mercandetti, the editor who bought my book in 2008 and whom I had known since 2002. Susan endured countless fits and starts as the project got under way, consistently finding new and inventive ways to put the screws to me without ever undermining my confidence in my ability to see the book through. Her staunch rejection of several bad early ideas was particularly important. The parts that she liked from the start became, after long labor, the seeds of the book that you hold in your hands.

Susan departed Random House before the book was complete, and in that moment of great uncertainty Ben Steinberg stepped in to steady the ship. Ben had been working with Susan and had been reading my drafts all along. He has a keen eye and a great ear, and his comments about one particularly unfruitful diversion in the draft manuscript reminded me of what I was doing, and of what I shouldn't be doing. He also kept me sane for much of this process, and for that alone I can't thank him enough. From small details to the big picture of how a book should read, look, and feel, he shepherded me along and made important contributions at every stage. His future is bright.

I don't know that I could have finished the book, or felt as good about the finished product as I do, if Andy Ward hadn't come aboard during the final months. He is the best editor I have ever worked with, the kind of editor a writer hopes to have. I trust him and his judgment completely. (Among other things, he saved me from myself more times than I can count.) He always made time for me, always listened to me, and always took the problems I encountered along the way as seriously as I did. Having him thinking with me, and standing with me, has been one of the best parts of working on this book.

Others at Random House outside of the editorial chain of command are also worthy of praise and thanks. Deborah Foley, the head of the permissions department, endured an onslaught of emails and phone calls as we sorted our way through the tangle of permissions required for a book of this length and complexity. Our discussion about the copyright properties of a lipstick smudge was particularly memorable. Thanks to Janet Wygal, who oversaw the copyediting of this book. And, of course, none of this would have been possible at all without the support of Susan Kamil, the publisher of Random

House, and Gina Centrello, the president, who believed in me and in this book from the start. I also thank Benjamin Dreyer, who oversaw a complex production process, and Barbara Fillon and Sally Marvin, who helped with publicity, and Chayenne Skeete, for her help with the paperback.

Great chunks of this book were organized, written, and rewritten in Rapidan, Virginia, at the weekend home of my in-laws, Jan and Elizabeth Lodal. Their generous willingness to let me take over portions of their house for weeks at a time allowed me to make leaps I could never have made otherwise. Alan and Nancy Nixon, neighbors and friends, also paid welcome visits when I was out there by myself. They brought me everything from fresh vegetables to a chance to make conversation with another human being, all of which I needed.

With the arrival of my daughter, my home office disappeared, as did my willingness to be away for long stretches. Into the breach stepped my dad and his law firm, Beveridge & Diamond. For the last year, as I was making the final push, they have allowed me free rein with an unused office in one of their suites. That kindness was transformative. I want to thank Katherine Harris, the firm's chief operating officer, for tolerating and supporting my presence. I also want to thank Gloria Joshua and Sarah Sullivan, the two women who have allowed me to get to the office in the first place by taking such good care of my daughter during the week.

My siblings—my brother-in-law, Eric Lodal, my brother, Ken, and my sister, Liza—provided counsel at crucial moments. Eric, a writer himself, was a constant source of inspiration and advice. Ken gave an early draft of the manuscript a hard and thoughtful read, at a time when I needed more feedback than I knew. He helped me feel good about some of the tougher decisions, and his effort to do it all in the midst of his own busy life was a great kindness to me. And Liza has saved me throughout the last year, from stepping in to look after my daughter when deadlines loomed and babysitters bailed to simply being on the other end of the phone when I needed her.

This book is dedicated to my grandparents, which tells you everything that you need to know about what they mean to me except for their names: Walter and Connie Burke (Pops and Cee Cee), and Sol and Helen Himmelman (Baba and Grandma).

I also want to thank my parents, Harold and Bonnie, though as a new parent myself I realize there is no way to thank them enough. In addition to providing me with office space, my dad has been my one-man legal team and sympathetic devil's advocate, while my mom helped me to maintain a healthy skepticism, provided song-filled babysitting support, and kept me nourished, perhaps slightly more than I needed to be. They are wonderful grandparents and wonderful company, and as I've gotten older I realize how lucky I am to have them in my life.

Finally, I thank my wife, Kirsten, without whom there is no living person named Jeff Himmelman, no book to read, no music to listen to. Since the moment we got together she has been the driving force behind everything that is good in my life, always seeing the best in me, never letting me settle, defending me to myself whenever I despaired that I'd lost my way. Her patience with my idiocies is the most renewable resource I have ever encountered. The work that she does at LIFT, but also (perhaps as important) the way in which she does that work, is a source of constant humility and inspiration for me. The home that we have made together is the only place on this earth that I ever want to be.

And, of course, Kirsten brought to me, to us, the truest joy in our lives: our daughter, Billie. This book came into being as she did, and my thoughts of her—what she will think of her daddy, who she will know him to be—were always with me as I stared down the blank page. This book is for her as much as for anybody. Little Billie: I love dancing with you the most. If you are going to take one lesson from Ben, or from me, I hope it will be that you should always do your best to speak the truth.

Jeff Himmelman
Washington, D.C., December 2017

April 2, 1993

Dear Dr. Parle,

You have a good point about Ben Bradlee's title. I fear it's too late to change.

Truthfully, I don't think anyone is aware of Ben's title. Ben is Ben and needs no title. He contributes a lot as he always has.

Sincerely,

Katharine Graham

INDEX

IMAGE CREDITS

AP/World Wide (p. 54)
Tony Bradlee (p. 273)
Herblock (p. 253)
Jeff Himmelman (p. 211)
David R. Legge/The Washington Post (p. 248)
Kirsten Lodal (p. 28)
Harry Naltchayan/The Washington Post (p. 263)
Neshan Naltchayan (p. 441)
Cecil Stoughton (p. 310)
Tulsa Tribune (p. 406)
Courtesy of United Features Syndicate (p. 327)
The Washington Post (pp. 8, 15, 17, 25, 42, 55, 56, 57, 77, 105, 118, 119, 141, 165, 186, 222, 235, 241–245, 250, 339, 342, 351, 355–356, 359, 374, 377, 391, 392, 401, 407, 416, 421, 423–425, 428, 433, 452, 482)

PHOTO: © SARAH BERNARDI

JEFF HIMMELMAN is a contributing writer at *The New York Times Magazine,* where he has been a finalist for a National Magazine Award; his writing has also appeared in *New York, GQ, Washingtonian,* and *The Washington Post.* His work with a team of reporters at the *Post* helped the paper secure the national reporting Pulitzer Prize for its post-9/11 coverage. He is also a professional musician who writes, records, and performs under the name Down Dexter. He lives in Washington, D.C., with his wife and three daughters.

yoursintruth.com

ABOUT THE TYPE

This book was set in Bembo, a typeface based on an old-style Roman face that was used for Cardinal Bembo's tract *De Aetna* in 1495. Bembo was cut by Francisco Griffo in the early sixteenth century. The Lanston Monotype Machine Company of Philadelphia brought the well-proportioned letter forms of Bembo to the United States in the 1930s.